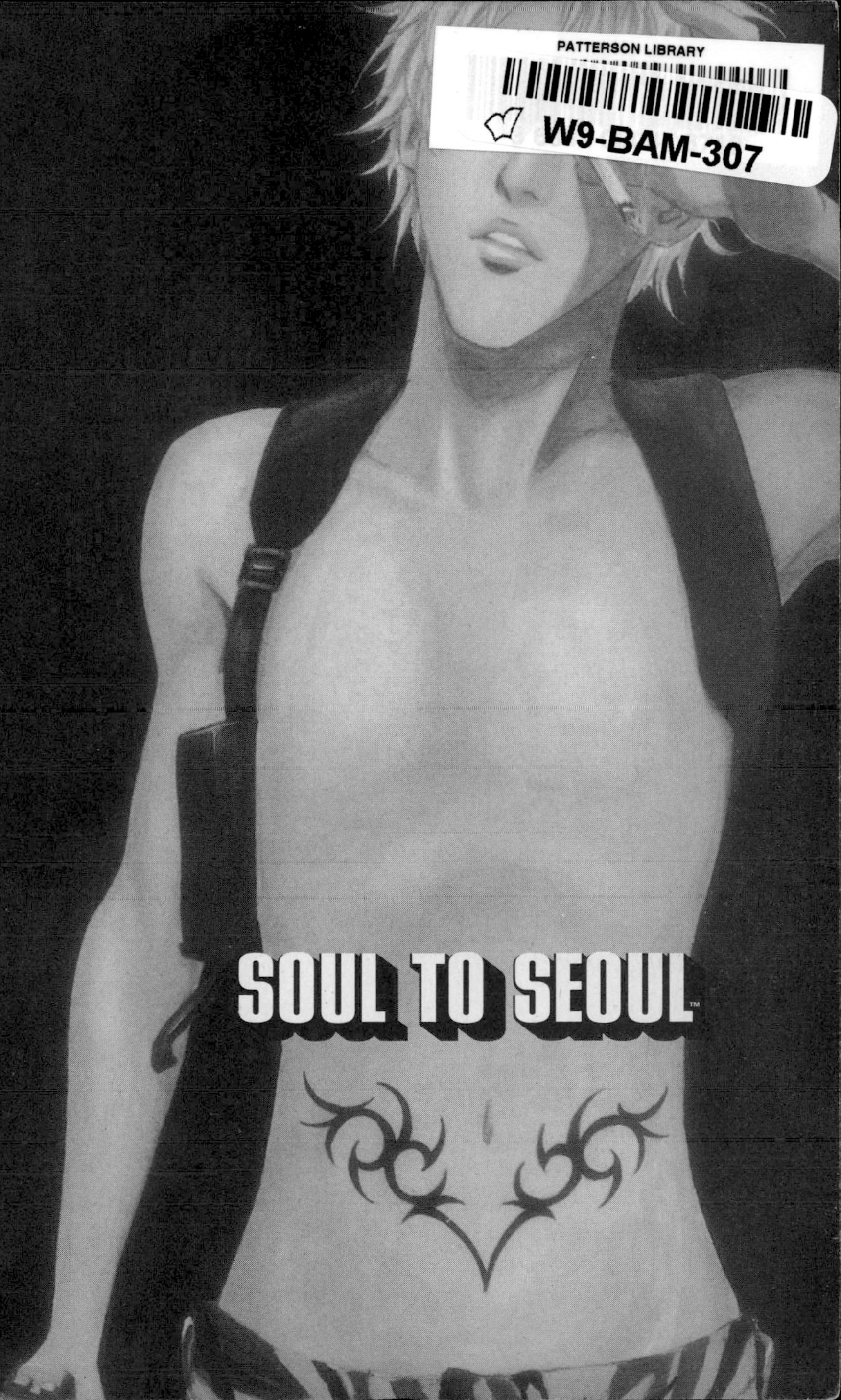
SOUL TO SEOUL™

Soul to Seoul Vol. 4
created by Kim Jea Eun

Translation	-	Ellen Choi
English Adaptation	-	Marc Goldsmith
Retouch and Lettering	-	Corey Whitfield
Production Artist	-	Mike Estacio
Cover Design	-	James Lee

Editor	-	Troy Lewter
Digital Imaging Manager	-	Chris Buford
Production Managers	-	Elisabeth Brizzi
Managing Editor	-	Sheldon Drzka
VP of Production	-	Ron Klamert
Editor-In-Chief	-	Rob Tokar
Publisher	-	Mike Kiley
President and C.O.O.	-	John Parker
C.E.O. and Chief Creative Officer	-	Stuart Levy

A  Manga

TOKYOPOP Inc.
5900 Wilshire Blvd. Suite 2000
Los Angeles, CA 90036

E-mail: info@TOKYOPOP.com
Come visit us online at www.TOKYOPOP.com

© 2001 KIM JEA EUN, DAIWON C.I. Inc. All Rights Reserved. All rights reserved. No portion of this book may be
First published in Korea in 2001 by DAIWON C.I. Inc. reproduced or transmitted in any form or by any means
English translation rights in North America, UK, NZ, and without written permission from the copyright holders.
Australia arranged by DAIWON C.I. Inc. This manga is a work of fiction. Any resemblance to
actual events or locales or persons, living or dead, is
English text copyright © 2006 TOKYOPOP Inc. entirely coincidental.

ISBN: 1-59532-315-5

First TOKYOPOP printing: August 2006
10 9 8 7 6 5 4 3 2 1
Printed in the USA

SOUL TO SEOUL

4

Kim Jea Eun

TOKYOPOP

HAMBURG // LONDON // LOS ANGELES // TOKYO

Character Introductions

A Korean and white mix
Hobbies: Collecting army uniforms
Specialty: Lying, shooting
Wants to be: Gangster
Life motto: "Life is meaningless, cruel and foolish, yet glamorous."

Kai Lee (Kangil Lee) 17 years old
177 cm / 67 kg / Blood type AB

A Korean immigrant
Hobbies: Swimming, dancing
Specialty: Tae Kwon Do
Wants to be: Traveler
Life motto: "It could be enjoyable to live in a place where you don't know anyone."

Sunil Sohn 17 years old
172 cm / 52 kg / Blood type O

Second-generation Korean American
Hobbies: Making dolls
Specialty: Screaming
Wants to be: Too young to decide that yet, don't you think?
Life motto: "I'm too young to think about that stuff..."

Gelda (Heesun Lee) 14 years old
158 cm / 48kg / Blood type A

Korean Adoptee
Hobbies: Read anything you can read
Specialty: Doing makeup
Wants to be: Punk rock musician
Life motto: "Anything you learn from pain is touching."

J.J. (Judas Jesus) 14 years old
163 cm / 51 kg / Blood type AB

A Korean and black mix
Hobbies: Working out
Specialty: Rap
Wants to be: A dad
Life motto: "Don't ever let them see you sweat."

Spike Washington. 17 years old
186cm/71 kg/ Blood type A

Exchange student from Korea
Hobbies: Hanging around
Specialty: Laughing at people
Wants to be: ......
Life motto: "I don't have a motto.."

Sangyul Choi 17 years old
165 cm / 58 kg / Blood type B

SOUL TO SEOUL™

Story So Far

Kai and Spike are best friends living in New York who have a lot in common--they are both half-Korean teens trying to discover their place in the world. However, the bonds of their friendship are broken when they both fall for Sunil, a Korean foreign exchange student. This creates a rift between the two friends, ultimately landing Spike in jail and causing Kai to go on the run after killing someone to earn Spike's bail money.

Later, when Spike reenters Kai's life, attending Kai's school as a famous model's bodyguard. If that wasn't enough, Sunil demands to know about the secret life Kai hides from her...so he reluctantly takes her to hang with his gangster friends. Unfortunately, a fight breaks out between a rival gang, and Kai gets shot while trying to shield Sunil. Meanwhile, J.J. is adopted and moves out of Kai's family's house, and Kai is half-sister Gelda (who has a secret crush on J.J.) is devastated.

Soul to Seoul

CONTENTS

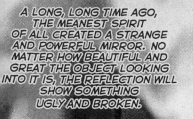

A LONG, LONG TIME AGO, THE MEANEST SPIRIT OF ALL CREATED A STRANGE AND POWERFUL MIRROR. NO MATTER HOW BEAUTIFUL AND GREAT THE OBJECT LOOKING INTO IT IS, THE REFLECTION WILL SHOW SOMETHING UGLY AND BROKEN.

NO MATTER HOW NOBLE AND GOOD YOUR THOUGHTS ARE, THIS MIRROR WILL CHANGE THEM INTO SOMETHING EVIL. OF COURSE, IF THE OBJECT IS ALREADY EVIL, THE MIRROR WILL MAKE IT LOOK THAT MUCH WORSE.

THE DEVIL WAS MOST AMUSED BY THIS AND CARRIED THE MIRROR ALL OVER THE WORLD, FORCING ALL THINGS TO LOOK INTO IT.

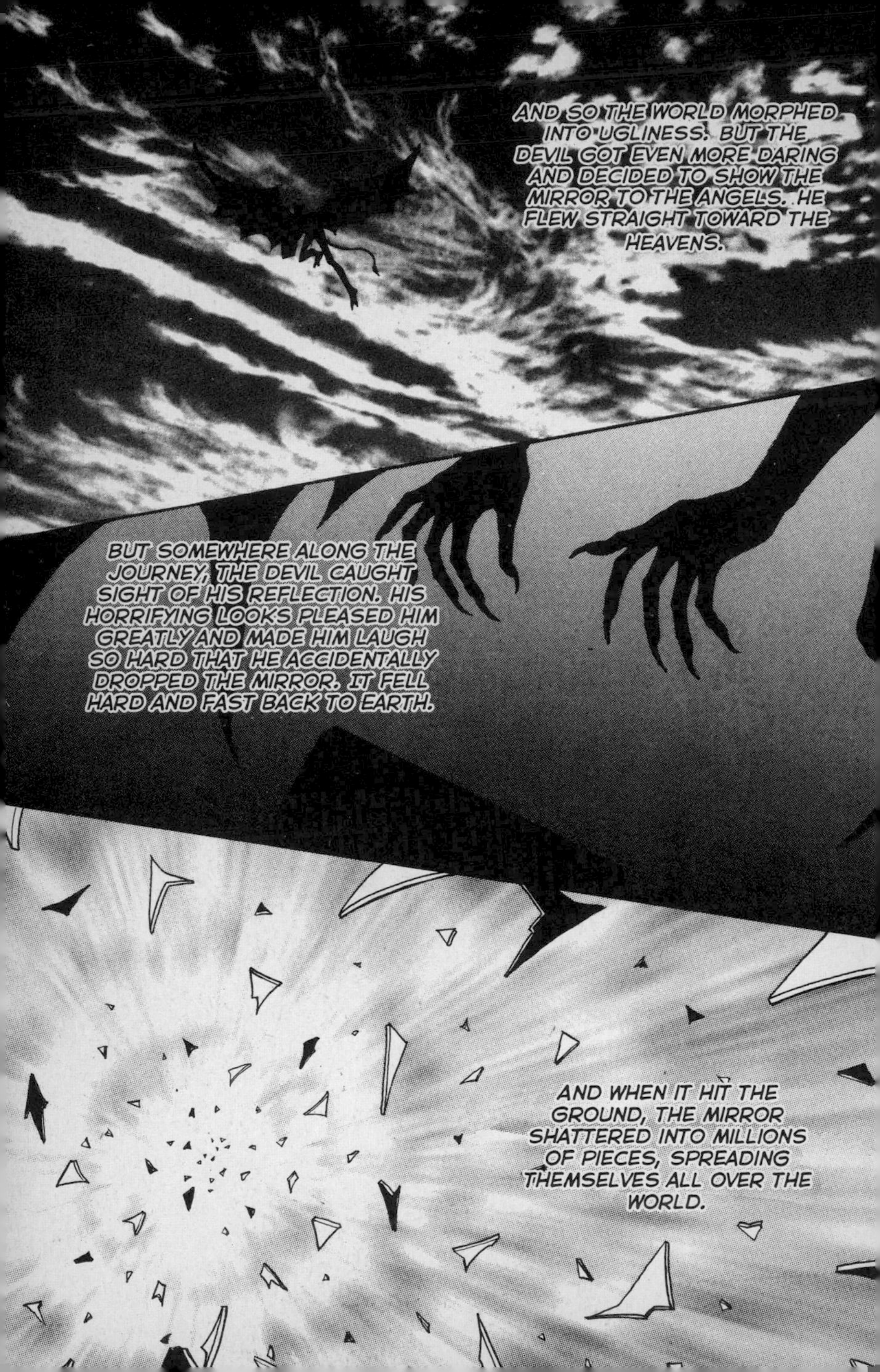
AND SO THE WORLD MORPHED INTO UGLINESS. BUT THE DEVIL GOT EVEN MORE DARING AND DECIDED TO SHOW THE MIRROR TO THE ANGELS. HE FLEW STRAIGHT TOWARD THE HEAVENS.
BUT SOMEWHERE ALONG THE JOURNEY, THE DEVIL CAUGHT SIGHT OF HIS REFLECTION. HIS HORRIFYING LOOKS PLEASED HIM GREATLY AND MADE HIM LAUGH SO HARD THAT HE ACCIDENTALLY DROPPED THE MIRROR. IT FELL HARD AND FAST BACK TO EARTH.
AND WHEN IT HIT THE GROUND, THE MIRROR SHATTERED INTO MILLIONS OF PIECES, SPREADING THEMSELVES ALL OVER THE WORLD.

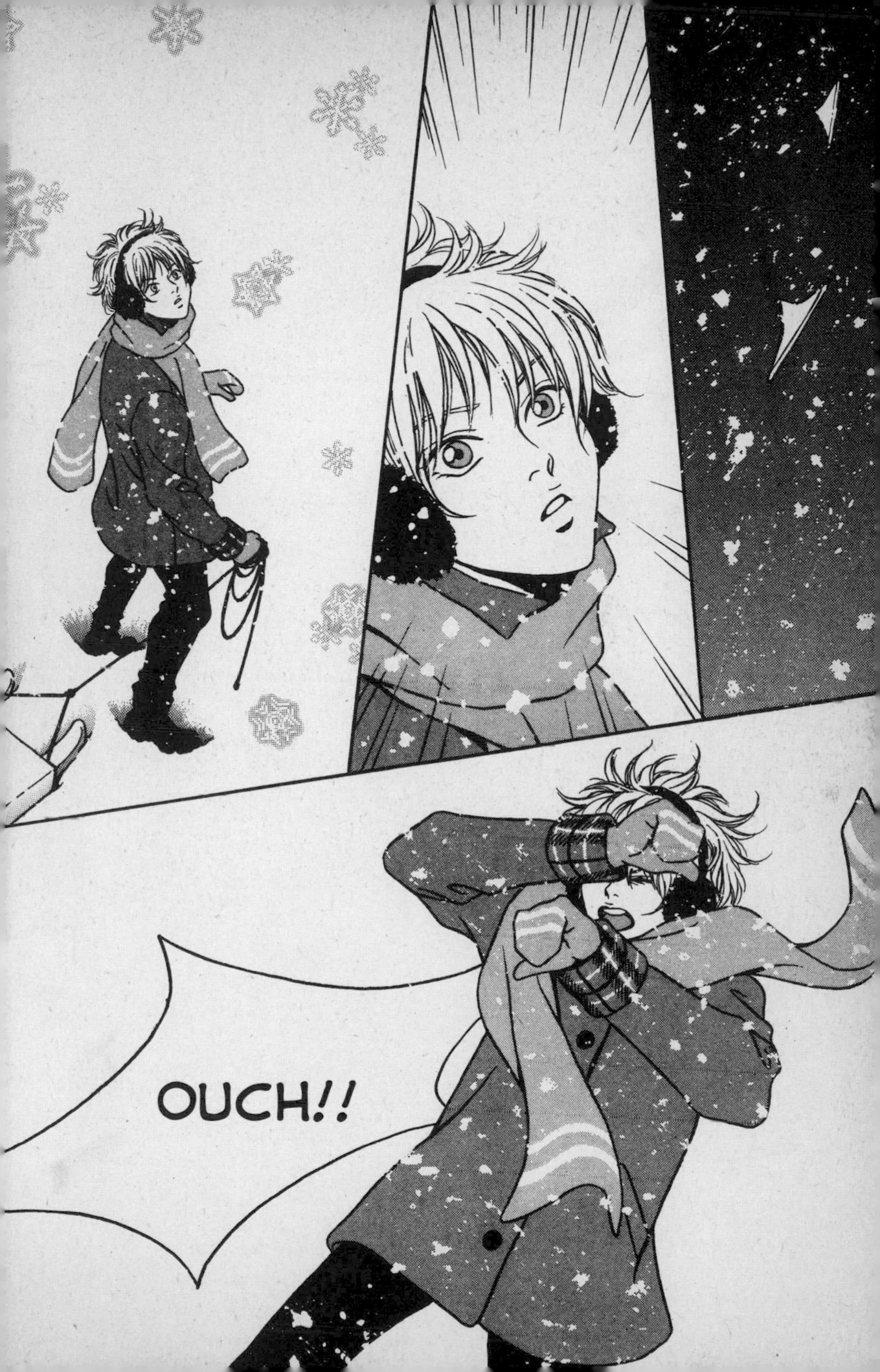
OUCH!!

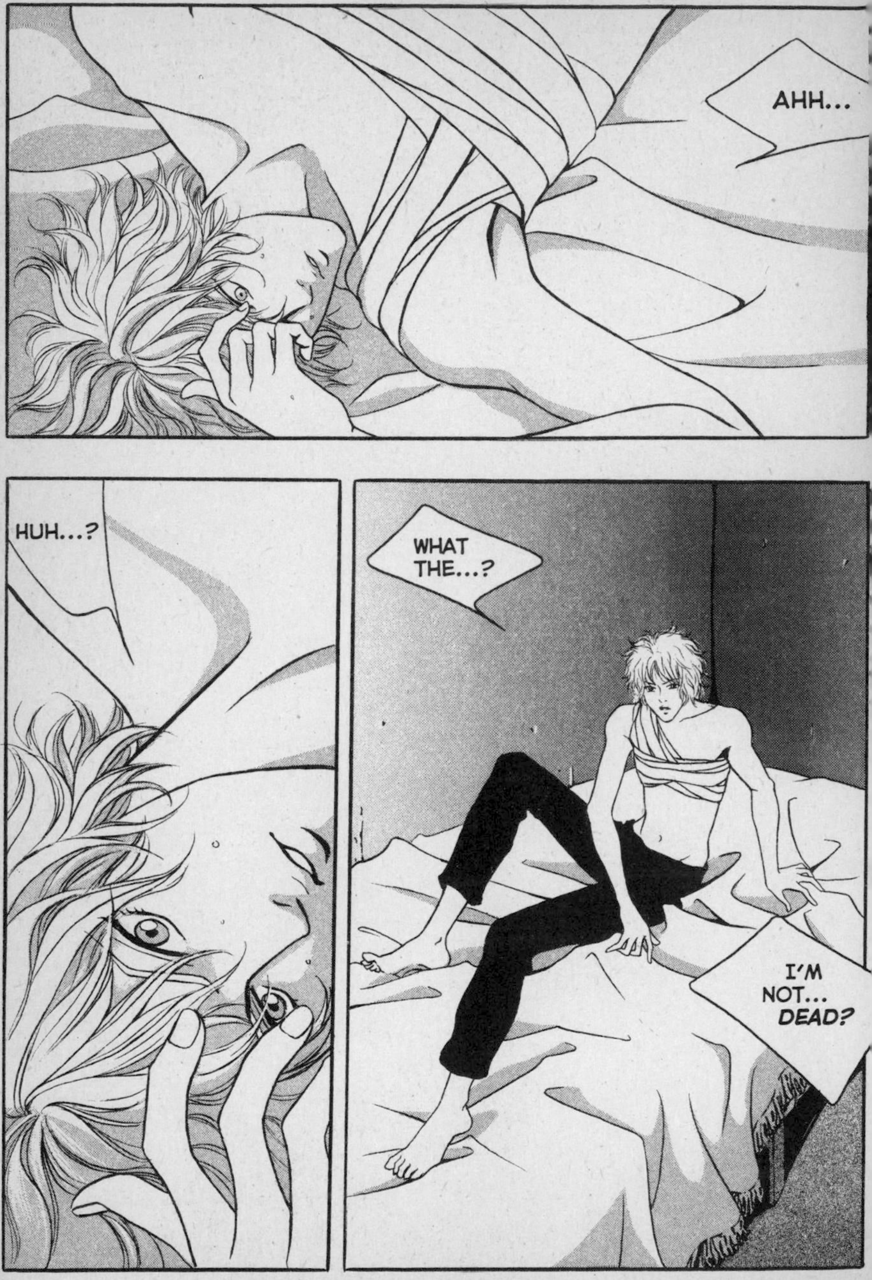
AHH...
HUH...?
WHAT THE...?
I'M NOT... *DEAD?*

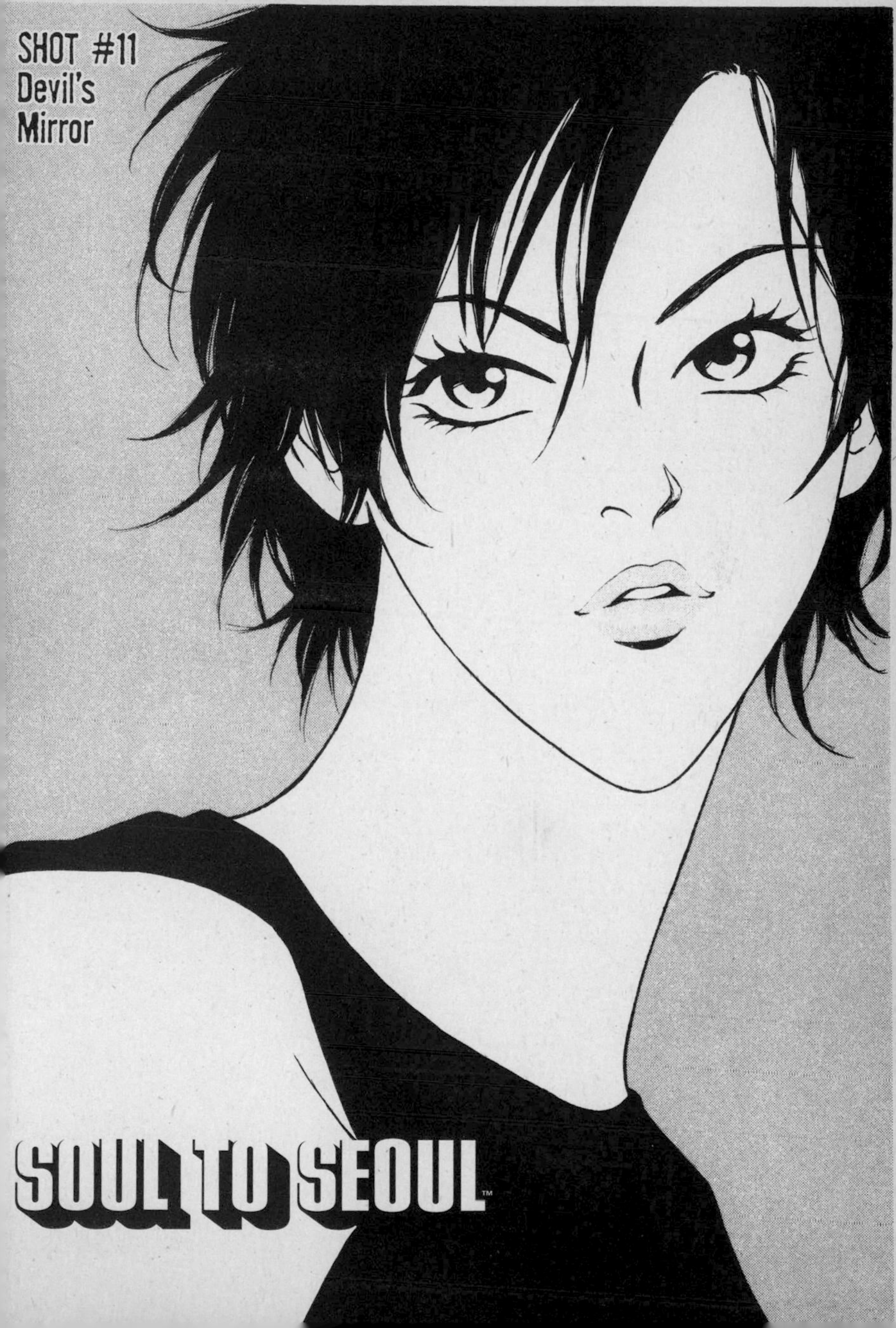
SHOT #11
Devil's
Mirror
SOUL TO SEOUL™

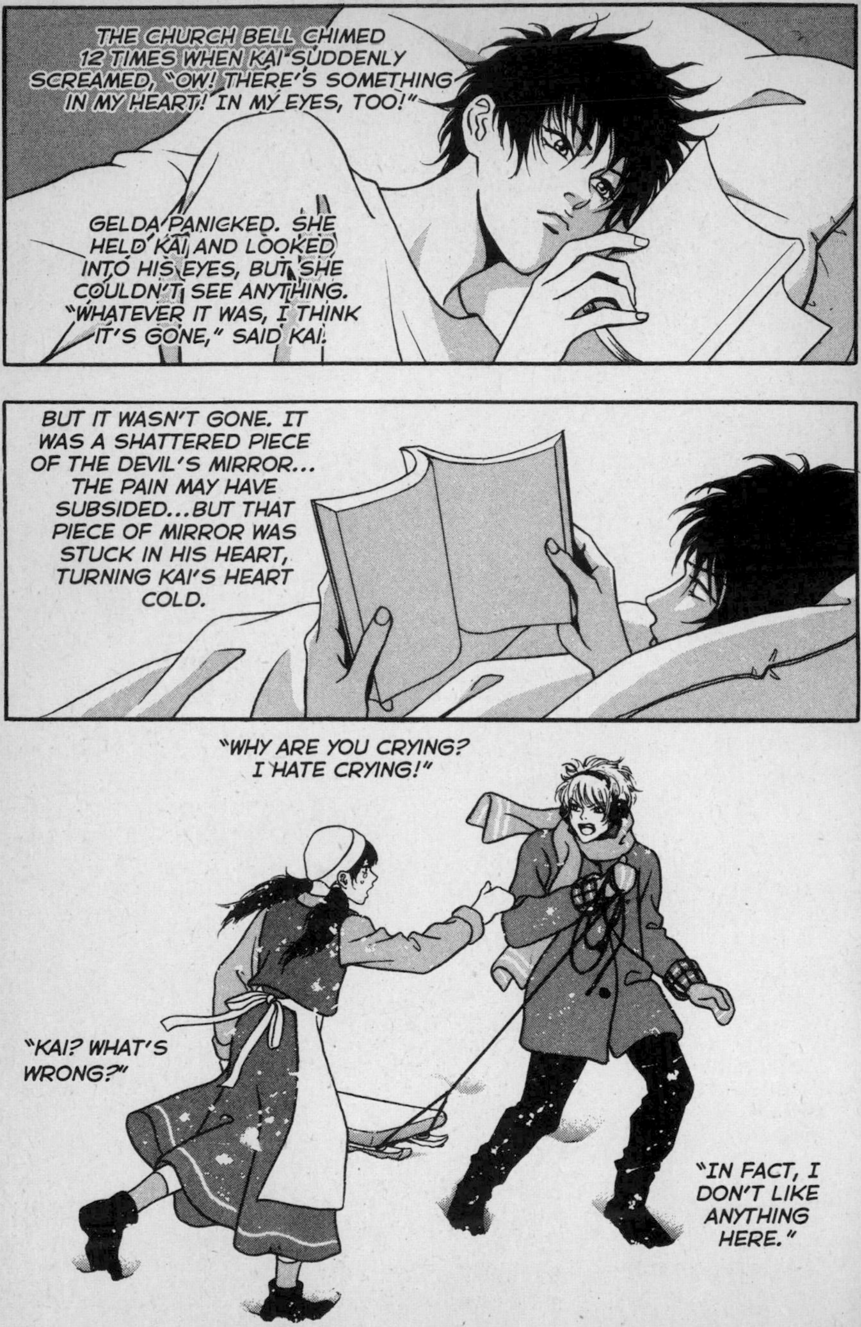
THE CHURCH BELL CHIMED 12 TIMES WHEN KAI SUDDENLY SCREAMED, "OW! THERE'S SOMETHING IN MY HEART! IN MY EYES, TOO!"
GELDA PANICKED. SHE HELD KAI AND LOOKED INTO HIS EYES, BUT SHE COULDN'T SEE ANYTHING. "WHATEVER IT WAS, I THINK IT'S GONE," SAID KAI.
BUT IT WASN'T GONE. IT WAS A SHATTERED PIECE OF THE DEVIL'S MIRROR... THE PAIN MAY HAVE SUBSIDED...BUT THAT PIECE OF MIRROR WAS STUCK IN HIS HEART, TURNING KAI'S HEART COLD.
"WHY ARE YOU CRYING? I HATE CRYING!"
"KAI? WHAT'S WRONG?"
"IN FACT, I DON'T LIKE ANYTHING HERE."

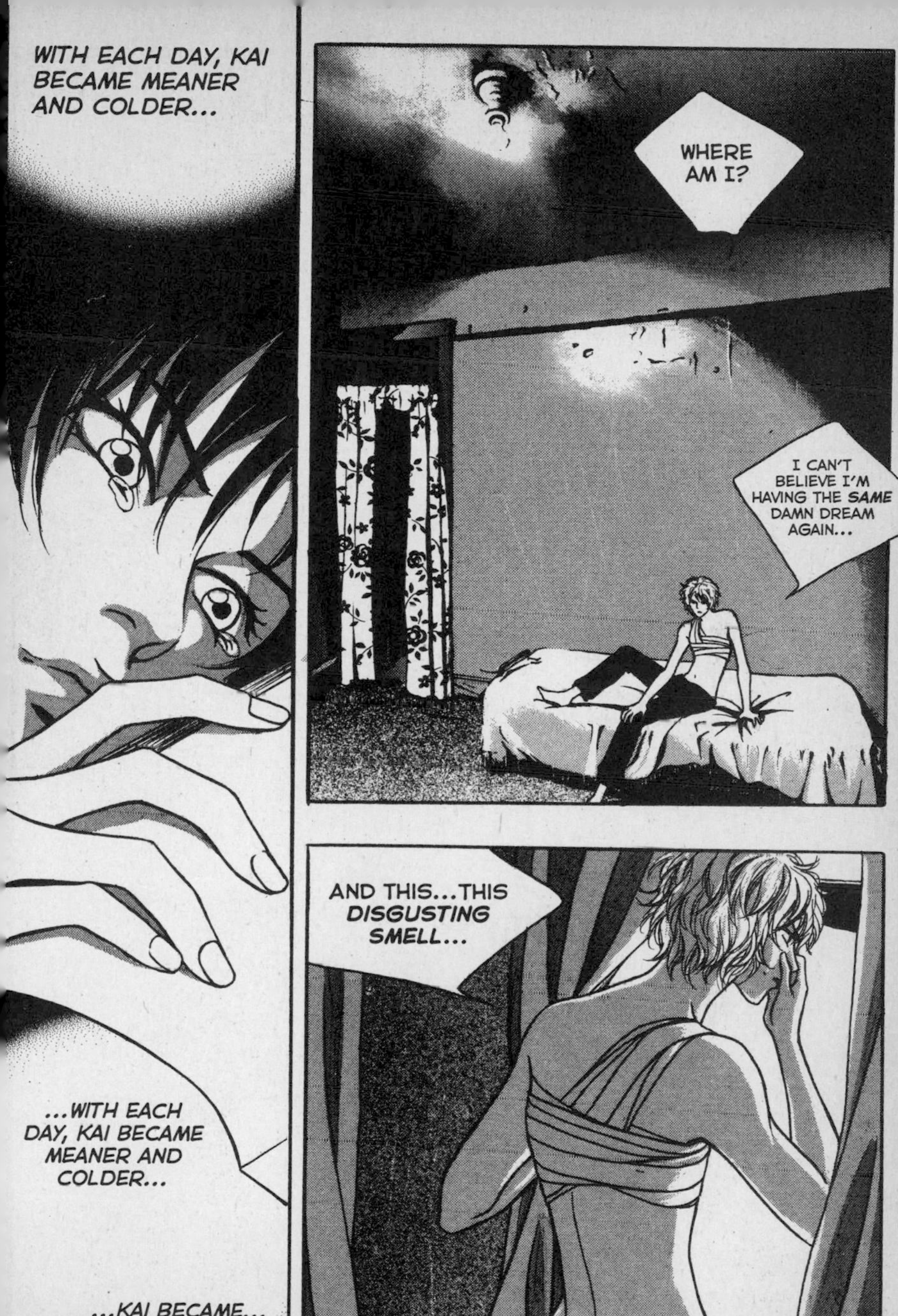
WHERE AM I?
I CAN'T BELIEVE I'M HAVING THE *SAME* DAMN DREAM AGAIN...
AND THIS...THIS *DISGUSTING* SMELL...
WITH EACH DAY, KAI BECAME MEANER AND COLDER...
...WITH EACH DAY, KAI BECAME MEANER AND COLDER...
...KAI BECAME...

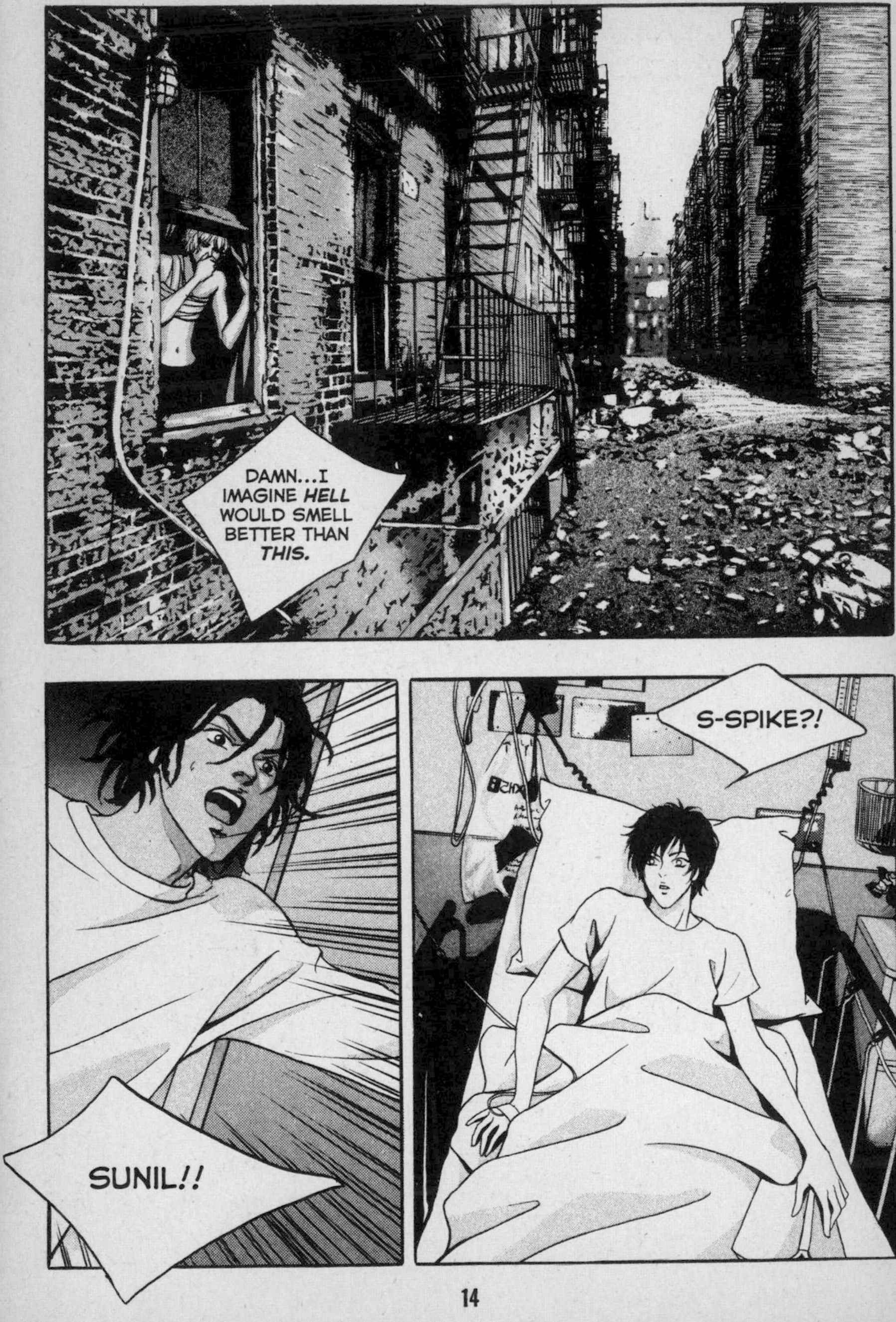
DAMN...I IMAGINE HELL WOULD SMELL BETTER THAN THIS.
SUNIL!!
S-SPIKE?!

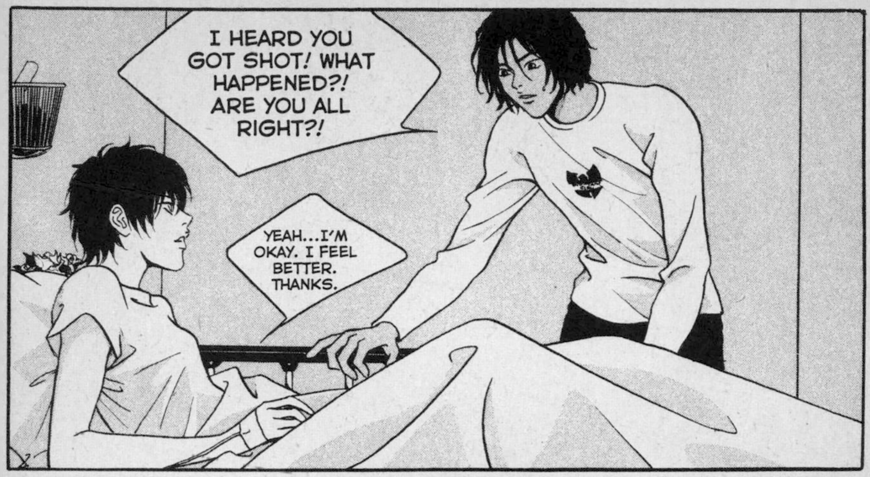
I HEARD YOU GOT SHOT! WHAT HAPPENED?! ARE YOU ALL RIGHT?!
YEAH...I'M OKAY. I FEEL BETTER. THANKS.

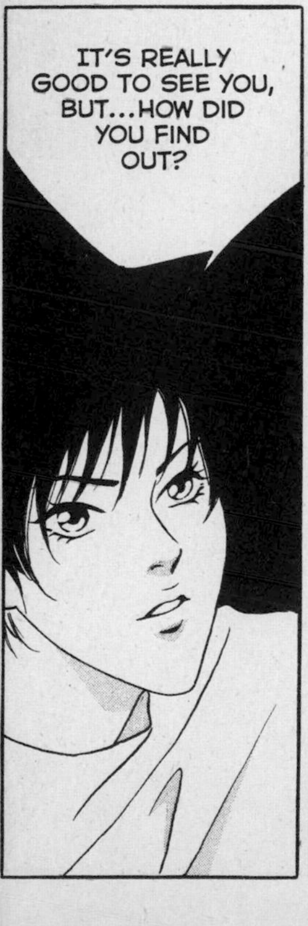
IT'S REALLY GOOD TO SEE YOU, BUT...HOW DID YOU FIND OUT?

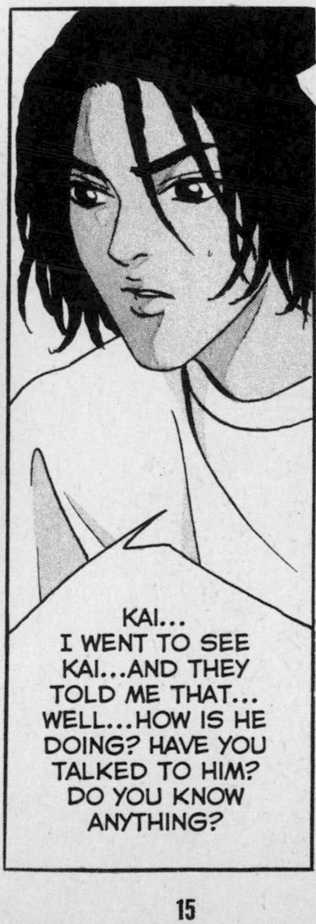
KAI... I WENT TO SEE KAI...AND THEY TOLD ME THAT... WELL...HOW IS HE DOING? HAVE YOU TALKED TO HIM? DO YOU KNOW ANYTHING?

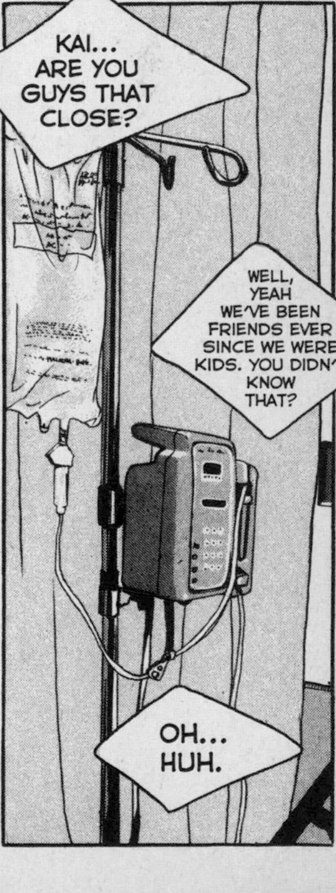
KAI... ARE YOU GUYS THAT CLOSE?
WELL, YEAH WE'VE BEEN FRIENDS EVER SINCE WE WERE KIDS. YOU DIDN'T KNOW THAT?
OH... HUH.

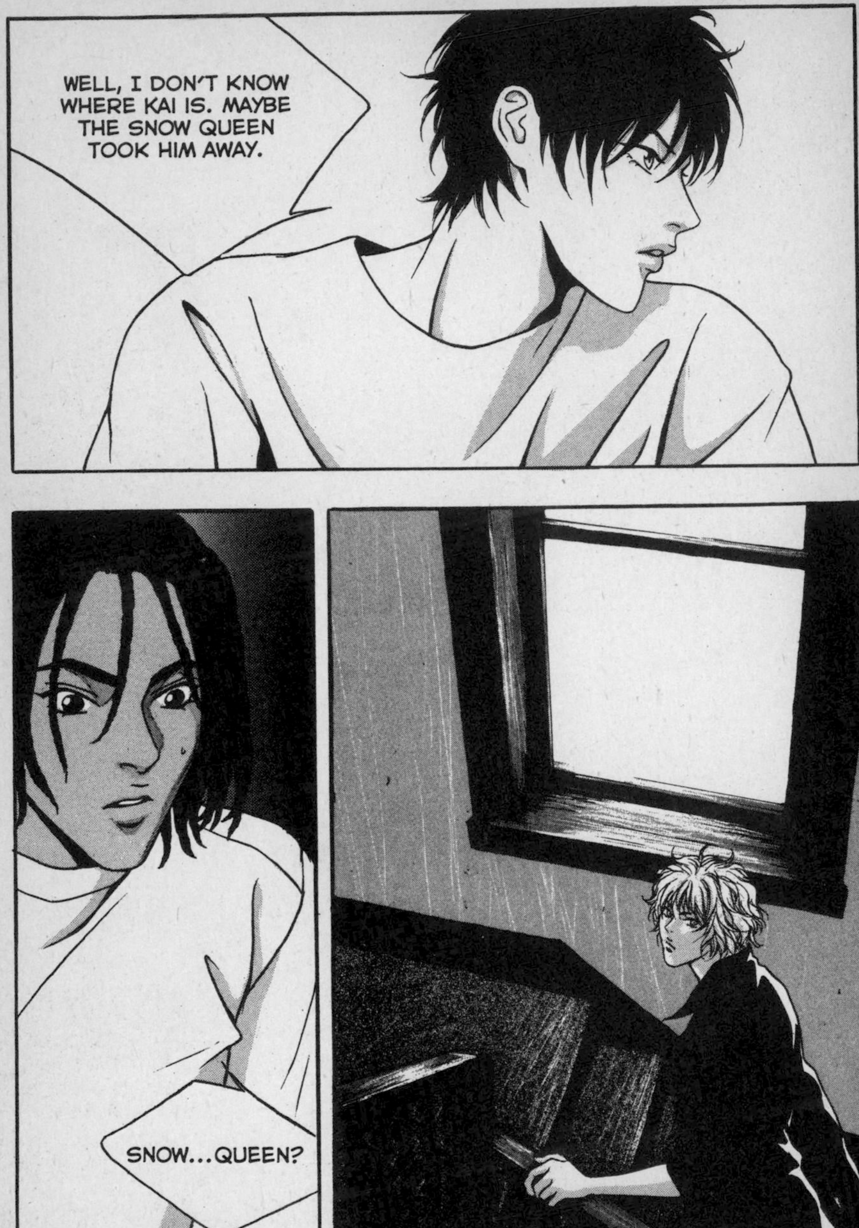
WELL, I DON'T KNOW WHERE KAI IS. MAYBE THE SNOW QUEEN TOOK HIM AWAY.
SNOW...QUEEN?

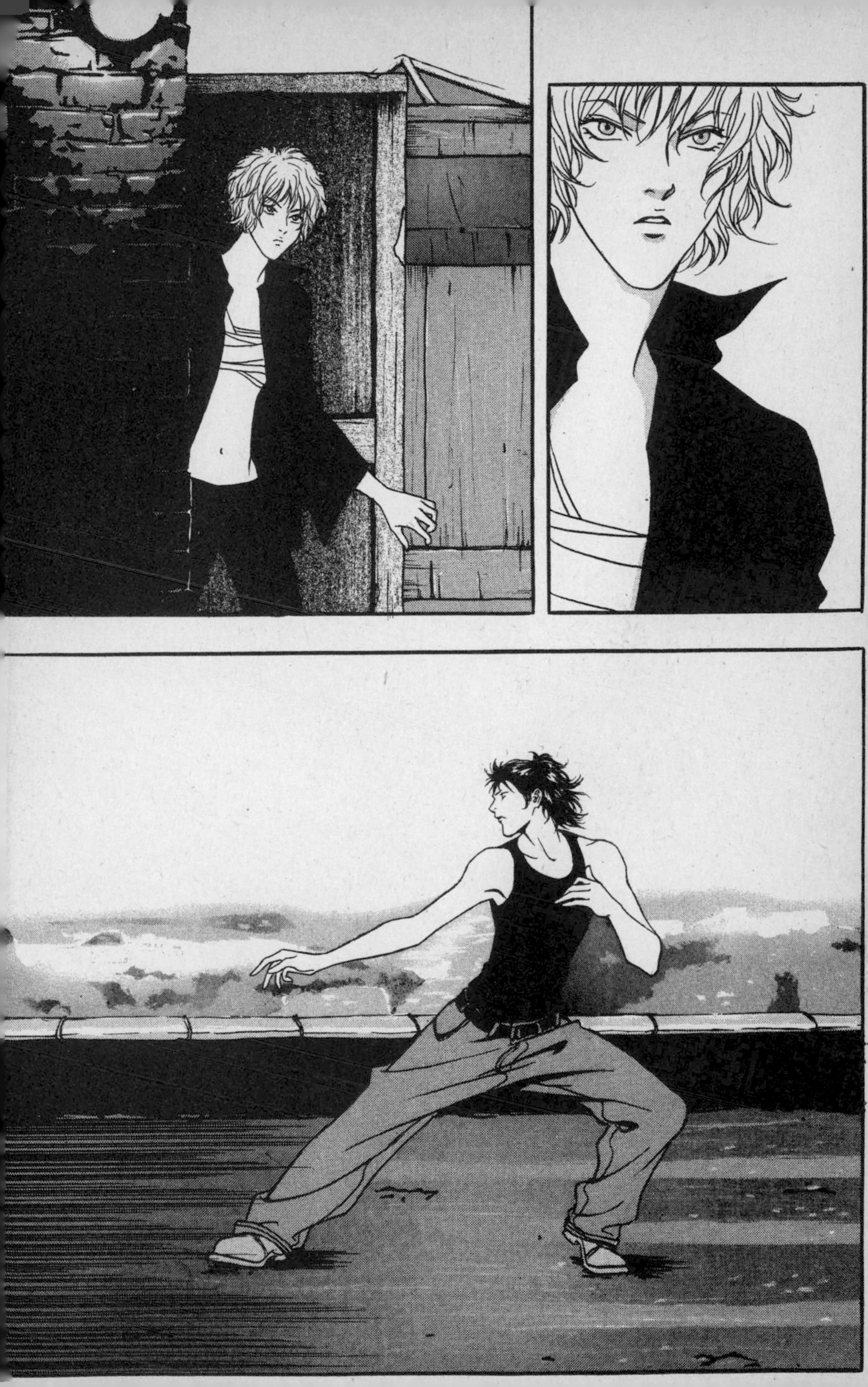

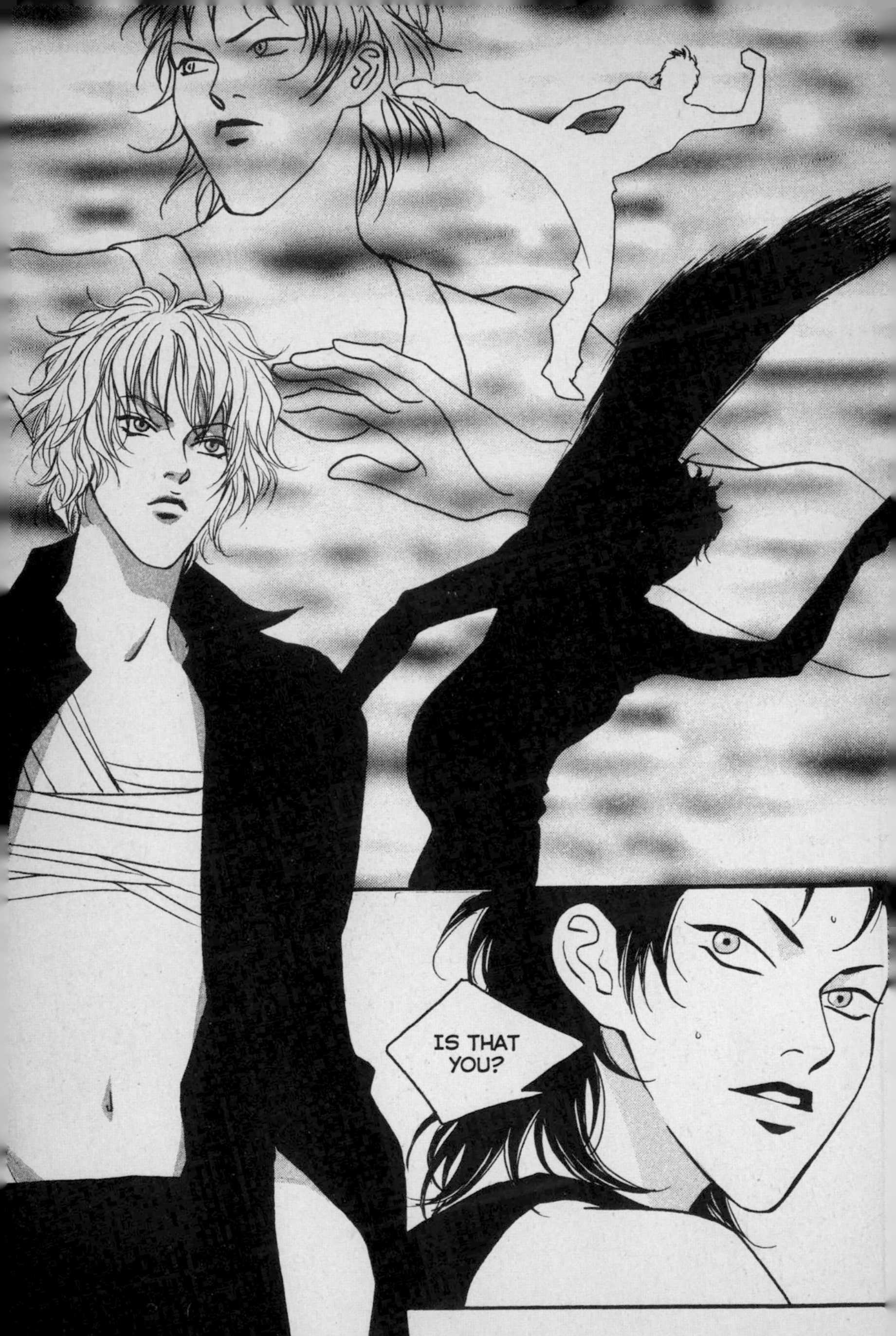
IS THAT
YOU?

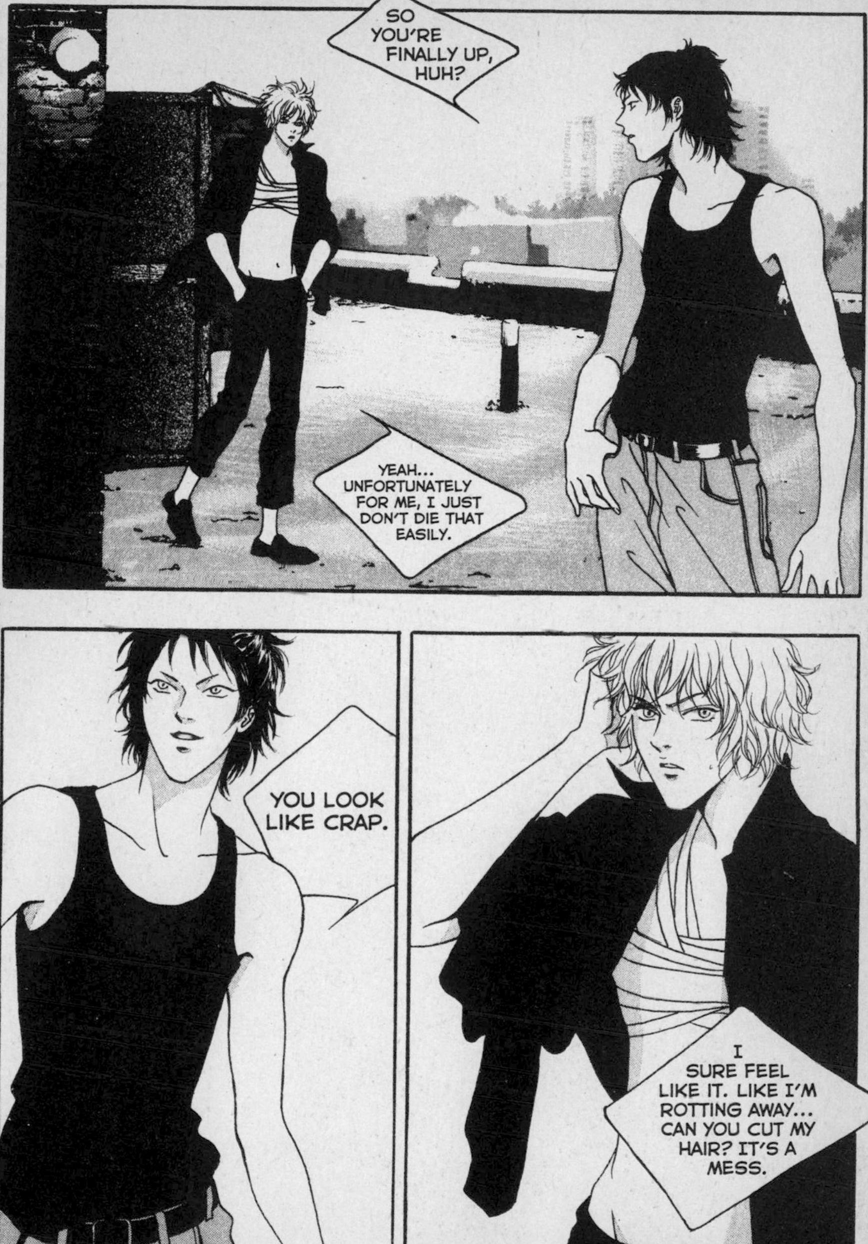
SO YOU'RE FINALLY UP, HUH?
YEAH... UNFORTUNATELY FOR ME, I JUST DON'T DIE THAT EASILY.
YOU LOOK LIKE CRAP.
I SURE FEEL LIKE IT. LIKE I'M ROTTING AWAY... CAN YOU CUT MY HAIR? IT'S A MESS.

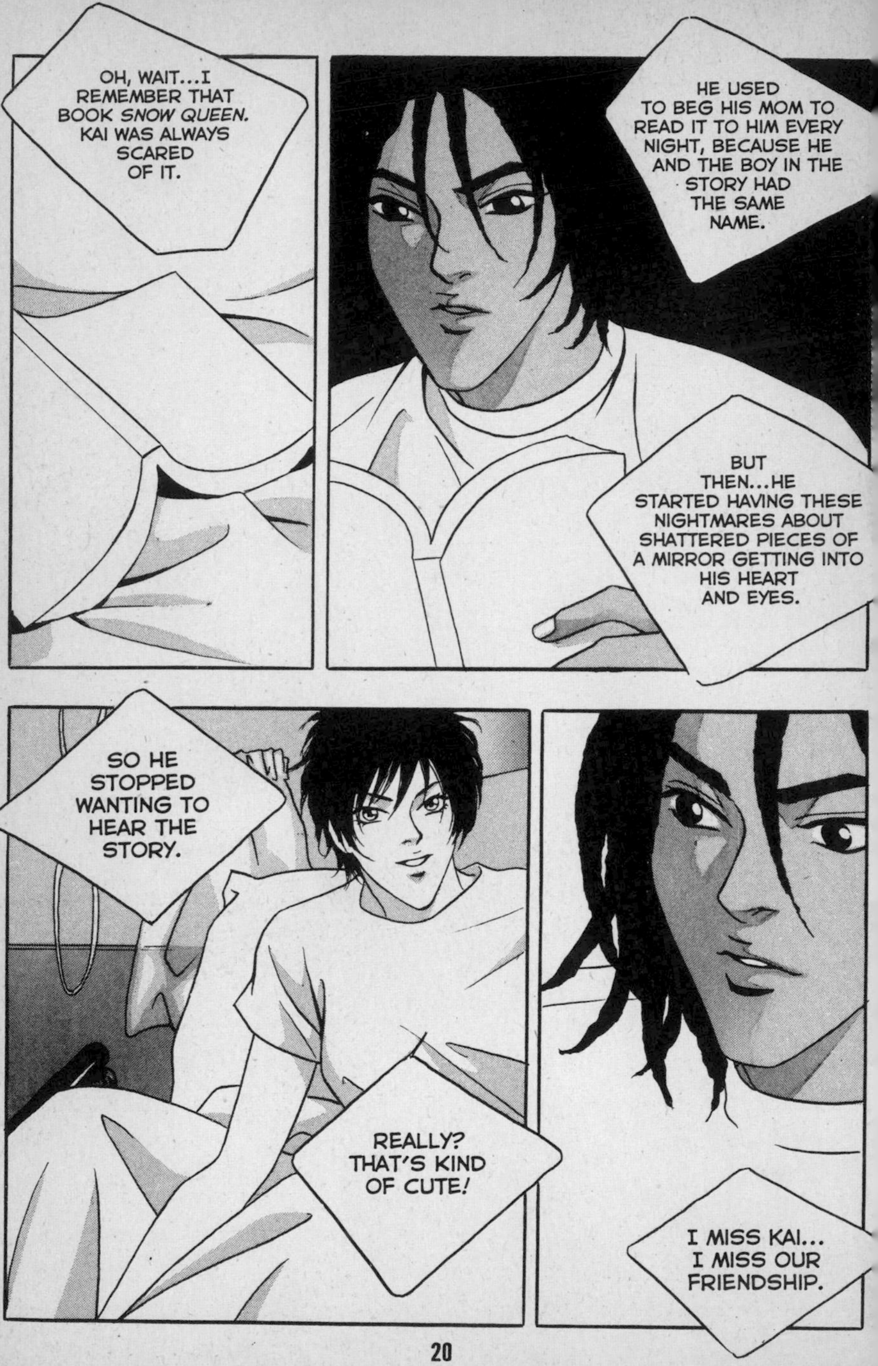
OH, WAIT...I REMEMBER THAT BOOK *SNOW QUEEN.* KAI WAS ALWAYS SCARED OF IT.
HE USED TO BEG HIS MOM TO READ IT TO HIM EVERY NIGHT, BECAUSE HE AND THE BOY IN THE STORY HAD THE SAME NAME.
BUT THEN...HE STARTED HAVING THESE NIGHTMARES ABOUT SHATTERED PIECES OF A MIRROR GETTING INTO HIS HEART AND EYES.
SO HE STOPPED WANTING TO HEAR THE STORY.
REALLY? THAT'S KIND OF CUTE!
I MISS KAI... I MISS OUR FRIENDSHIP.

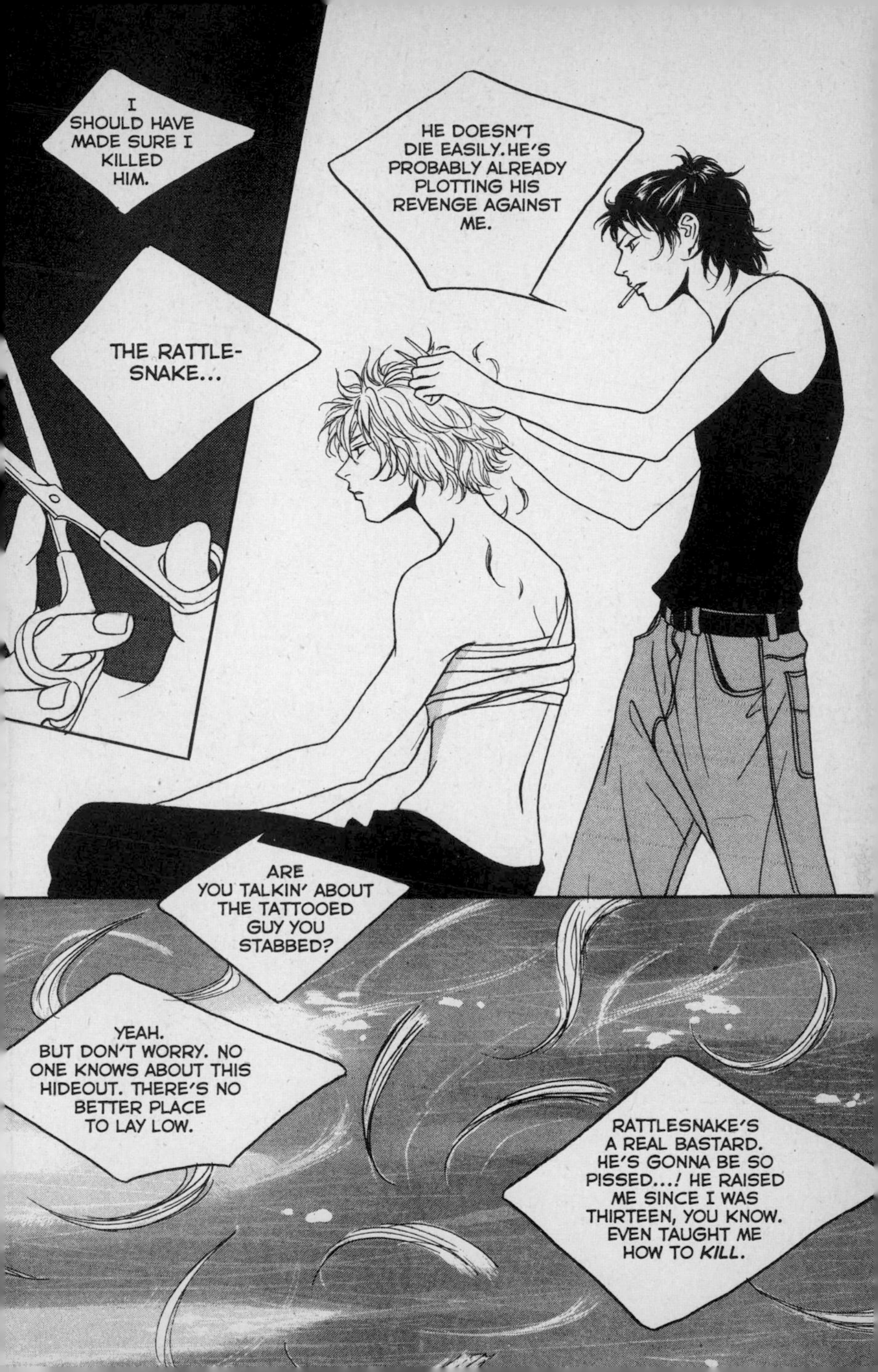
HE DOESN'T DIE EASILY. HE'S PROBABLY ALREADY PLOTTING HIS REVENGE AGAINST ME.
I SHOULD HAVE MADE SURE I KILLED HIM.
THE RATTLE-SNAKE...
ARE YOU TALKIN' ABOUT THE TATTOOED GUY YOU STABBED?
YEAH. BUT DON'T WORRY. NO ONE KNOWS ABOUT THIS HIDEOUT. THERE'S NO BETTER PLACE TO LAY LOW.
RATTLESNAKE'S A REAL BASTARD. HE'S GONNA BE SO PISSED...! HE RAISED ME SINCE I WAS THIRTEEN, YOU KNOW. EVEN TAUGHT ME HOW TO *KILL*.

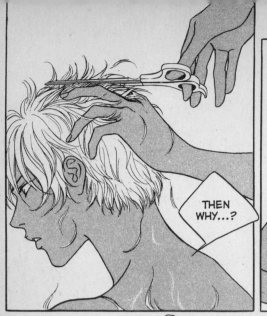

THEN WHY...?

WHY DID I BETRAY HIM?

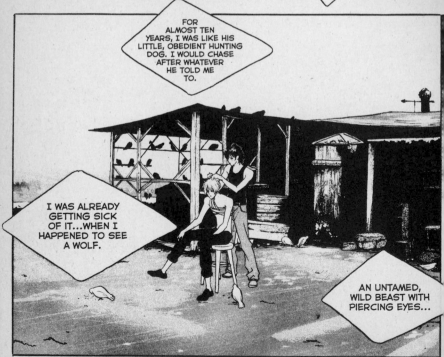

FOR ALMOST TEN YEARS, I WAS LIKE HIS LITTLE, OBEDIENT HUNTING DOG. I WOULD CHASE AFTER WHATEVER HE TOLD ME TO.

I WAS ALREADY GETTING SICK OF IT...WHEN I HAPPENED TO SEE A WOLF.

AN UNTAMED, WILD BEAST WITH PIERCING EYES...

22

I KNEW I COULD NEVER BECOME A WOLF MYSELF...BUT I COULD BECOME WILD AND FINALLY FOLLOW MY CALLING...MY *TRUE* NATURE!

SO THE DOG BIT ITS MASTER.

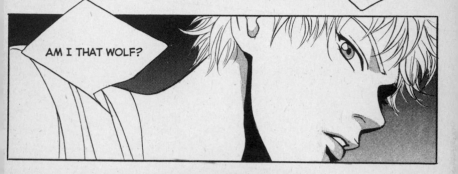

AM I THAT WOLF?

YES, YOU ARE. SO NOW YOU'LL TAKE CARE OF ME.

SO? WHAT DO YOU THINK? DO YOU LIKE IT?

23

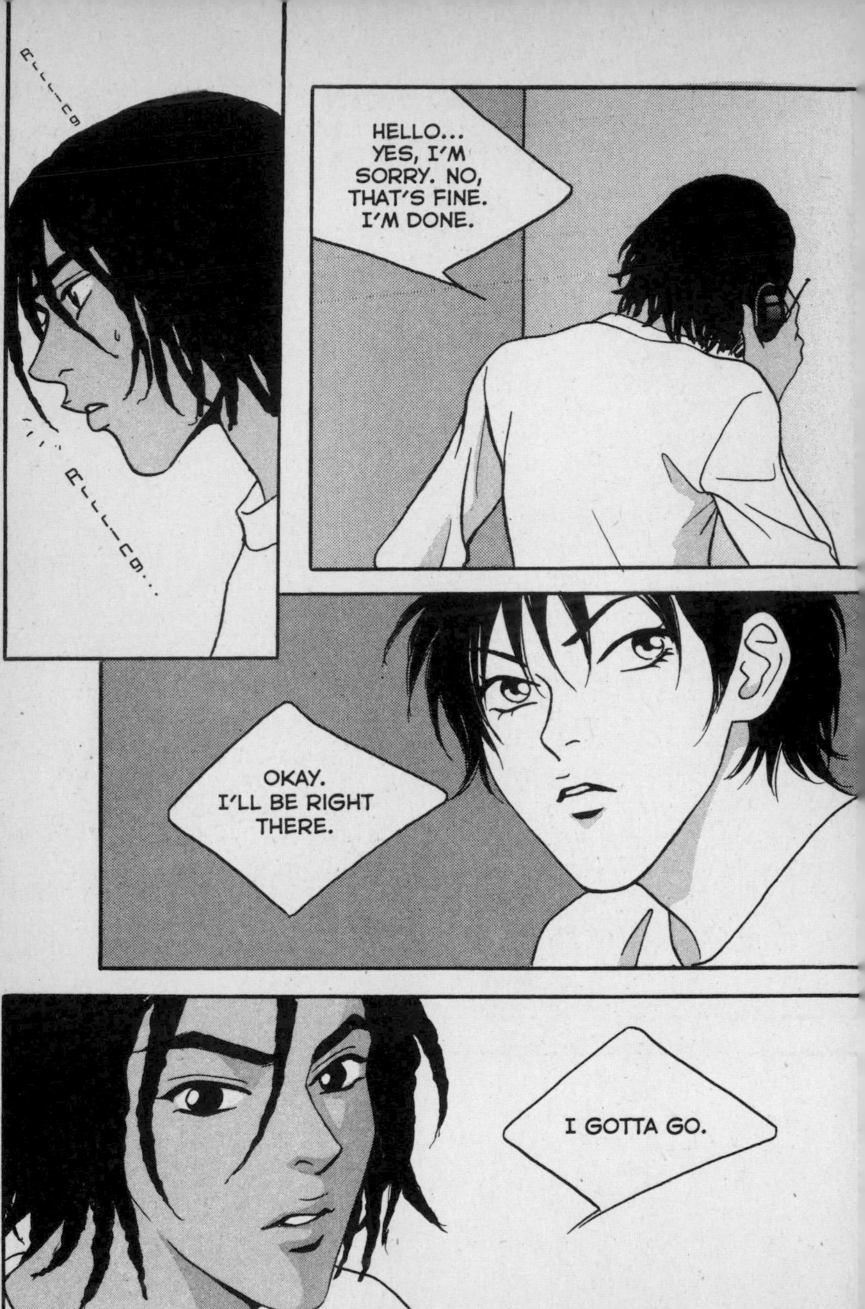
HELLO... YES, I'M SORRY. NO, THAT'S FINE. I'M DONE.
OKAY. I'LL BE RIGHT THERE.
I GOTTA GO.

THAT WAS HILLARY, WASN'T IT?

YEAH.

YOU TWO REALLY DO LOOK GOOD TOGETHER.

......

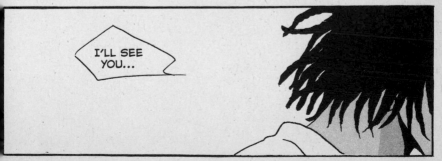

I'LL SEE YOU...

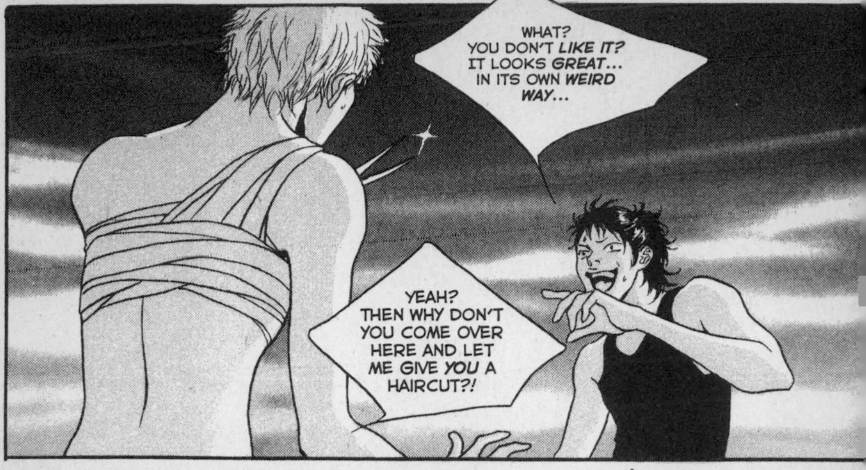
WHAT? YOU DON'T *LIKE IT?* IT LOOKS *GREAT...* IN ITS OWN *WEIRD WAY...*
YEAH? THEN WHY DON'T YOU COME OVER HERE AND LET ME GIVE *YOU* A HAIRCUT?!

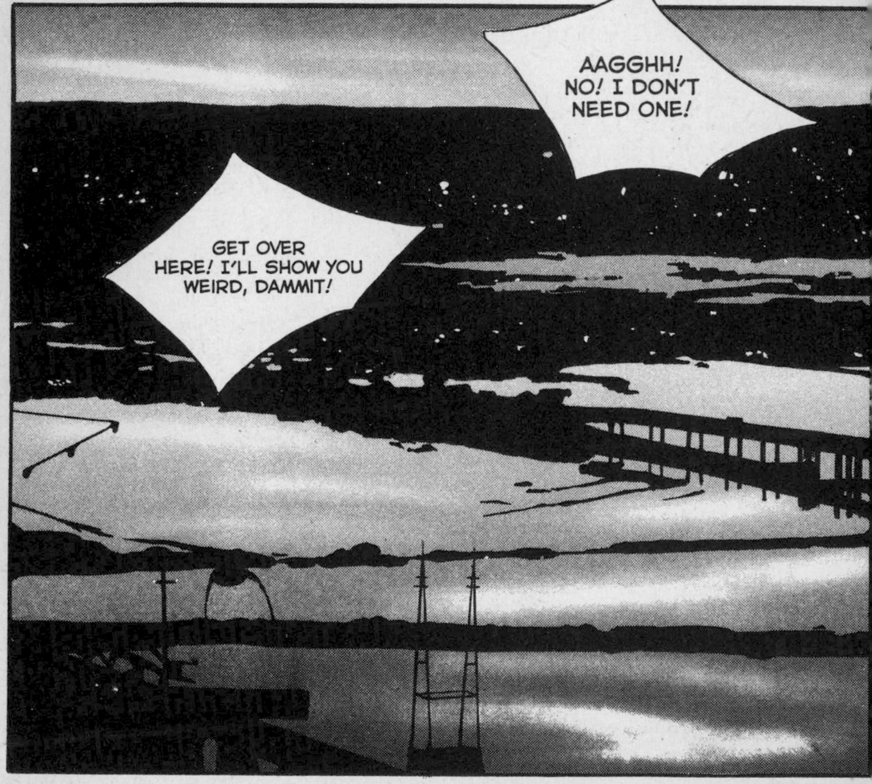
AAGGHH! NO! I DON'T NEED ONE!
GET OVER HERE! I'LL SHOW YOU WEIRD, DAMMIT!

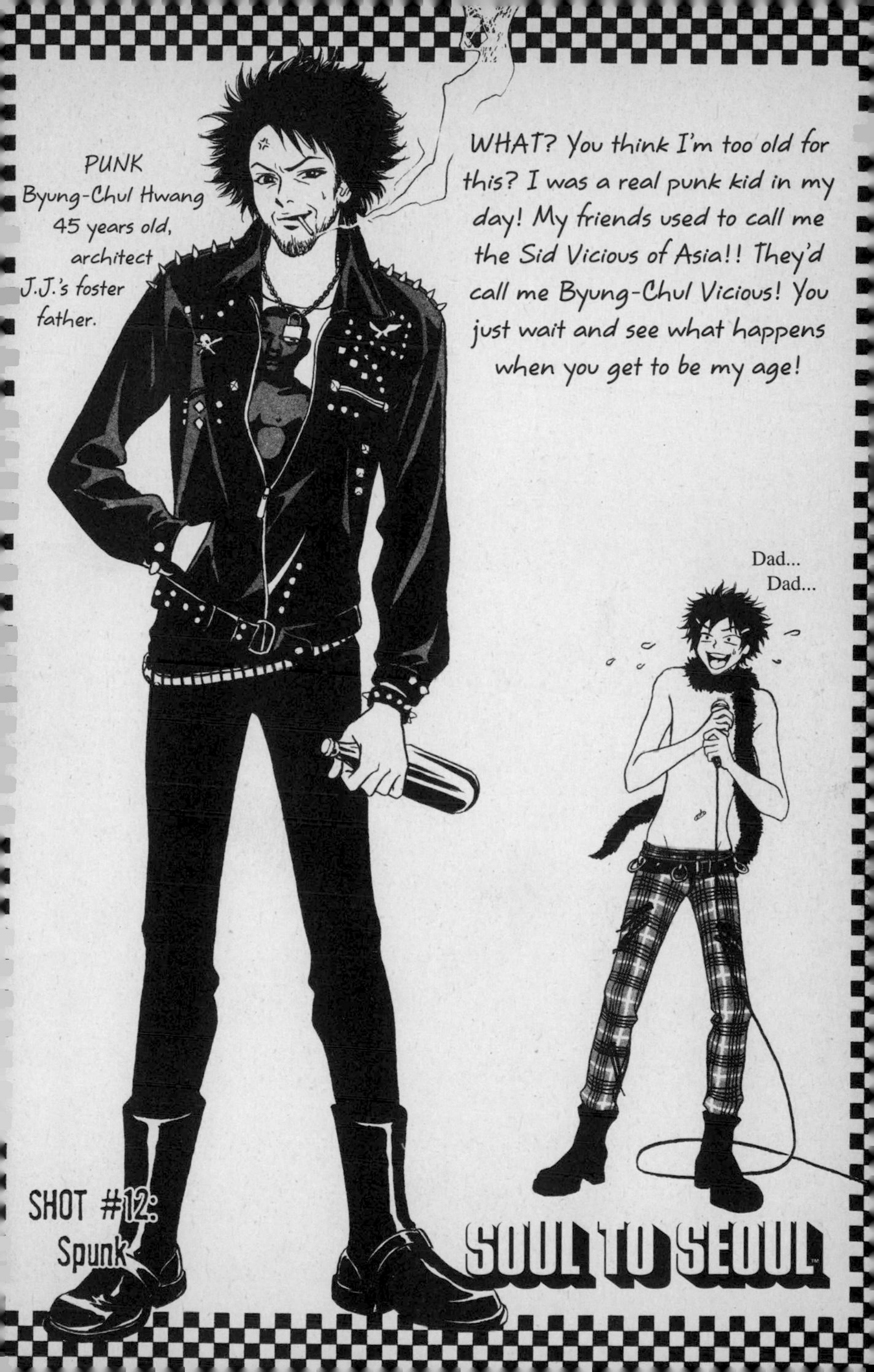
WHAT? You think I'm too old for this? I was a real punk kid in my day! My friends used to call me the Sid Vicious of Asia!! They'd call me Byung-Chul Vicious! You just wait and see what happens when you get to be my age!
PUNK
Byung-Chul Hwang
45 years old,
architect
J.J.'s foster father.
Dad... Dad...
SHOT #12:
Spunk
SOUL TO SEOUL

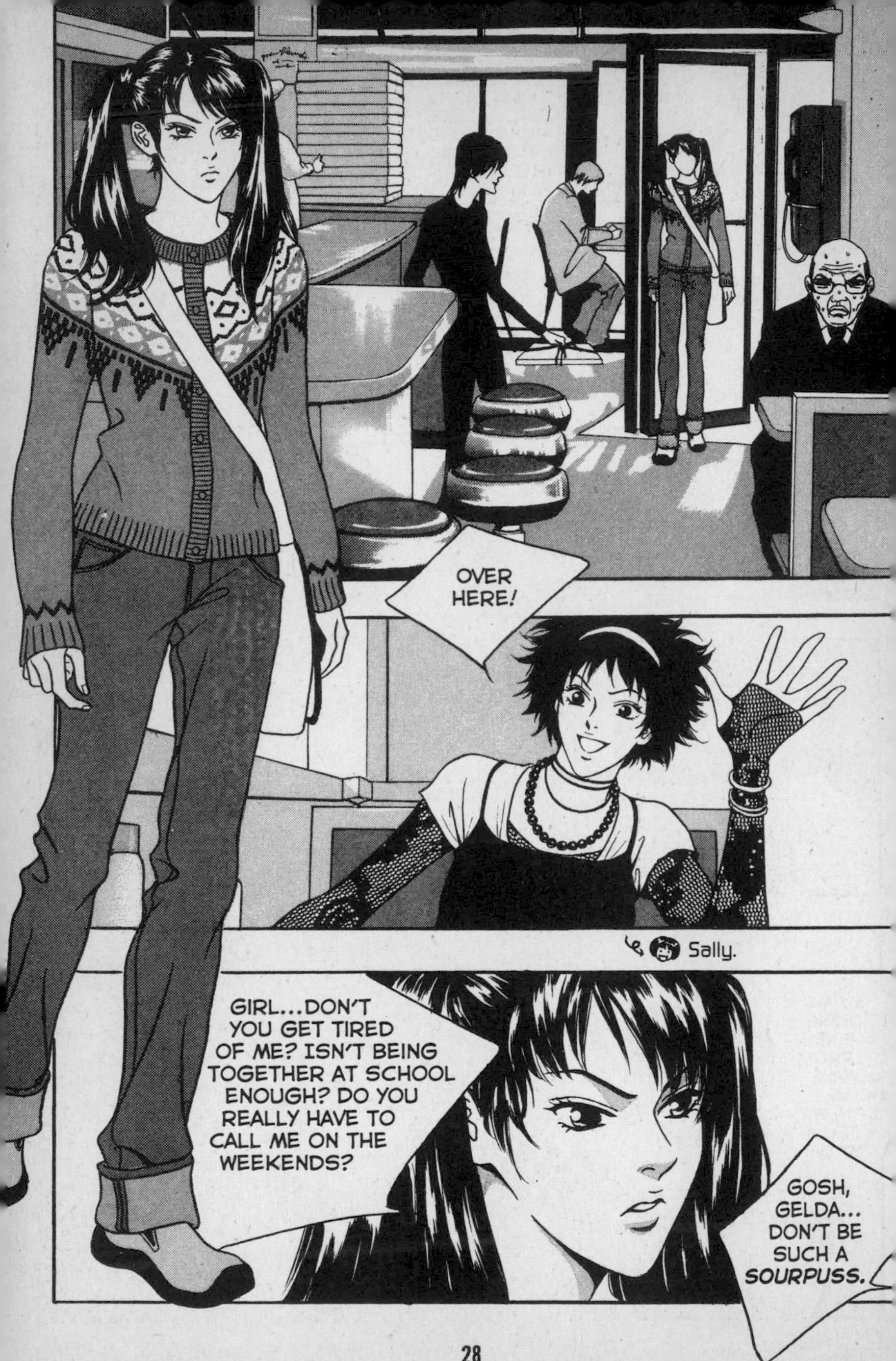
OVER HERE!
Sally.
GIRL...DON'T YOU GET TIRED OF ME? ISN'T BEING TOGETHER AT SCHOOL ENOUGH? DO YOU REALLY HAVE TO CALL ME ON THE WEEKENDS?
GOSH, GELDA... DON'T BE SUCH A *SOURPUSS.*

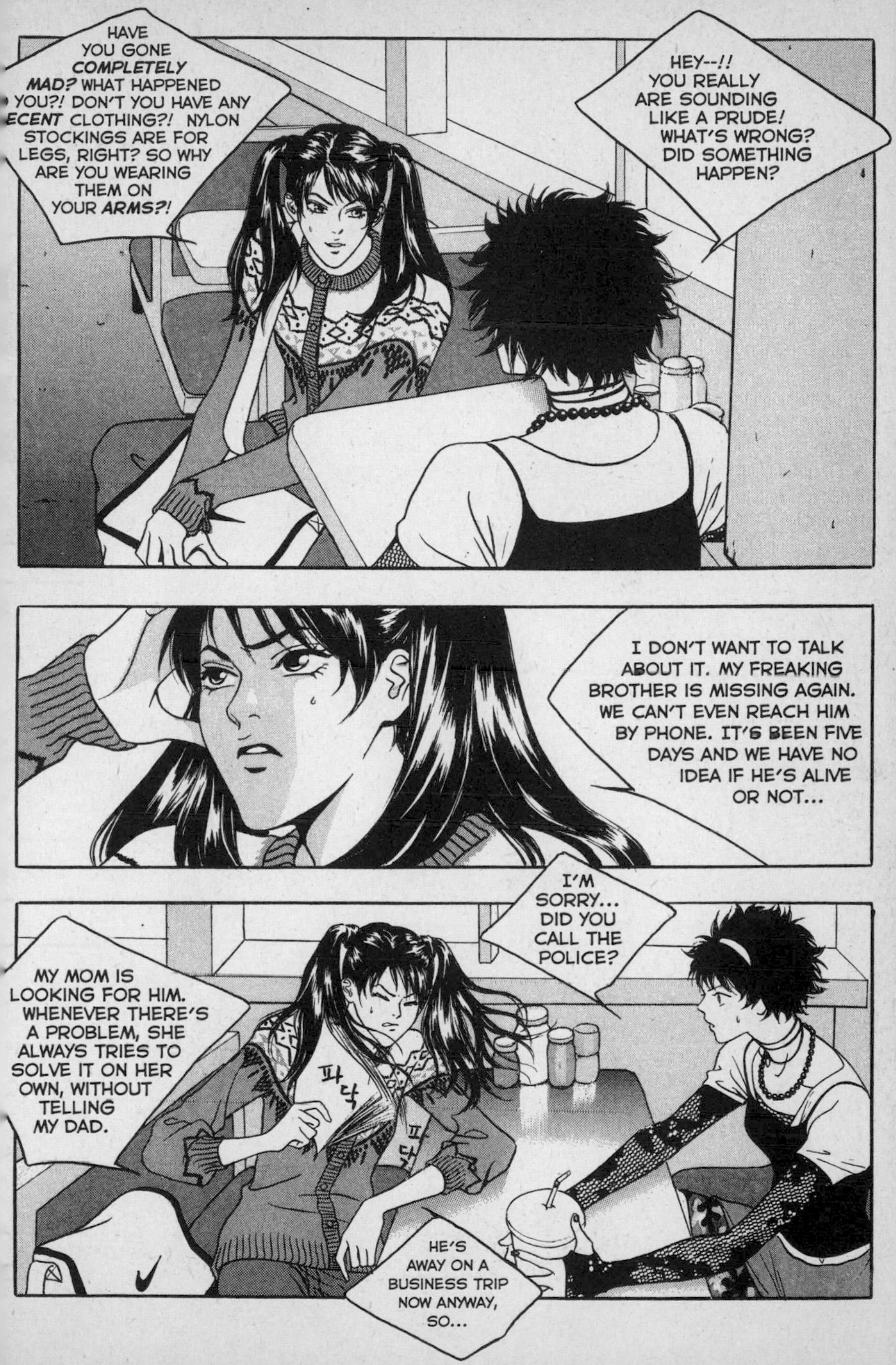
HAVE YOU GONE COMPLETELY MAD? WHAT HAPPENED YOU?! DON'T YOU HAVE ANY ECENT CLOTHING?! NYLON STOCKINGS ARE FOR LEGS, RIGHT? SO WHY ARE YOU WEARING THEM ON YOUR ARMS?!
HEY--!! YOU REALLY ARE SOUNDING LIKE A PRUDE! WHAT'S WRONG? DID SOMETHING HAPPEN?
I DON'T WANT TO TALK ABOUT IT. MY FREAKING BROTHER IS MISSING AGAIN. WE CAN'T EVEN REACH HIM BY PHONE. IT'S BEEN FIVE DAYS AND WE HAVE NO IDEA IF HE'S ALIVE OR NOT...
I'M SORRY... DID YOU CALL THE POLICE?
MY MOM IS LOOKING FOR HIM. WHENEVER THERE'S A PROBLEM, SHE ALWAYS TRIES TO SOLVE IT ON HER OWN, WITHOUT TELLING MY DAD.
파닥
파닥
HE'S AWAY ON A BUSINESS TRIP NOW ANYWAY, SO...

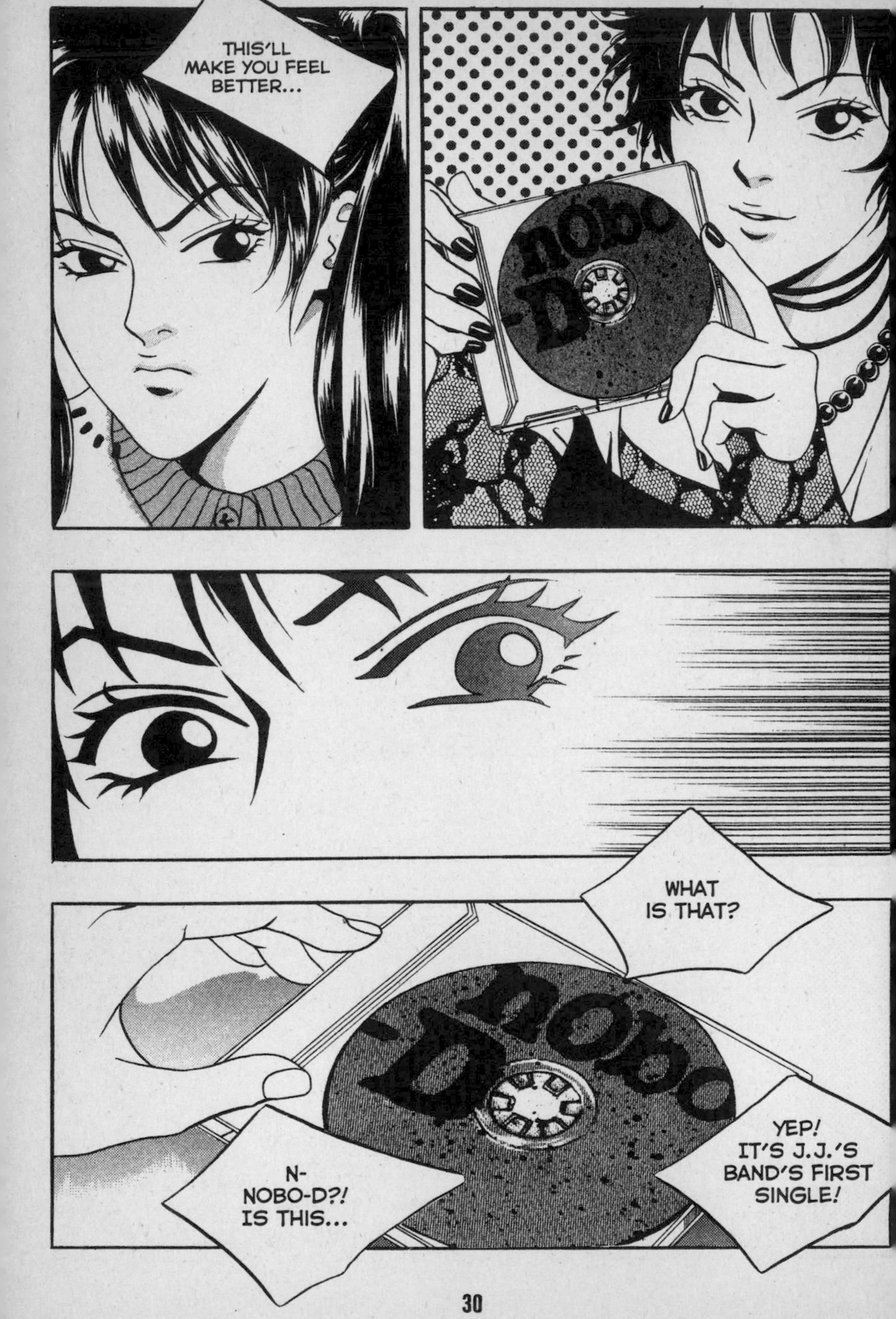
THIS'LL MAKE YOU FEEL BETTER...
WHAT IS THAT?
N-NOBO-D?! IS THIS...
YEP! IT'S J.J.'S BAND'S FIRST SINGLE!

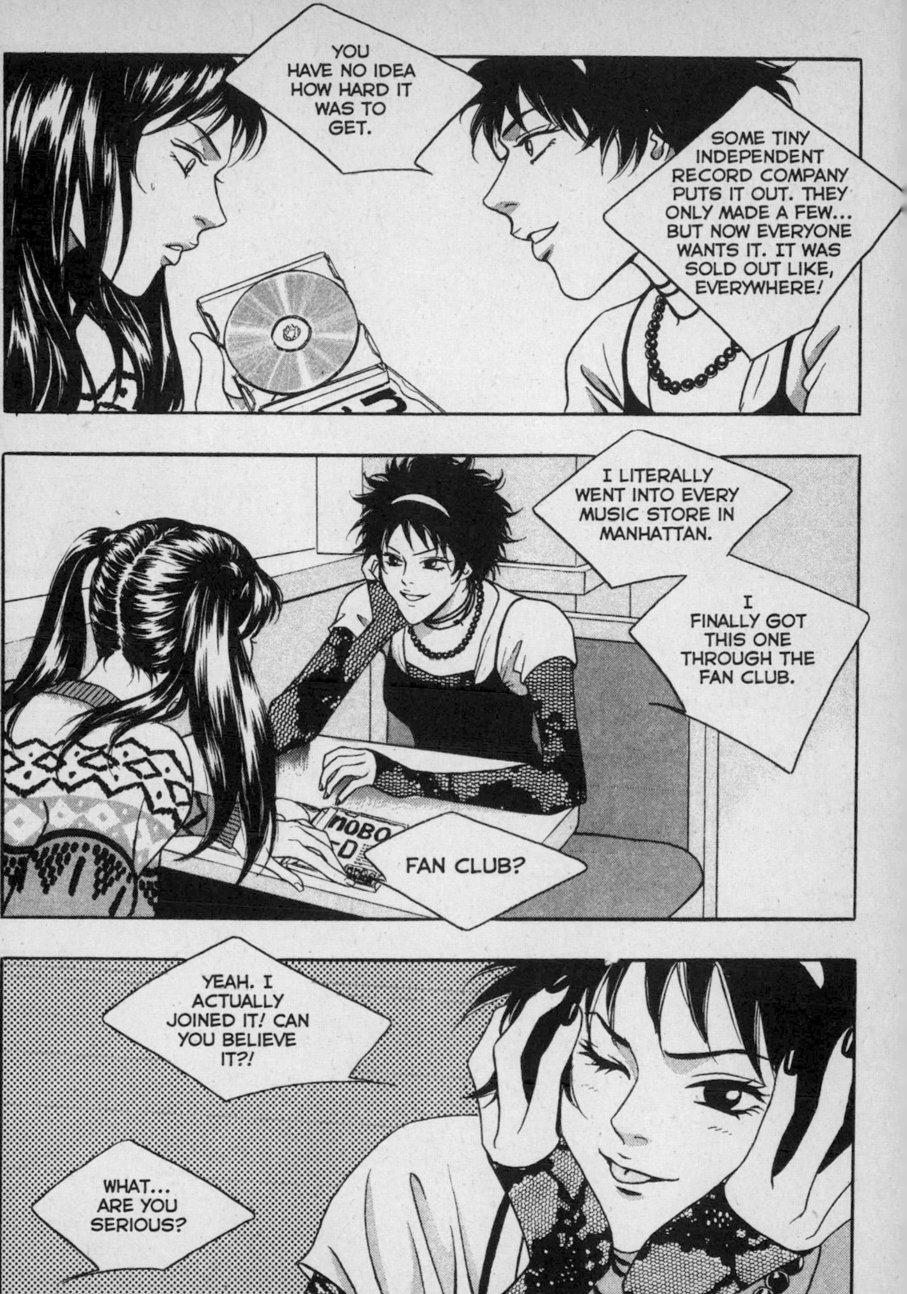
YOU HAVE NO IDEA HOW HARD IT WAS TO GET.
SOME TINY INDEPENDENT RECORD COMPANY PUTS IT OUT. THEY ONLY MADE A FEW... BUT NOW EVERYONE WANTS IT. IT WAS SOLD OUT LIKE, EVERYWHERE!
I LITERALLY WENT INTO EVERY MUSIC STORE IN MANHATTAN.
I FINALLY GOT THIS ONE THROUGH THE FAN CLUB.
FAN CLUB?
YEAH. I ACTUALLY JOINED IT! CAN YOU BELIEVE IT?!
WHAT... ARE YOU SERIOUS?

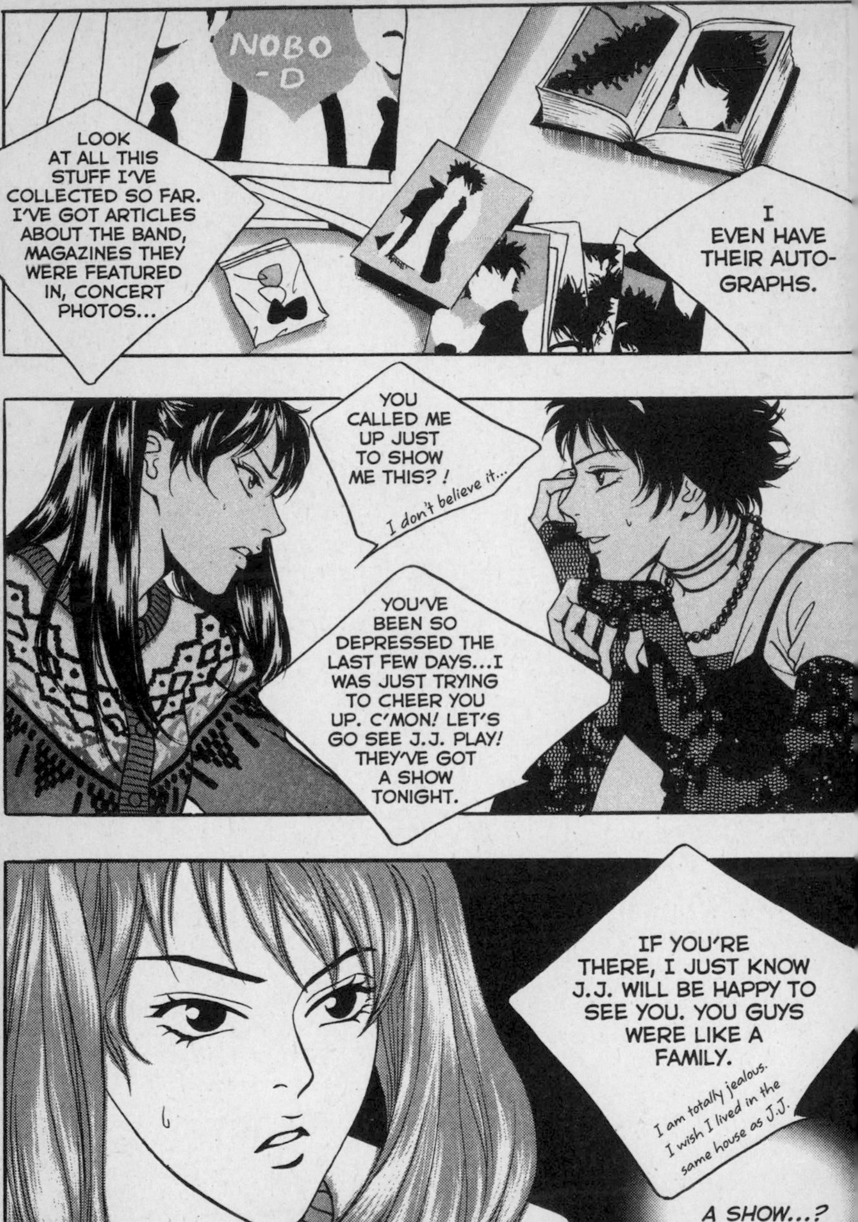
NOBO -D
LOOK AT ALL THIS STUFF I'VE COLLECTED SO FAR. I'VE GOT ARTICLES ABOUT THE BAND, MAGAZINES THEY WERE FEATURED IN, CONCERT PHOTOS...
I EVEN HAVE THEIR AUTO-GRAPHS.
YOU CALLED ME UP JUST TO SHOW ME THIS?!
I don't believe it...
YOU'VE BEEN SO DEPRESSED THE LAST FEW DAYS...I WAS JUST TRYING TO CHEER YOU UP. C'MON! LET'S GO SEE J.J. PLAY! THEY'VE GOT A SHOW TONIGHT.
IF YOU'RE THERE, I JUST KNOW J.J. WILL BE HAPPY TO SEE YOU. YOU GUYS WERE LIKE A FAMILY.
I am totally jealous. I wish I lived in the same house as J.J.
A SHOW...?

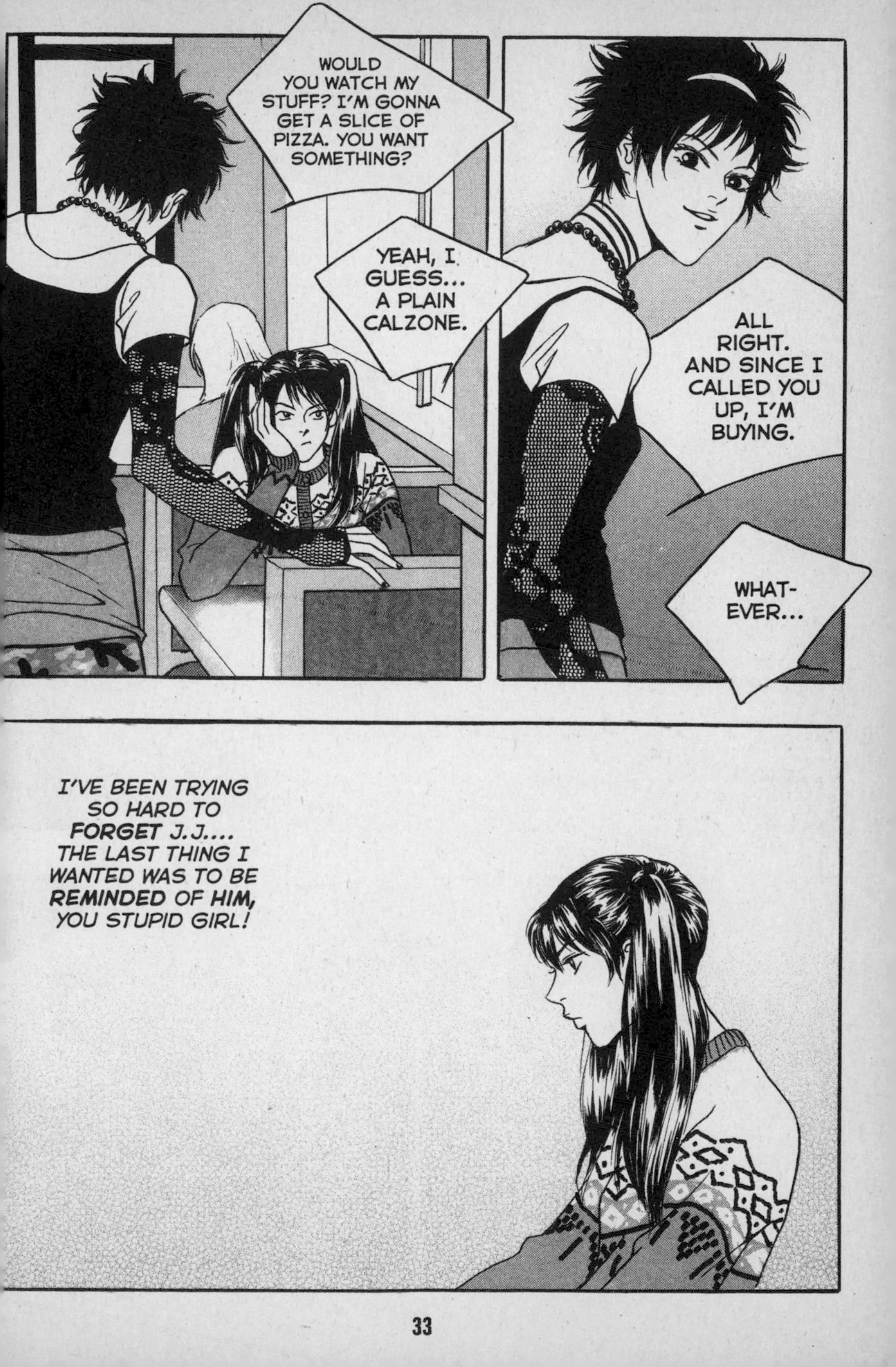
WOULD YOU WATCH MY STUFF? I'M GONNA GET A SLICE OF PIZZA. YOU WANT SOMETHING?
YEAH, I GUESS... A PLAIN CALZONE.
ALL RIGHT. AND SINCE I CALLED YOU UP, I'M BUYING.
WHAT-EVER...
I'VE BEEN TRYING SO HARD TO FORGET J.J.... THE LAST THING I WANTED WAS TO BE REMINDED OF HIM, YOU STUPID GIRL!

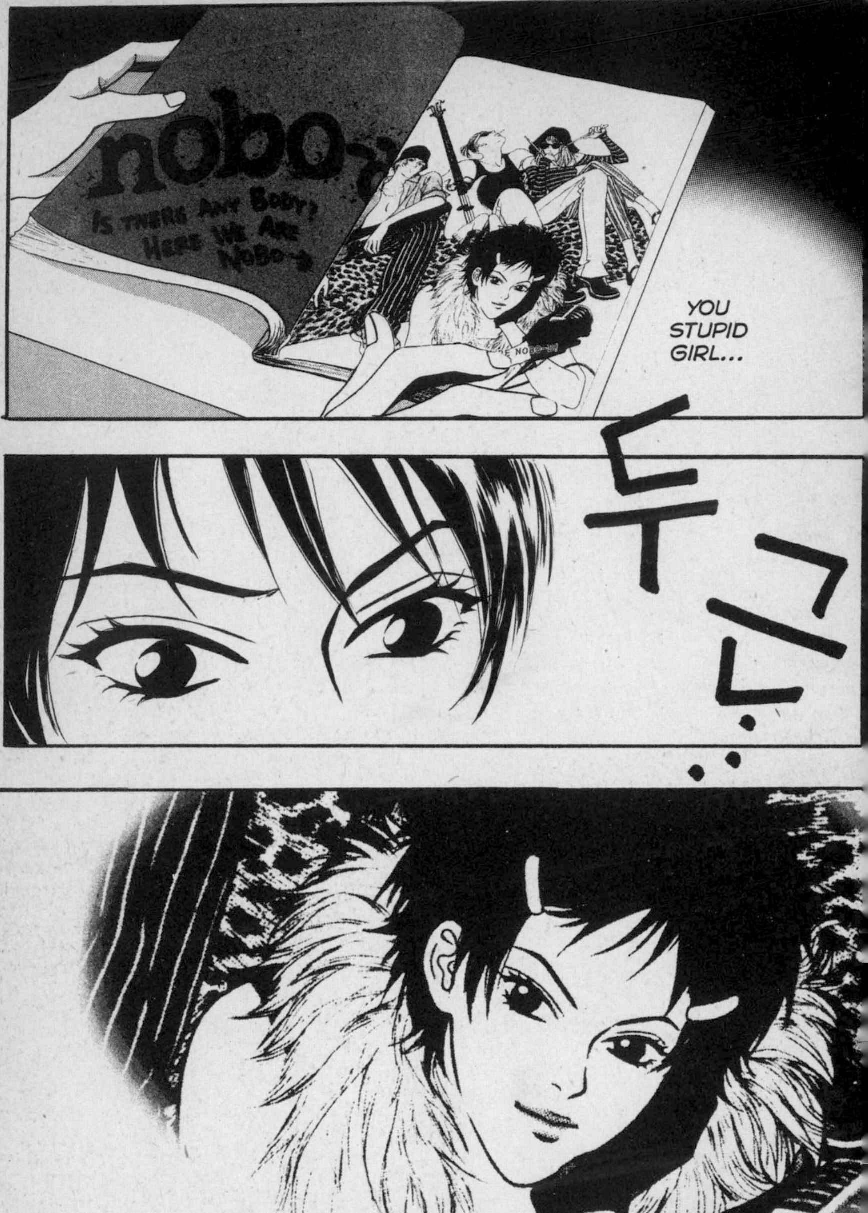
IS THERE ANY BODY?
HERE WE ARE NOBO-
YOU STUPID GIRL...

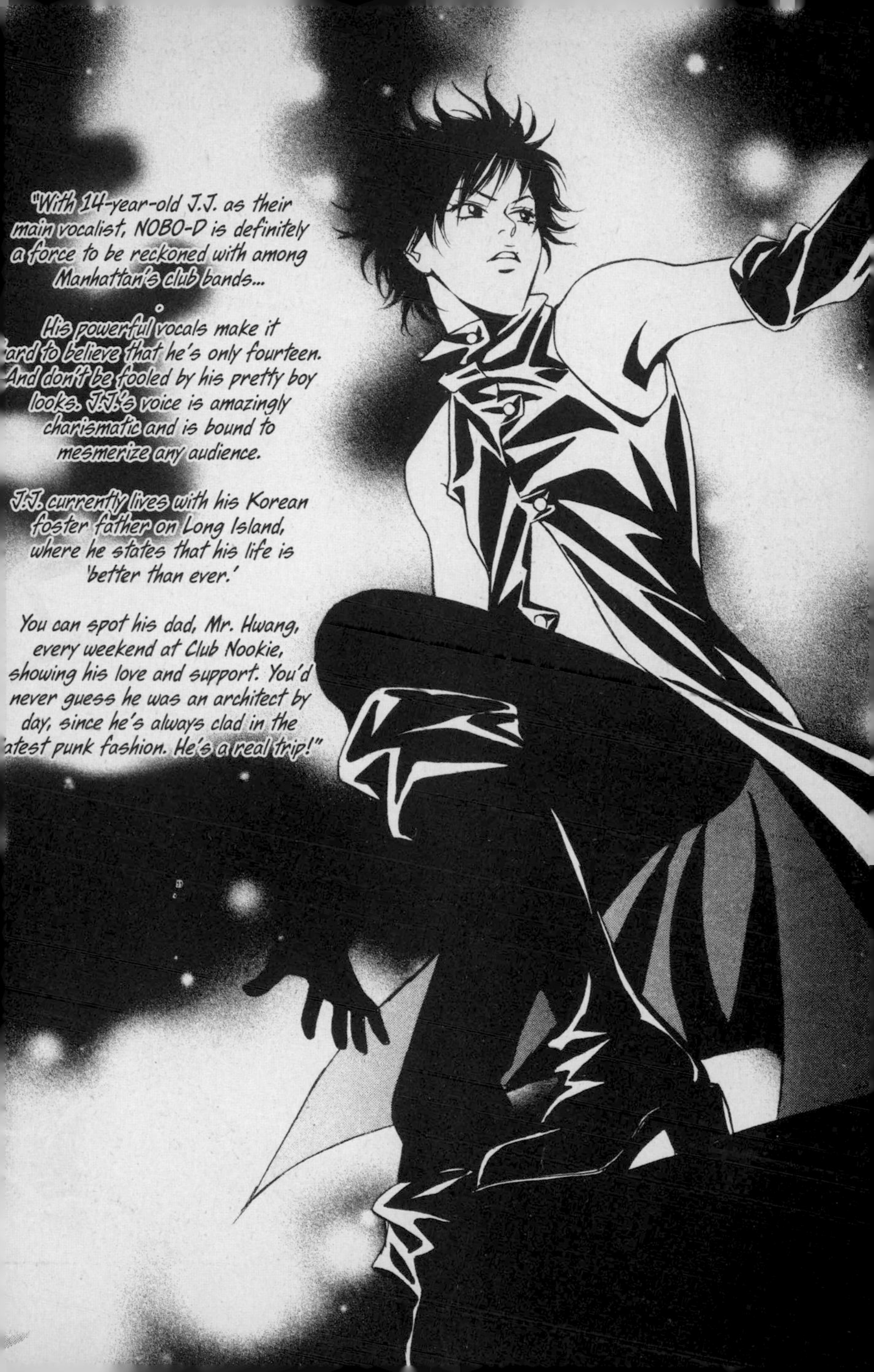
"With 14-year-old J.J. as their main vocalist, NOBO-D is definitely a force to be reckoned with among Manhattan's club bands...
His powerful vocals make it ard to believe that he's only fourteen. And don't be fooled by his pretty boy looks. J.J.'s voice is amazingly charismatic and is bound to mesmerize any audience.
J.J. currently lives with his Korean foster father on Long Island, where he states that his life is 'better than ever.'
You can spot his dad, Mr. Hwang, every weekend at Club Nookie, showing his love and support. You'd never guess he was an architect by day, since he's always clad in the atest punk fashion. He's a real trip!"

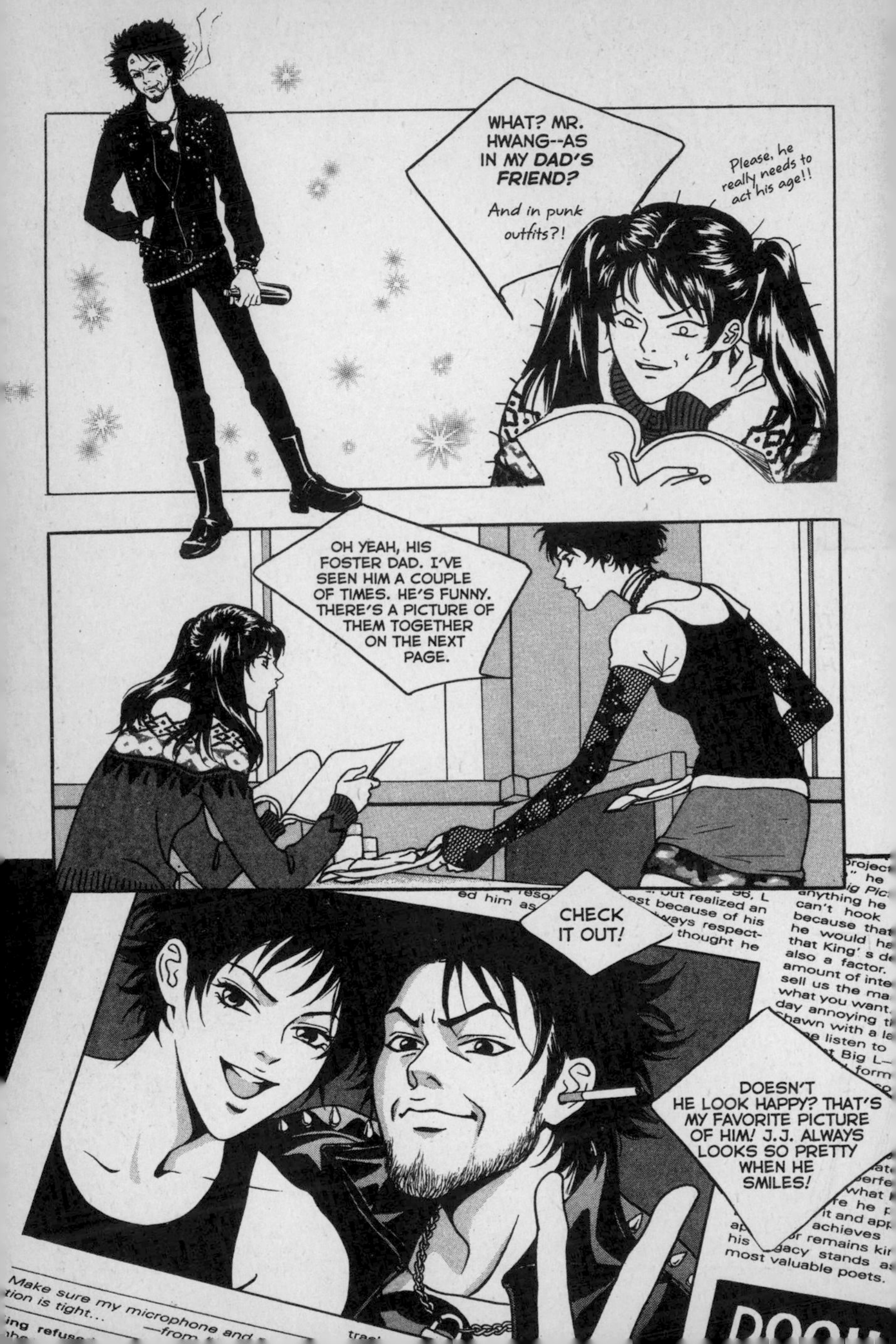
WHAT? MR. HWANG--AS IN MY DAD'S FRIEND?
And in punk outfits?!
Please, he really needs to act his age!!
OH YEAH, HIS FOSTER DAD. I'VE SEEN HIM A COUPLE OF TIMES. HE'S FUNNY. THERE'S A PICTURE OF THEM TOGETHER ON THE NEXT PAGE.
CHECK IT OUT!
DOESN'T HE LOOK HAPPY? THAT'S MY FAVORITE PICTURE OF HIM! J.J. ALWAYS LOOKS SO PRETTY WHEN HE SMILES!

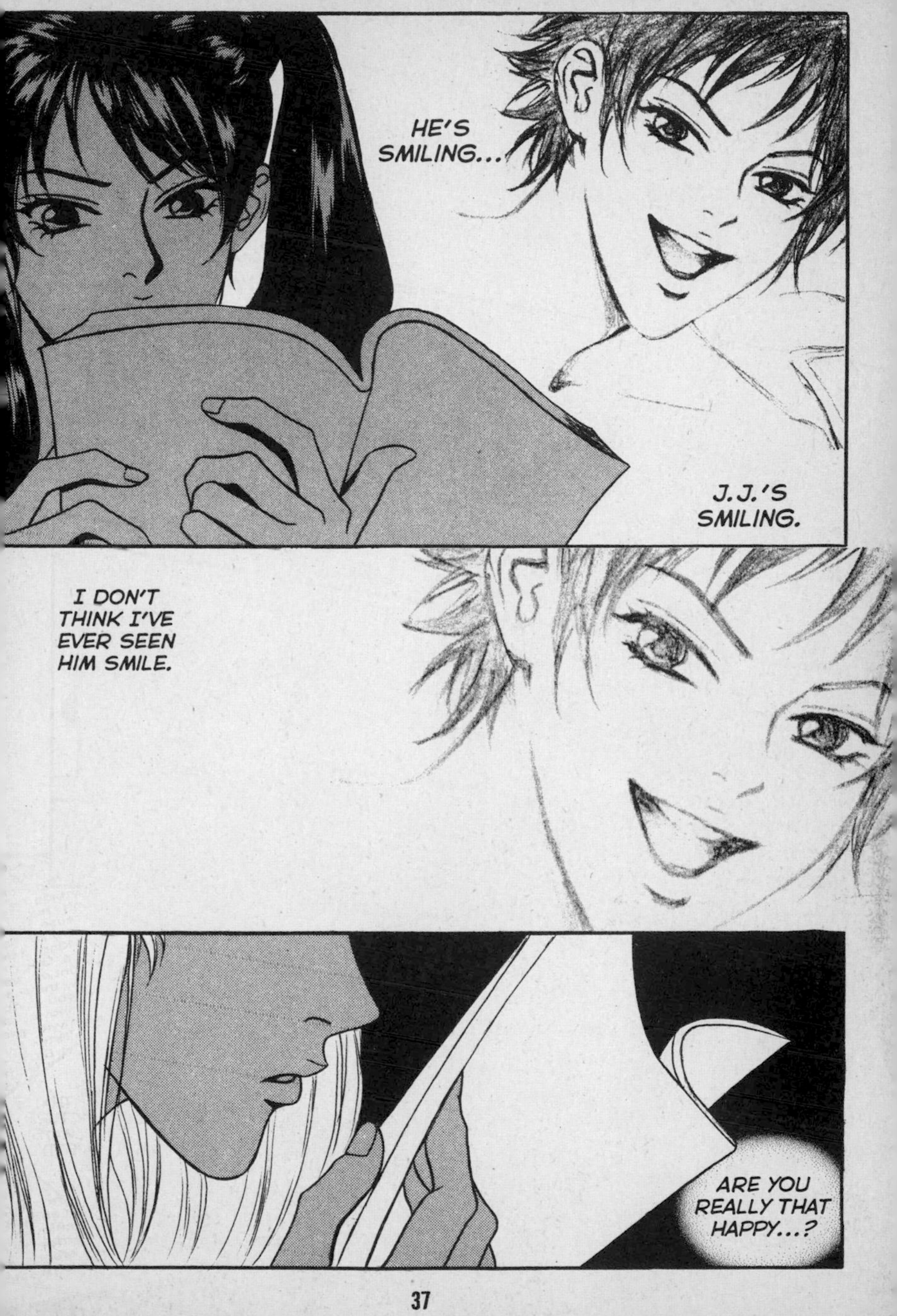
HE'S SMILING...
J.J.'S SMILING.
I DON'T THINK I'VE EVER SEEN HIM SMILE.
ARE YOU REALLY THAT HAPPY...?

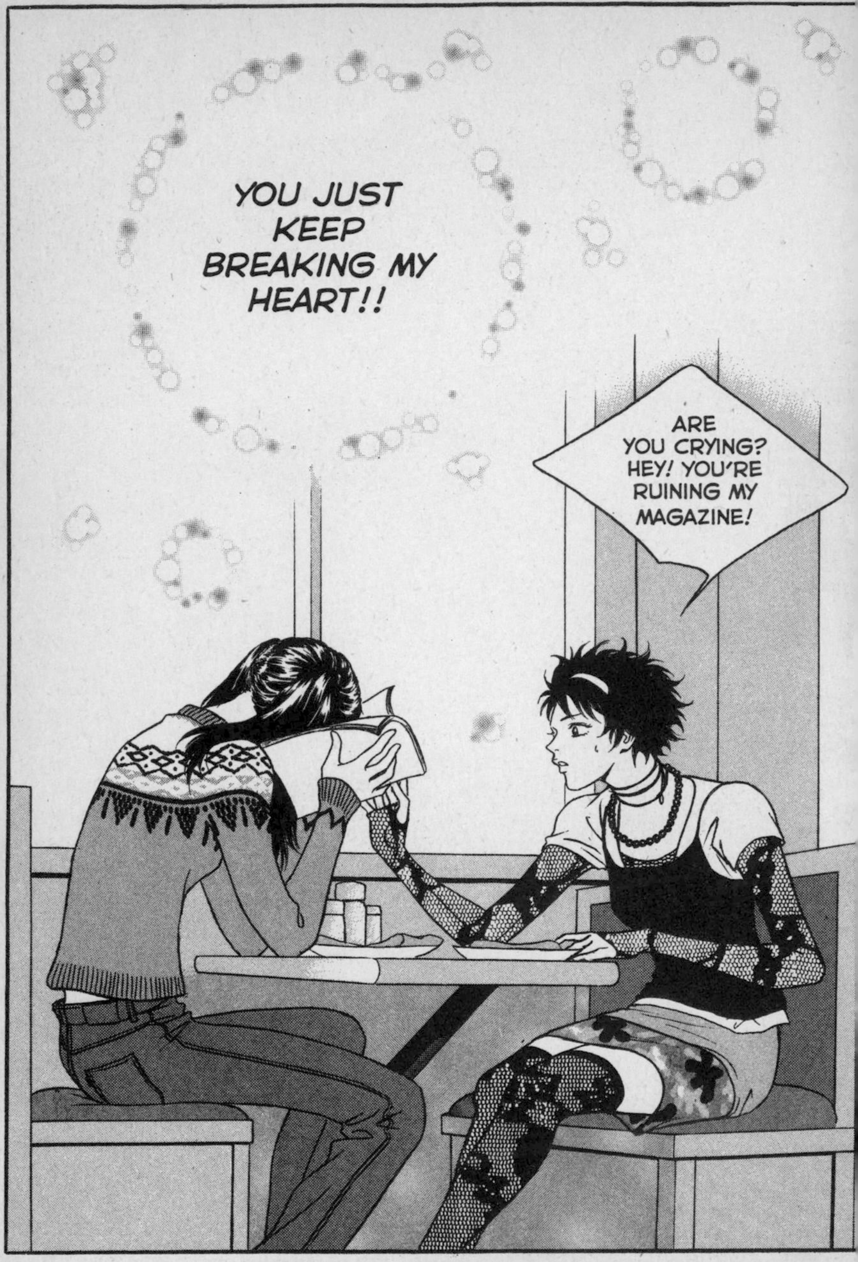
YOU JUST KEEP BREAKING MY HEART!!
ARE YOU CRYING? HEY! YOU'RE RUINING MY MAGAZINE!

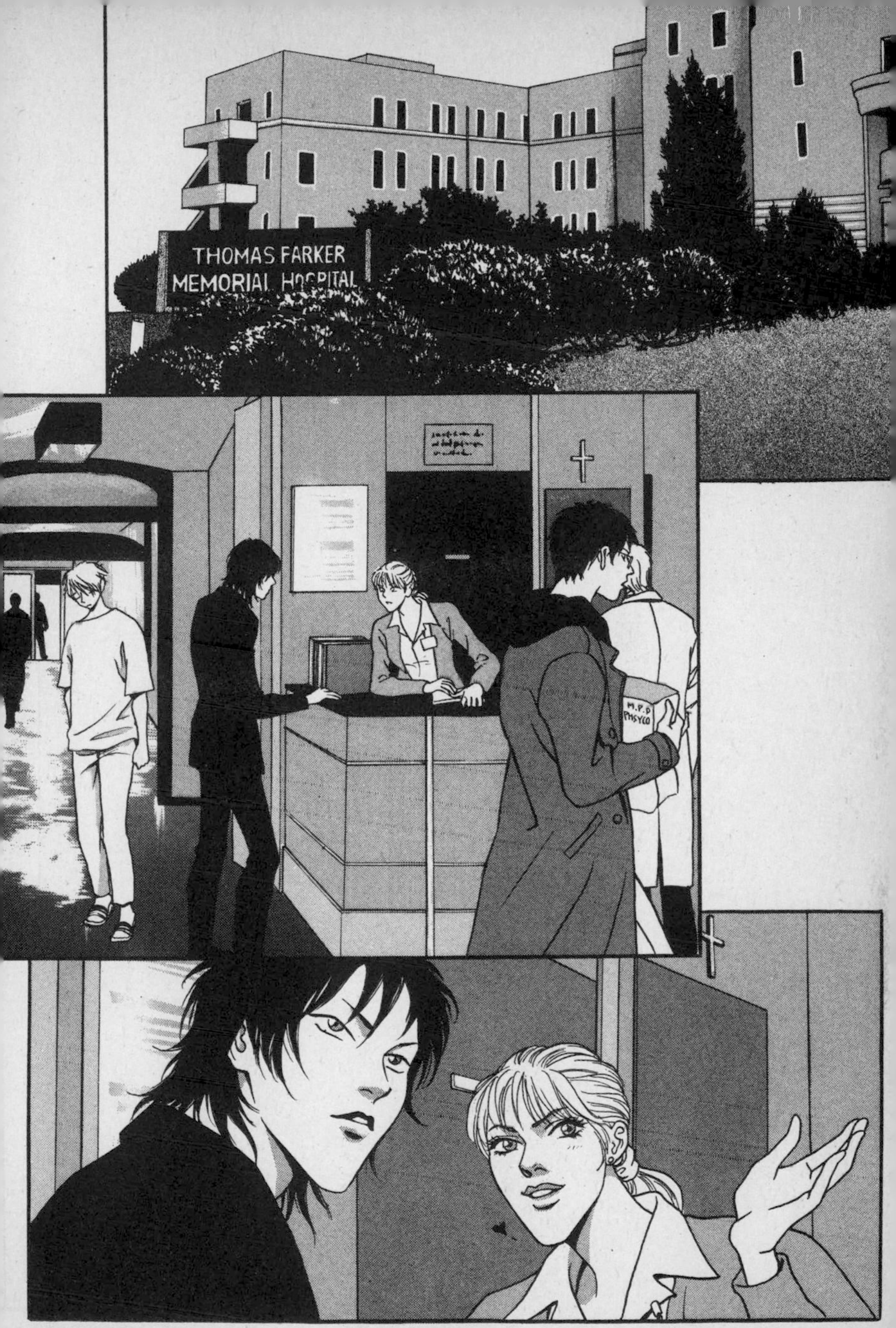
THOMAS FARKER
MEMORIAL HOSPITAL
M.P.D
PHSYCO

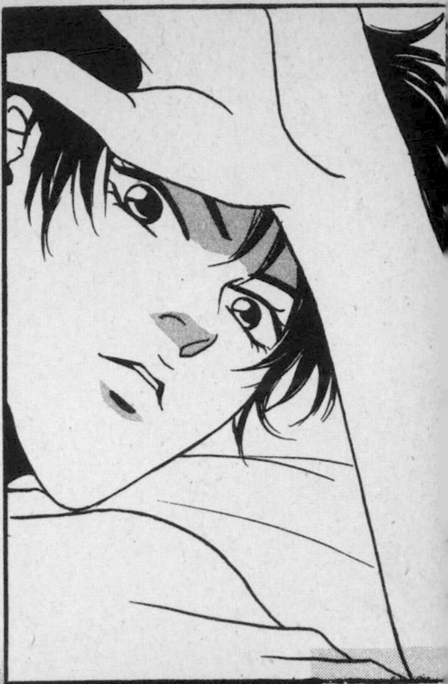
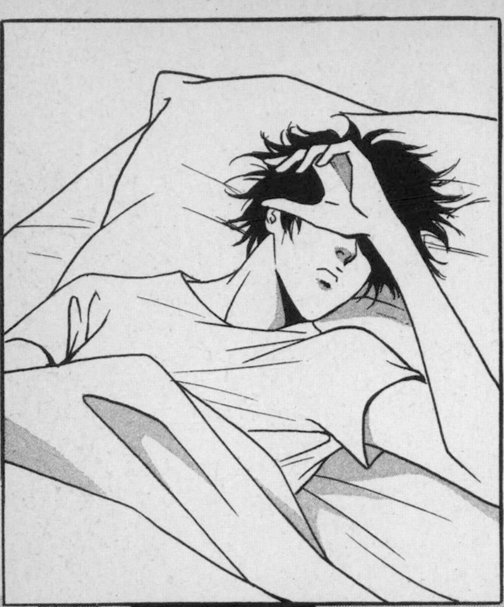
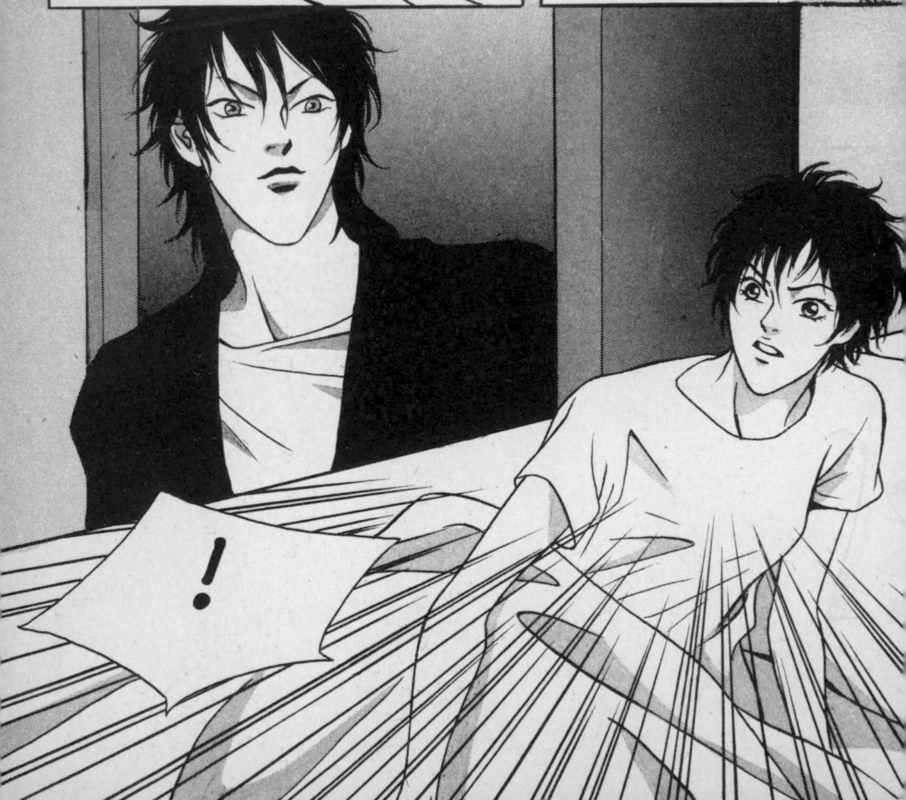
!

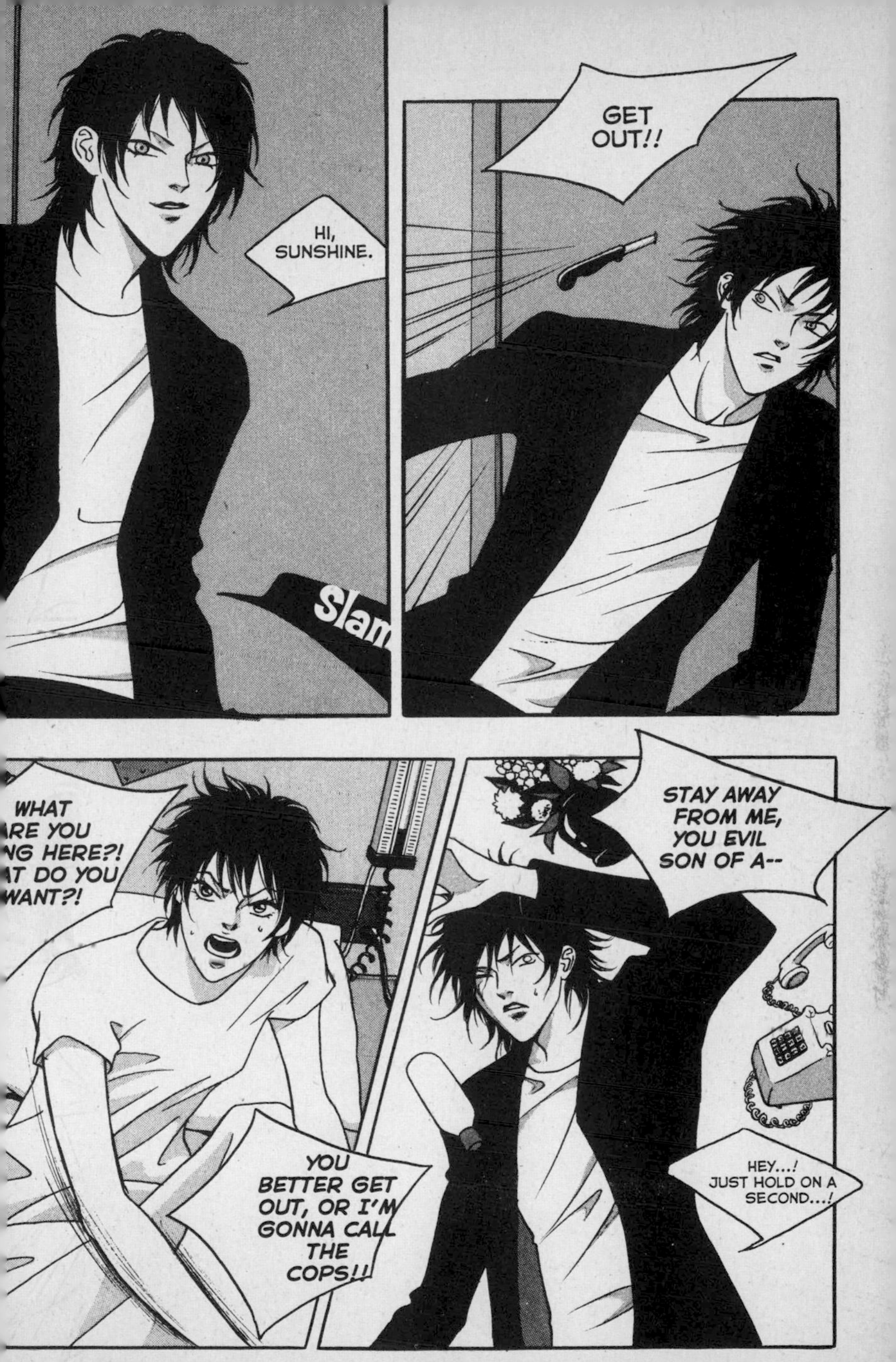
HI, SUNSHINE.
Slam
GET OUT!!
WHAT ARE YOU NG HERE?! AT DO YOU WANT?!
YOU BETTER GET OUT, OR I'M GONNA CALL THE COPS!!
STAY AWAY FROM ME, YOU EVIL SON OF A--
HEY...! JUST HOLD ON A SECOND...!

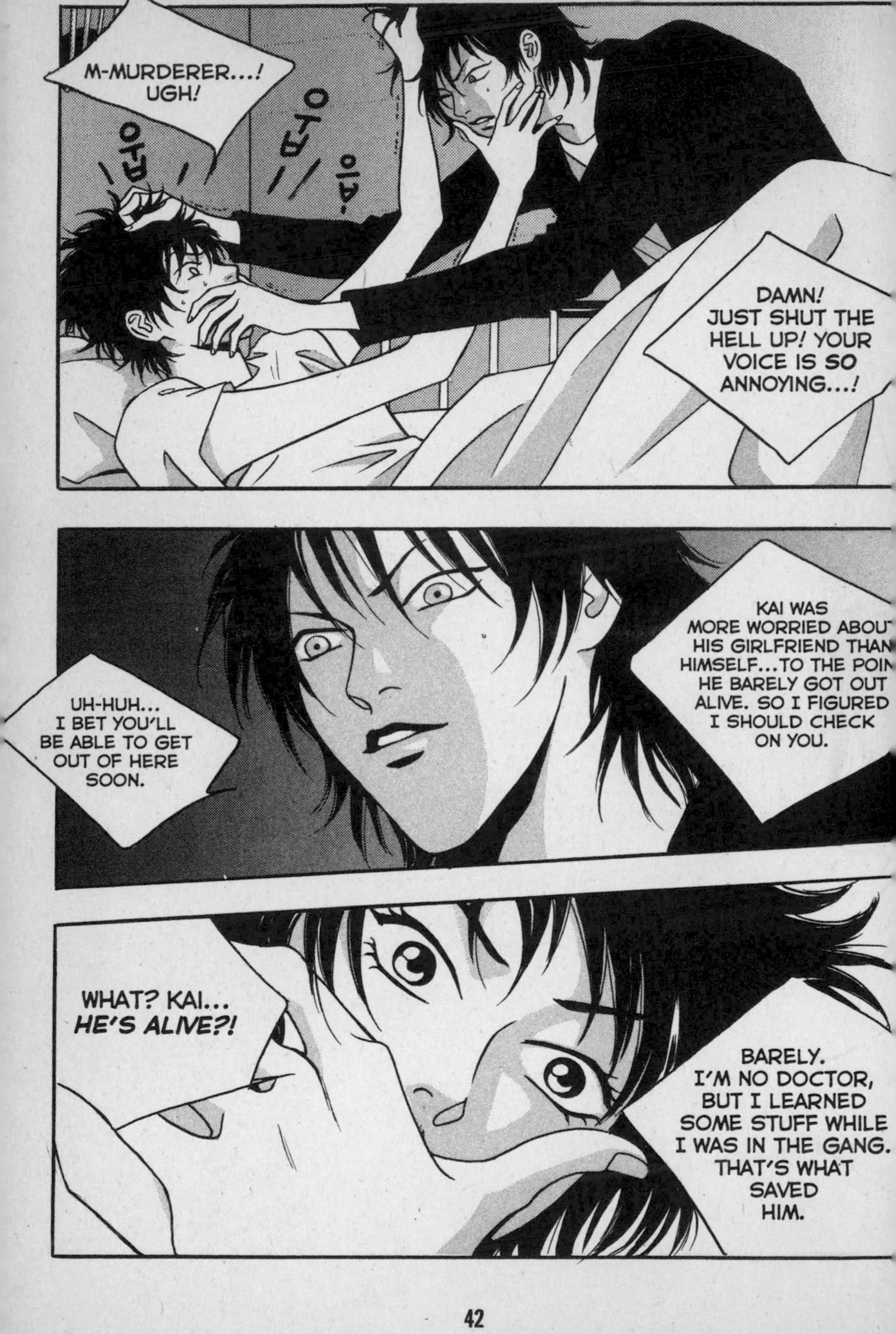
M-MURDERER...! UGH!
DAMN! JUST SHUT THE HELL UP! YOUR VOICE IS SO ANNOYING...!
KAI WAS MORE WORRIED ABOUT HIS GIRLFRIEND THAN HIMSELF...TO THE POIN HE BARELY GOT OUT ALIVE. SO I FIGURED I SHOULD CHECK ON YOU.
UH-HUH... I BET YOU'LL BE ABLE TO GET OUT OF HERE SOON.
WHAT? KAI... *HE'S ALIVE?!*
BARELY. I'M NO DOCTOR, BUT I LEARNED SOME STUFF WHILE I WAS IN THE GANG. THAT'S WHAT SAVED HIM.

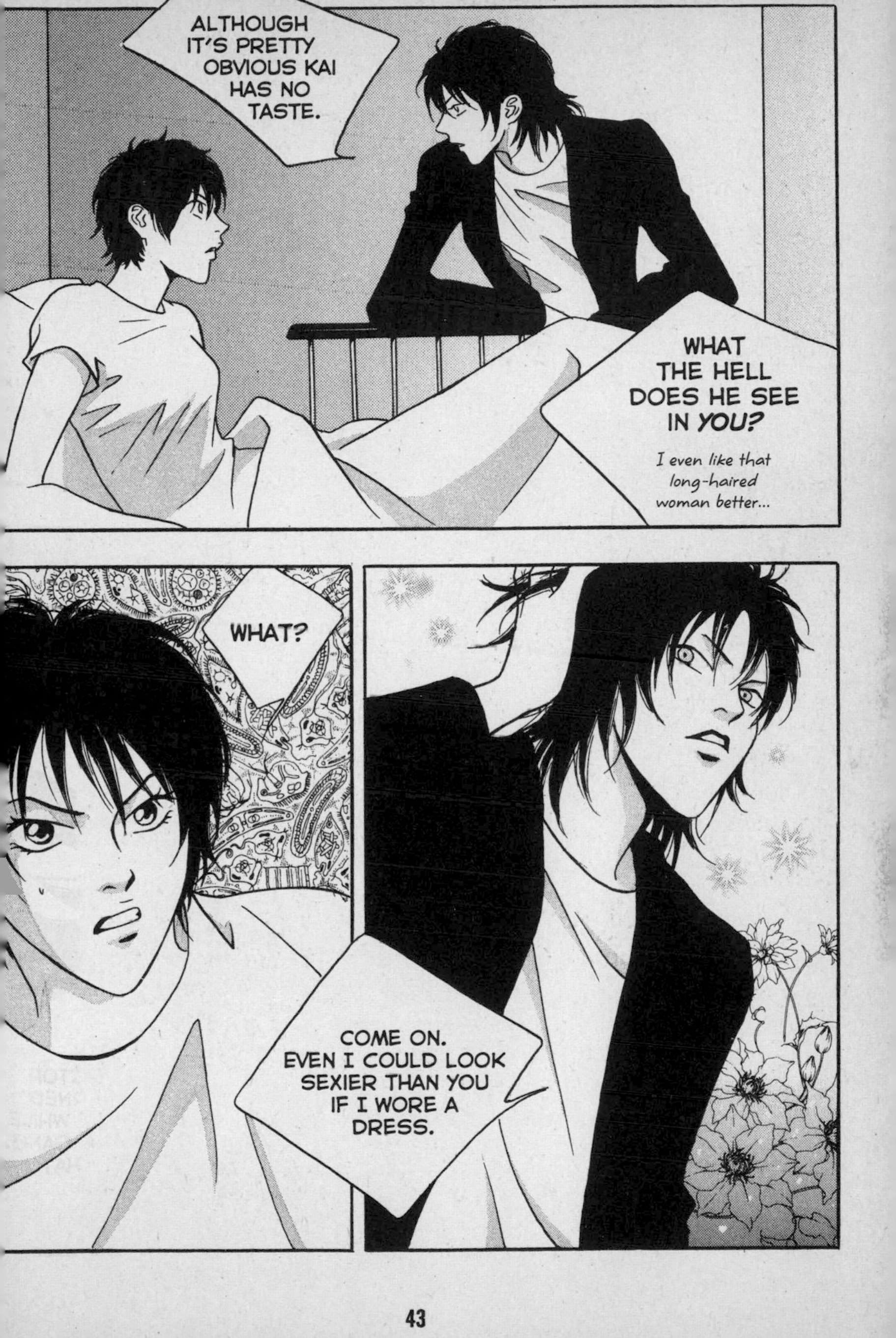
ALTHOUGH IT'S PRETTY OBVIOUS KAI HAS NO TASTE.
WHAT THE HELL DOES HE SEE IN *YOU?*
I even like that long-haired woman better...
WHAT?
COME ON. EVEN I COULD LOOK SEXIER THAN YOU IF I WORE A DRESS.

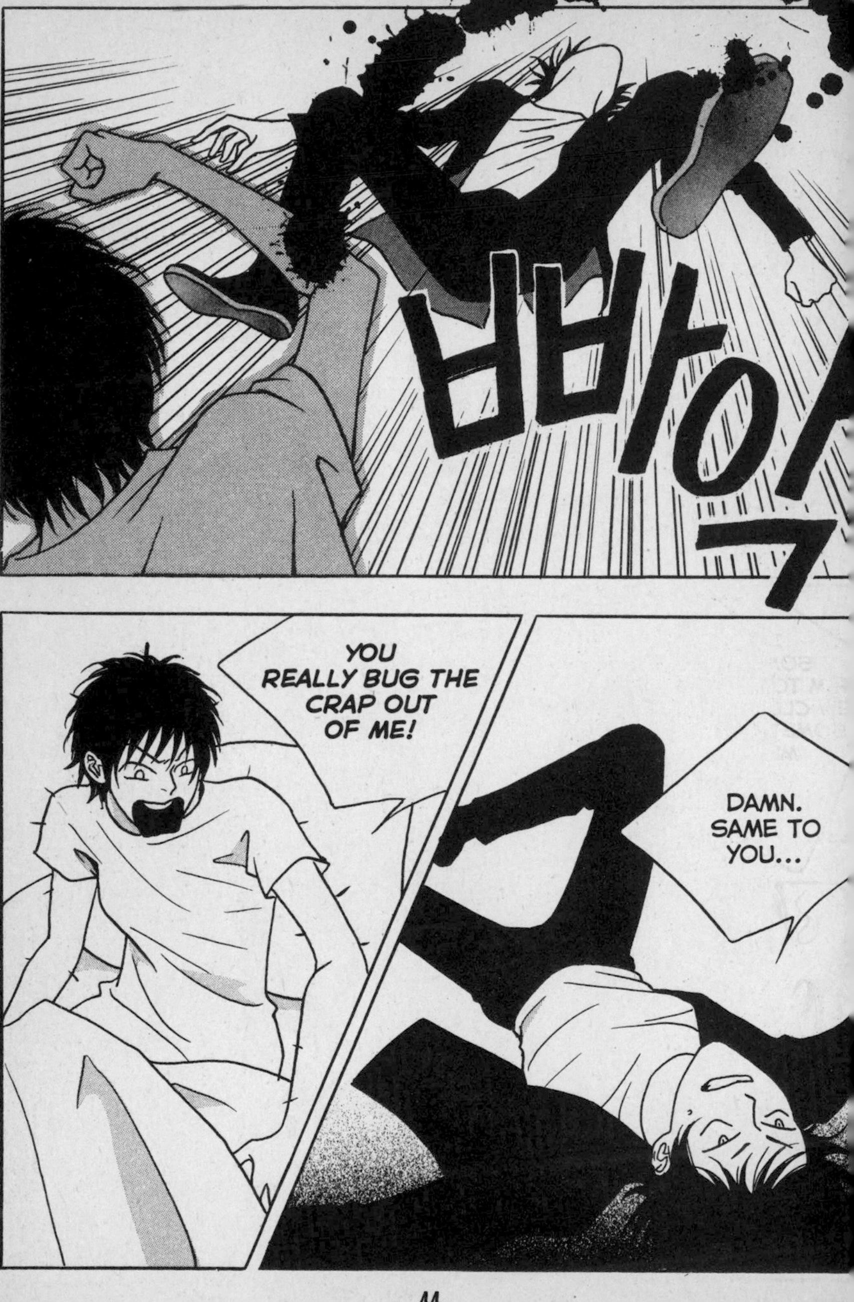
YOU REALLY BUG THE CRAP OUT OF ME!
DAMN. SAME TO YOU...

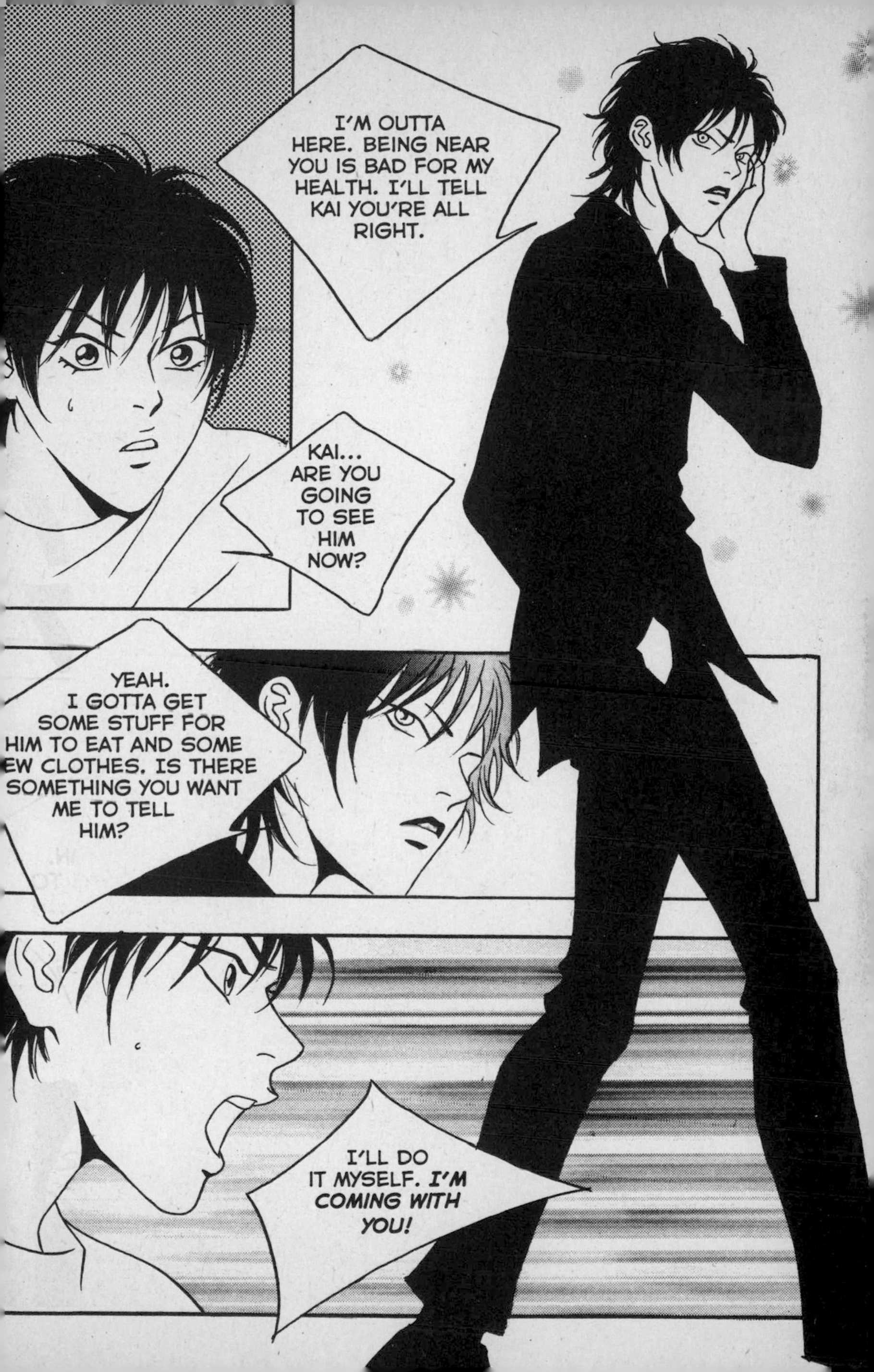
I'M OUTTA HERE. BEING NEAR YOU IS BAD FOR MY HEALTH. I'LL TELL KAI YOU'RE ALL RIGHT.
KAI... ARE YOU GOING TO SEE HIM NOW?
YEAH. I GOTTA GET SOME STUFF FOR HIM TO EAT AND SOME EW CLOTHES. IS THERE SOMETHING YOU WANT ME TO TELL HIM?
I'LL DO IT MYSELF. I'M COMING WITH YOU!

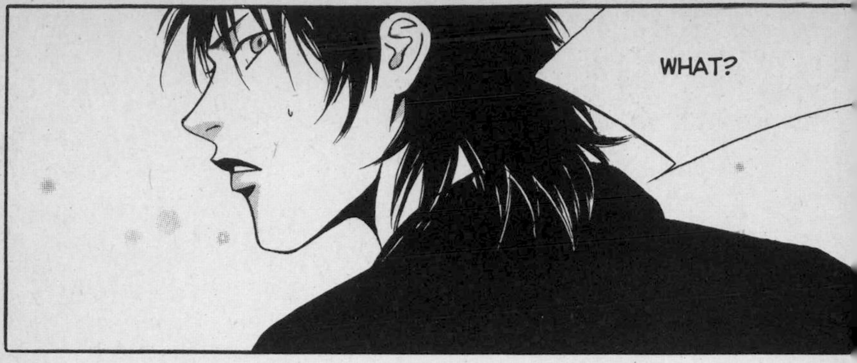
WHAT?

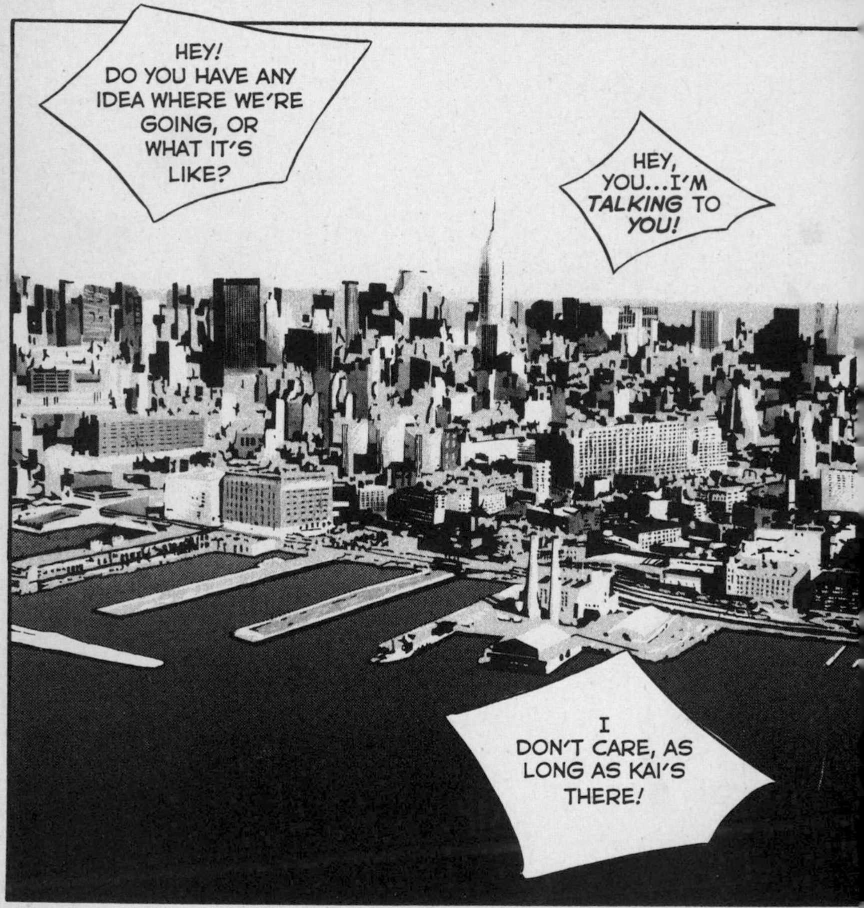
HEY, YOU...I'M *TALKING* TO *YOU!*
HEY! DO YOU HAVE ANY IDEA WHERE WE'RE GOING, OR WHAT IT'S LIKE?
I DON'T CARE, AS LONG AS KAI'S THERE!

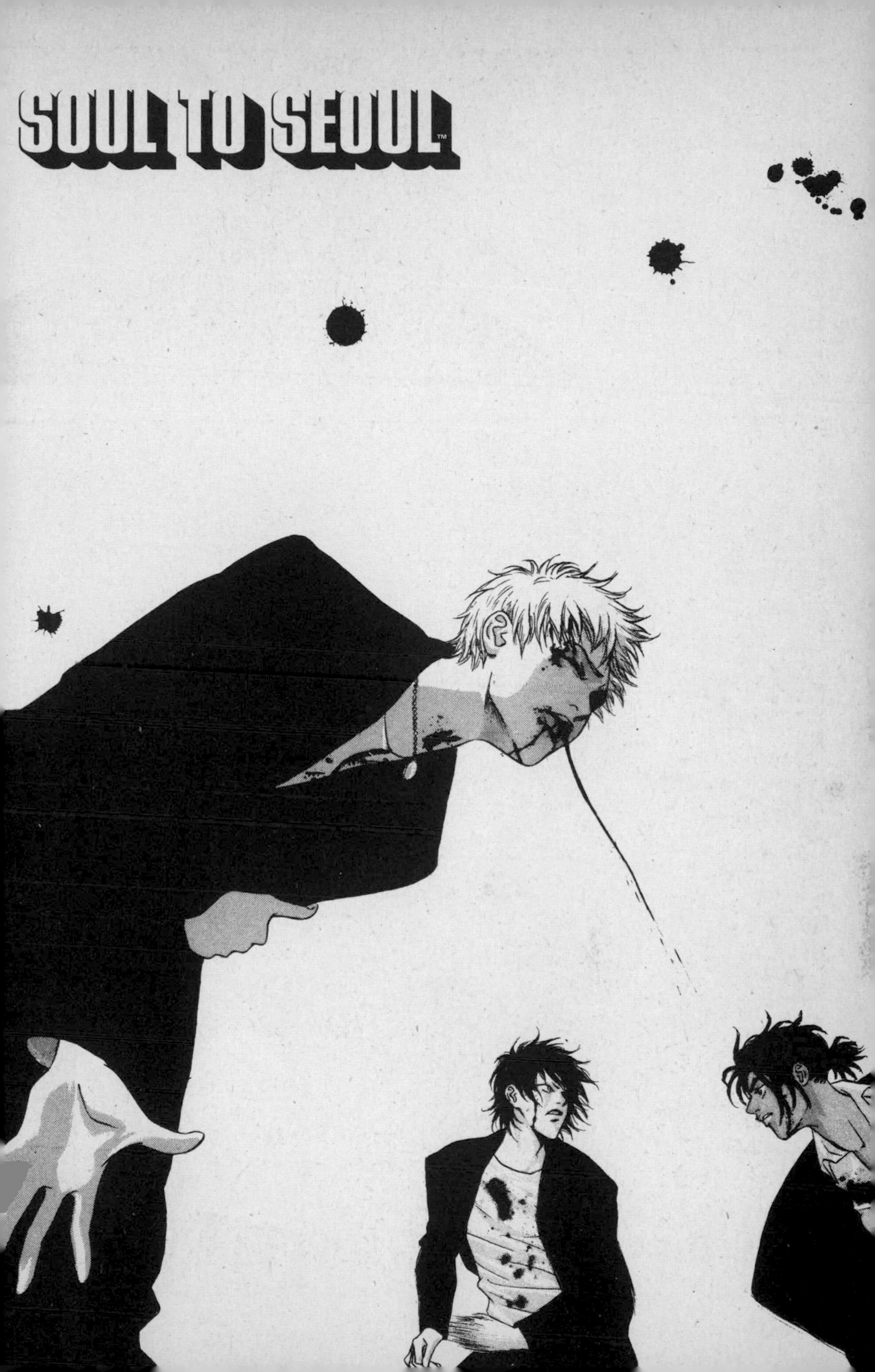
SOUL TO SEOUL™

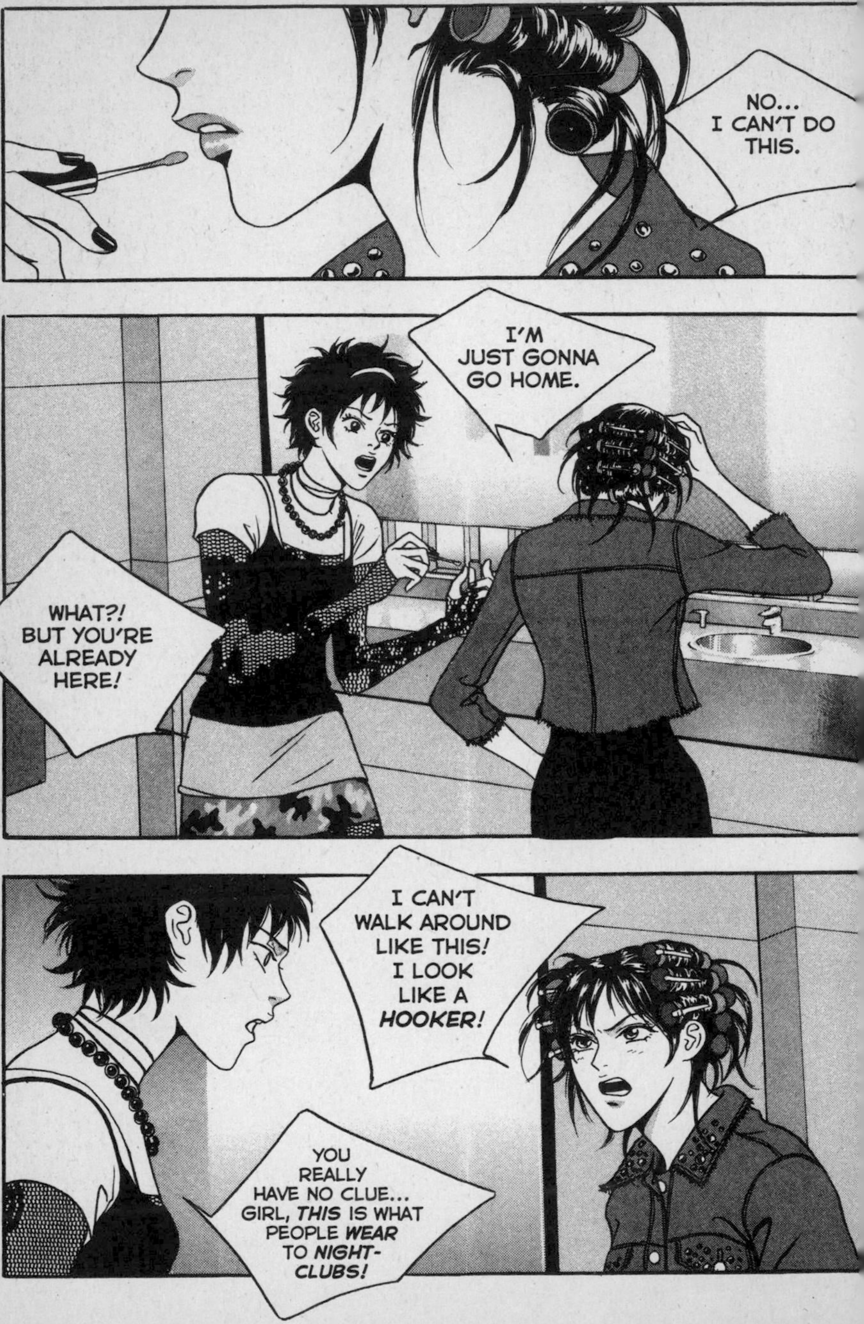
NO... I CAN'T DO THIS.
I'M JUST GONNA GO HOME.
WHAT?! BUT YOU'RE ALREADY HERE!
I CAN'T WALK AROUND LIKE THIS! I LOOK LIKE A *HOOKER*!
YOU REALLY HAVE NO CLUE... GIRL, *THIS* IS WHAT PEOPLE *WEAR* TO *NIGHT-CLUBS*!

GELDA, DON'T WORRY. YOU LOOK PRETTY...

IF YOU LIKE IT SO MUCH, THEN *YOU* WEAR IT!

FINE*!* THEN WEAR THIS! IT'S WHAT I WORE TO SNEAK OUT OF MY HOUSE. THOUGH I DON'T KNOW IF IT'LL FIT...

BUT AT LEAST YOU'LL FEEL BETTER IN IT.

WHAT DO YOU THINK? IT LOOKS OKAY, RIGHT? LET'S JUST PUT ON A LITTLE MAKEUP...

WHY?

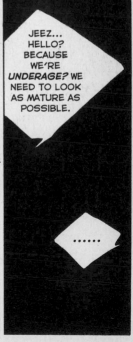

JEEZ... HELLO? BECAUSE WE'RE *UNDERAGE?* WE NEED TO LOOK AS MATURE AS POSSIBLE.

......

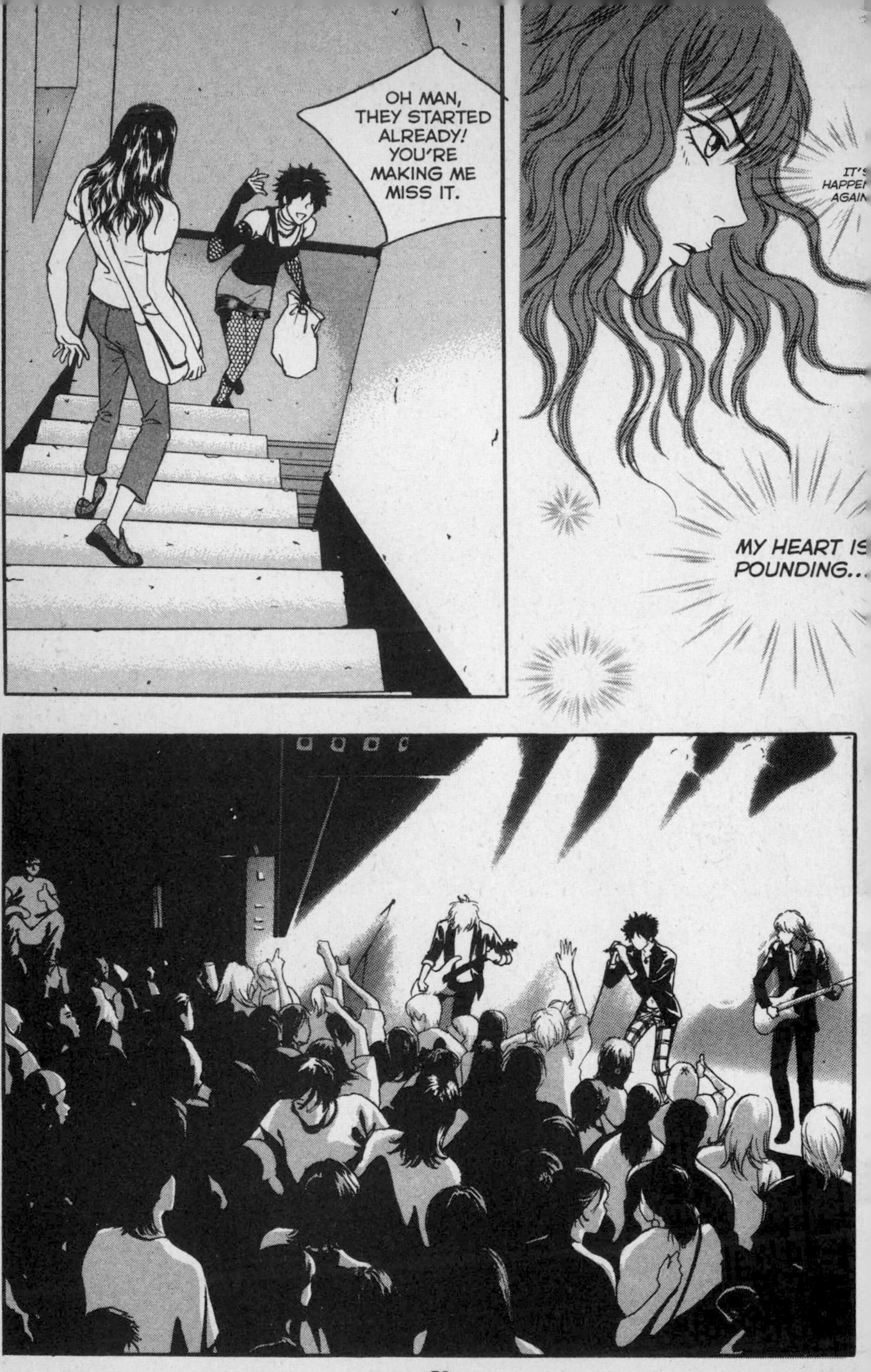
IT'S HAPPEN AGAIN
MY HEART IS POUNDING...
OH MAN, THEY STARTED ALREADY! YOU'RE MAKING ME MISS IT.

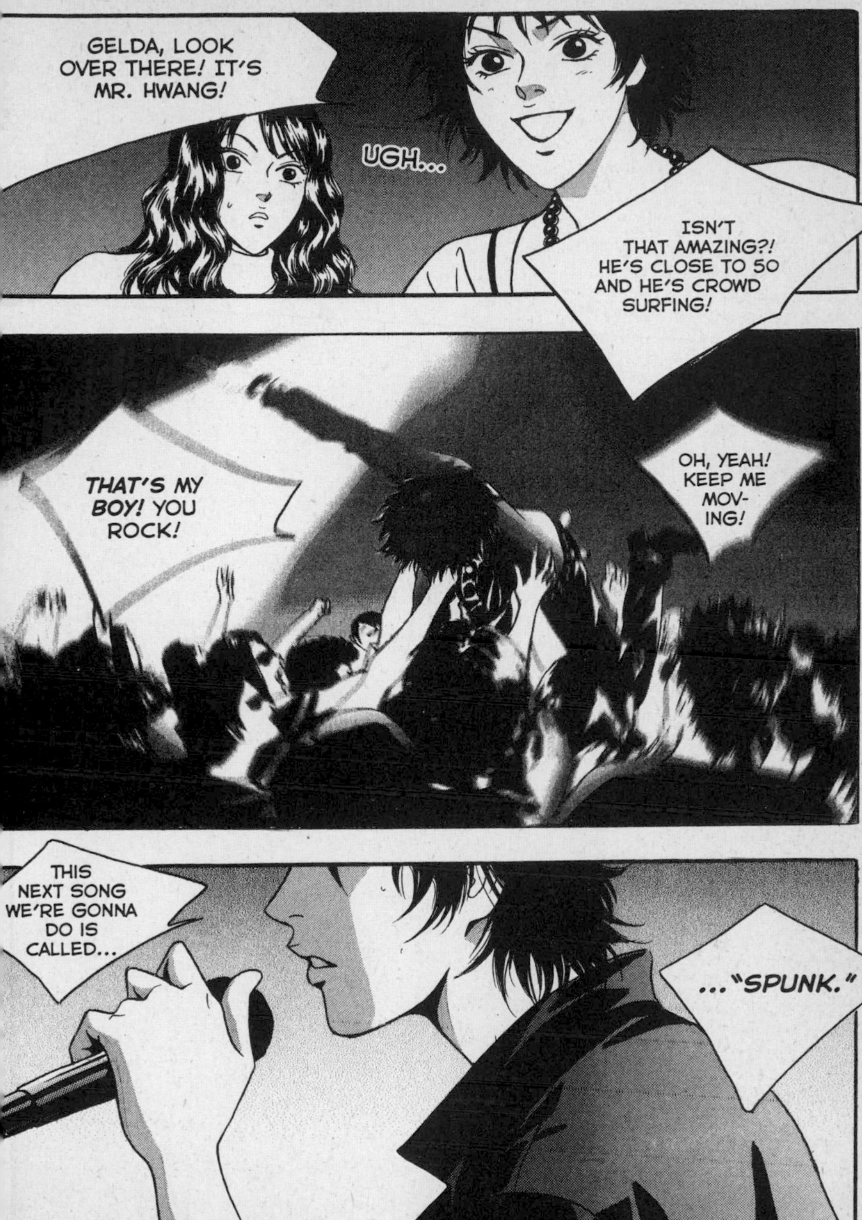
GELDA, LOOK OVER THERE! IT'S MR. HWANG!
UGH...
ISN'T THAT AMAZING?! HE'S CLOSE TO 50 AND HE'S CROWD SURFING!
THAT'S MY BOY! YOU ROCK!
OH, YEAH! KEEP ME MOV-ING!
THIS NEXT SONG WE'RE GONNA DO IS CALLED...
..."SPUNK."

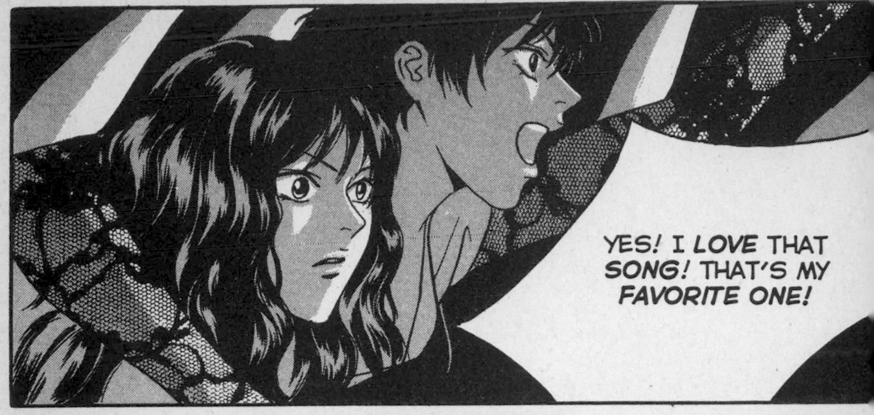
YES! I LOVE THAT SONG! THAT'S MY FAVORITE ONE!
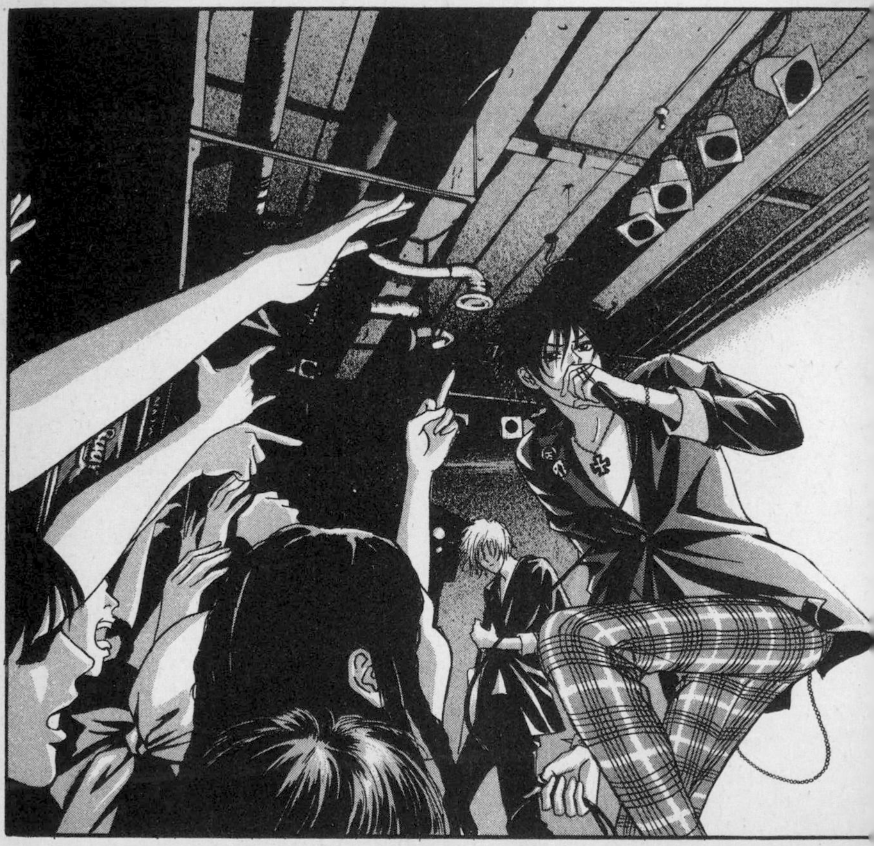

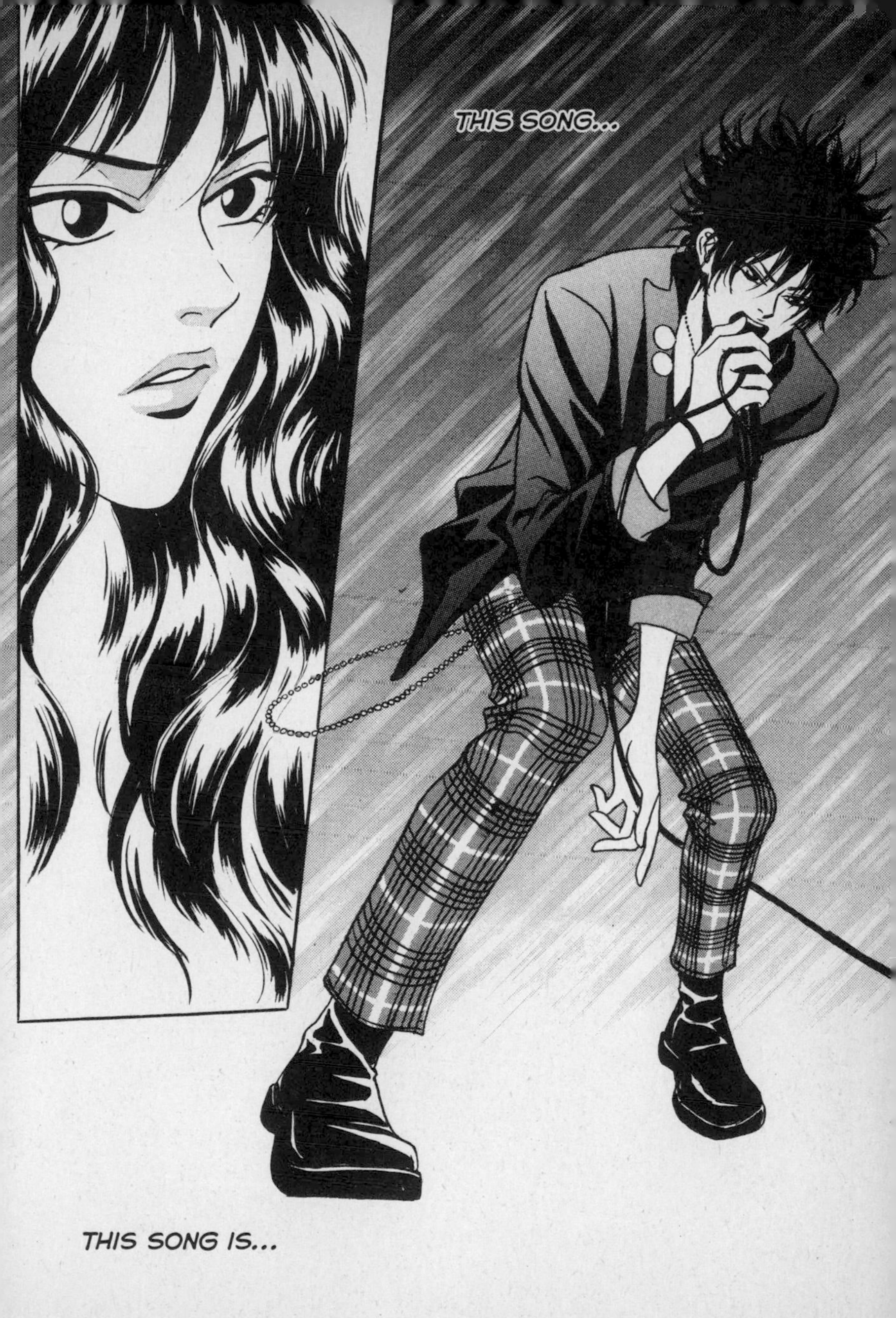
THIS SONG...
THIS SONG IS...

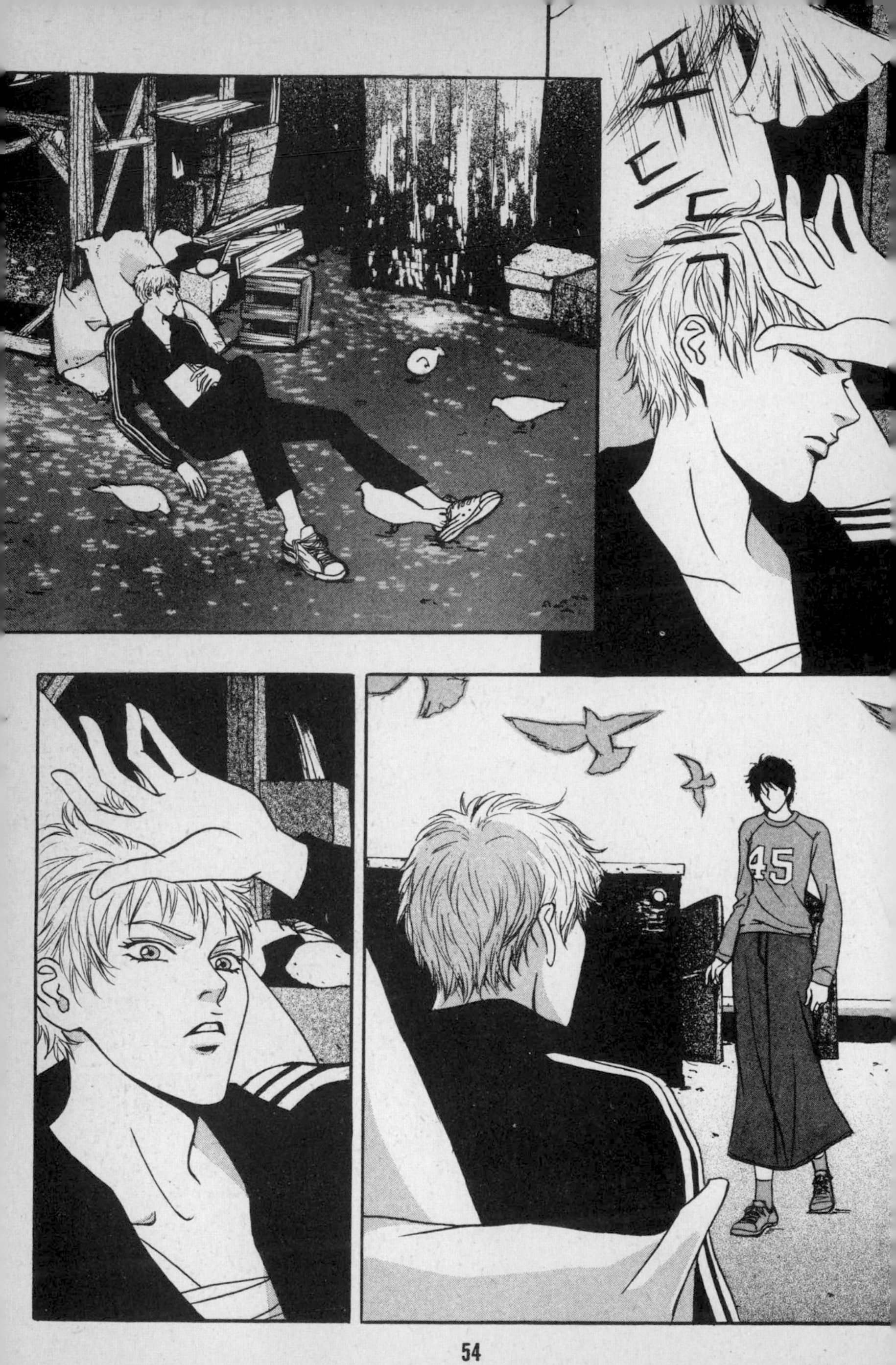
푸드득

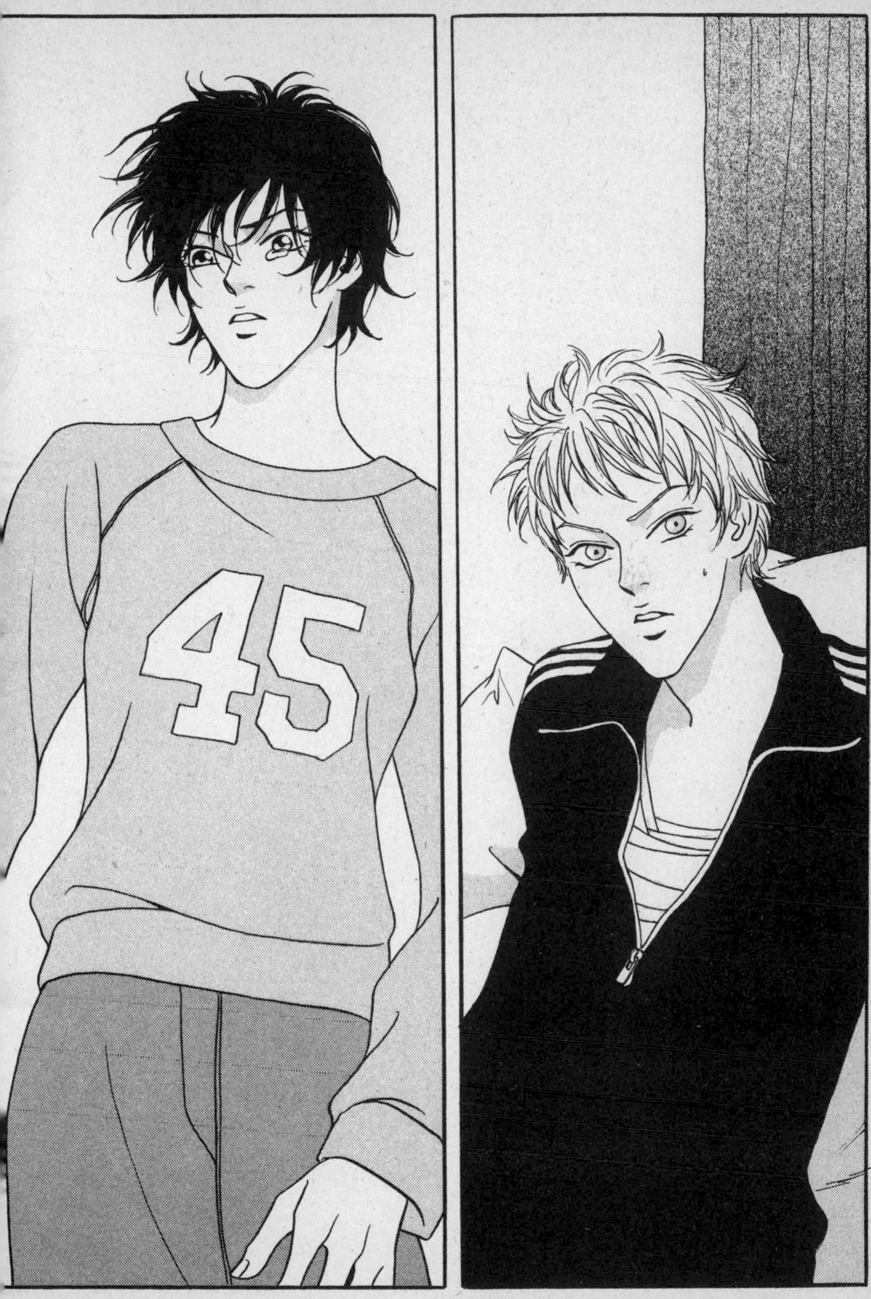
45

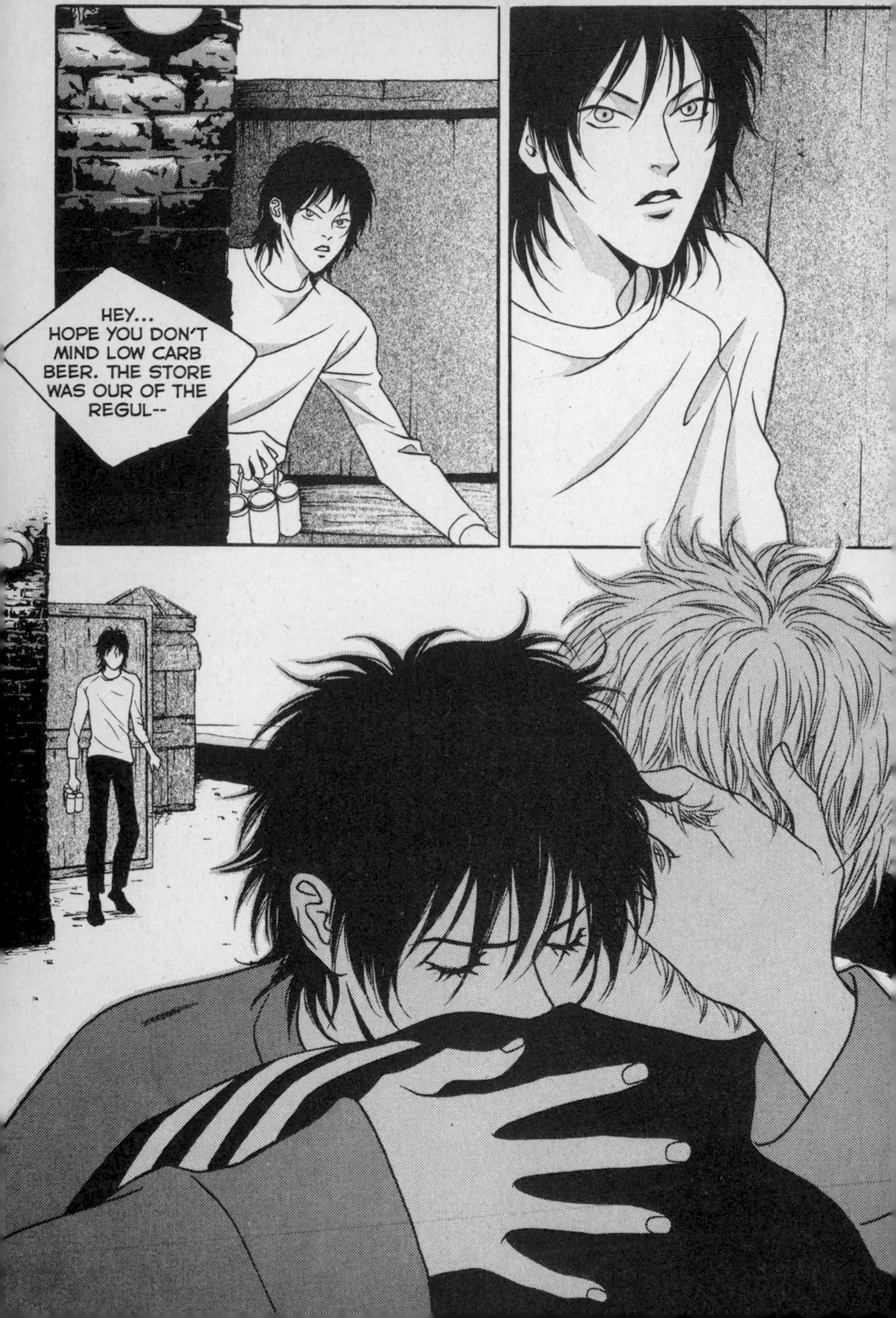
HEY... HOPE YOU DON'T MIND LOW CARB BEER. THE STORE WAS OUR OF THE REGUL--

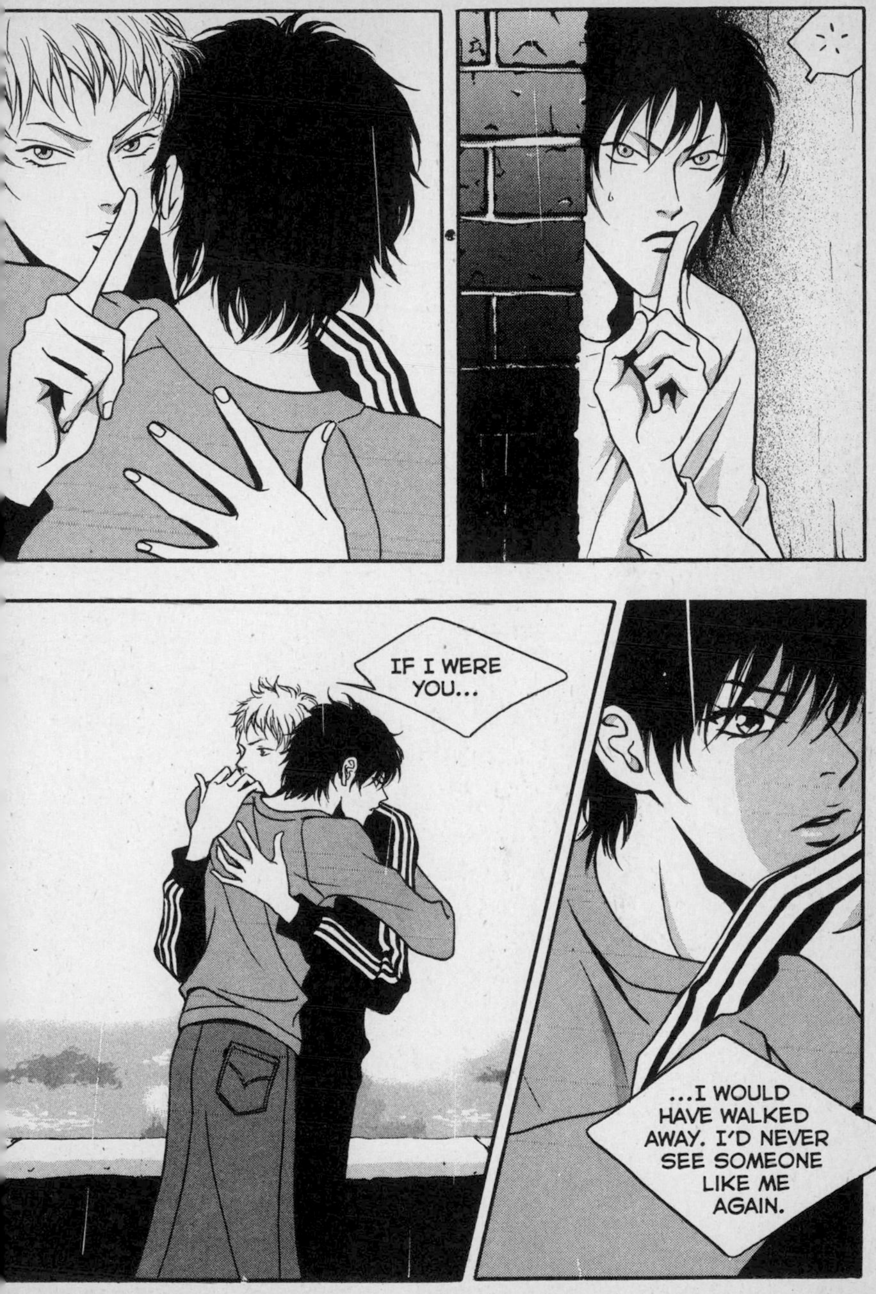
IF I WERE YOU...
...I WOULD HAVE WALKED AWAY. I'D NEVER SEE SOMEONE LIKE ME AGAIN.

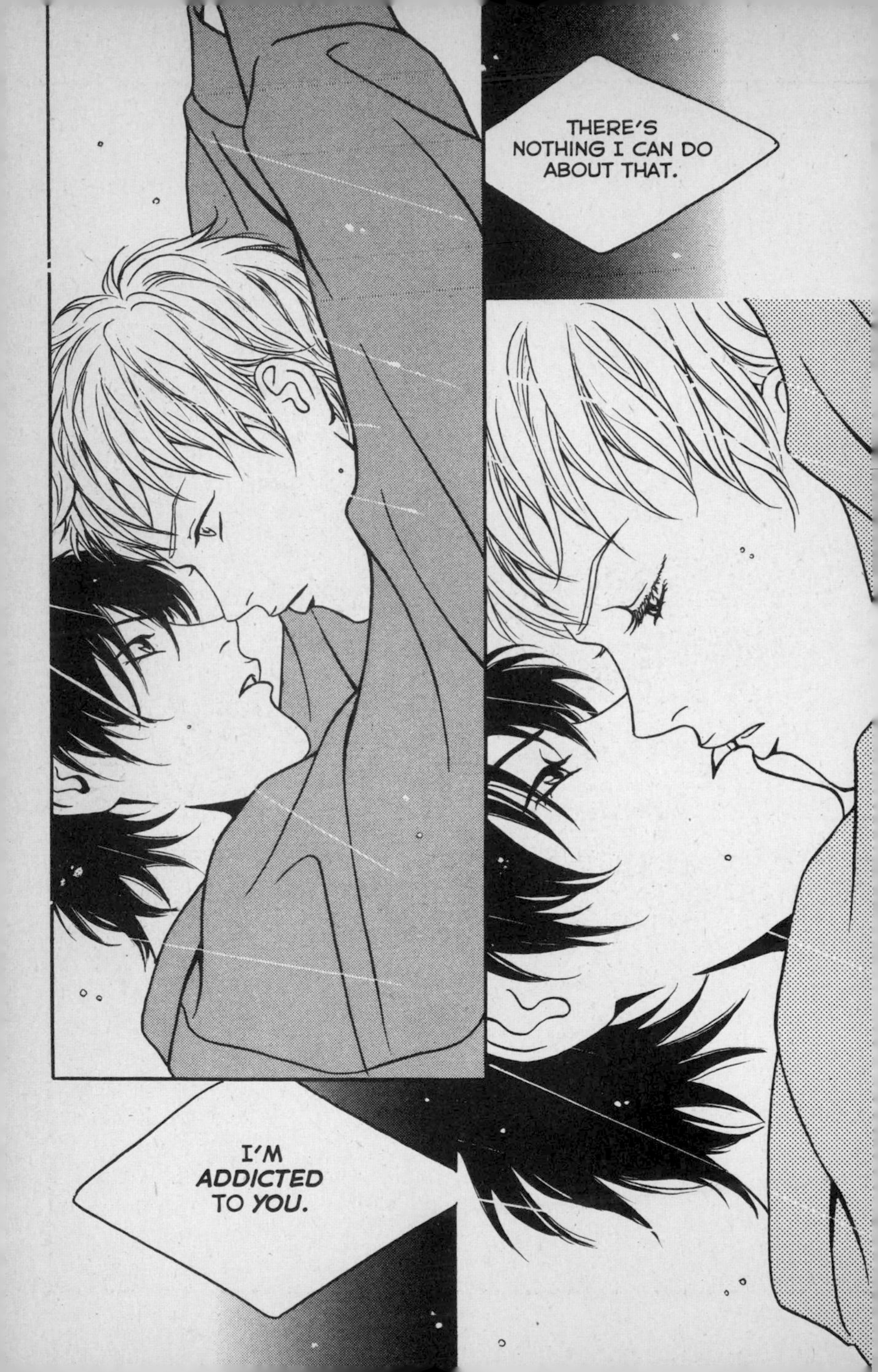
THERE'S NOTHING I CAN DO ABOUT THAT.
I'M *ADDICTED* TO *YOU.*

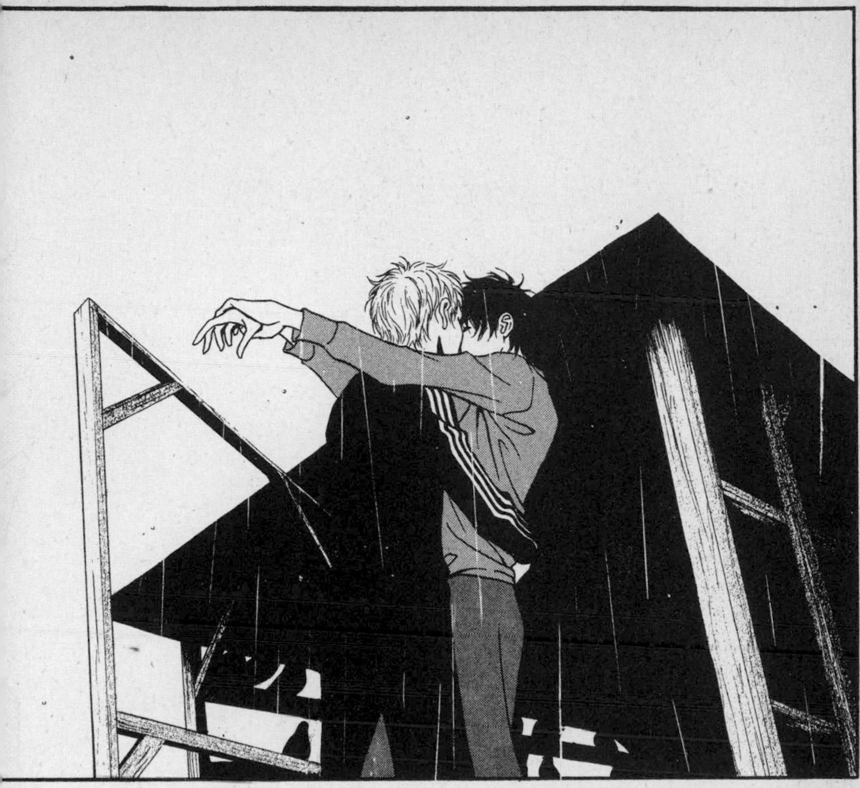
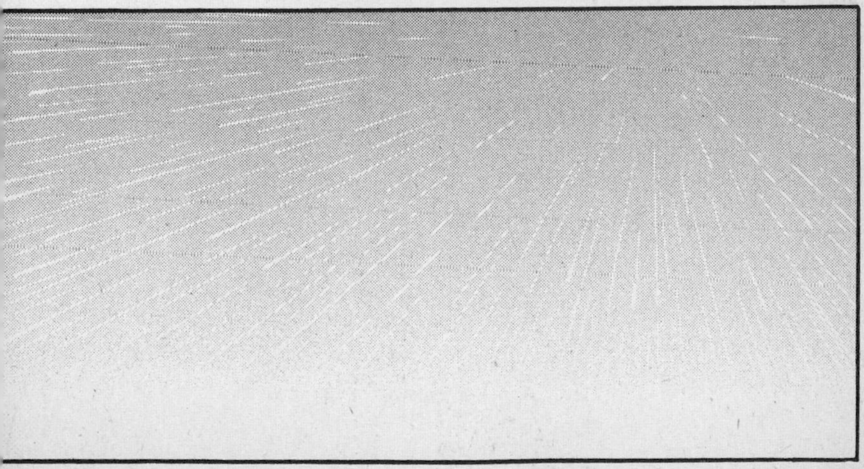

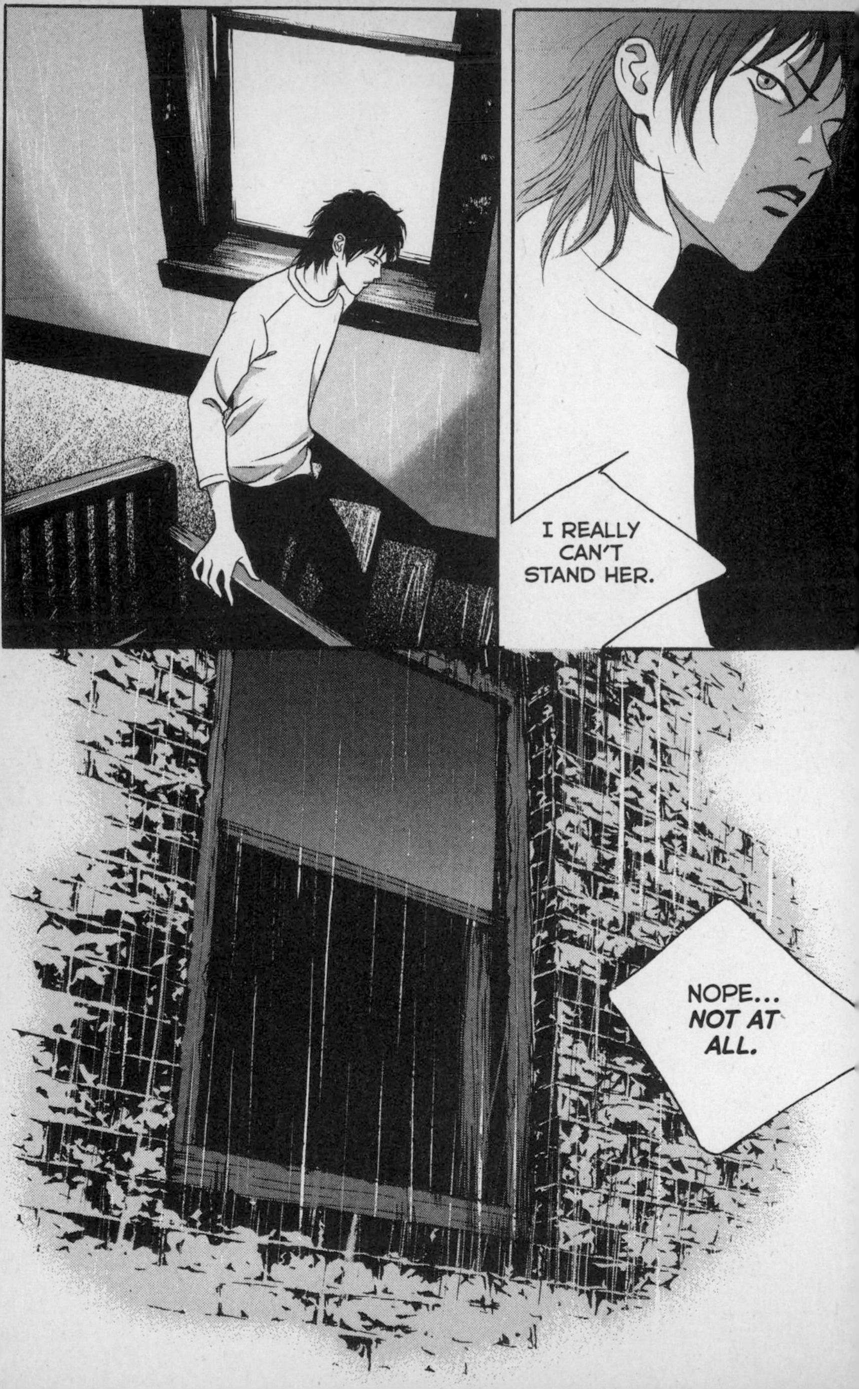
I REALLY CAN'T STAND HER.
NOPE... *NOT AT ALL.*

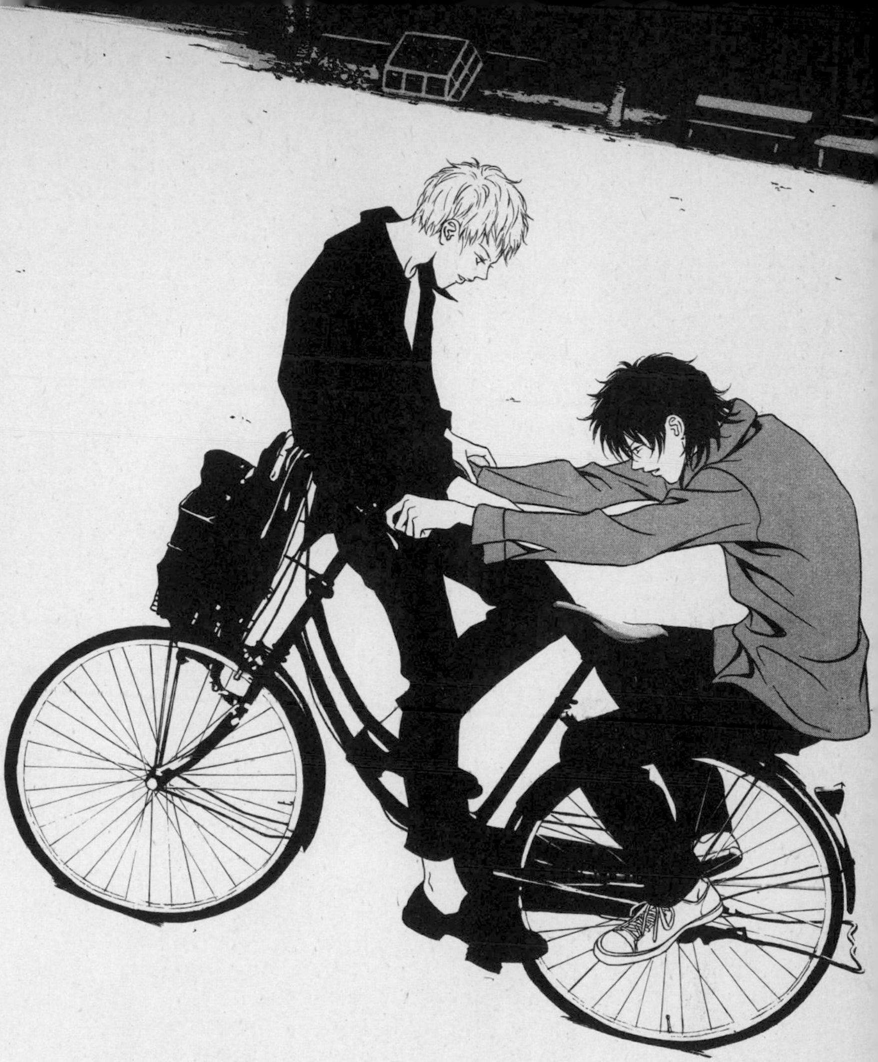

SOUL TO SEOUL™

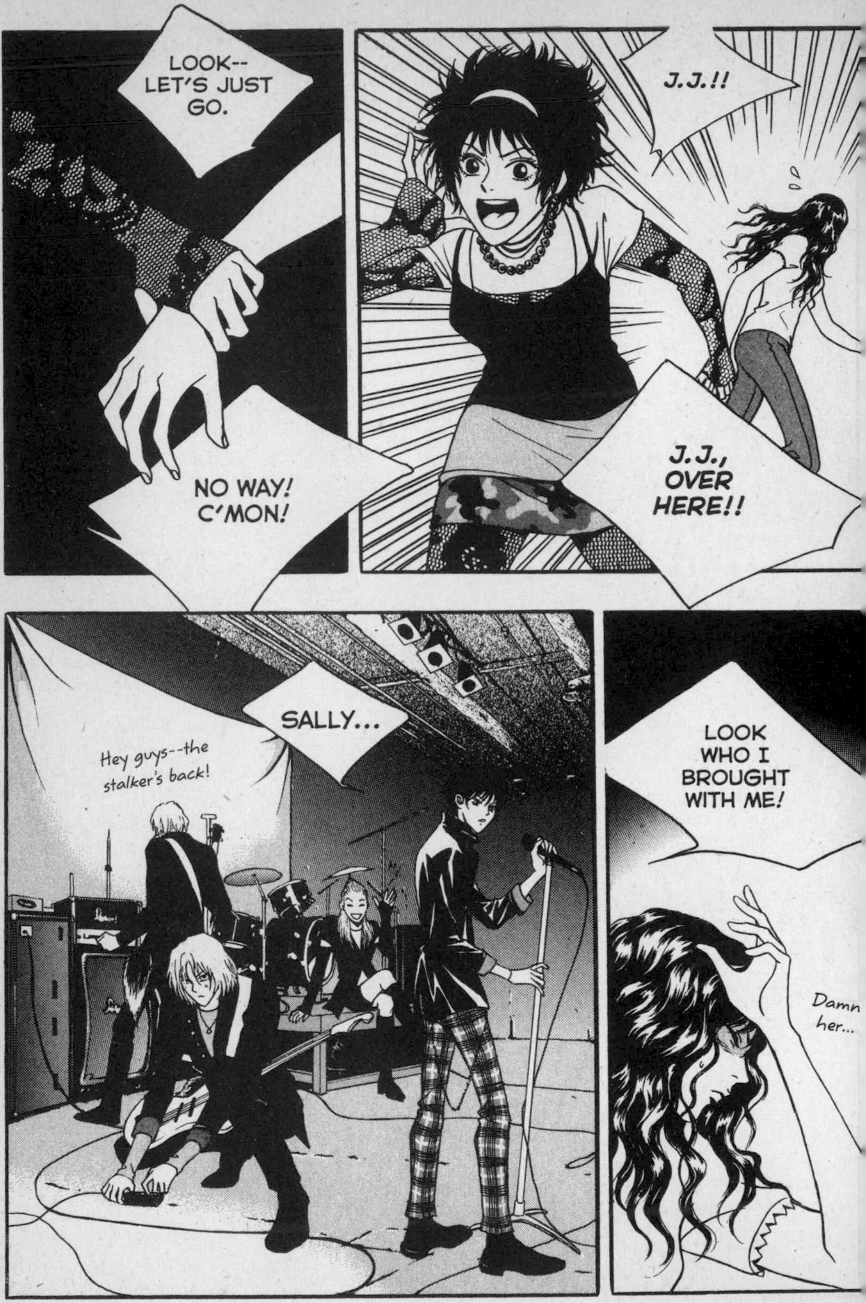
LOOK-- LET'S JUST GO.
NO WAY! C'MON!
J.J.!!
J.J., OVER HERE!!
SALLY...
Hey guys--the stalker's back!
LOOK WHO I BROUGHT WITH ME!
Damn her...

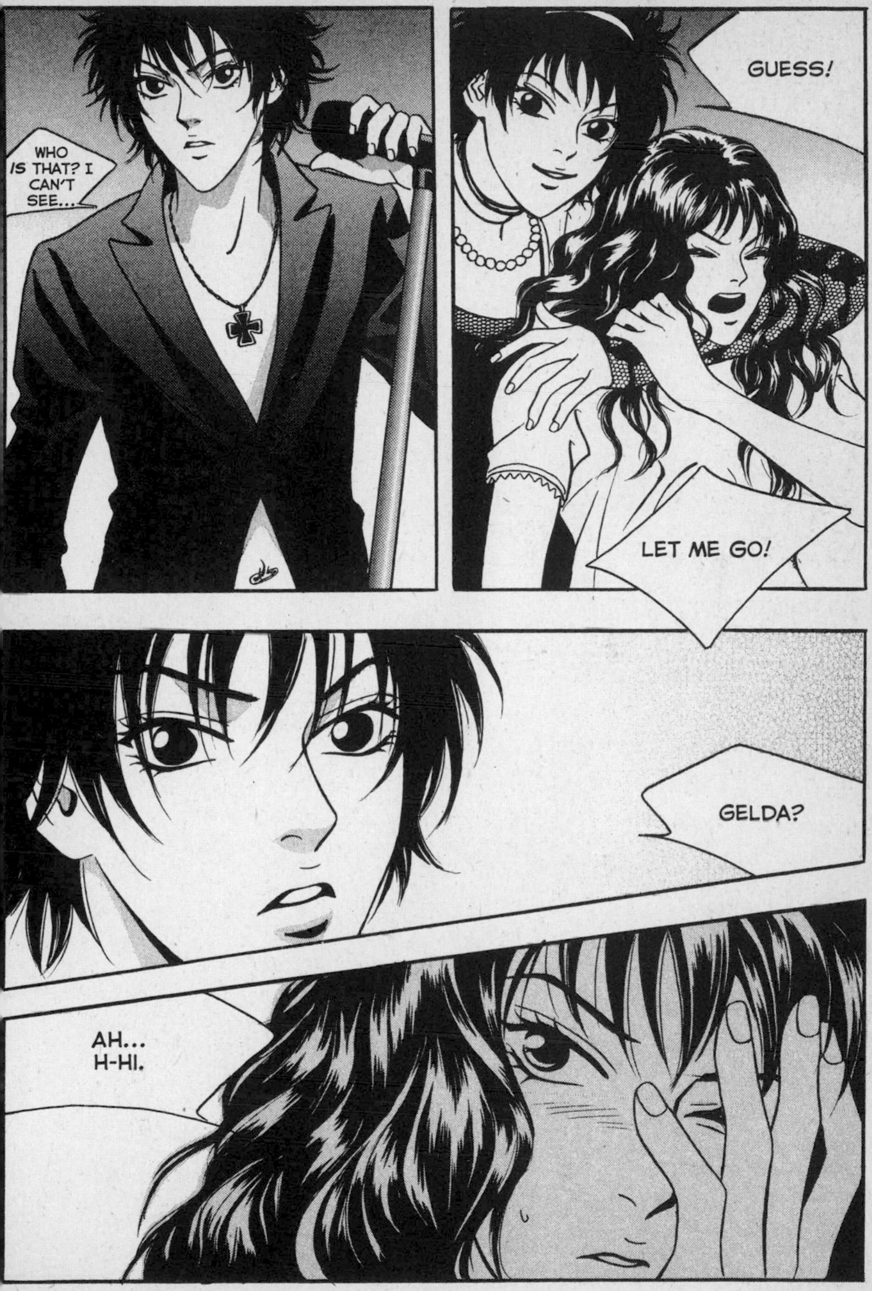
WHO IS THAT? I CAN'T SEE...
GUESS!
LET ME GO!
GELDA?
AH... H-HI.

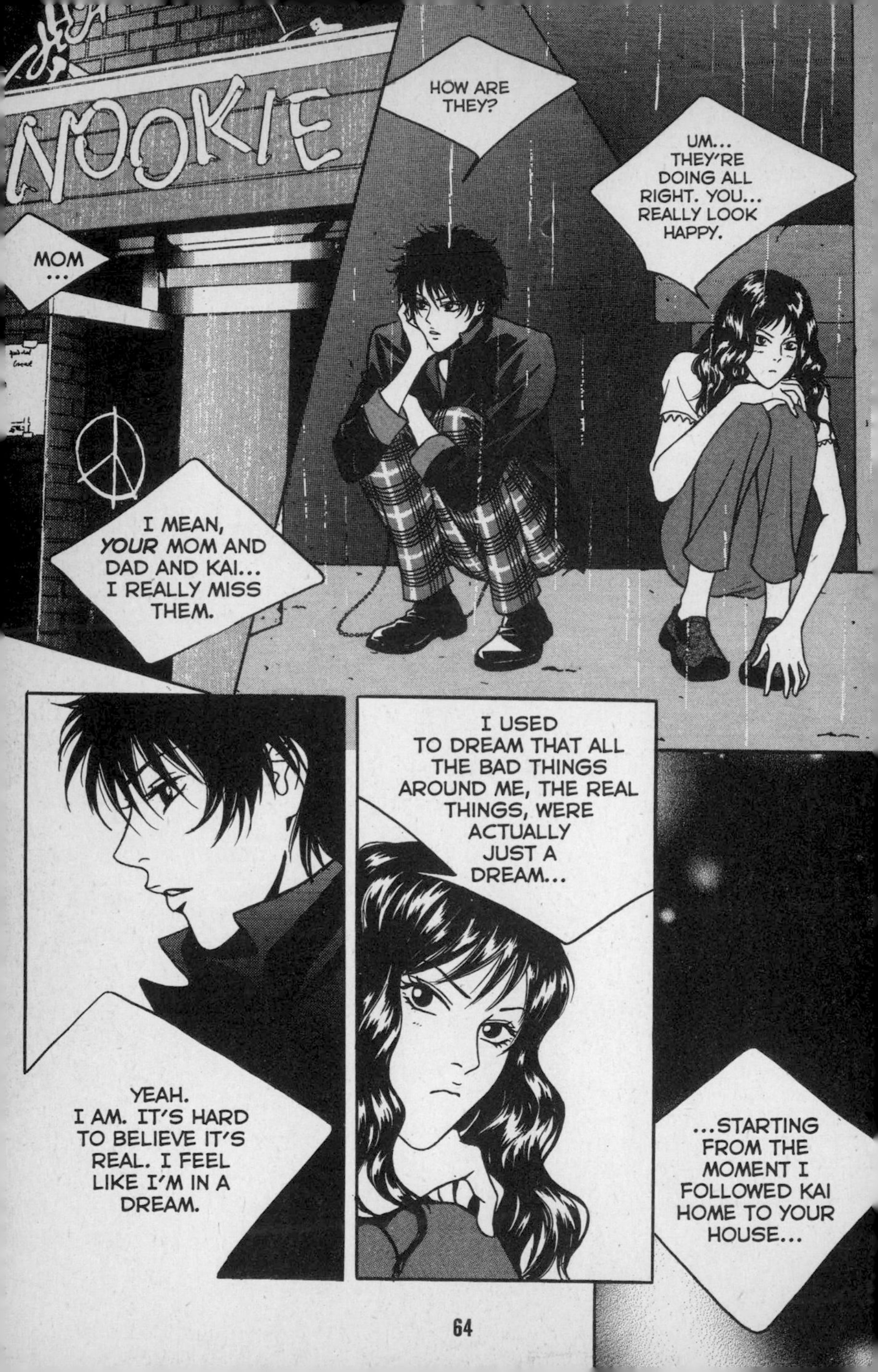
NOOKIE
MOM ...
HOW ARE THEY?
I MEAN, *YOUR* MOM AND DAD AND KAI... I REALLY MISS THEM.
UM... THEY'RE DOING ALL RIGHT. YOU... REALLY LOOK HAPPY.
YEAH. I AM. IT'S HARD TO BELIEVE IT'S REAL. I FEEL LIKE I'M IN A DREAM.
I USED TO DREAM THAT ALL THE BAD THINGS AROUND ME, THE REAL THINGS, WERE ACTUALLY JUST A DREAM...
...STARTING FROM THE MOMENT I FOLLOWED KAI HOME TO YOUR HOUSE...

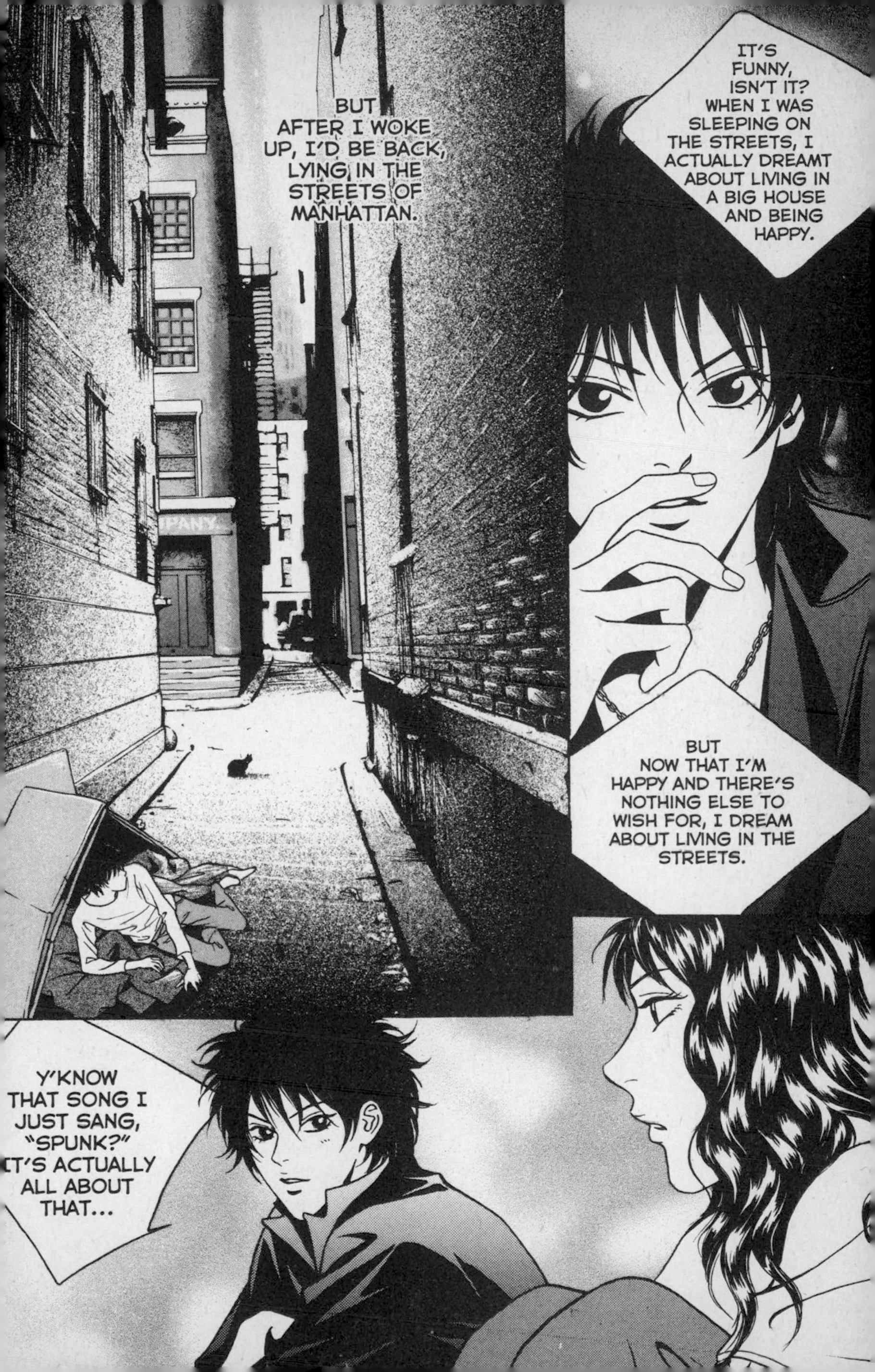
IT'S FUNNY, ISN'T IT? WHEN I WAS SLEEPING ON THE STREETS, I ACTUALLY DREAMT ABOUT LIVING IN A BIG HOUSE AND BEING HAPPY.
BUT NOW THAT I'M HAPPY AND THERE'S NOTHING ELSE TO WISH FOR, I DREAM ABOUT LIVING IN THE STREETS.
BUT AFTER I WOKE UP, I'D BE BACK, LYING IN THE STREETS OF MANHATTAN.
Y'KNOW THAT SONG I JUST SANG, "SPUNK?" IT'S ACTUALLY ALL ABOUT THAT...

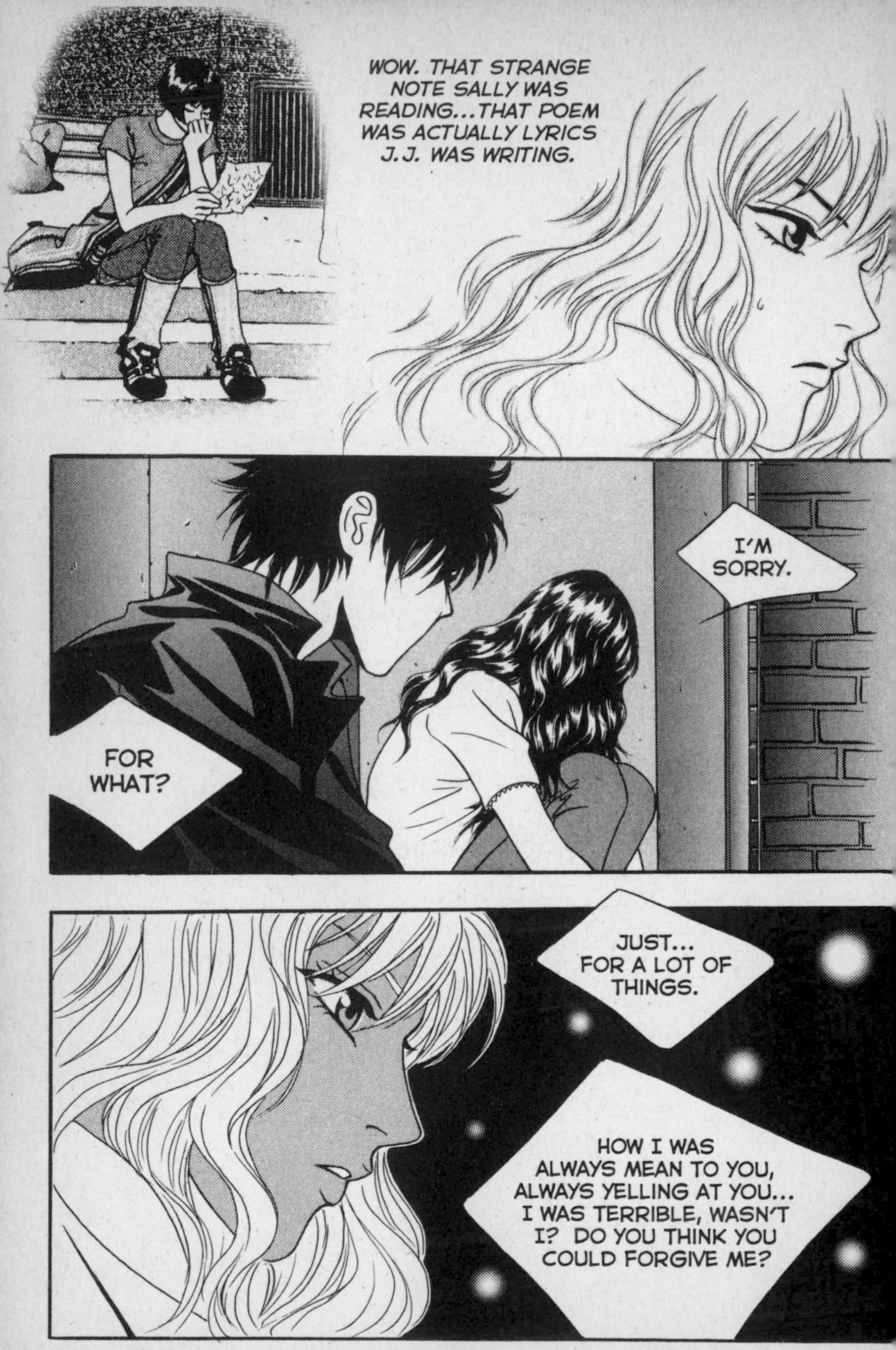
WOW. THAT STRANGE NOTE SALLY WAS READING...THAT POEM WAS ACTUALLY LYRICS J.J. WAS WRITING.
I'M SORRY.
FOR WHAT?
JUST... FOR A LOT OF THINGS.
HOW I WAS ALWAYS MEAN TO YOU, ALWAYS YELLING AT YOU... I WAS TERRIBLE, WASN'T I? DO YOU THINK YOU COULD FORGIVE ME?

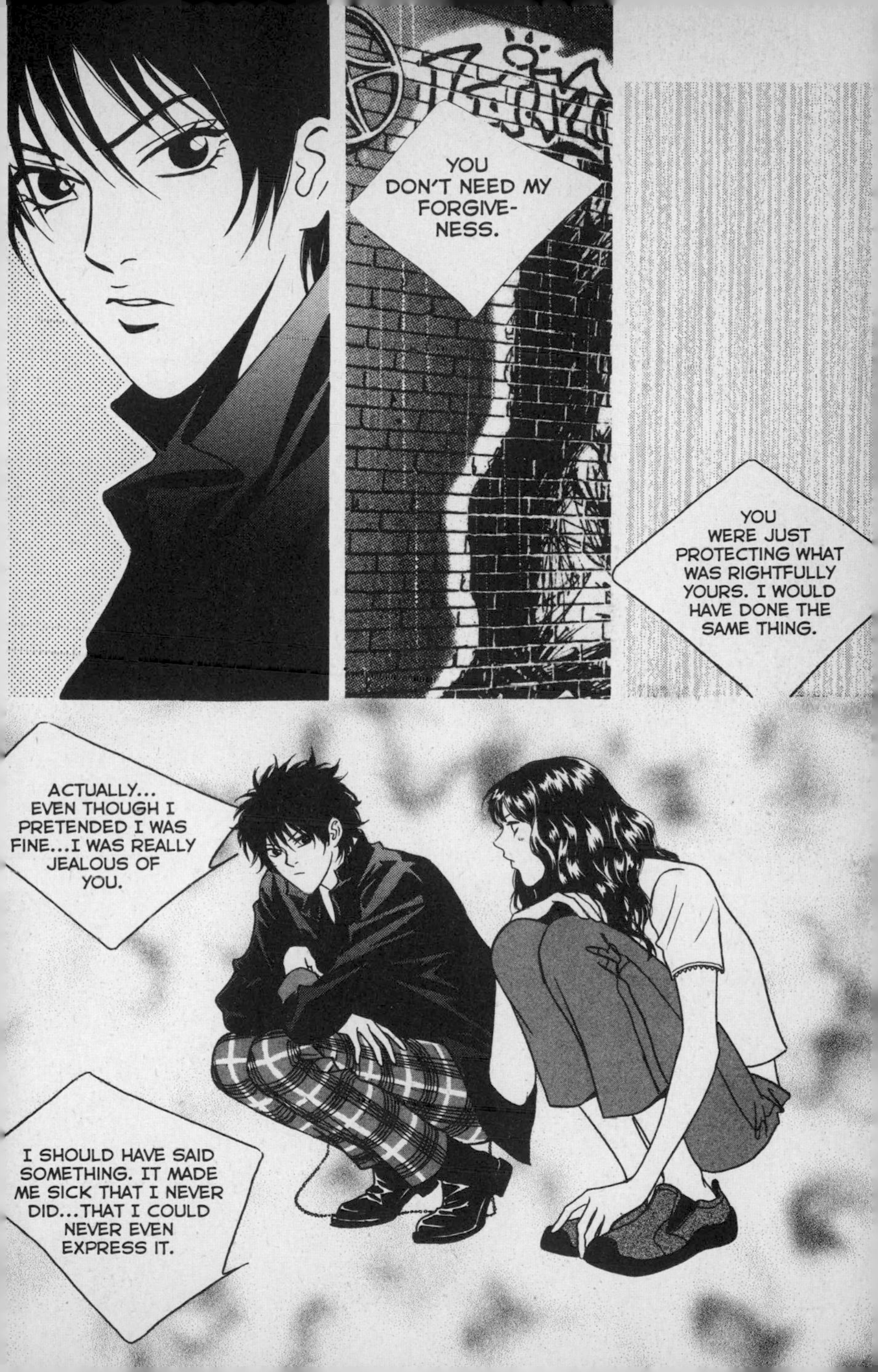
YOU DON'T NEED MY FORGIVE- NESS.
YOU WERE JUST PROTECTING WHAT WAS RIGHTFULLY YOURS. I WOULD HAVE DONE THE SAME THING.
ACTUALLY... EVEN THOUGH I PRETENDED I WAS FINE...I WAS REALLY JEALOUS OF YOU.
I SHOULD HAVE SAID SOMETHING. IT MADE ME SICK THAT I NEVER DID...THAT I COULD NEVER EVEN EXPRESS IT.

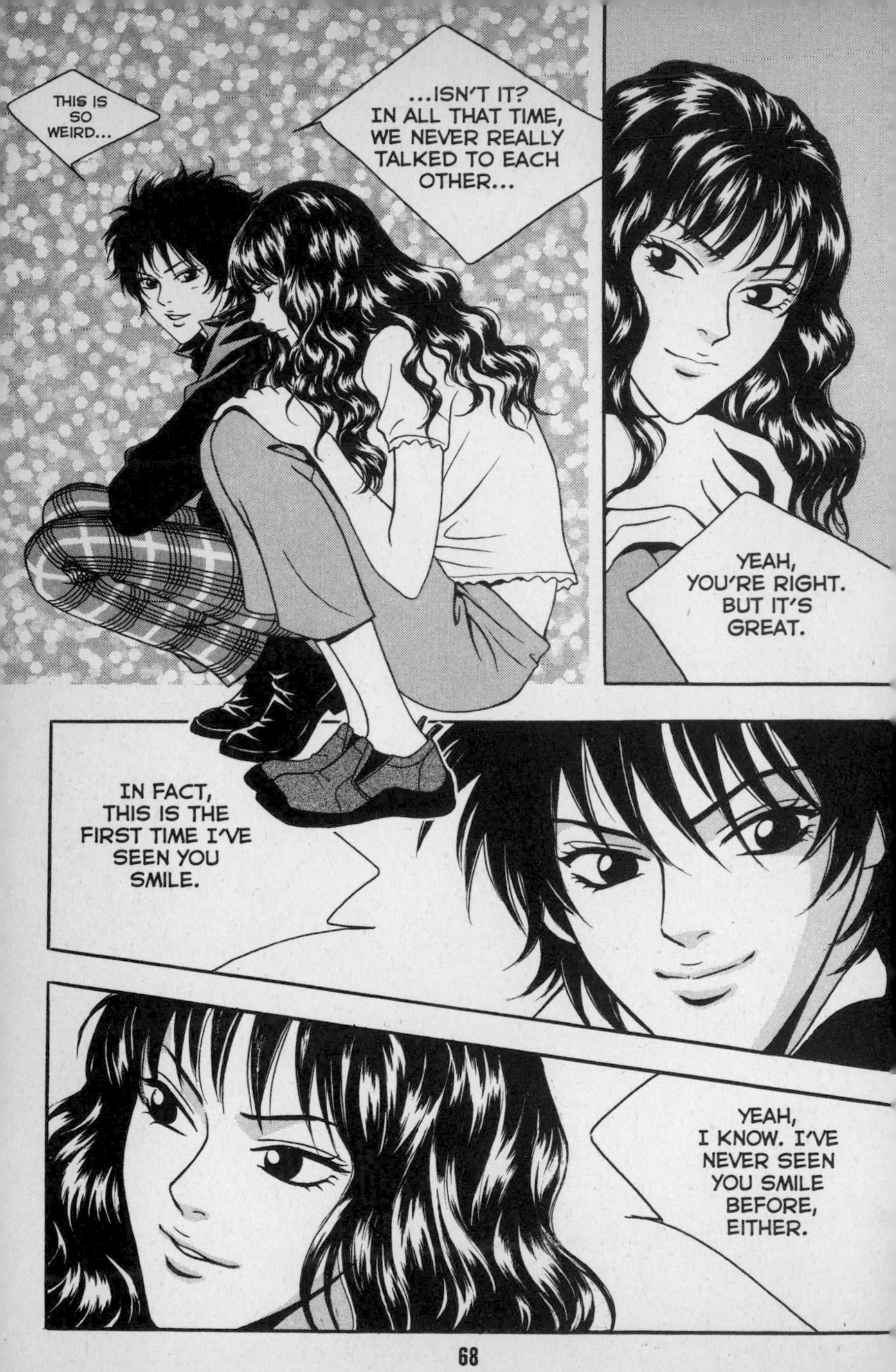
THIS IS SO WEIRD...
...ISN'T IT? IN ALL THAT TIME, WE NEVER REALLY TALKED TO EACH OTHER...
YEAH, YOU'RE RIGHT. BUT IT'S GREAT.
IN FACT, THIS IS THE FIRST TIME I'VE SEEN YOU SMILE.
YEAH, I KNOW. I'VE NEVER SEEN YOU SMILE BEFORE, EITHER.

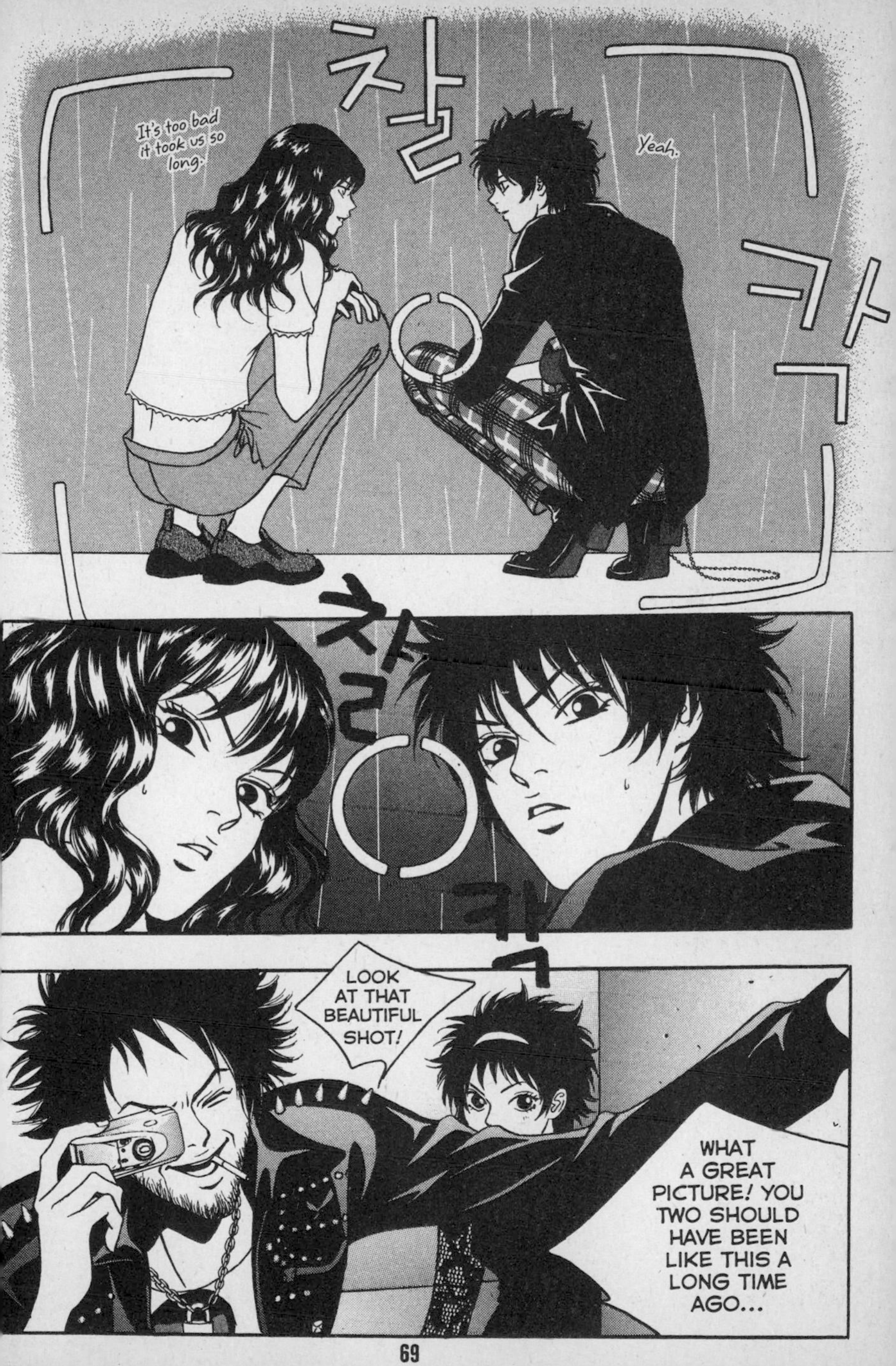
찰칵
It's too bad it took us so long.
Yeah.
찰칵
LOOK AT THAT BEAUTIFUL SHOT!
WHAT A GREAT PICTURE! YOU TWO SHOULD HAVE BEEN LIKE THIS A LONG TIME AGO...

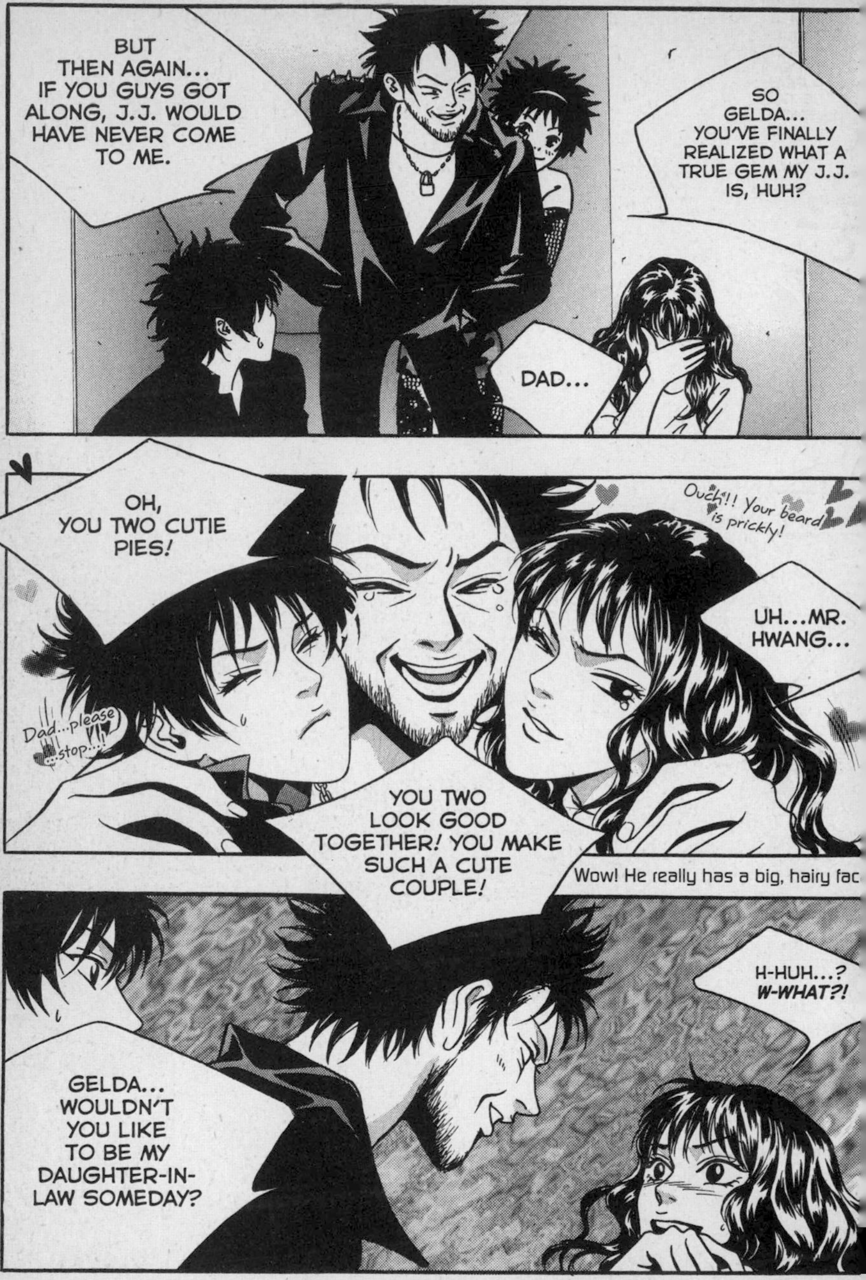
BUT THEN AGAIN... IF YOU GUYS GOT ALONG, J.J. WOULD HAVE NEVER COME TO ME.
SO GELDA... YOU'VE FINALLY REALIZED WHAT A TRUE GEM MY J.J. IS, HUH?
DAD...
OH, YOU TWO CUTIE PIES!
Dad...please stop...
Ouch!! Your beard is prickly!
UH...MR. HWANG...
YOU TWO LOOK GOOD TOGETHER! YOU MAKE SUCH A CUTE COUPLE!
Wow! He really has a big, hairy fac
GELDA... WOULDN'T YOU LIKE TO BE MY DAUGHTER-IN-LAW SOMEDAY?
H-HUH...? *W-WHAT?!*

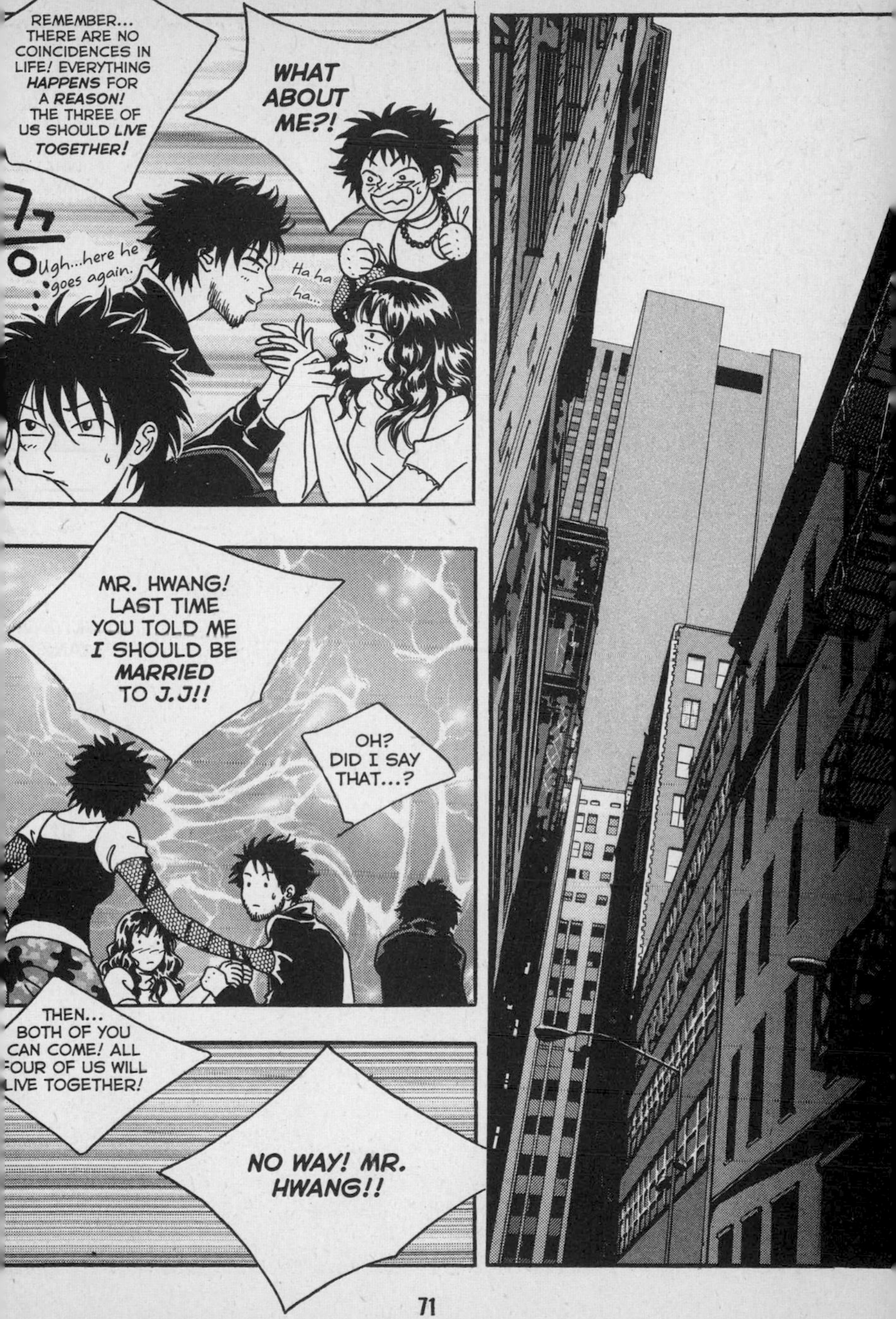
REMEMBER... THERE ARE NO COINCIDENCES IN LIFE! EVERYTHING HAPPENS FOR A REASON! THE THREE OF US SHOULD LIVE TOGETHER!
WHAT ABOUT ME?!
Ugh...here he goes again.
Ha ha ha...
MR. HWANG! LAST TIME YOU TOLD ME I SHOULD BE MARRIED TO J.J!!
OH? DID I SAY THAT...?
THEN... BOTH OF YOU CAN COME! ALL FOUR OF US WILL LIVE TOGETHER!
NO WAY! MR. HWANG!!

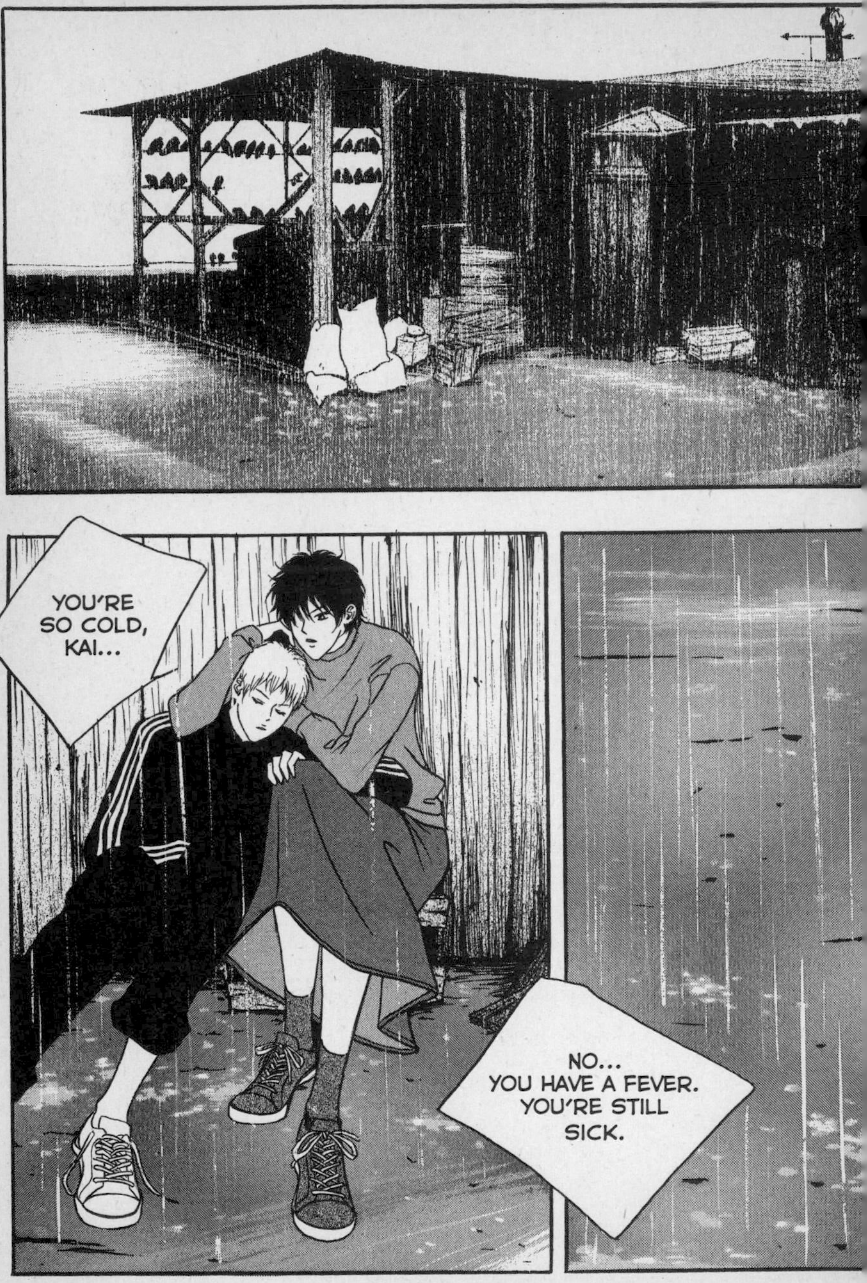
YOU'RE SO COLD, KAI...
NO... YOU HAVE A FEVER. YOU'RE STILL SICK.

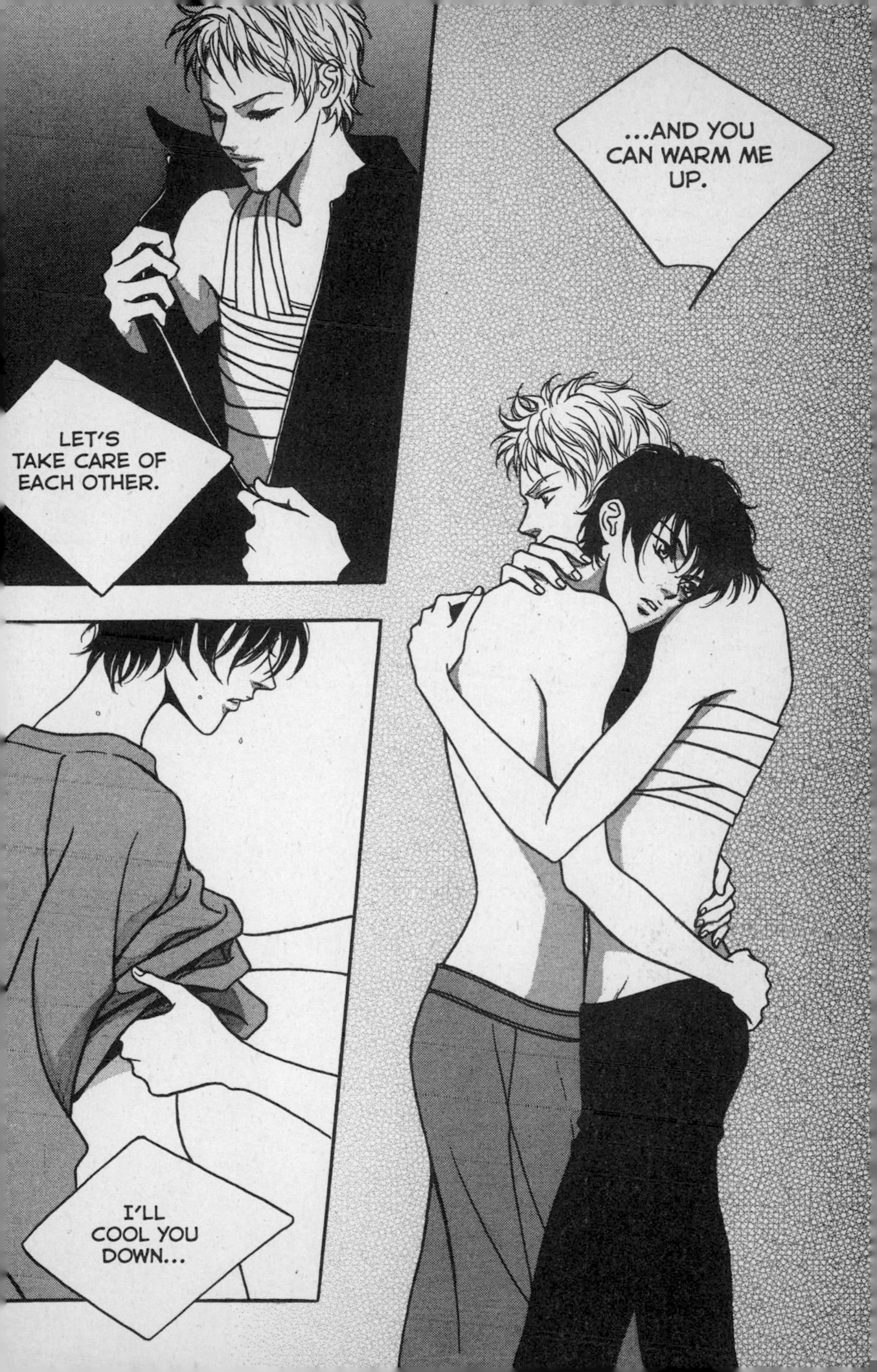
LET'S TAKE CARE OF EACH OTHER.
I'LL COOL YOU DOWN...
...AND YOU CAN WARM ME UP.

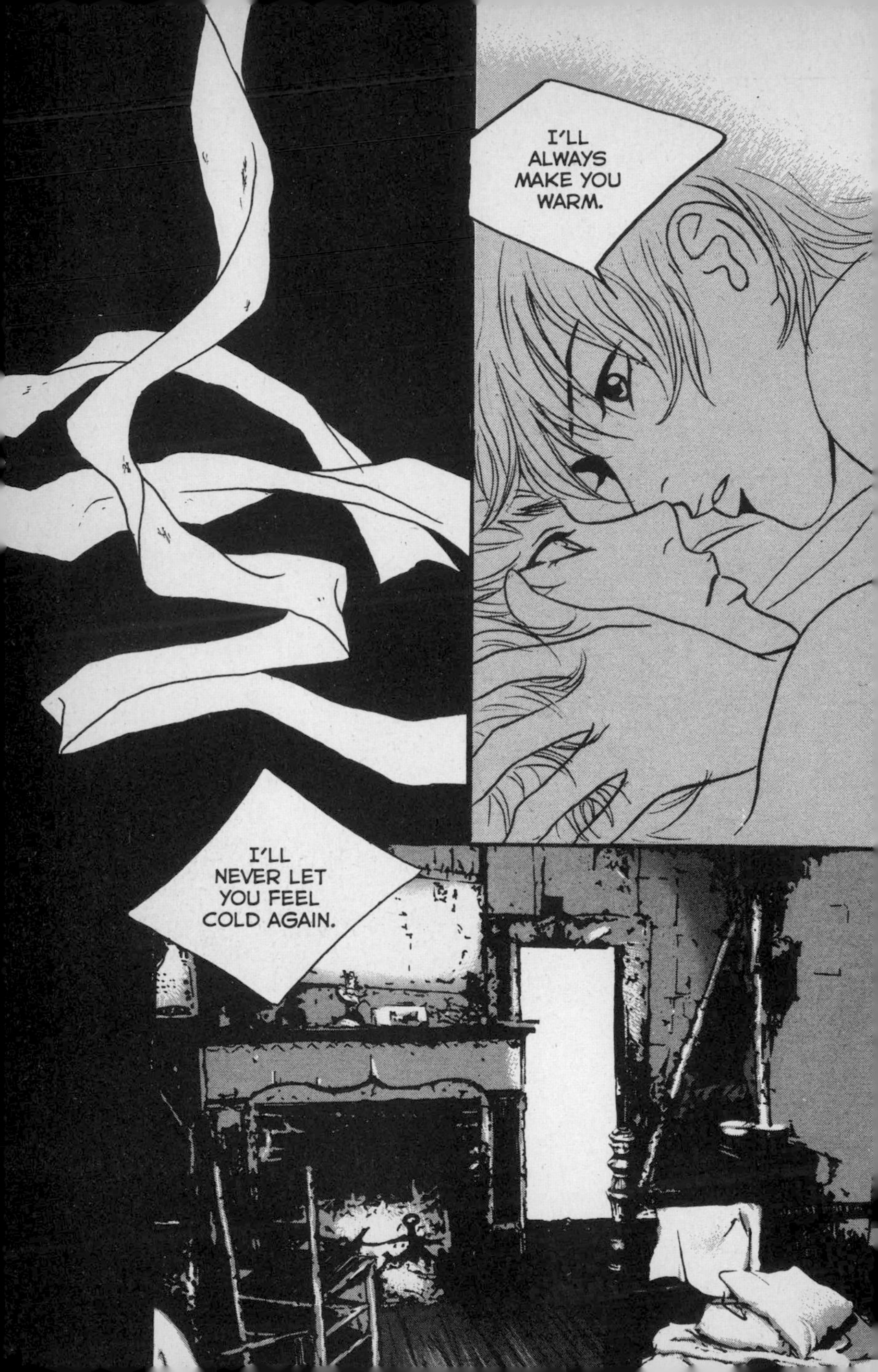
I'LL ALWAYS MAKE YOU WARM.
I'LL NEVER LET YOU FEEL COLD AGAIN.

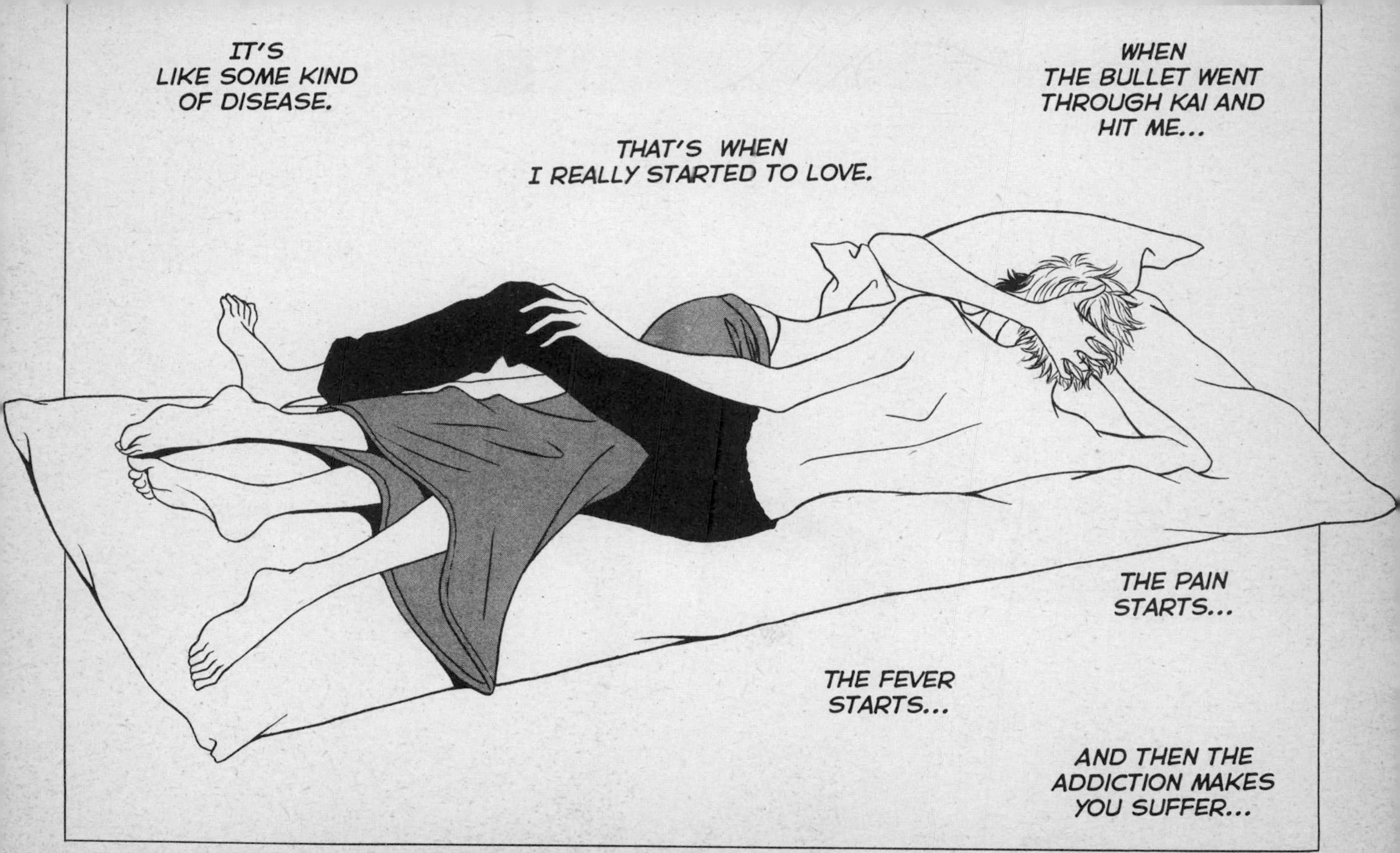
WHEN THE BULLET WENT THROUGH KAI AND HIT ME...
THE PAIN STARTS...
AND THEN THE ADDICTION MAKES YOU SUFFER...
THAT'S WHEN I REALLY STARTED TO LOVE.
THE FEVER STARTS...
IT'S LIKE SOME KIND OF DISEASE.

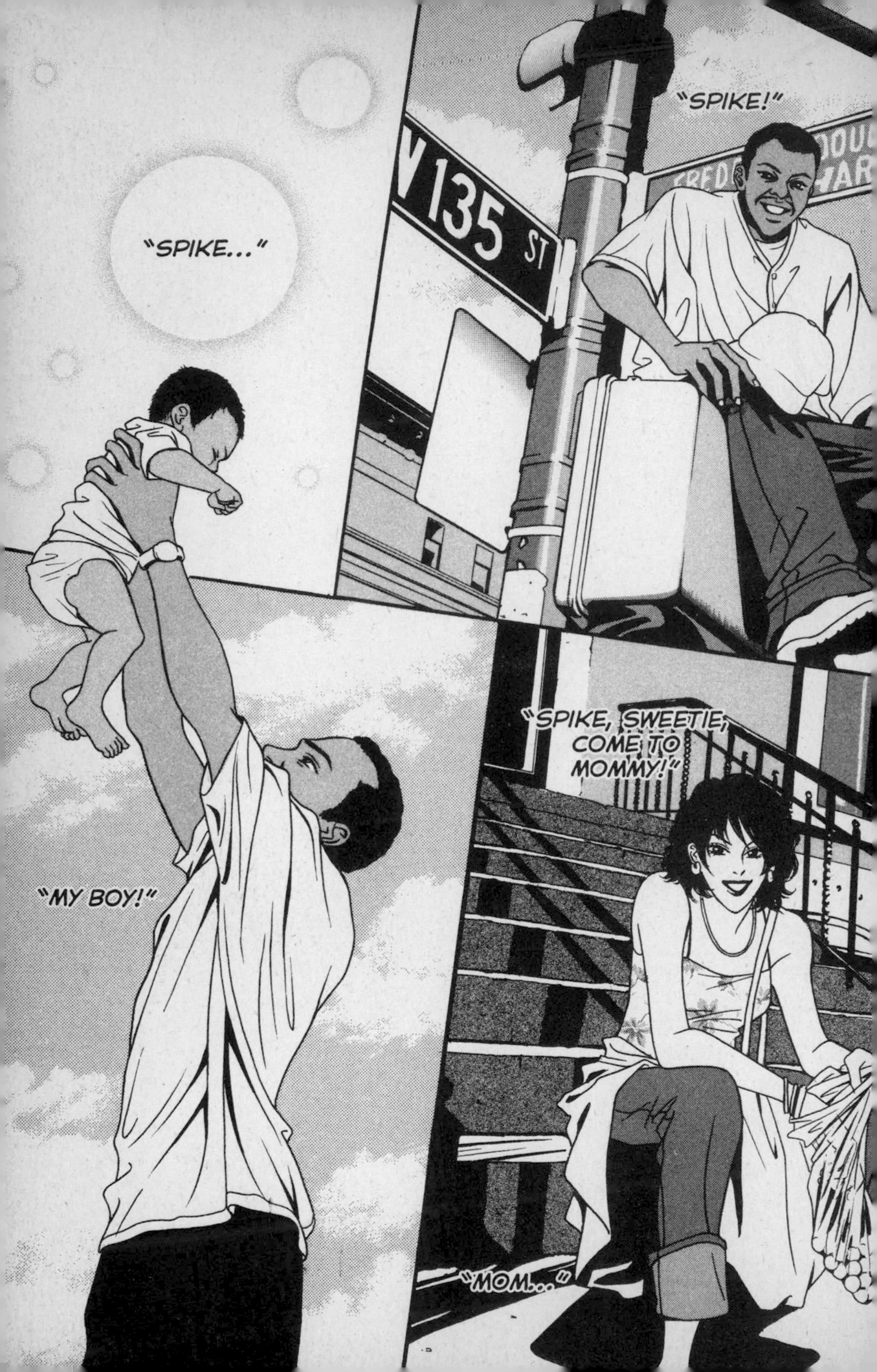
"SPIKE!"
"SPIKE..."
"SPIKE, SWEETIE, COME TO MOMMY!"
"MOM..."
"MY BOY!"

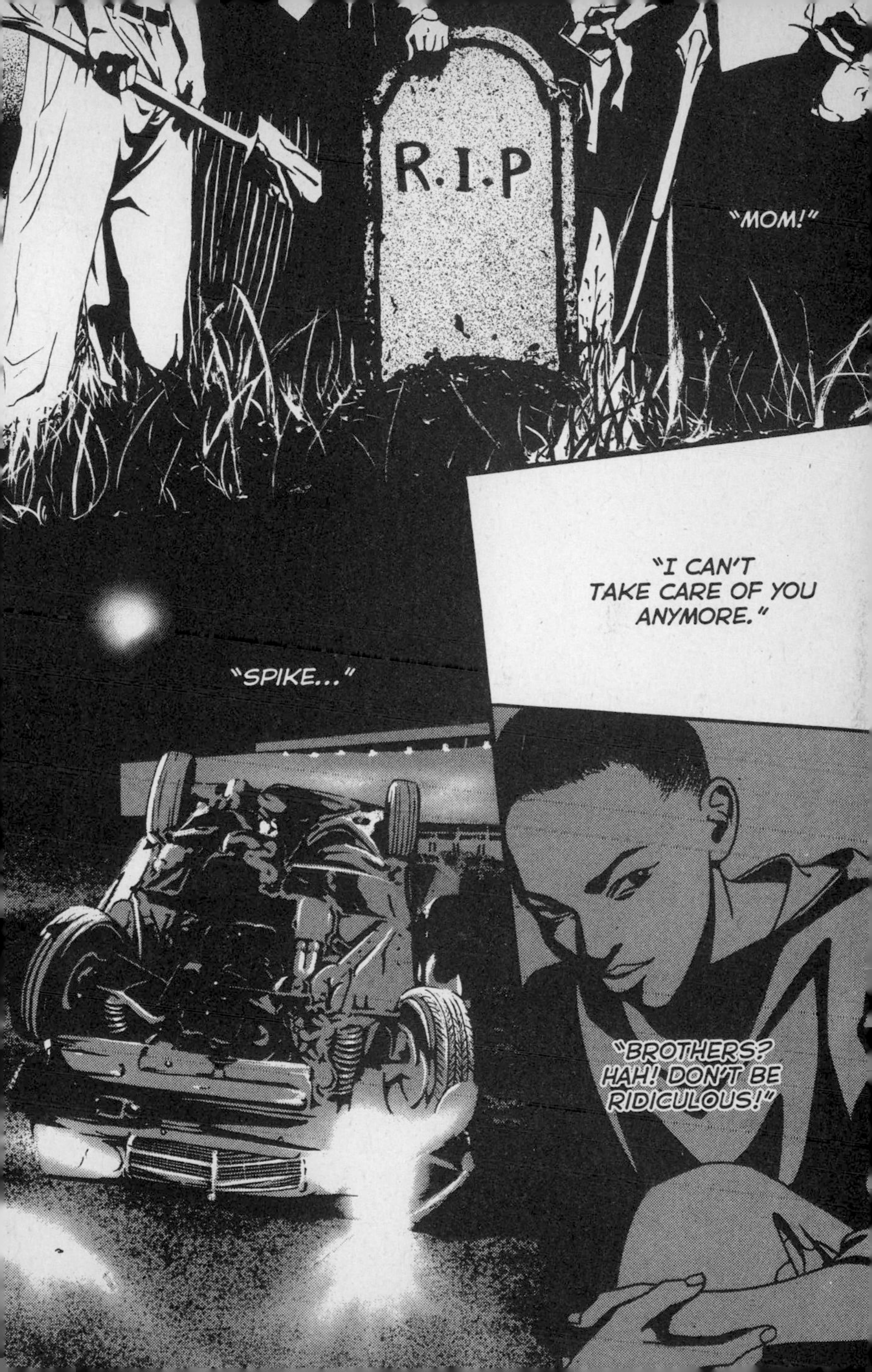
R.I.P
"MOM!"
"I CAN'T TAKE CARE OF YOU ANYMORE."
"SPIKE..."
"BROTHERS? HAH! DON'T BE RIDICULOUS!"

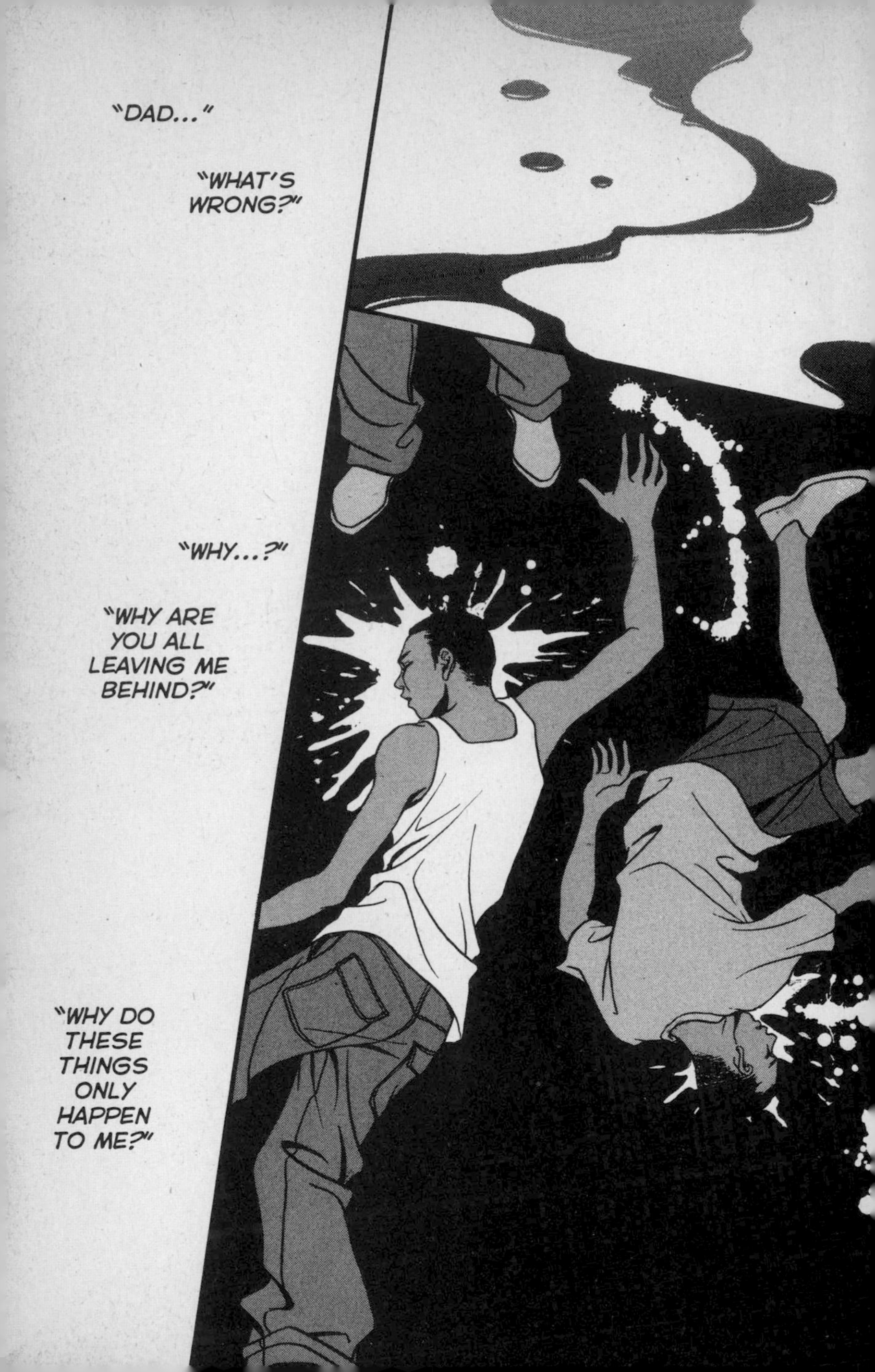
"DAD..."
"WHAT'S WRONG?"
"WHY...?"
"WHY ARE YOU ALL LEAVING ME BEHIND?"
"WHY DO THESE THINGS ONLY HAPPEN TO ME?"

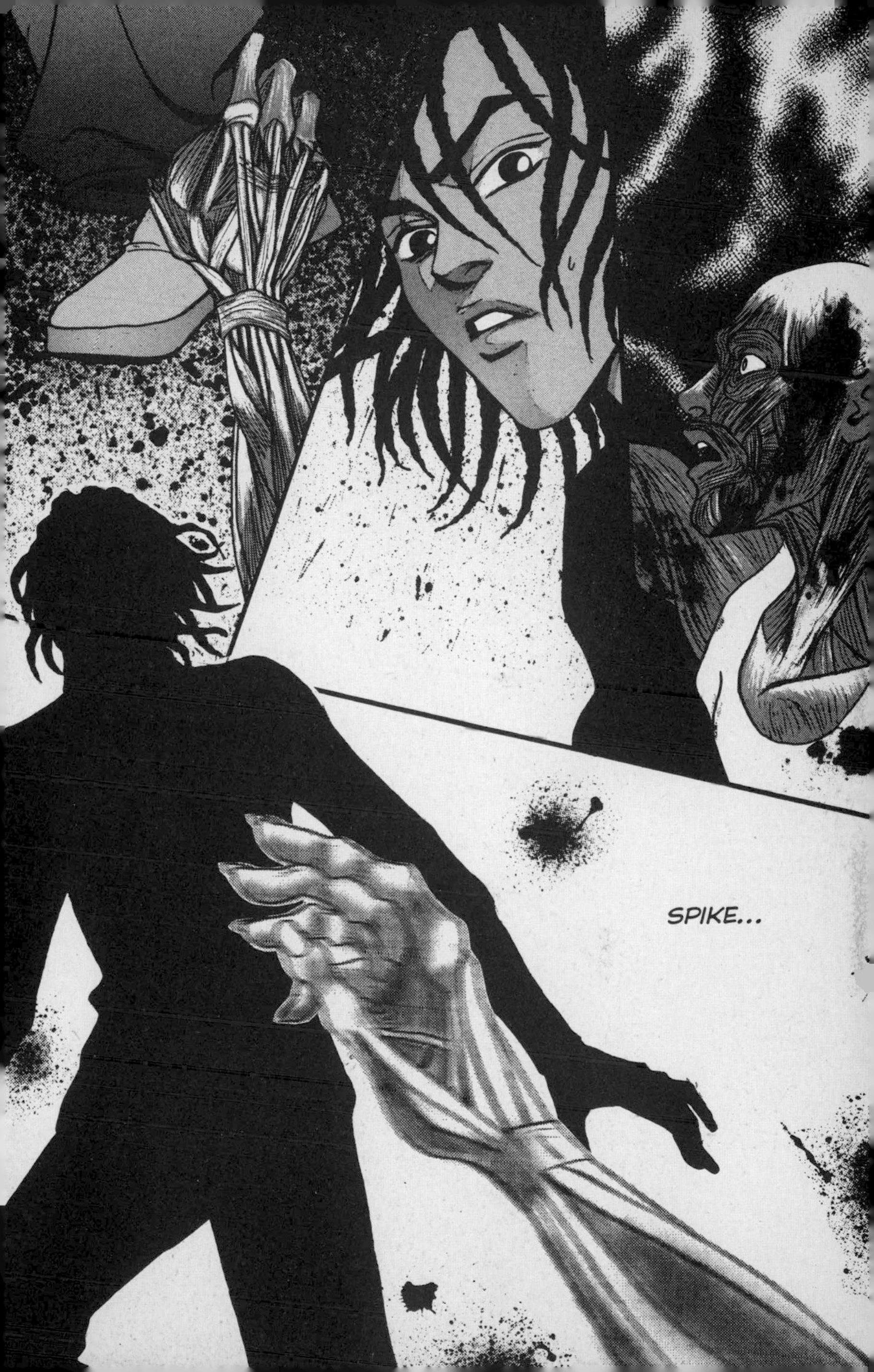
SPIKE...

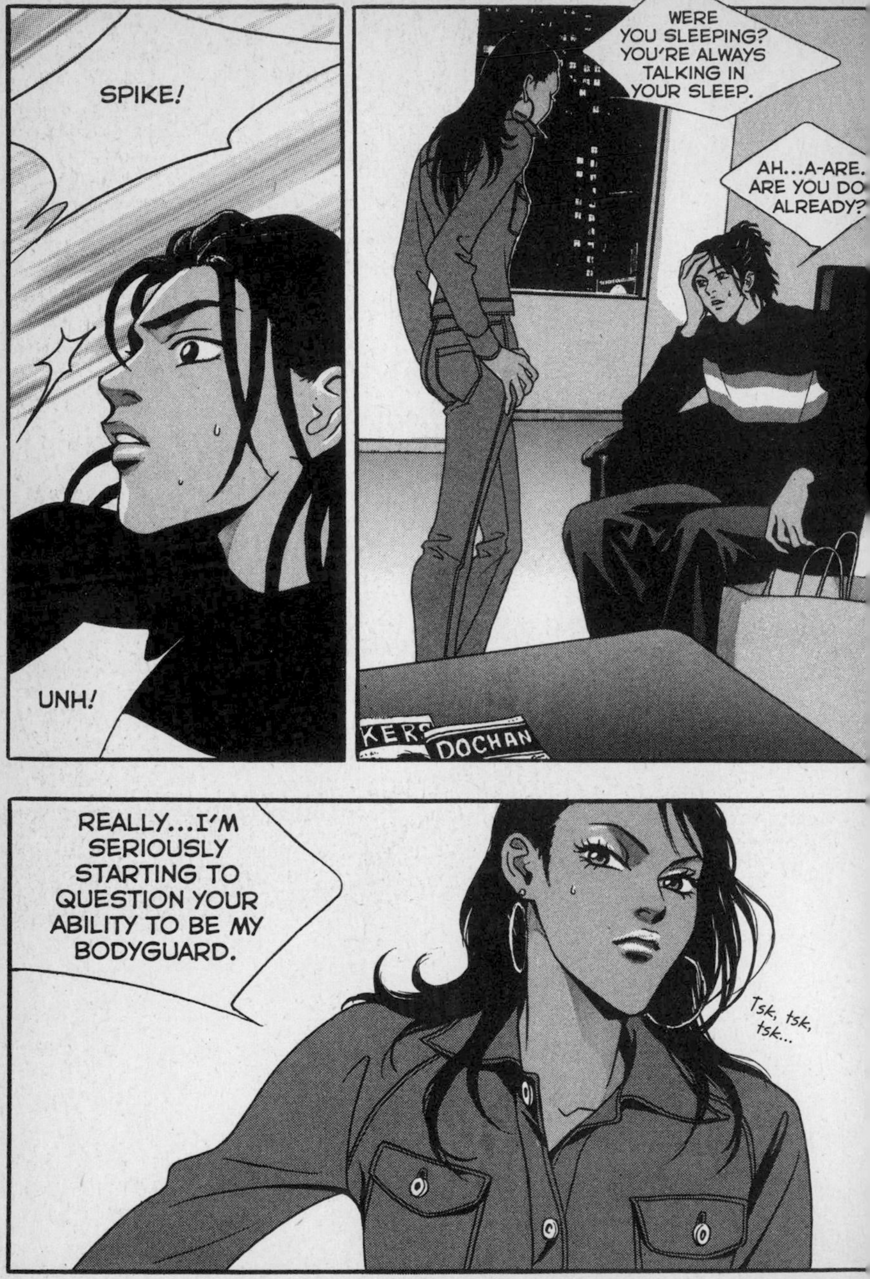
SPIKE!
UNH!
WERE YOU SLEEPING? YOU'RE ALWAYS TALKING IN YOUR SLEEP.
AH...A-ARE. ARE YOU DO ALREADY?
KERS
DOCHAN
REALLY...I'M SERIOUSLY STARTING TO QUESTION YOUR ABILITY TO BE MY BODYGUARD.
Tsk, tsk, tsk...

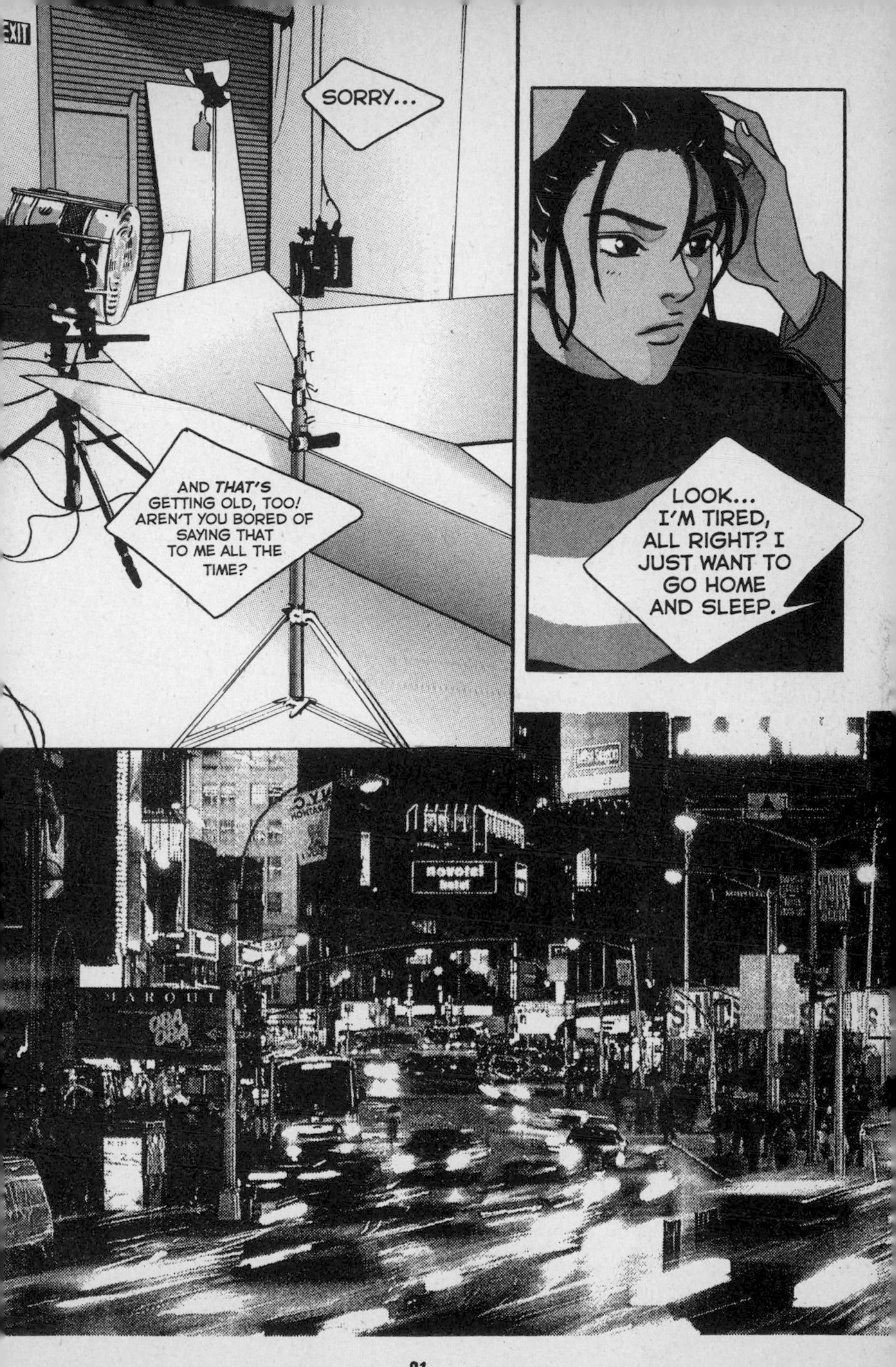
EXIT
SORRY...
AND *THAT'S* GETTING OLD, TOO! AREN'T YOU BORED OF SAYING THAT TO ME ALL THE TIME?
LOOK... I'M TIRED, ALL RIGHT? I JUST WANT TO GO HOME AND SLEEP.
novotel hotel

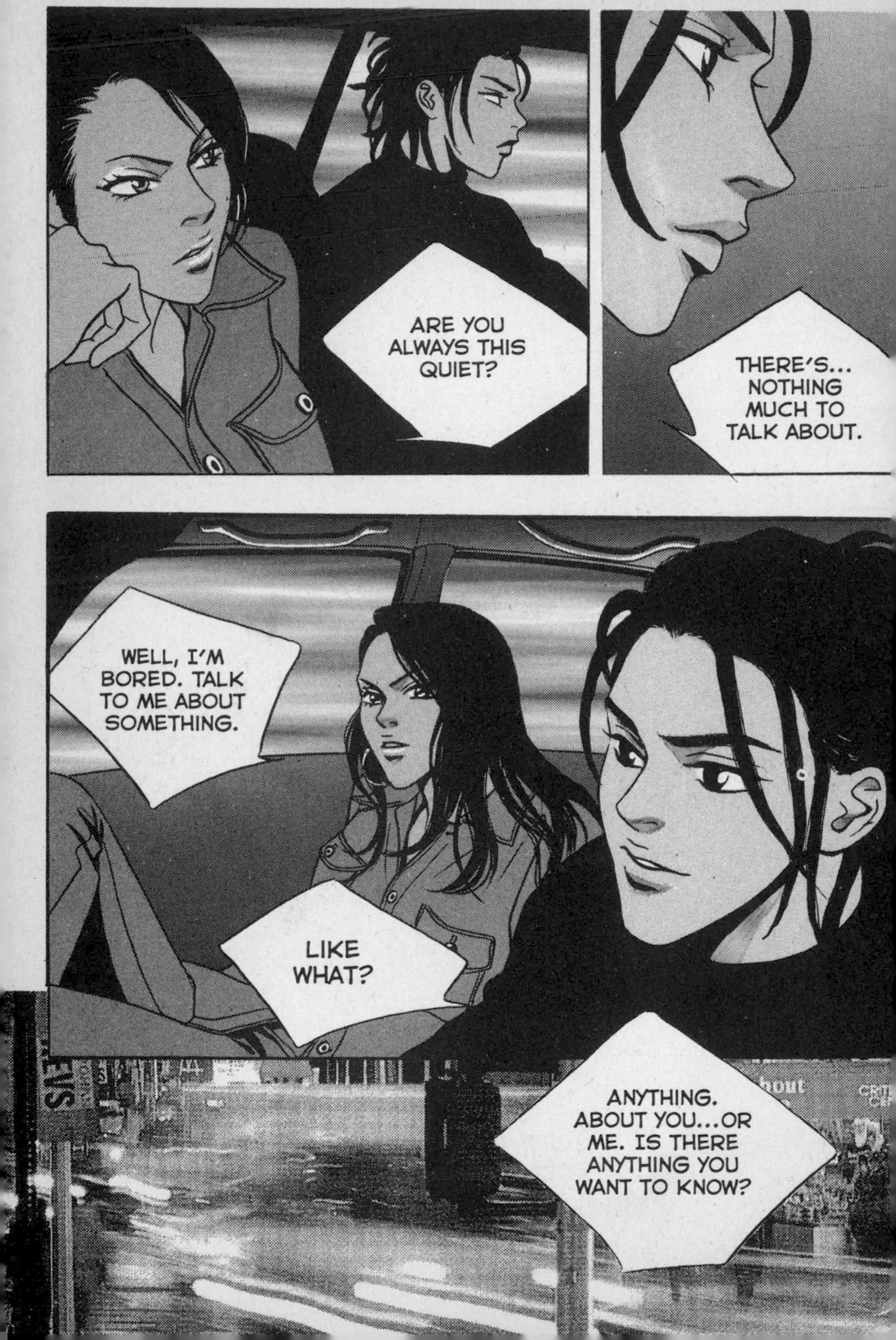
ARE YOU ALWAYS THIS QUIET?
THERE'S... NOTHING MUCH TO TALK ABOUT.
WELL, I'M BORED. TALK TO ME ABOUT SOMETHING.
LIKE WHAT?
ANYTHING. ABOUT YOU...OR ME. IS THERE ANYTHING YOU WANT TO KNOW?

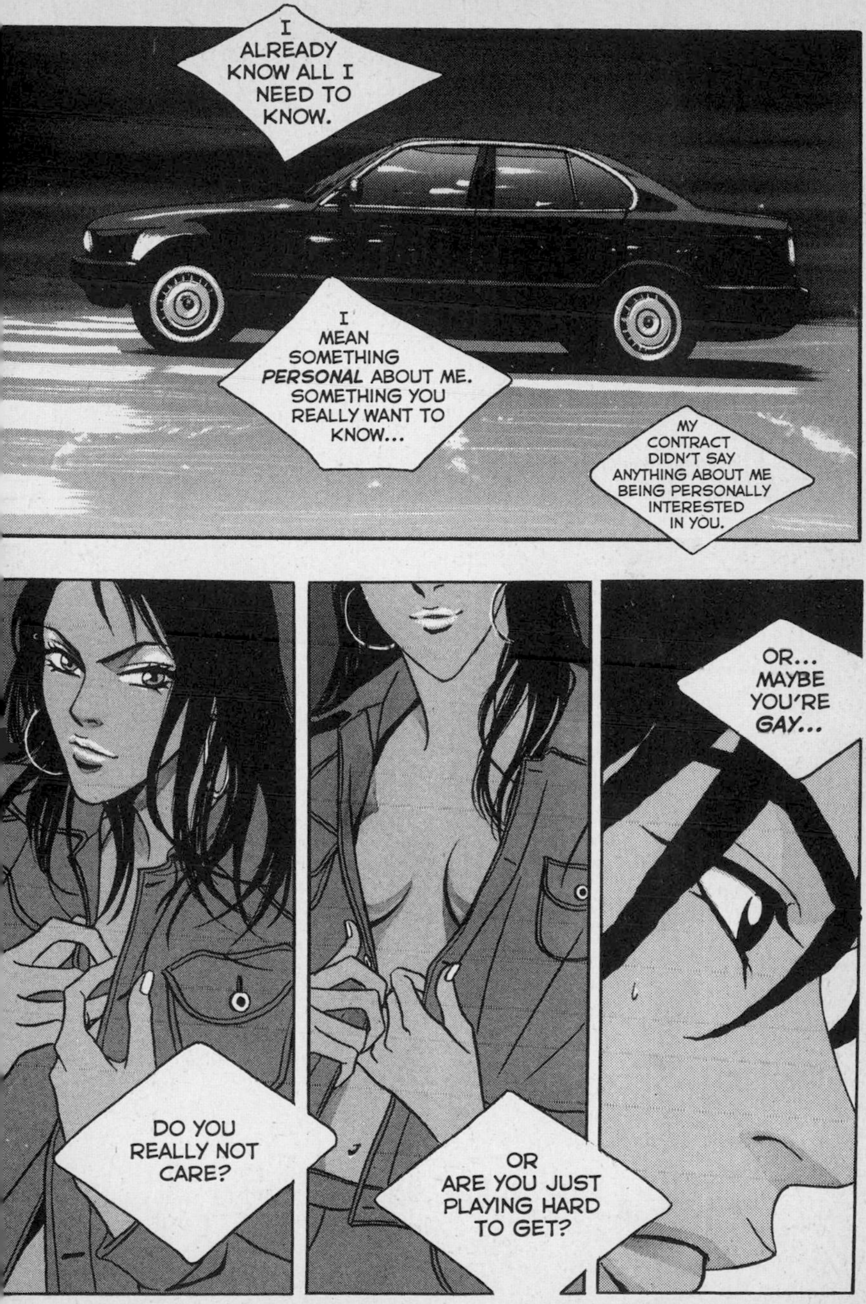
I ALREADY KNOW ALL I NEED TO KNOW.
I MEAN SOMETHING *PERSONAL* ABOUT ME. SOMETHING YOU REALLY WANT TO KNOW...
MY CONTRACT DIDN'T SAY ANYTHING ABOUT ME BEING PERSONALLY INTERESTED IN YOU.
DO YOU REALLY NOT CARE?
OR ARE YOU JUST PLAYING HARD TO GET?
OR... MAYBE YOU'RE *GAY*...

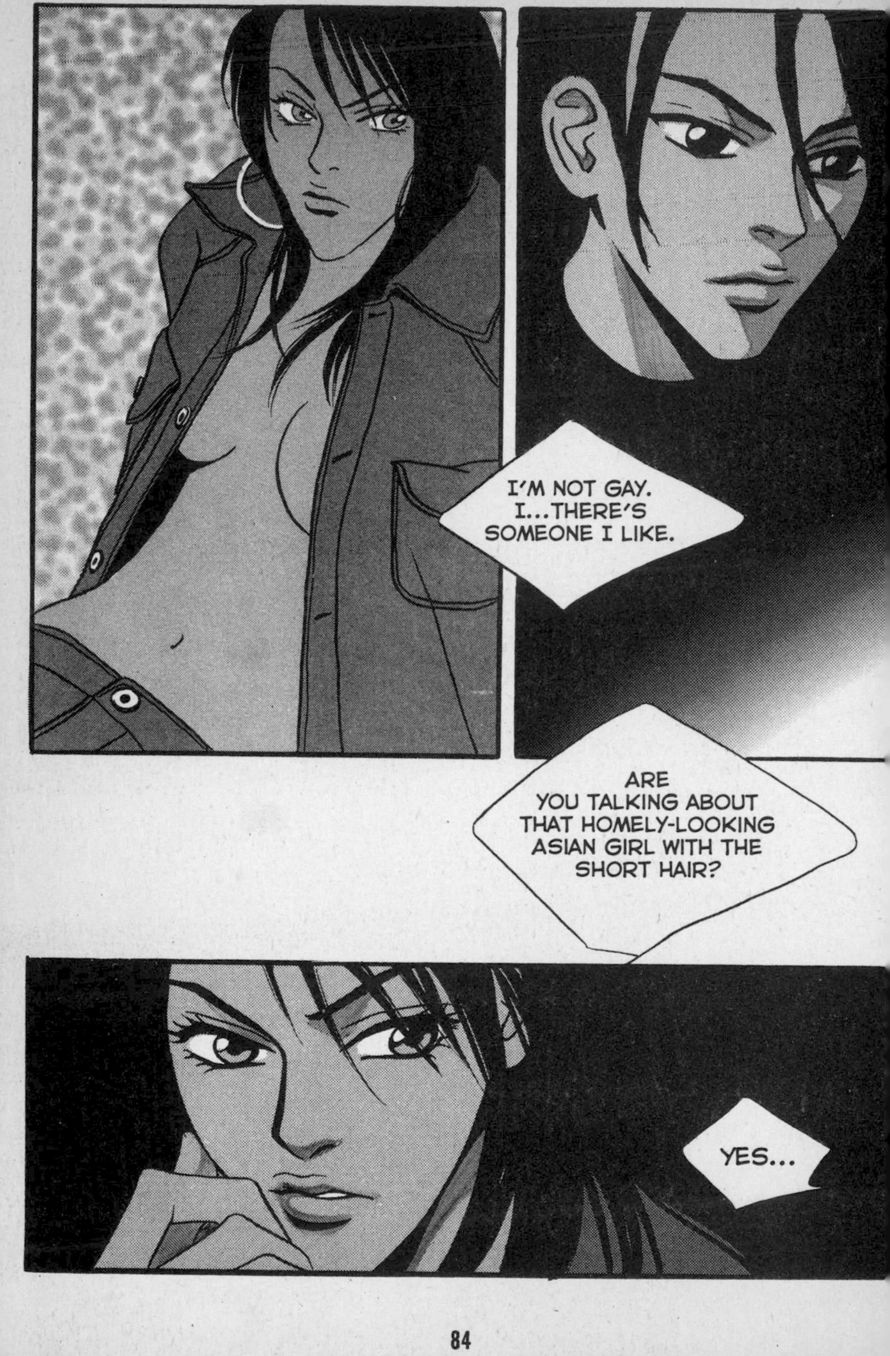
I'M NOT GAY. I...THERE'S SOMEONE I LIKE.
ARE YOU TALKING ABOUT THAT HOMELY-LOOKING ASIAN GIRL WITH THE SHORT HAIR?
YES...

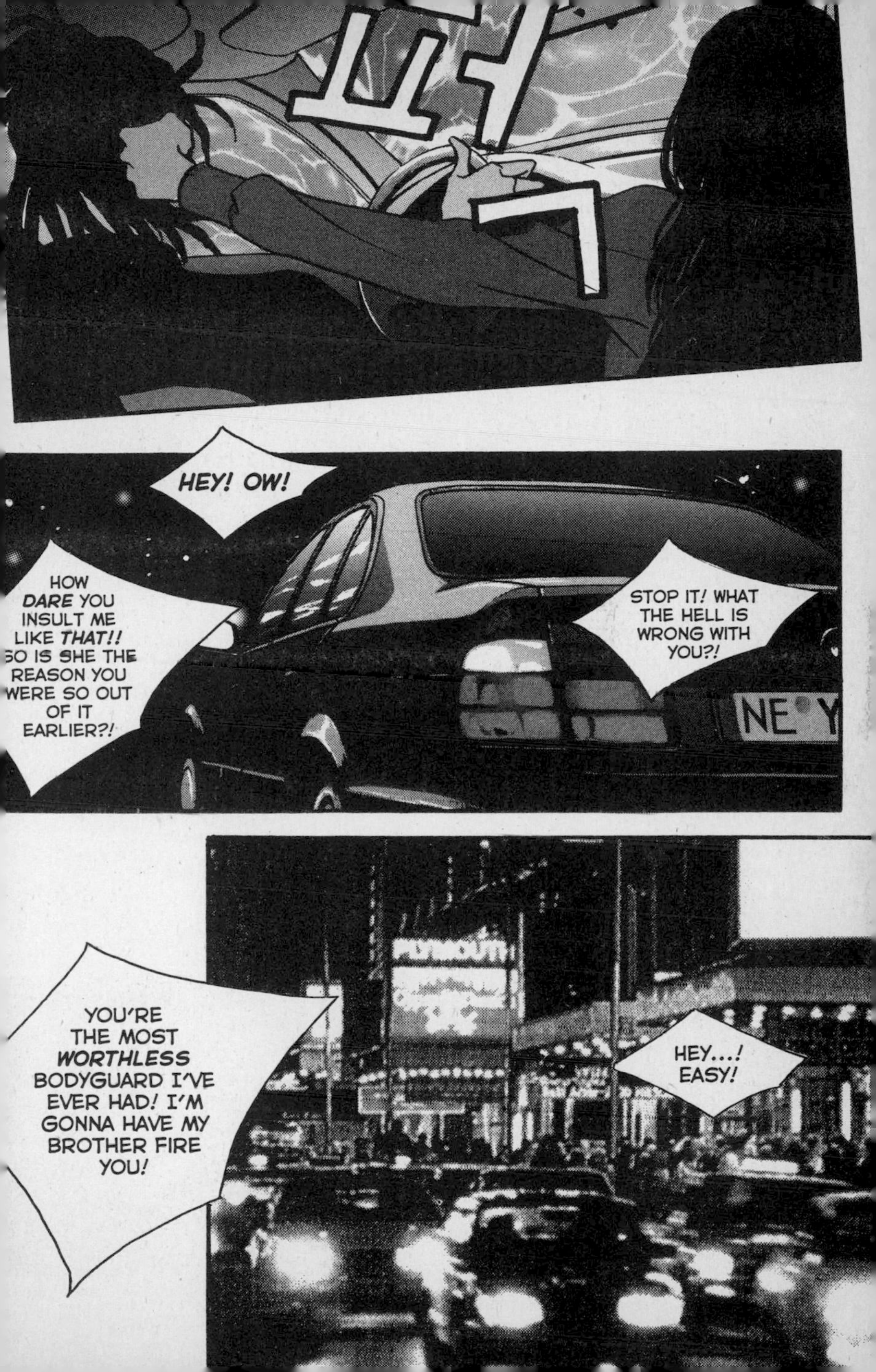
HEY! OW!
HOW DARE YOU INSULT ME LIKE THAT!! SO IS SHE THE REASON YOU WERE SO OUT OF IT EARLIER?!
STOP IT! WHAT THE HELL IS WRONG WITH YOU?!
NE Y
YOU'RE THE MOST WORTHLESS BODYGUARD I'VE EVER HAD! I'M GONNA HAVE MY BROTHER FIRE YOU!
HEY...! EASY!

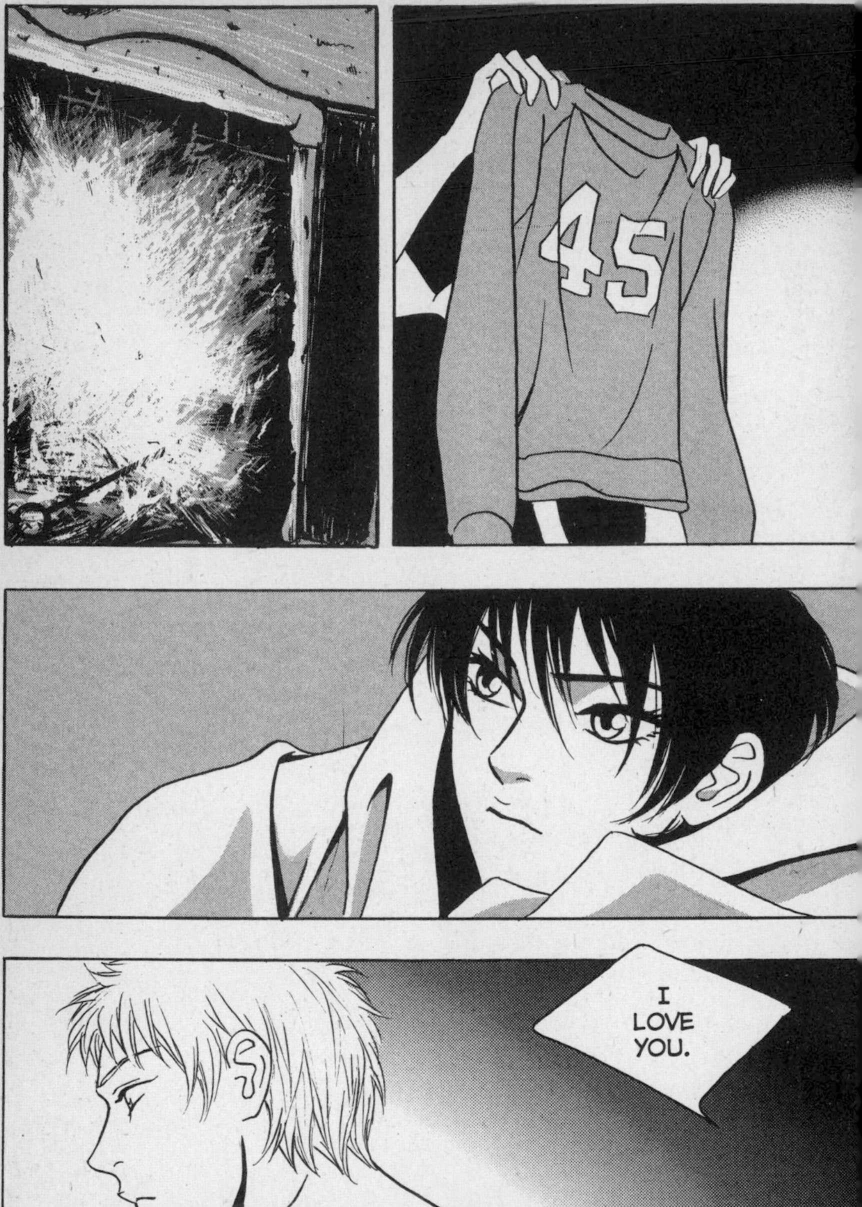
45
I LOVE YOU.

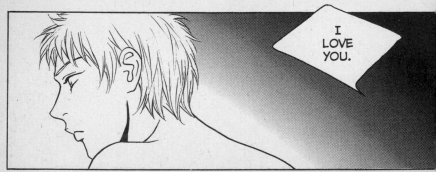

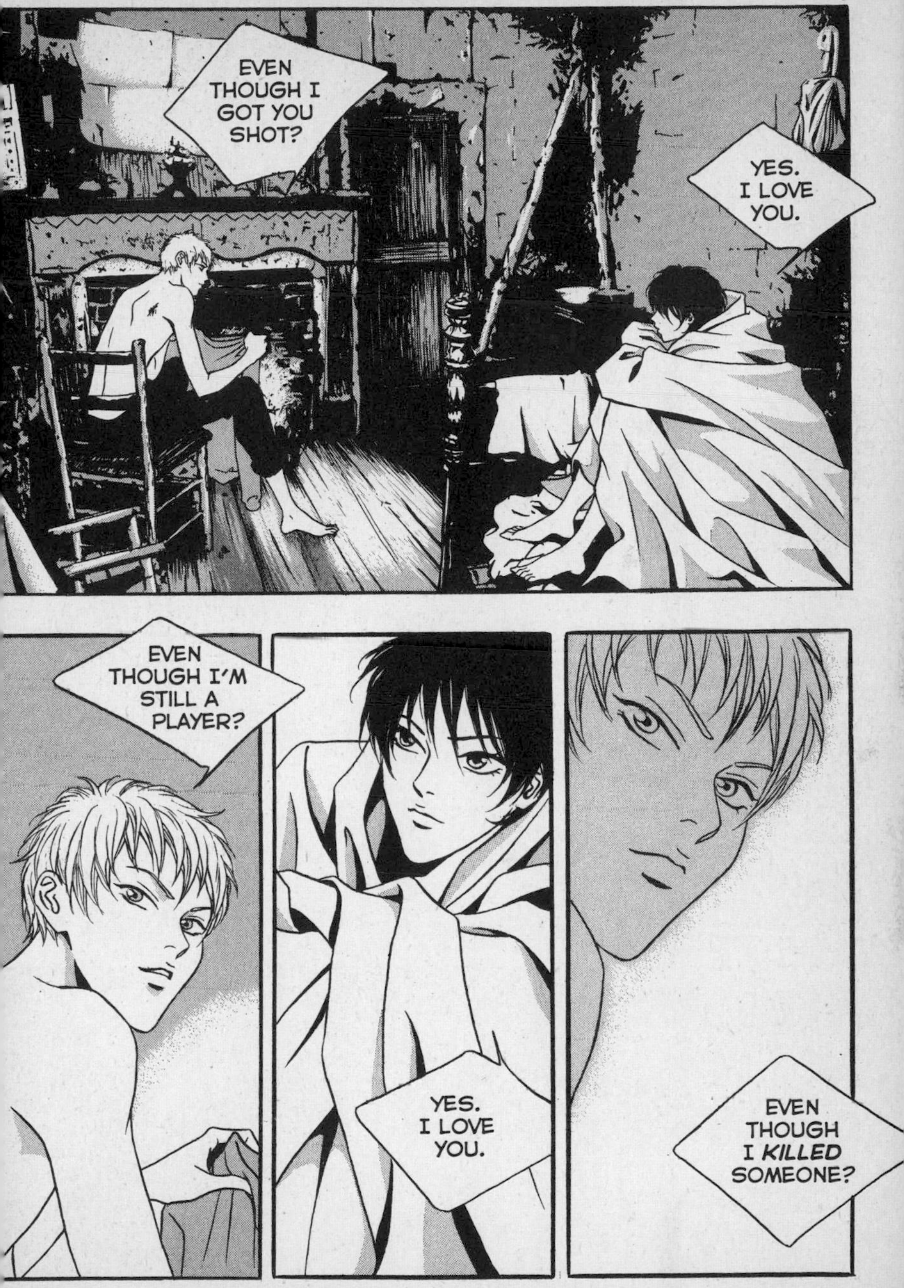
EVEN THOUGH I GOT YOU SHOT?
YES. I LOVE YOU.
EVEN THOUGH I'M STILL A PLAYER?
YES. I LOVE YOU.
EVEN THOUGH I *KILLED* SOMEONE?

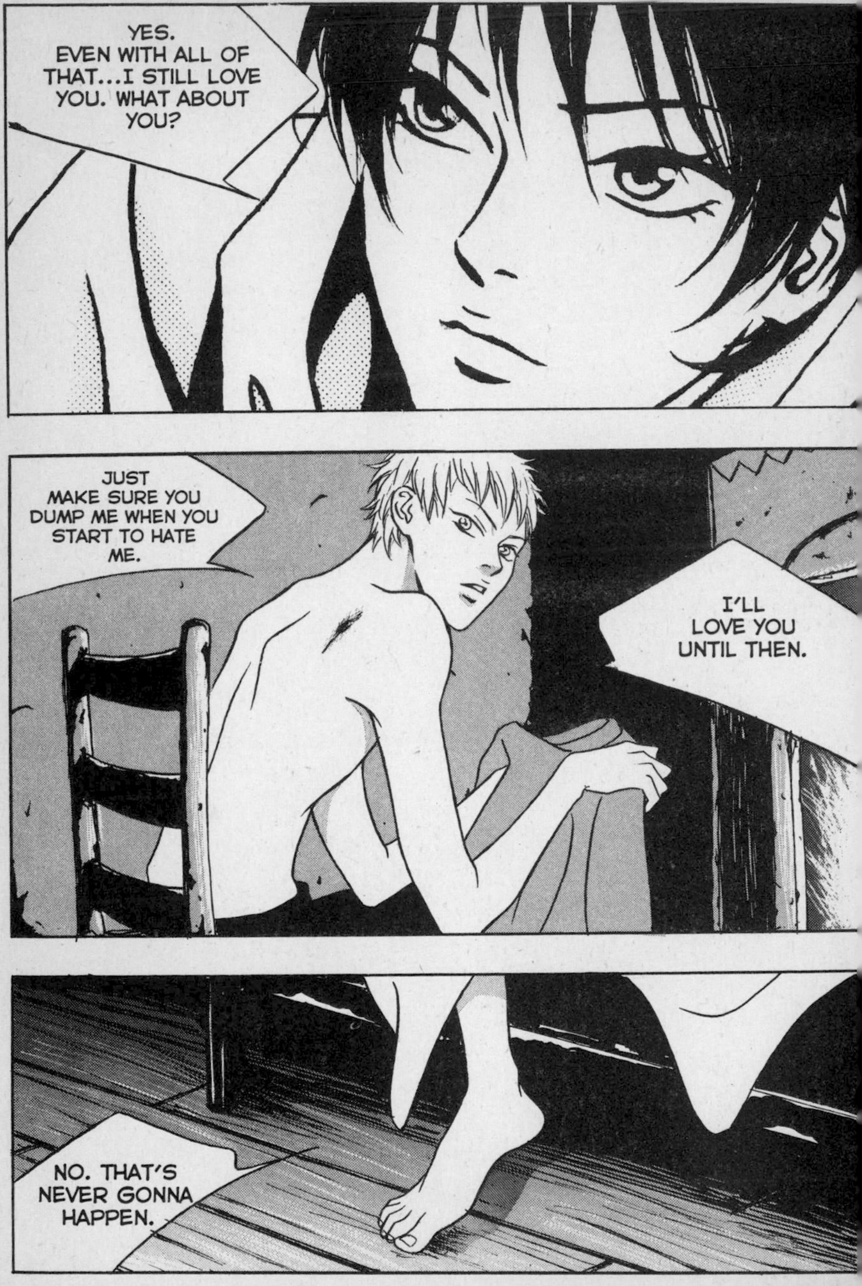
YES. EVEN WITH ALL OF THAT...I STILL LOVE YOU. WHAT ABOUT YOU?
JUST MAKE SURE YOU DUMP ME WHEN YOU START TO HATE ME.
I'LL LOVE YOU UNTIL THEN.
NO. THAT'S NEVER GONNA HAPPEN.

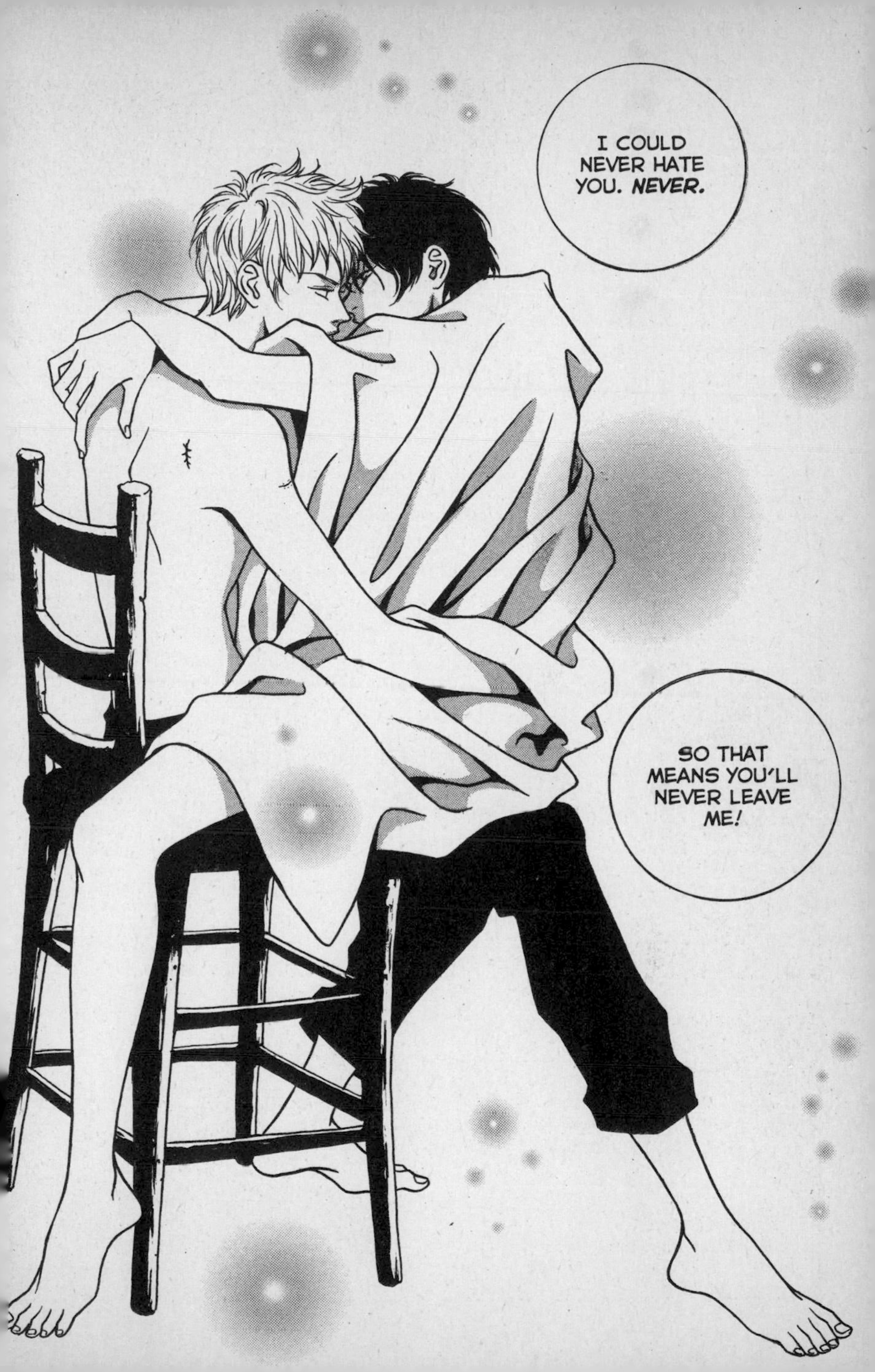
I COULD NEVER HATE YOU. ***NEVER.***
SO THAT MEANS YOU'LL NEVER LEAVE ME!

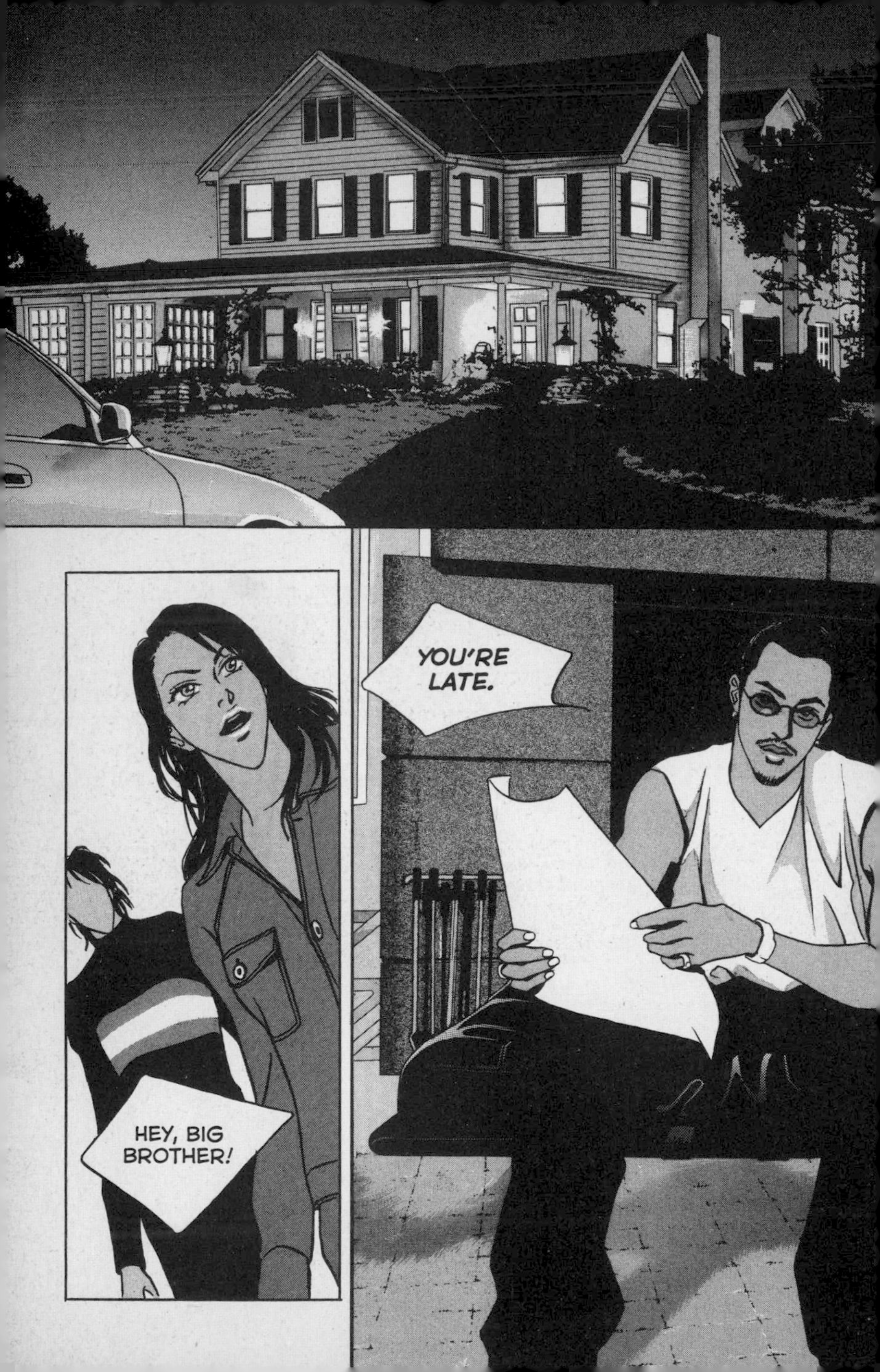
YOU'RE LATE.
HEY, BIG BROTHER!

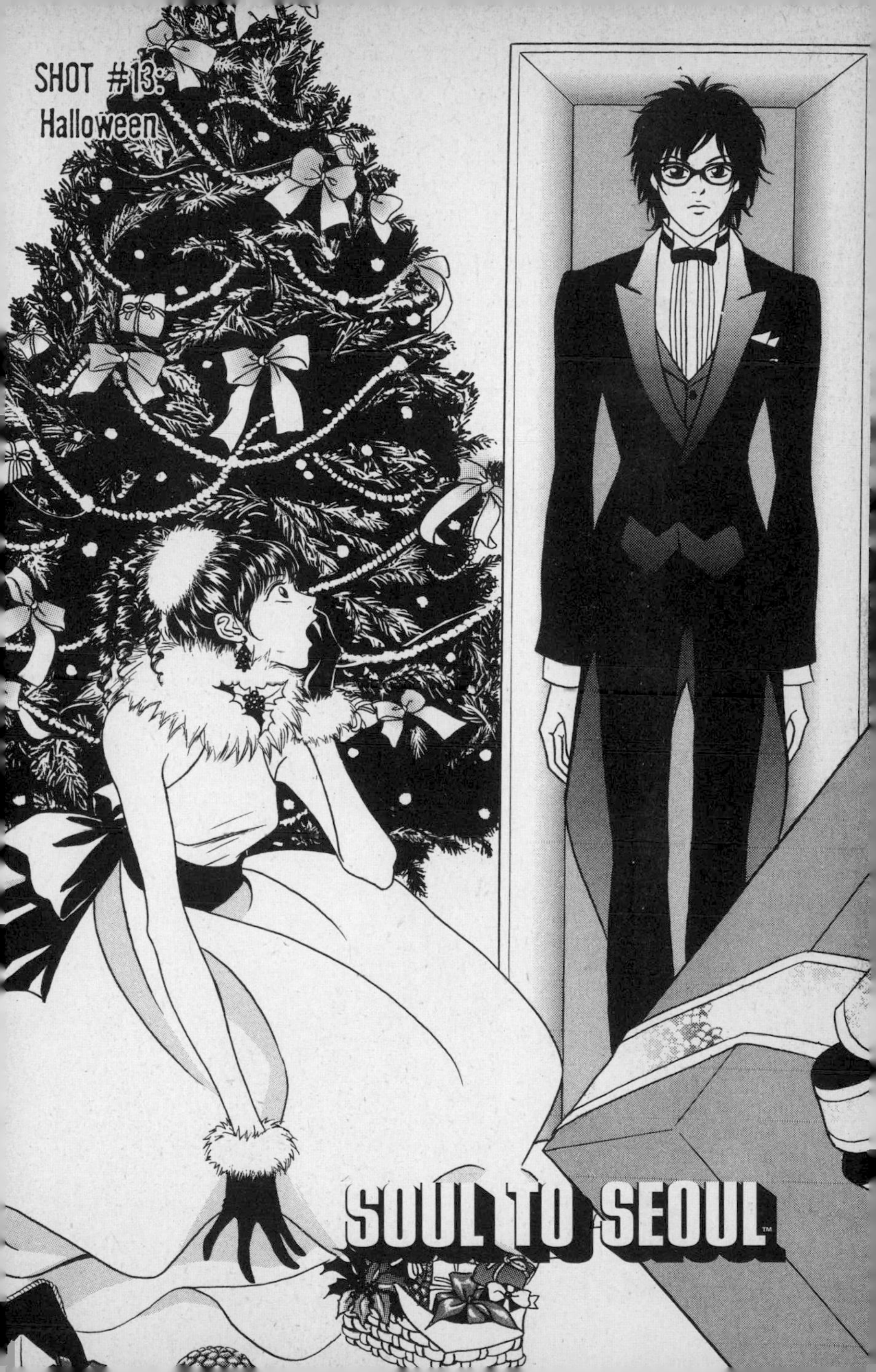
SHOT #13: Halloween
SOUL TO SEOUL™

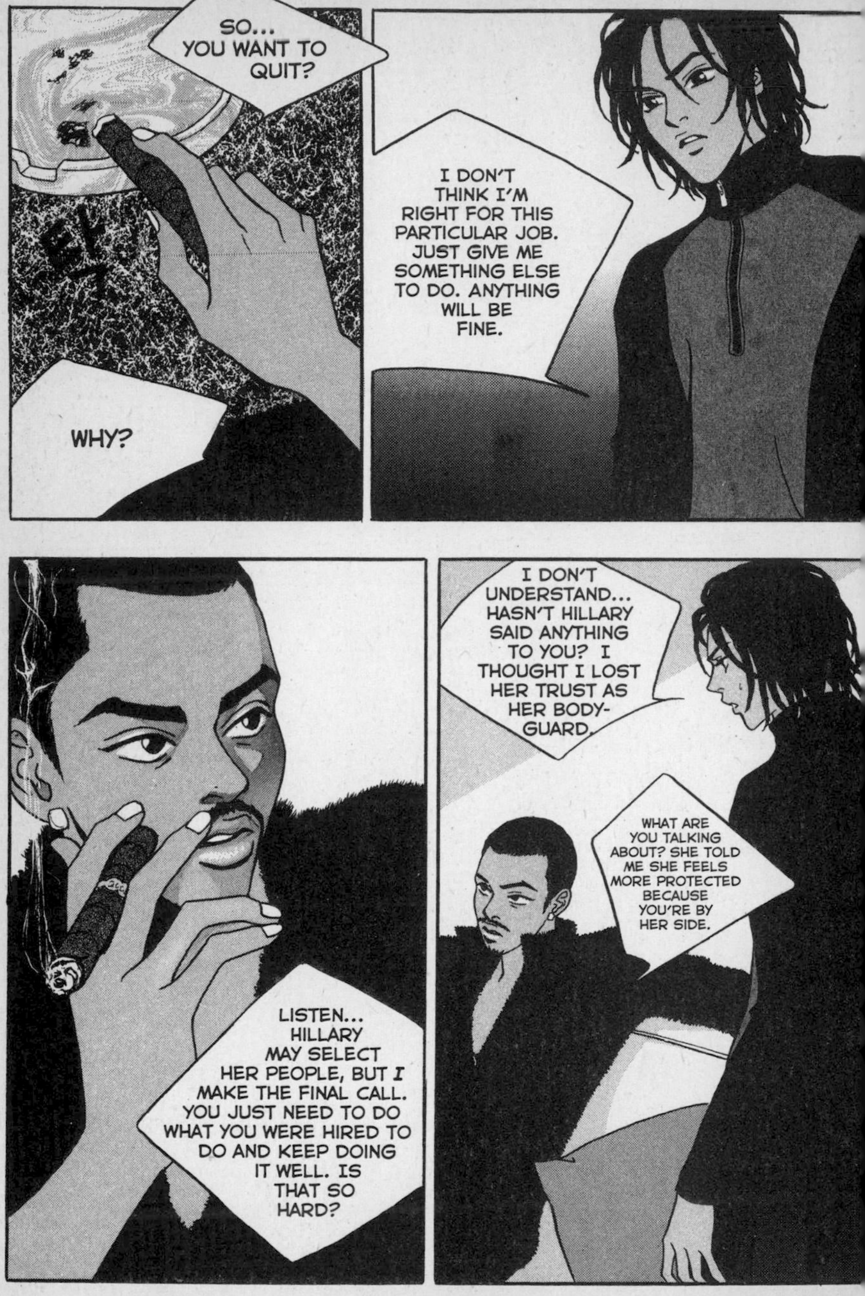
SO... YOU WANT TO QUIT?
WHY?
I DON'T THINK I'M RIGHT FOR THIS PARTICULAR JOB. JUST GIVE ME SOMETHING ELSE TO DO. ANYTHING WILL BE FINE.
LISTEN... HILLARY MAY SELECT HER PEOPLE, BUT *I* MAKE THE FINAL CALL. YOU JUST NEED TO DO WHAT YOU WERE HIRED TO DO AND KEEP DOING IT WELL. IS THAT SO HARD?
I DON'T UNDERSTAND... HASN'T HILLARY SAID ANYTHING TO YOU? I THOUGHT I LOST HER TRUST AS HER BODY-GUARD.
WHAT ARE YOU TALKING ABOUT? SHE TOLD ME SHE FEELS MORE PROTECTED BECAUSE YOU'RE BY HER SIDE.

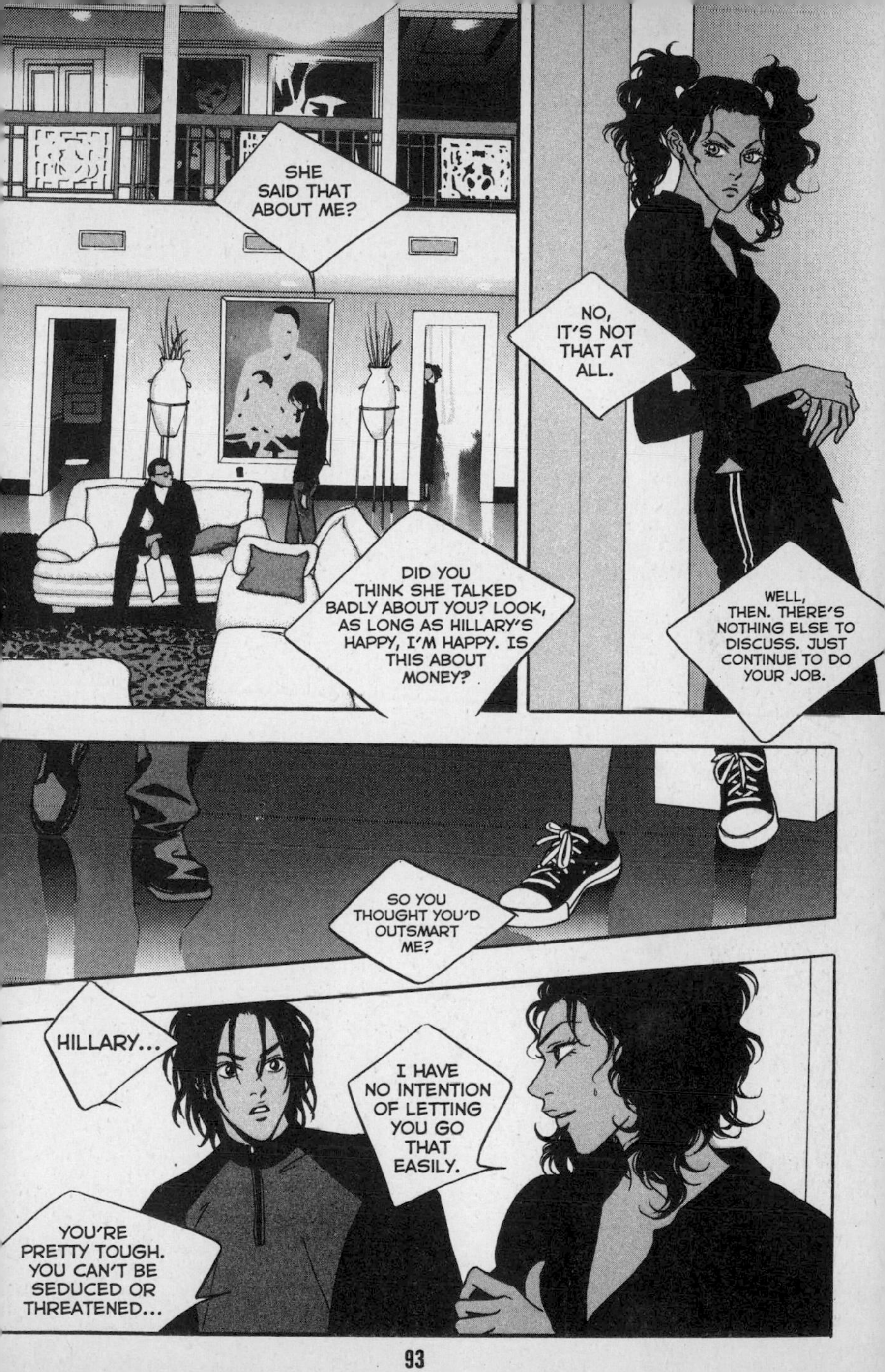

SHE SAID THAT ABOUT ME?
DID YOU THINK SHE TALKED BADLY ABOUT YOU? LOOK, AS LONG AS HILLARY'S HAPPY, I'M HAPPY. IS THIS ABOUT MONEY?
NO, IT'S NOT THAT AT ALL.
WELL, THEN. THERE'S NOTHING ELSE TO DISCUSS. JUST CONTINUE TO DO YOUR JOB.
SO YOU THOUGHT YOU'D OUTSMART ME?
HILLARY...
YOU'RE PRETTY TOUGH. YOU CAN'T BE SEDUCED OR THREATENED...
I HAVE NO INTENTION OF LETTING YOU GO THAT EASILY.

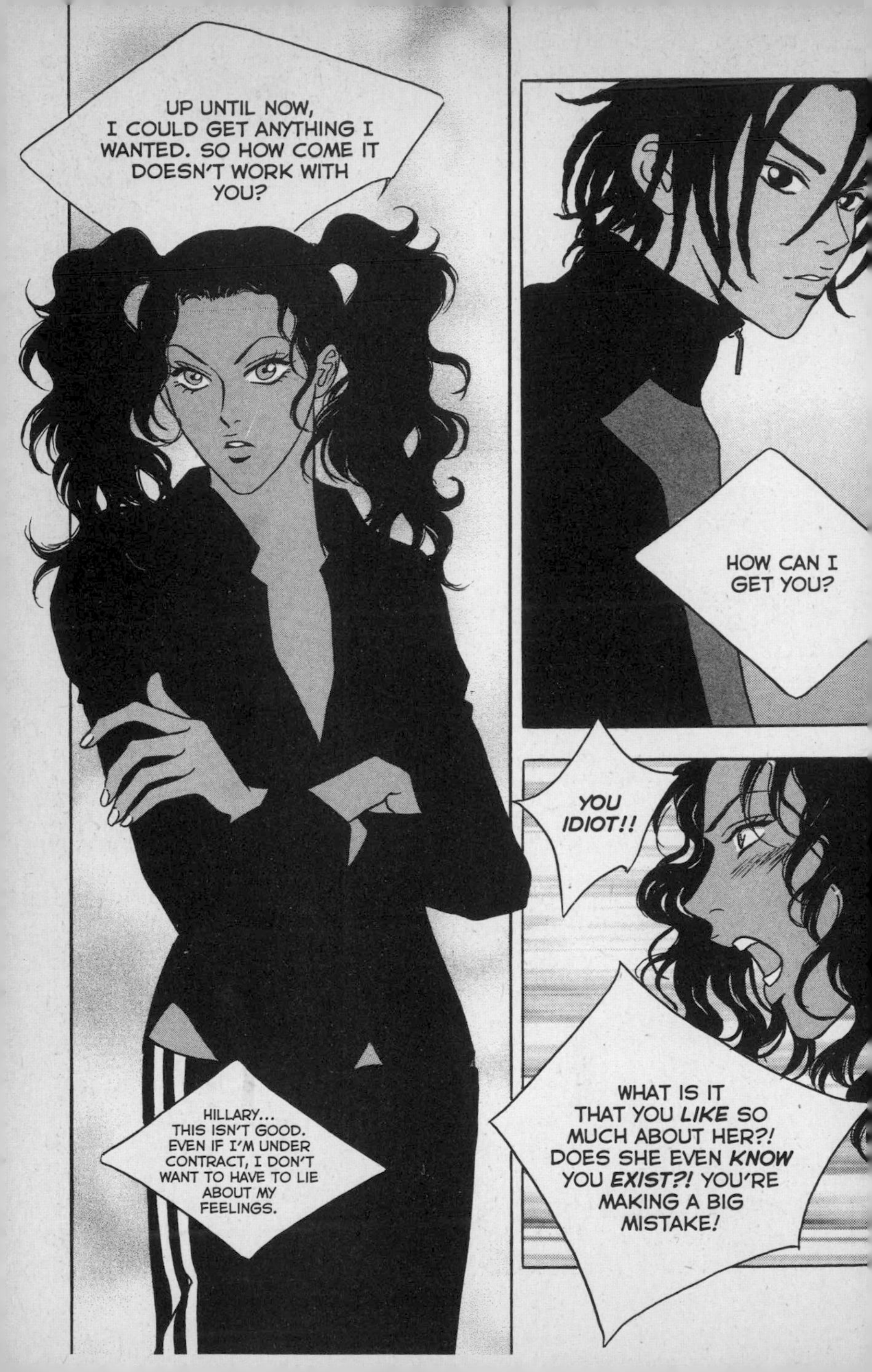
UP UNTIL NOW, I COULD GET ANYTHING I WANTED. SO HOW COME IT DOESN'T WORK WITH YOU?
HILLARY... THIS ISN'T GOOD. EVEN IF I'M UNDER CONTRACT, I DON'T WANT TO HAVE TO LIE ABOUT MY FEELINGS.
HOW CAN I GET YOU?
YOU IDIOT!!
WHAT IS IT THAT YOU LIKE SO MUCH ABOUT HER?! DOES SHE EVEN KNOW YOU EXIST?! YOU'RE MAKING A BIG MISTAKE!

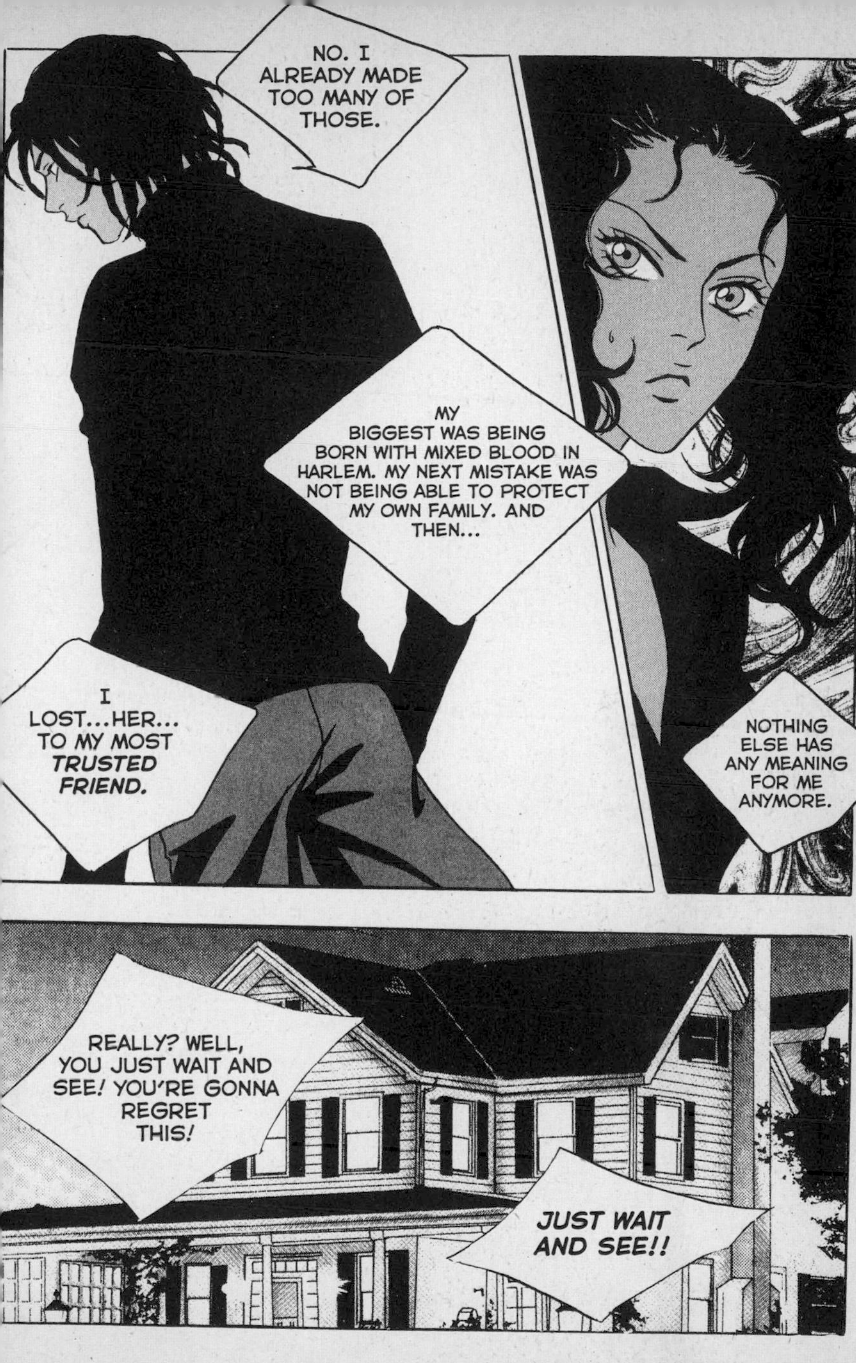
NO. I ALREADY MADE TOO MANY OF THOSE.
MY BIGGEST WAS BEING BORN WITH MIXED BLOOD IN HARLEM. MY NEXT MISTAKE WAS NOT BEING ABLE TO PROTECT MY OWN FAMILY. AND THEN...
I LOST...HER... TO MY MOST *TRUSTED FRIEND.*
NOTHING ELSE HAS ANY MEANING FOR ME ANYMORE.
REALLY? WELL, YOU JUST WAIT AND SEE! YOU'RE GONNA REGRET THIS!
JUST WAIT AND SEE!!

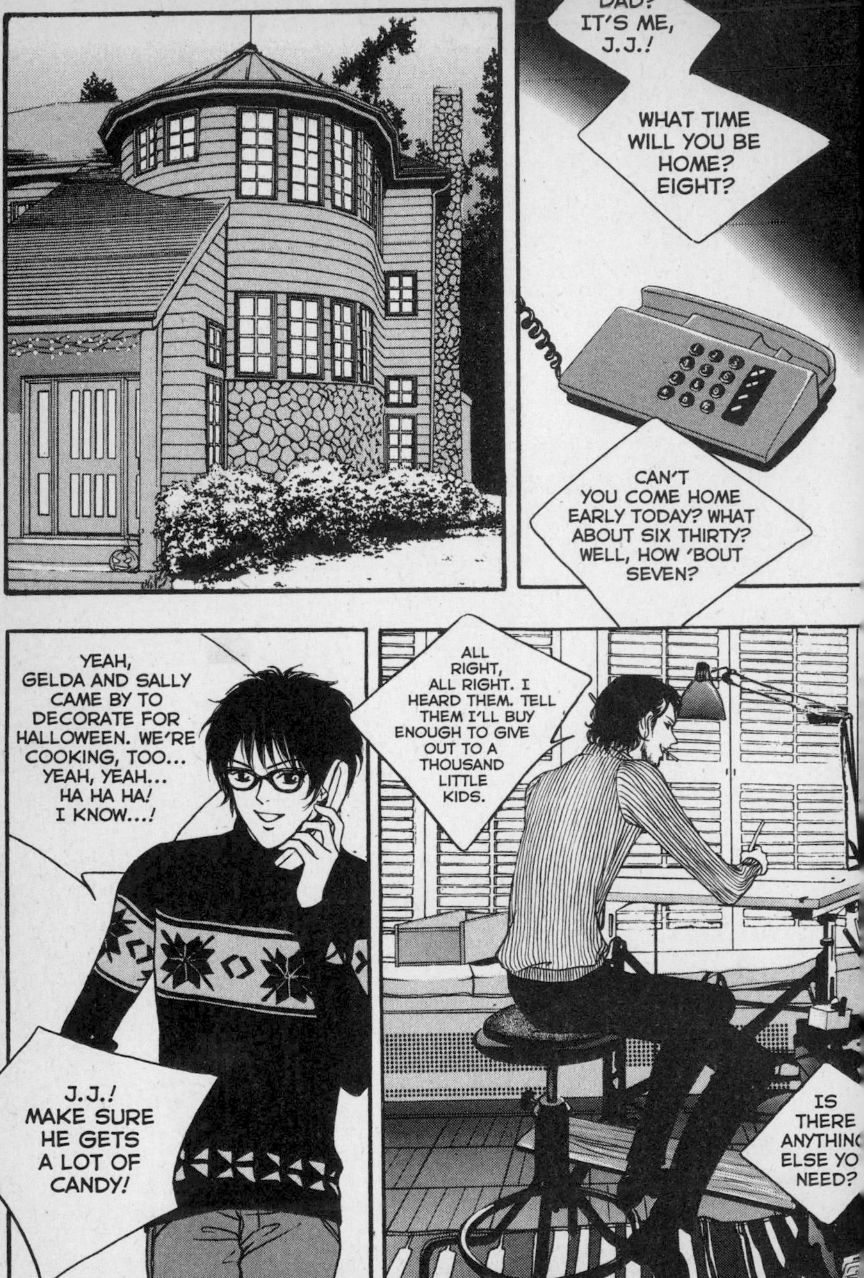
DAD? IT'S ME, J.J.!
WHAT TIME WILL YOU BE HOME? EIGHT?
CAN'T YOU COME HOME EARLY TODAY? WHAT ABOUT SIX THIRTY? WELL, HOW 'BOUT SEVEN?
YEAH, GELDA AND SALLY CAME BY TO DECORATE FOR HALLOWEEN. WE'RE COOKING, TOO... YEAH, YEAH... HA HA HA! I KNOW...!
J.J.! MAKE SURE HE GETS A LOT OF CANDY!
ALL RIGHT, ALL RIGHT. I HEARD THEM. TELL THEM I'LL BUY ENOUGH TO GIVE OUT TO A THOUSAND LITTLE KIDS.
IS THERE ANYTHING ELSE YOU NEED?

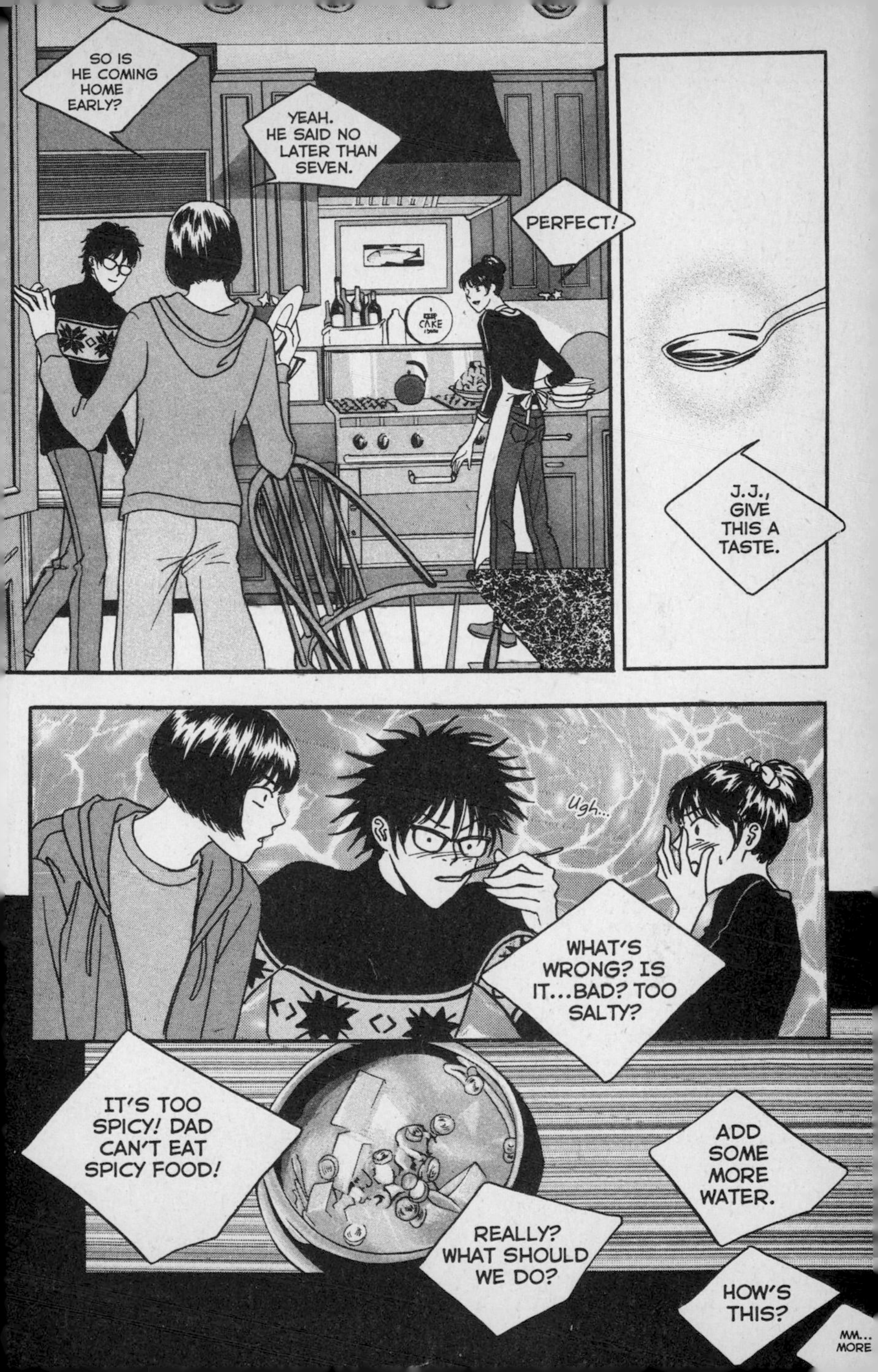
SO IS HE COMING HOME EARLY?
YEAH. HE SAID NO LATER THAN SEVEN.
PERFECT!
J.J., GIVE THIS A TASTE.
Ugh...
WHAT'S WRONG? IS IT...BAD? TOO SALTY?
IT'S TOO SPICY! DAD CAN'T EAT SPICY FOOD!
REALLY? WHAT SHOULD WE DO?
ADD SOME MORE WATER.
HOW'S THIS?
MM... MORE

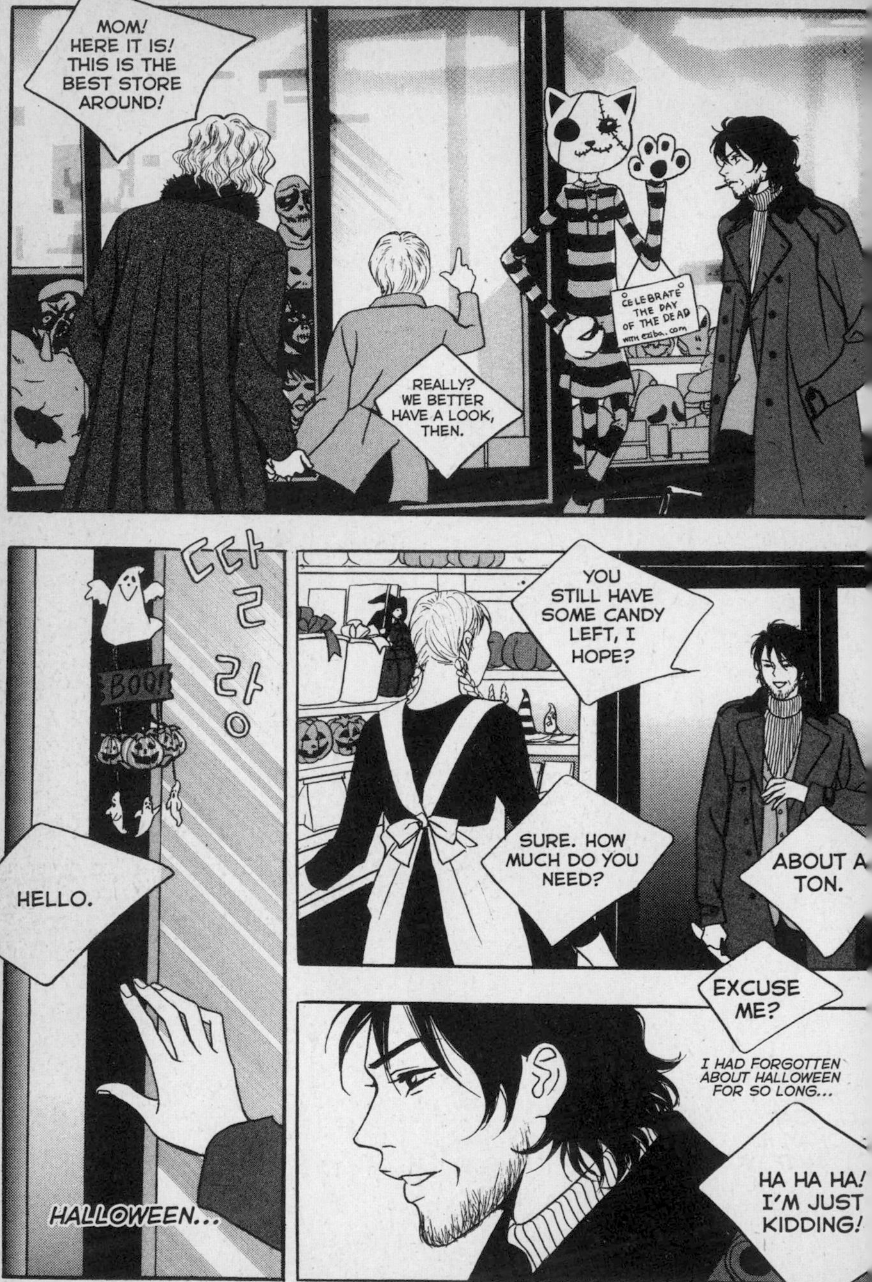
MOM! HERE IT IS! THIS IS THE BEST STORE AROUND!
CELEBRATE THE DAY OF THE DEAD with eziba.com
REALLY? WE BETTER HAVE A LOOK, THEN.
딸랑
BOO!
HELLO.
HALLOWEEN...
YOU STILL HAVE SOME CANDY LEFT, I HOPE?
SURE. HOW MUCH DO YOU NEED?
ABOUT A TON.
EXCUSE ME?
I HAD FORGOTTEN ABOUT HALLOWEEN FOR SO LONG...
HA HA HA! I'M JUST KIDDING!

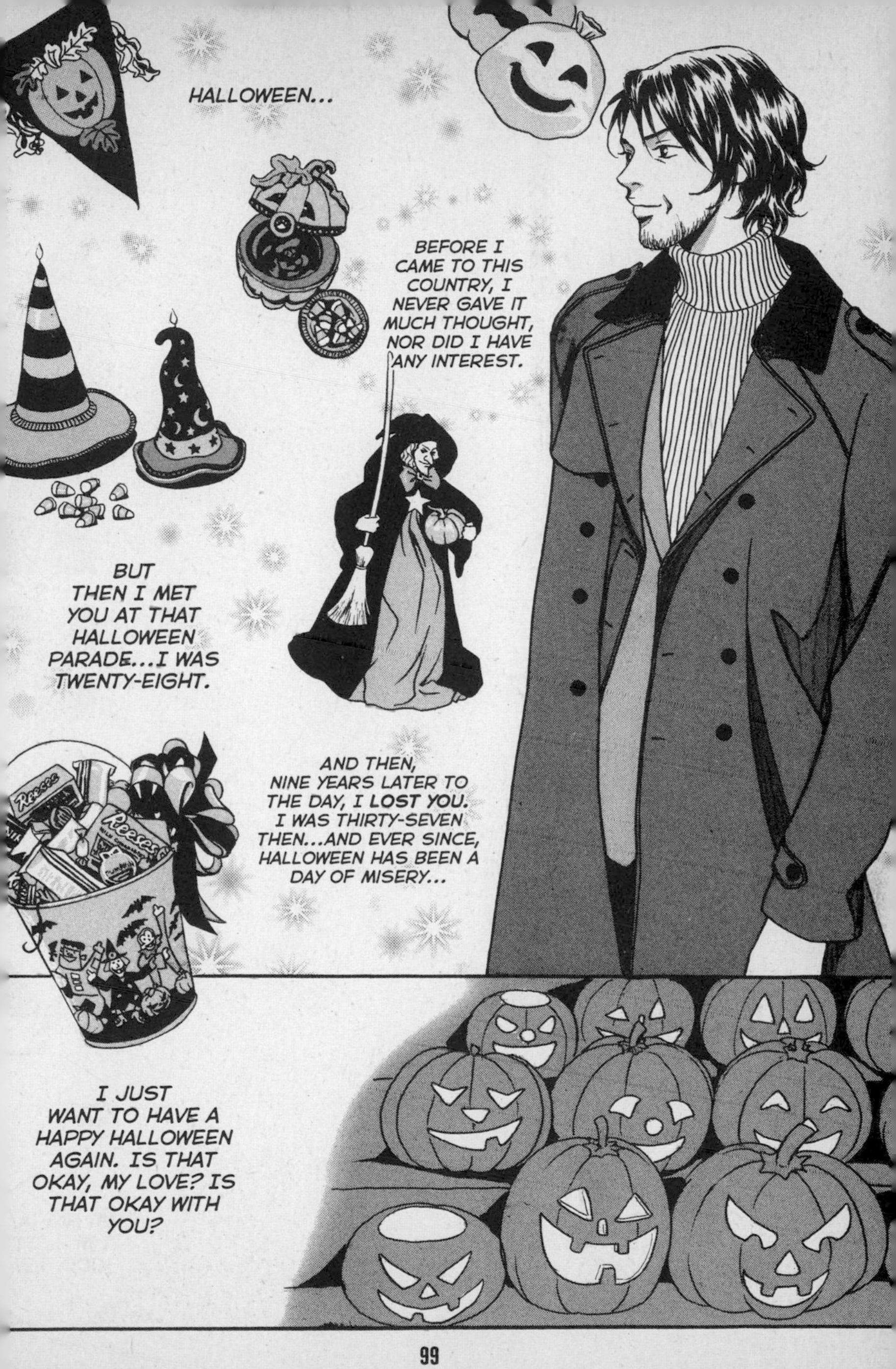
HALLOWEEN...
BEFORE I CAME TO THIS COUNTRY, I NEVER GAVE IT MUCH THOUGHT, NOR DID I HAVE ANY INTEREST.
BUT THEN I MET YOU AT THAT HALLOWEEN PARADE...I WAS TWENTY-EIGHT.
AND THEN, NINE YEARS LATER TO THE DAY, I **LOST YOU.** I WAS THIRTY-SEVEN THEN...AND EVER SINCE, HALLOWEEN HAS BEEN A DAY OF MISERY...
I JUST WANT TO HAVE A HAPPY HALLOWEEN AGAIN. IS THAT OKAY, MY LOVE? IS THAT OKAY WITH YOU?

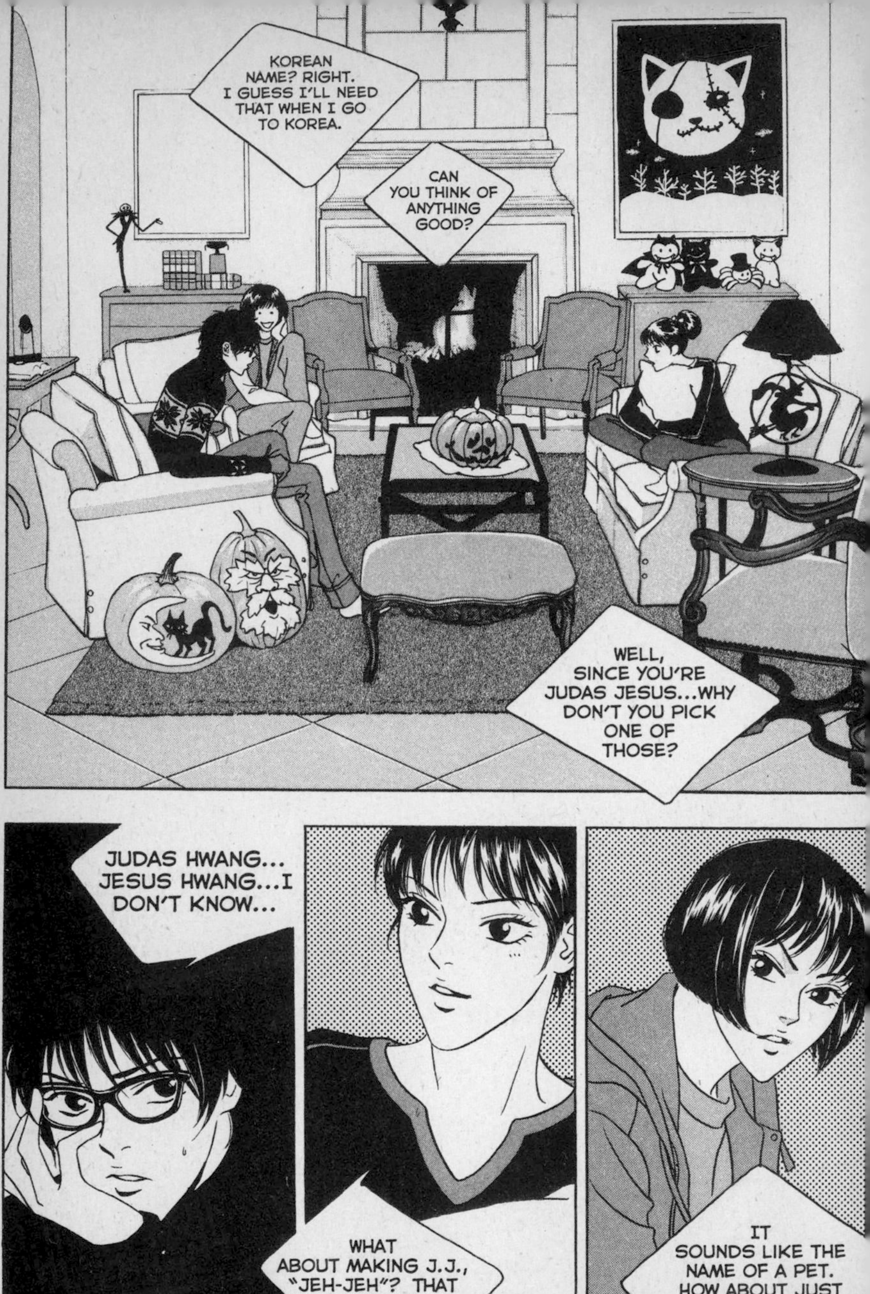
KOREAN NAME? RIGHT. I GUESS I'LL NEED THAT WHEN I GO TO KOREA.
CAN YOU THINK OF ANYTHING GOOD?
WELL, SINCE YOU'RE JUDAS JESUS...WHY DON'T YOU PICK ONE OF THOSE?
JUDAS HWANG... JESUS HWANG...I DON'T KNOW...
WHAT ABOUT MAKING J.J., "JEH-JEH"? THAT SOUNDS CUTE!
IT SOUNDS LIKE THE NAME OF A PET. HOW ABOUT JUST JEH? JEH HWANG!

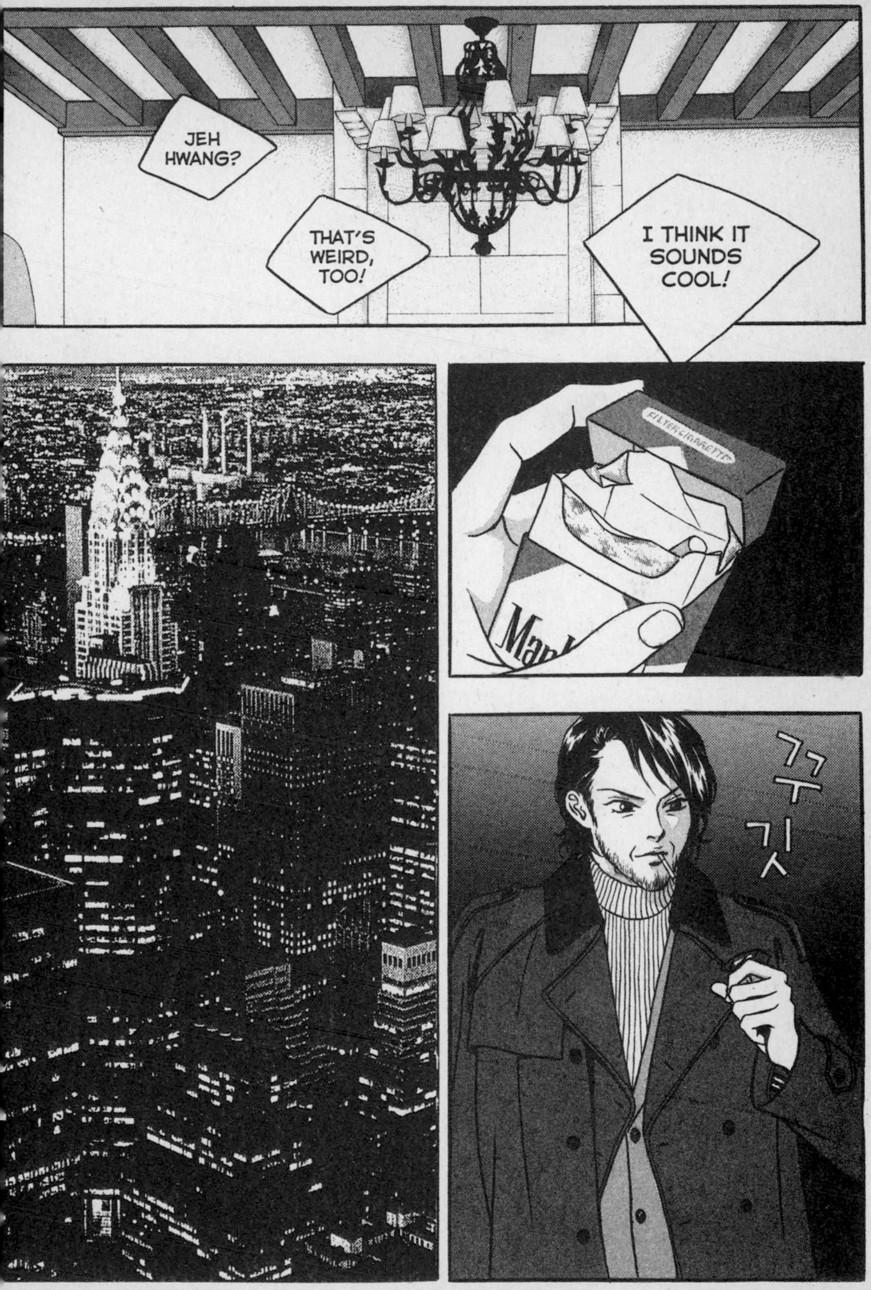
JEH HWANG?
THAT'S WEIRD, TOO!
I THINK IT SOUNDS COOL!

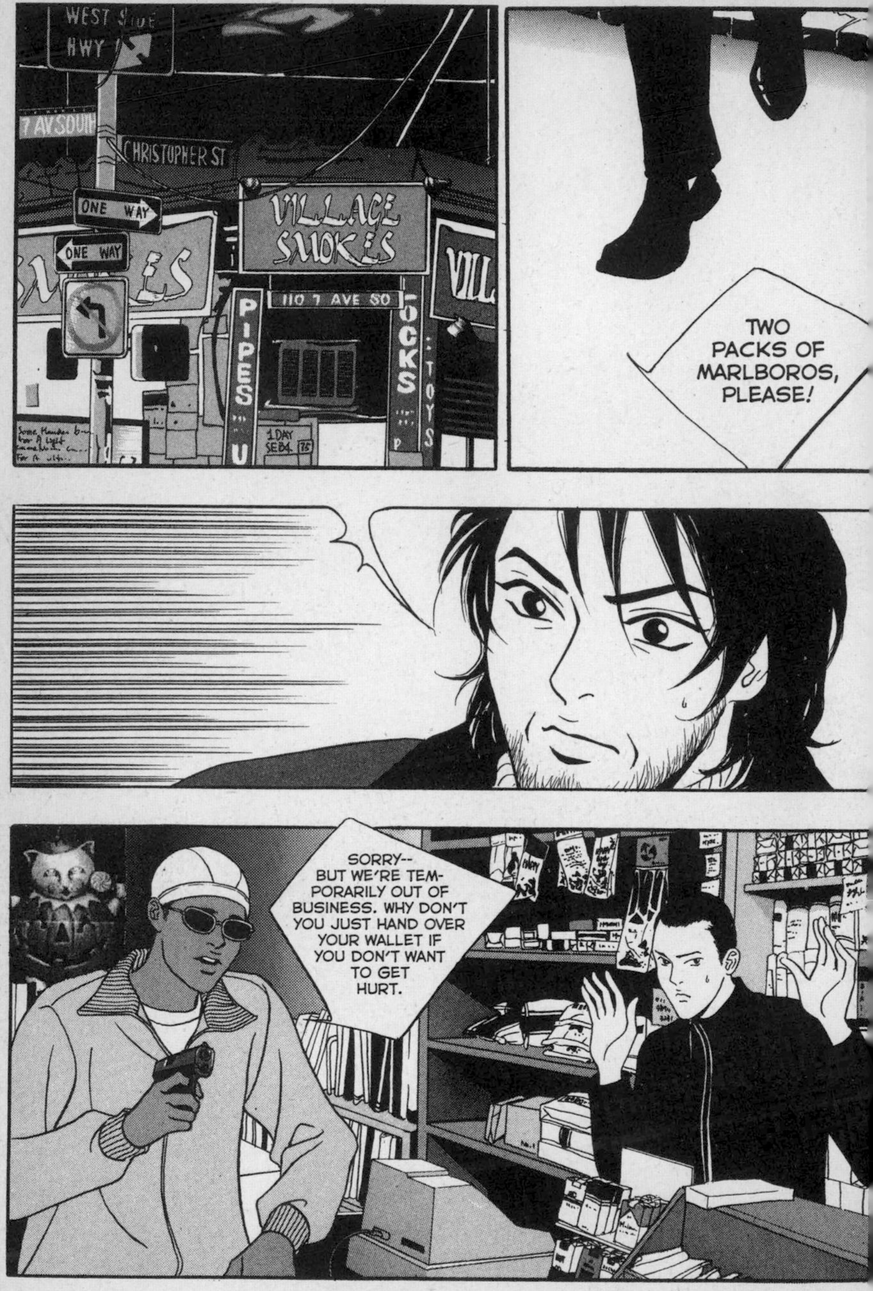

WEST SIDE HWY
7 AV SOUTH
CHRISTOPHER ST
ONE WAY
ONE WAY
VILLAGE SMOKES
110 7 AVE SO
PIPES
TOYS
TWO PACKS OF MARLBOROS, PLEASE!
SORRY-- BUT WE'RE TEMPORARILY OUT OF BUSINESS. WHY DON'T YOU JUST HAND OVER YOUR WALLET IF YOU DON'T WANT TO GET HURT.

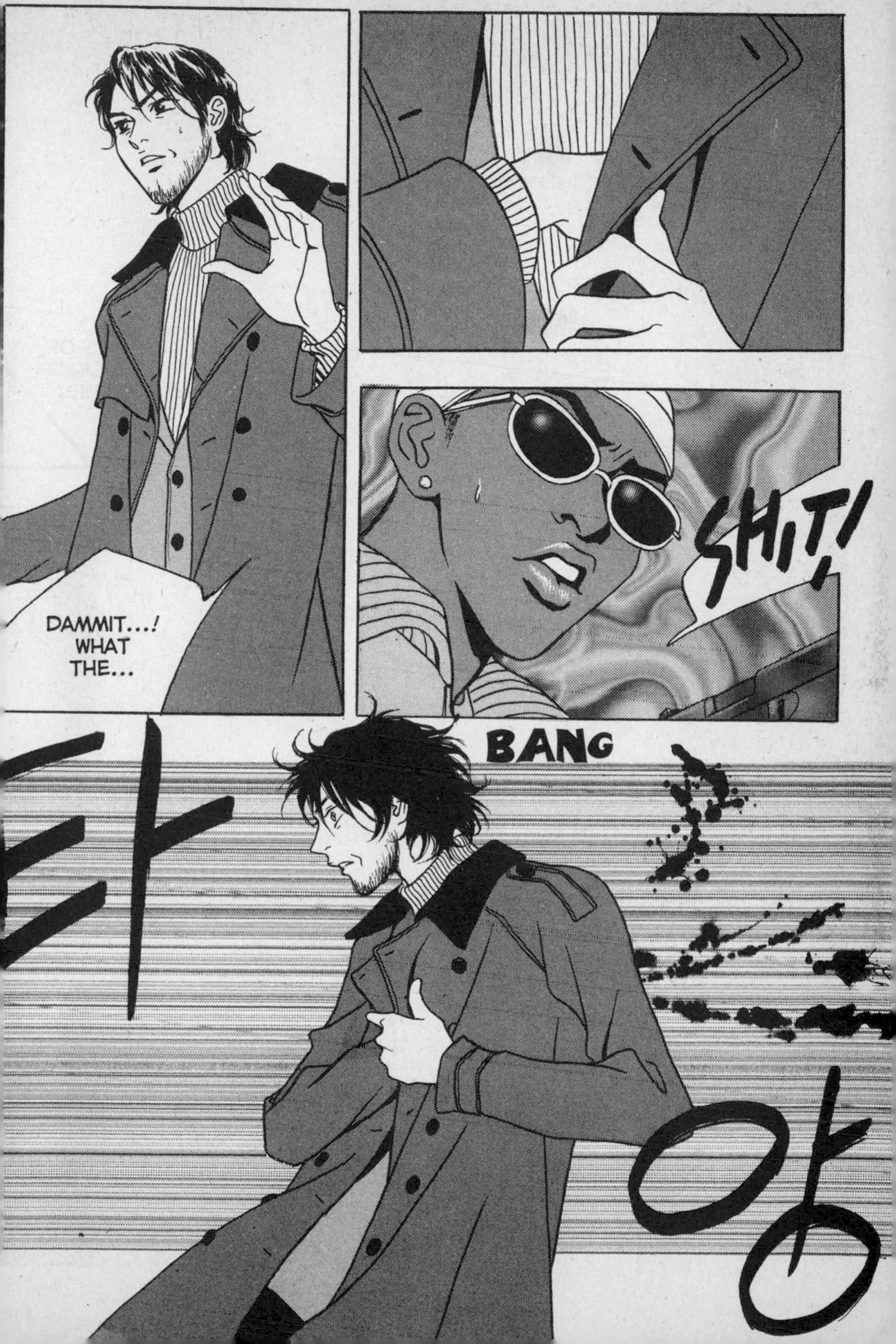
SHIT!
DAMMIT...! WHAT THE...
BANG

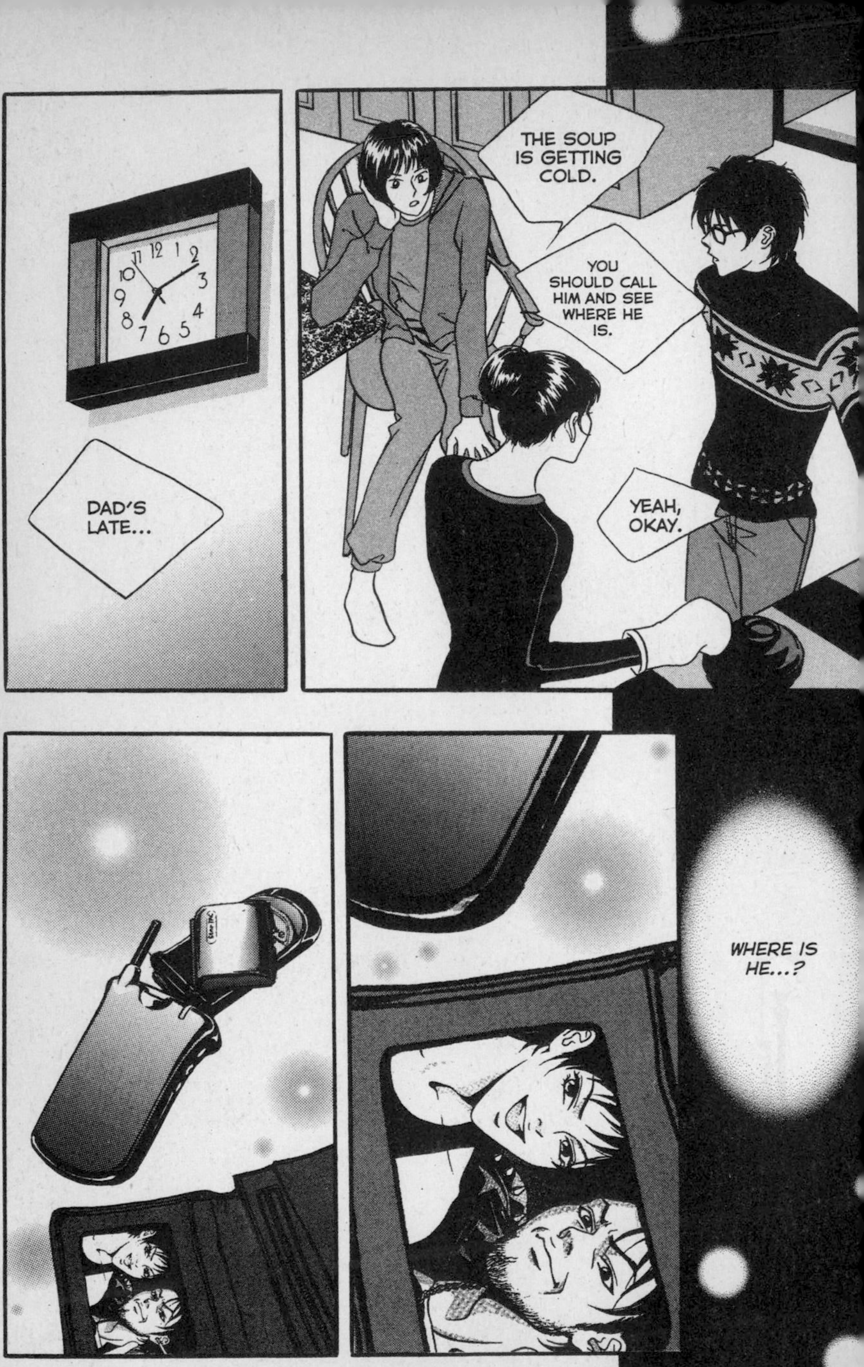
DAD'S LATE...
THE SOUP IS GETTING COLD.
YOU SHOULD CALL HIM AND SEE WHERE HE IS.
YEAH, OKAY.
WHERE IS HE...?

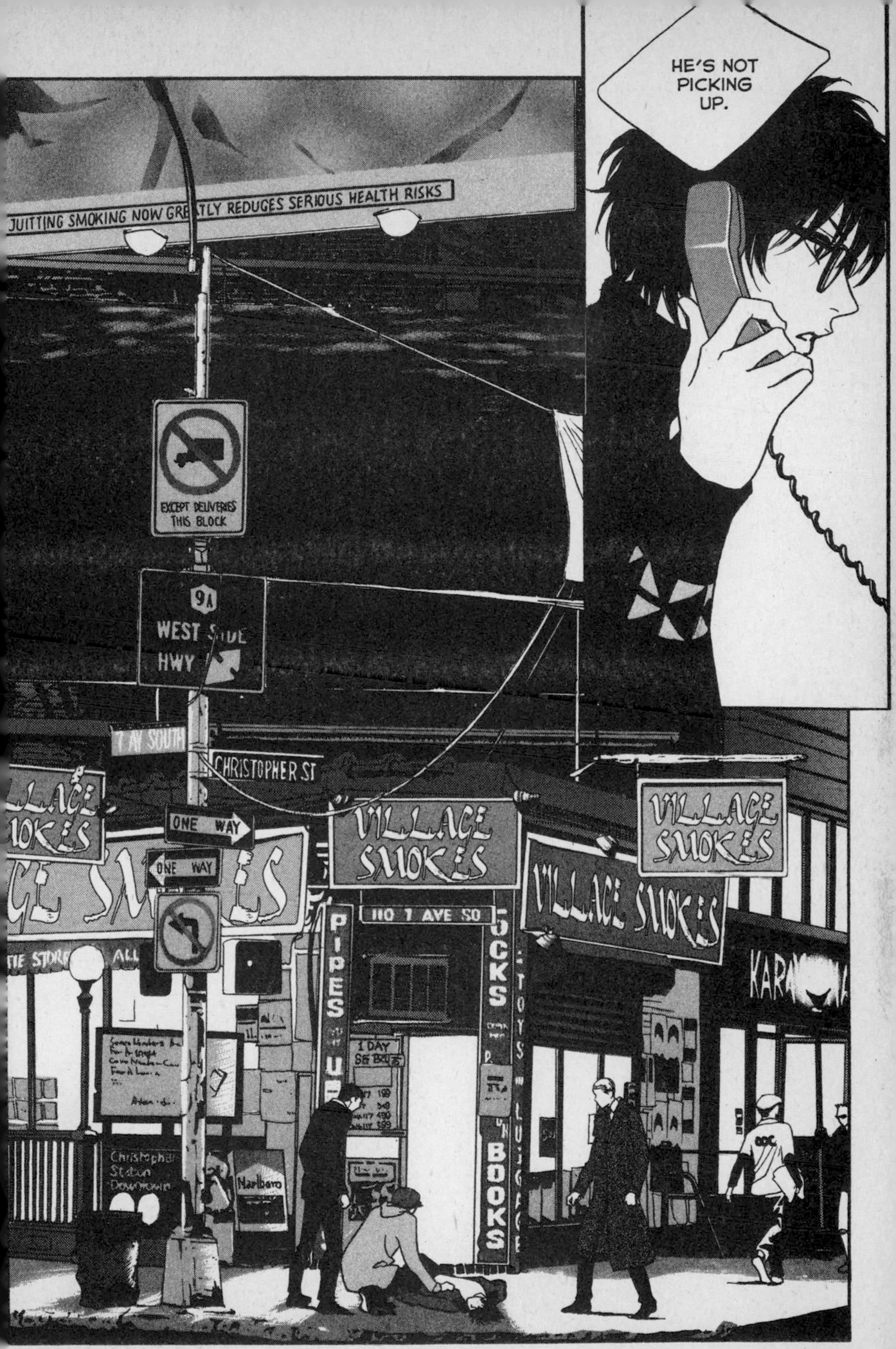
HE'S NOT PICKING UP.
QUITTING SMOKING NOW GREATLY REDUCES SERIOUS HEALTH RISKS
EXCEPT DELIVERIES THIS BLOCK
9A WEST SIDE HWY
7 AV SOUTH
CHRISTOPHER ST
ONE WAY
ONE WAY
VILLAGE SMOKES
VILLAGE SMOKES
VILLAGE SMOKES
VILLAGE SMOKES
110 7 AVE SO
PIPES
BOOKS
Marlboro

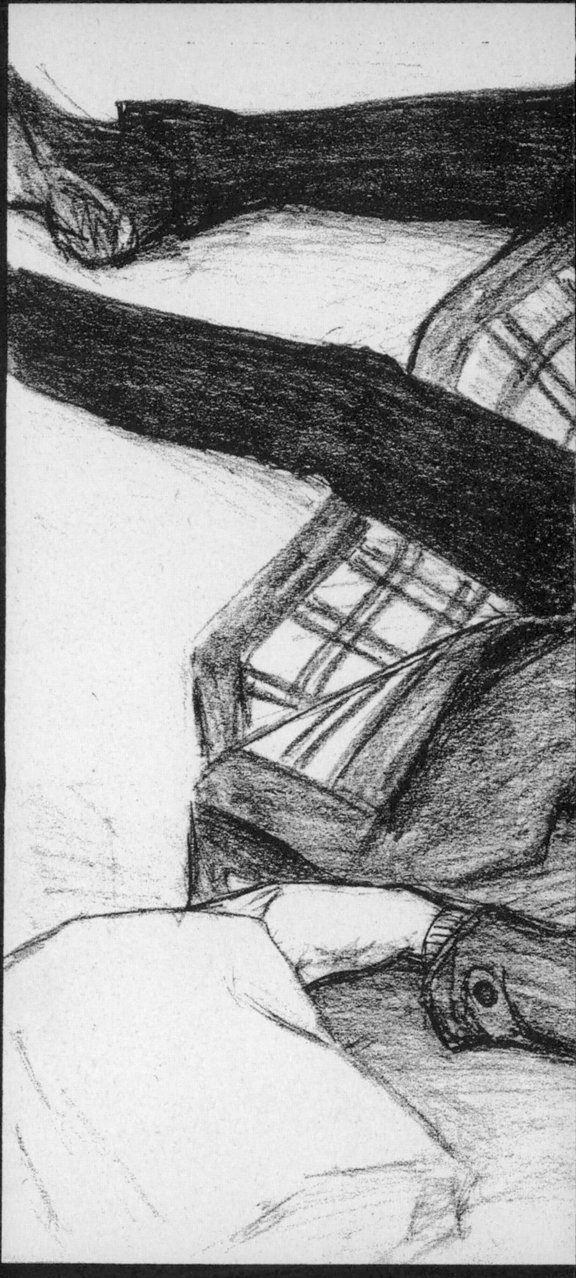

J.J....

I...
I NEED TO
GO TO J.J....
I NEED...
TO GO HOME
TO HIM...

WHAT...
WHAT TIME...
IS...IT...?

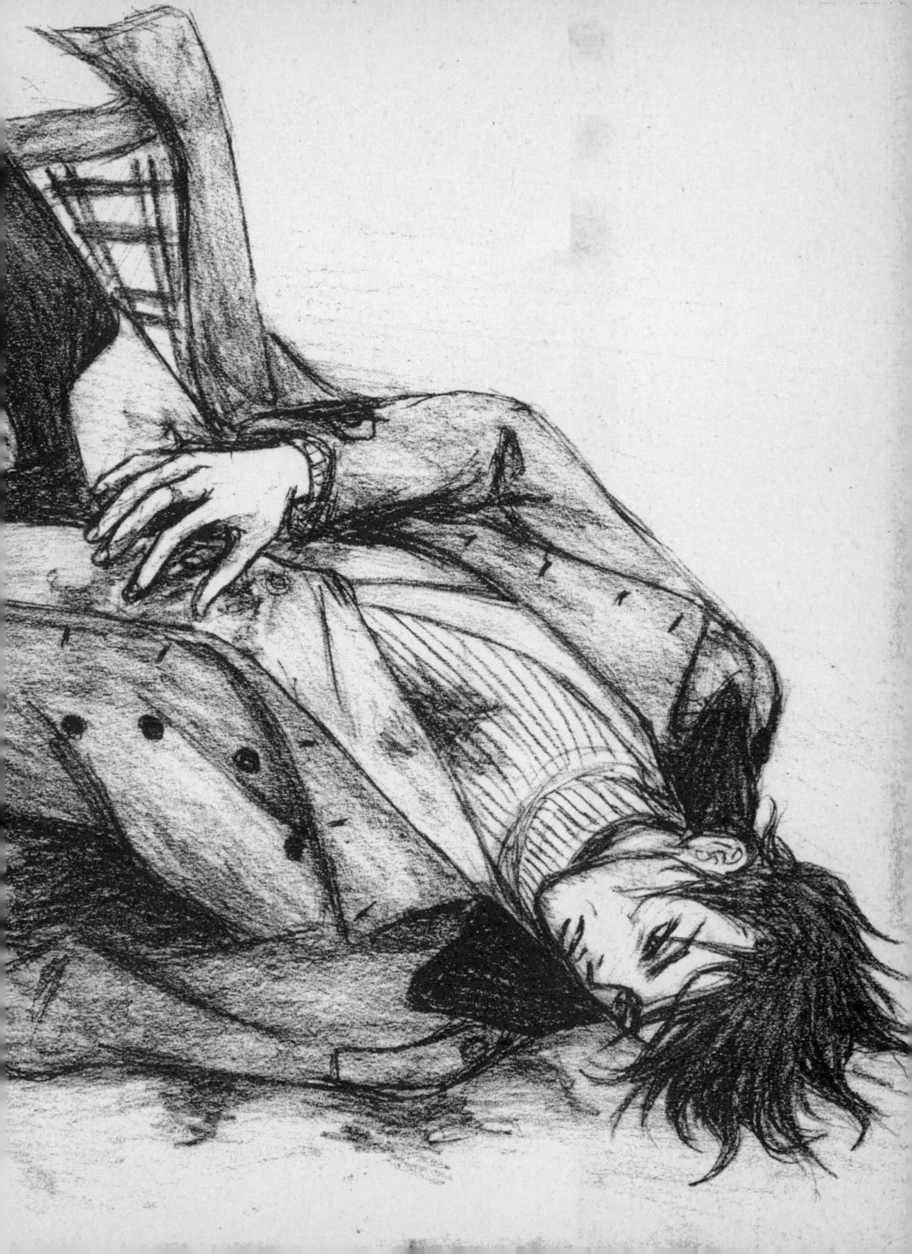

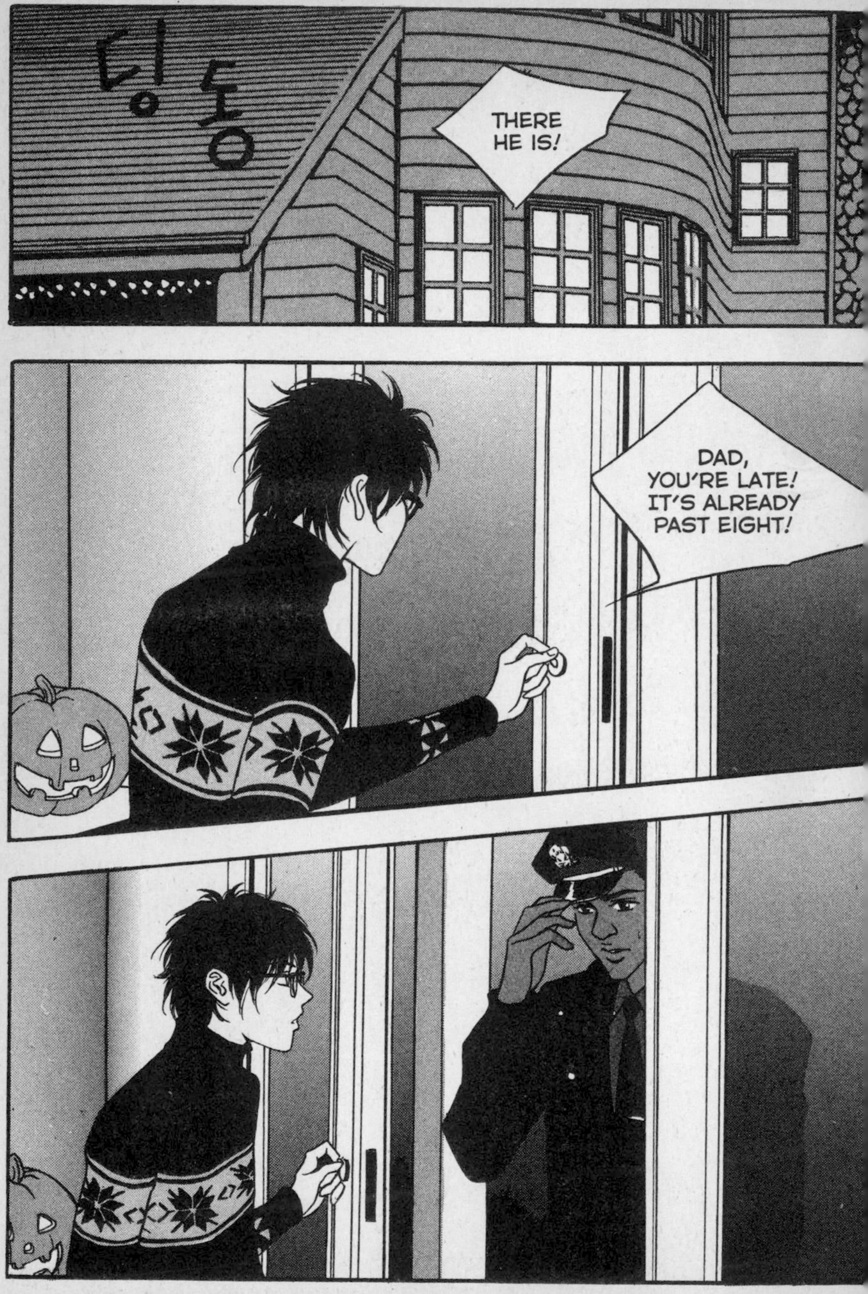
딩동
THERE HE IS!
DAD, YOU'RE LATE! IT'S ALREADY PAST EIGHT!

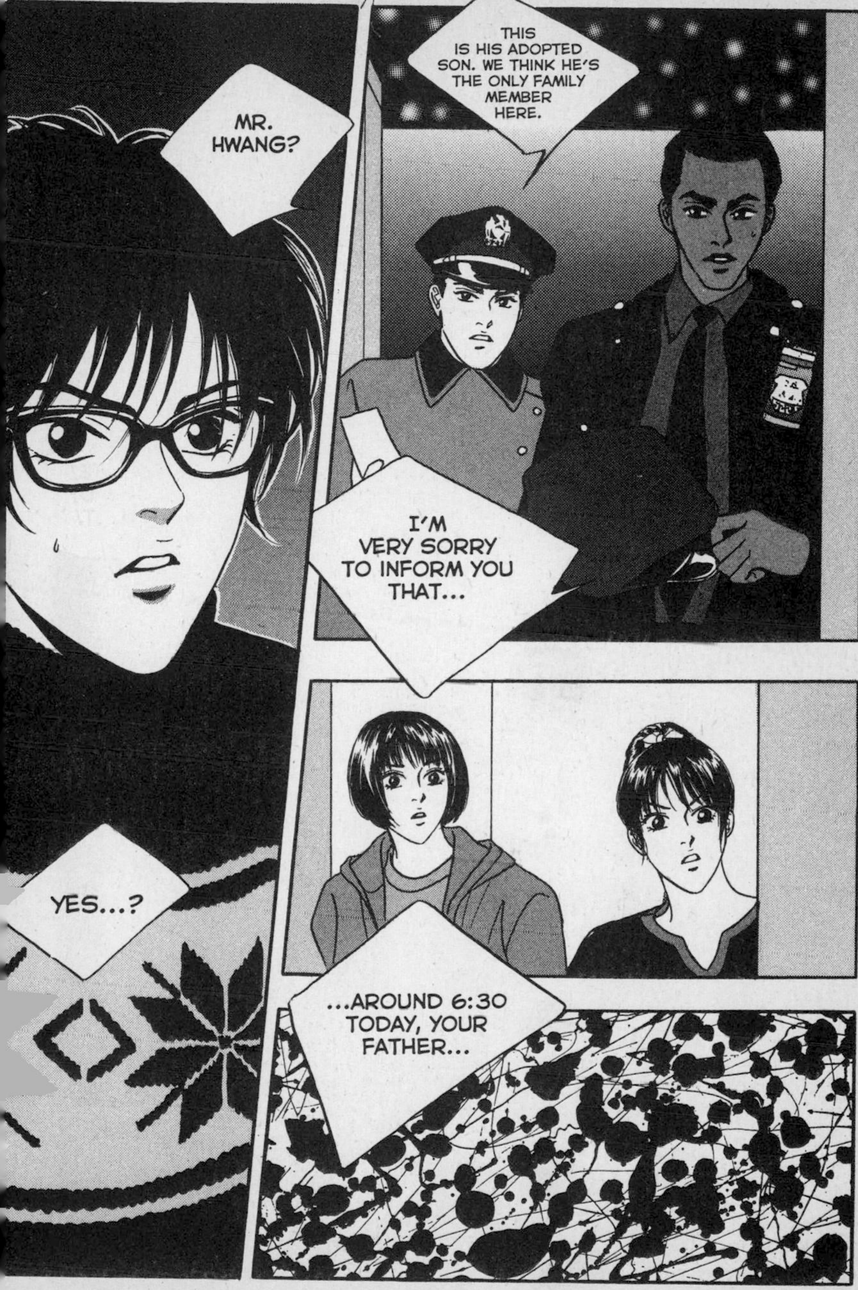
THIS IS HIS ADOPTED SON. WE THINK HE'S THE ONLY FAMILY MEMBER HERE.
MR. HWANG?
YES...?
I'M VERY SORRY TO INFORM YOU THAT...
...AROUND 6:30 TODAY, YOUR FATHER...

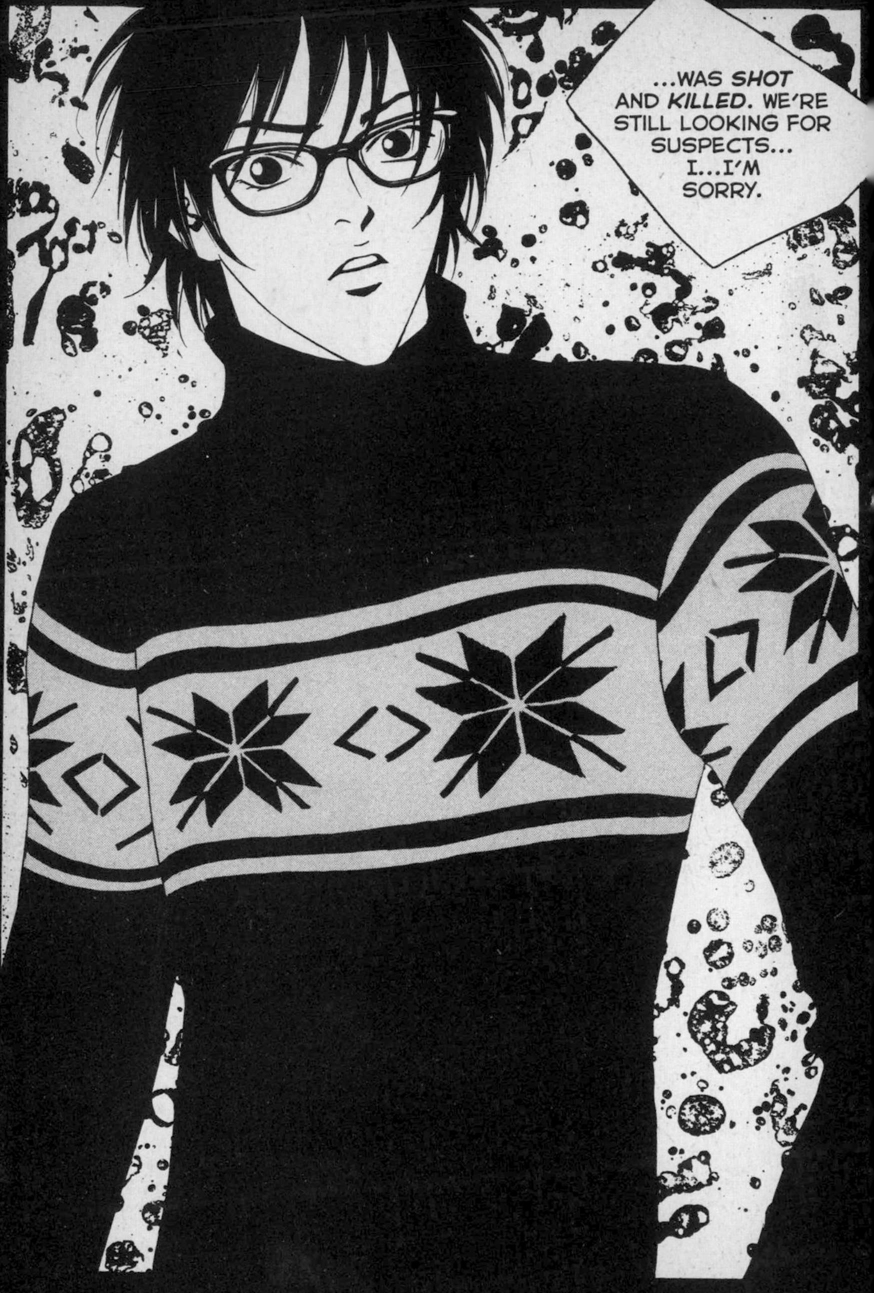
...WAS SHOT AND KILLED. WE'RE STILL LOOKING FOR SUSPECTS... I...I'M SORRY.

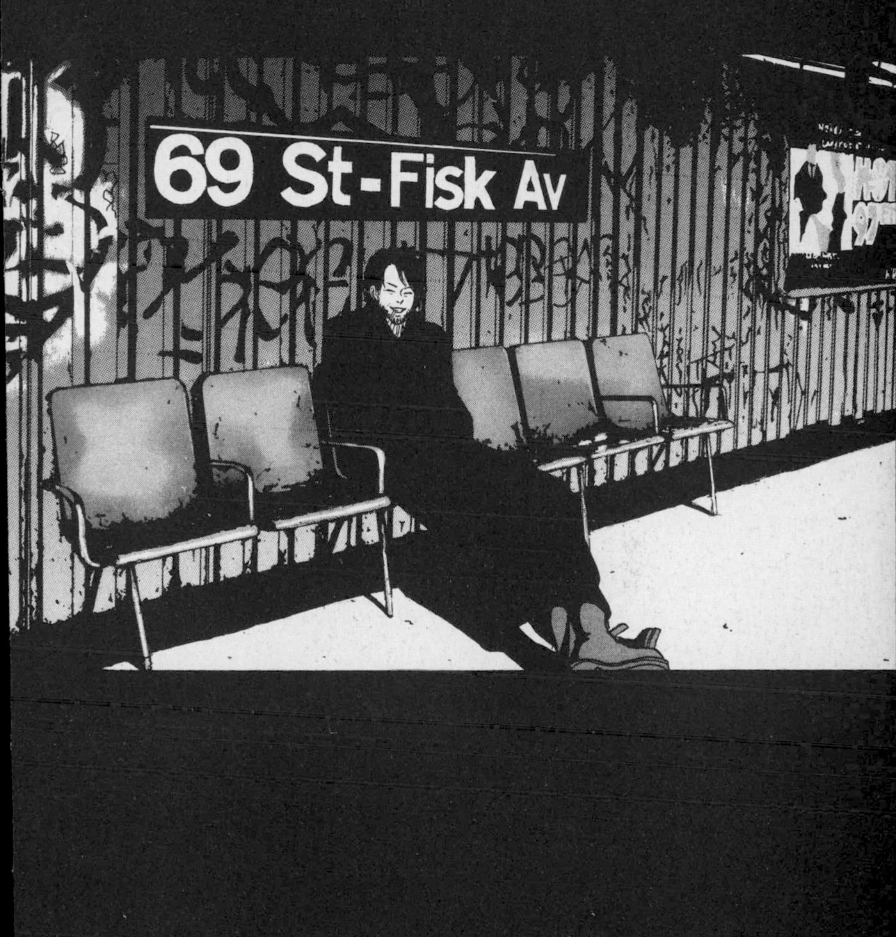
69 St-Fisk Av

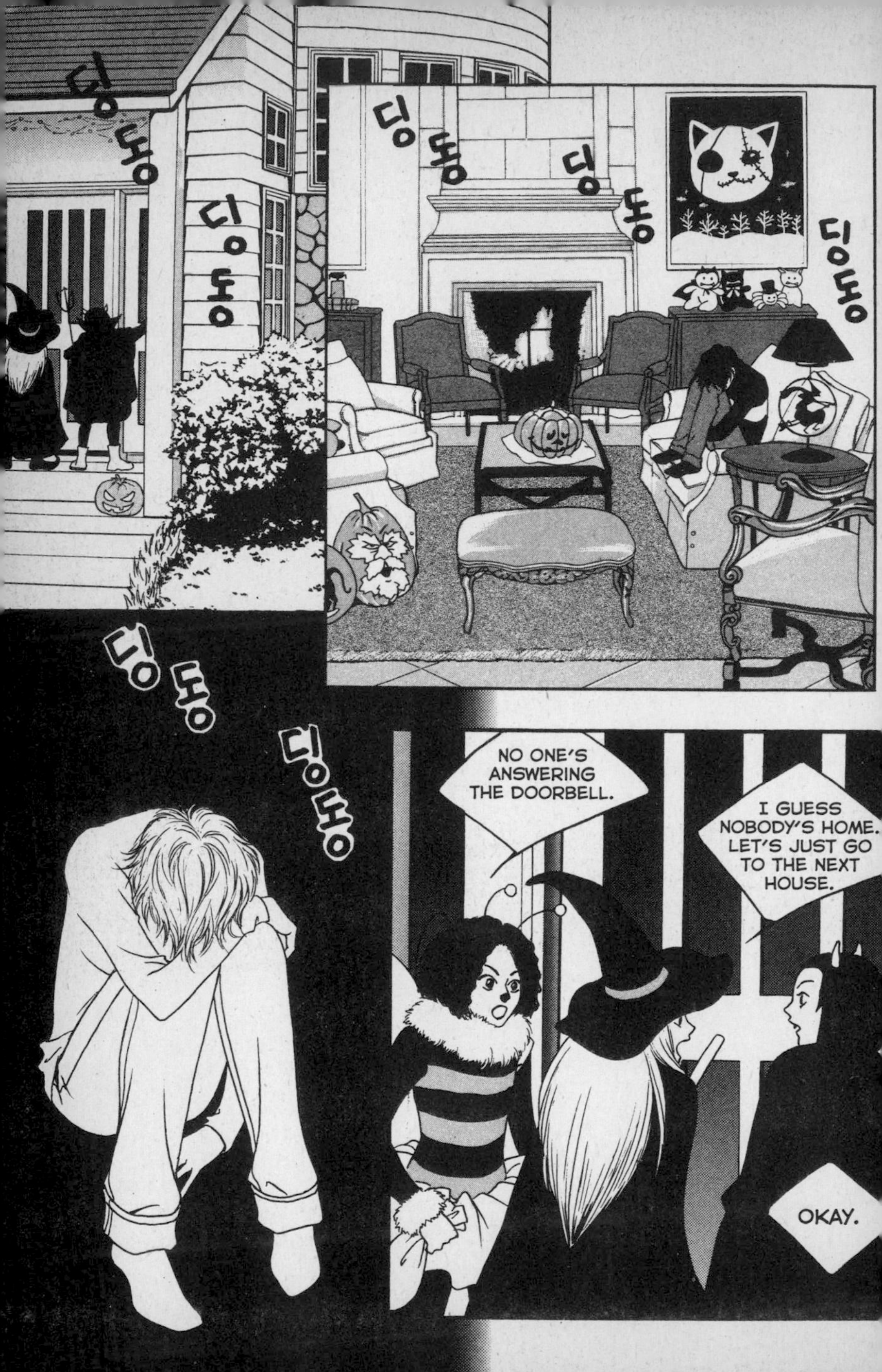

딩동
딩동
딩동
딩동
딩동
딩동
딩동
NO ONE'S ANSWERING THE DOORBELL.
I GUESS NOBODY'S HOME. LET'S JUST GO TO THE NEXT HOUSE.
OKAY.

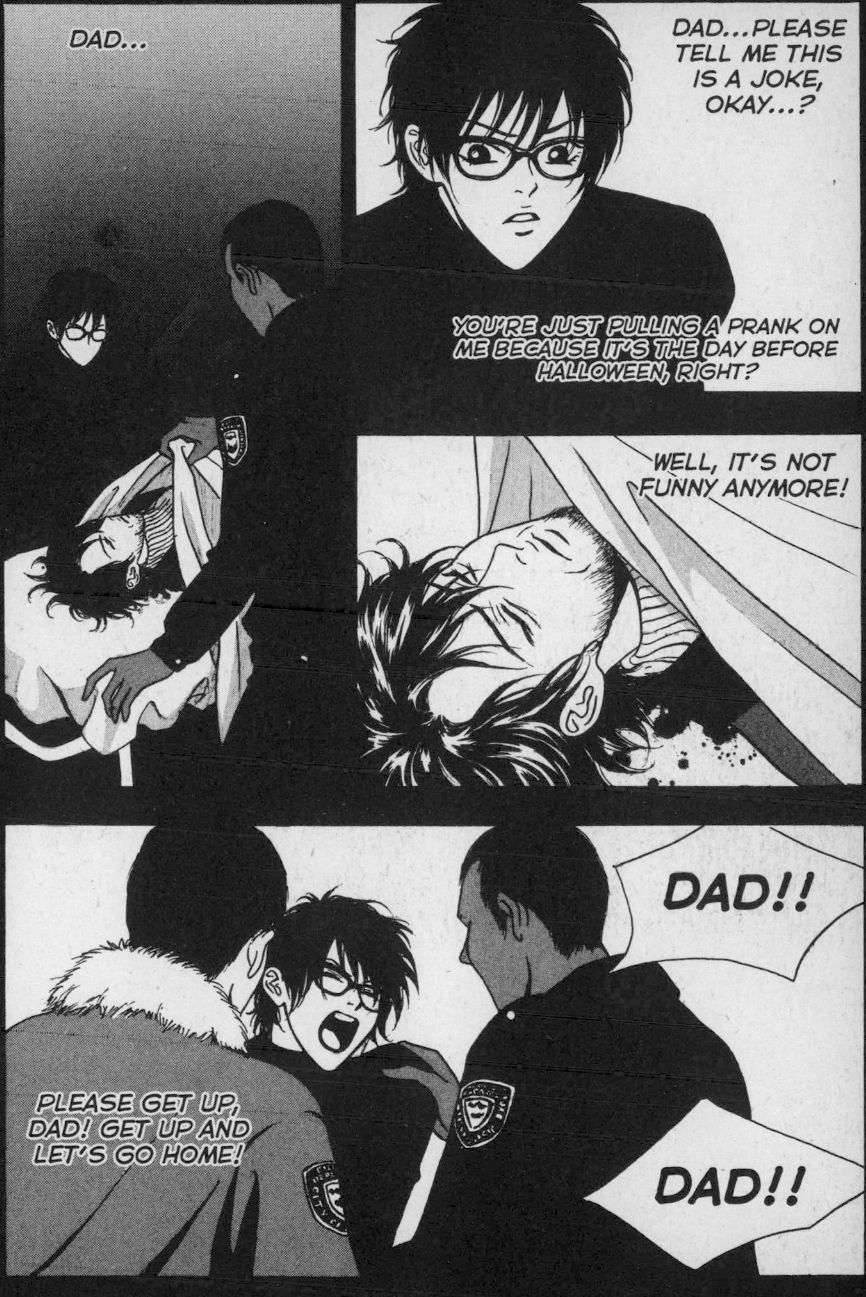
DAD...
DAD...PLEASE TELL ME THIS IS A JOKE, OKAY...?
YOU'RE JUST PULLING A PRANK ON ME BECAUSE IT'S THE DAY BEFORE HALLOWEEN, RIGHT?
WELL, IT'S NOT FUNNY ANYMORE!
DAD!!
PLEASE GET UP, DAD! GET UP AND LET'S GO HOME!
DAD!!

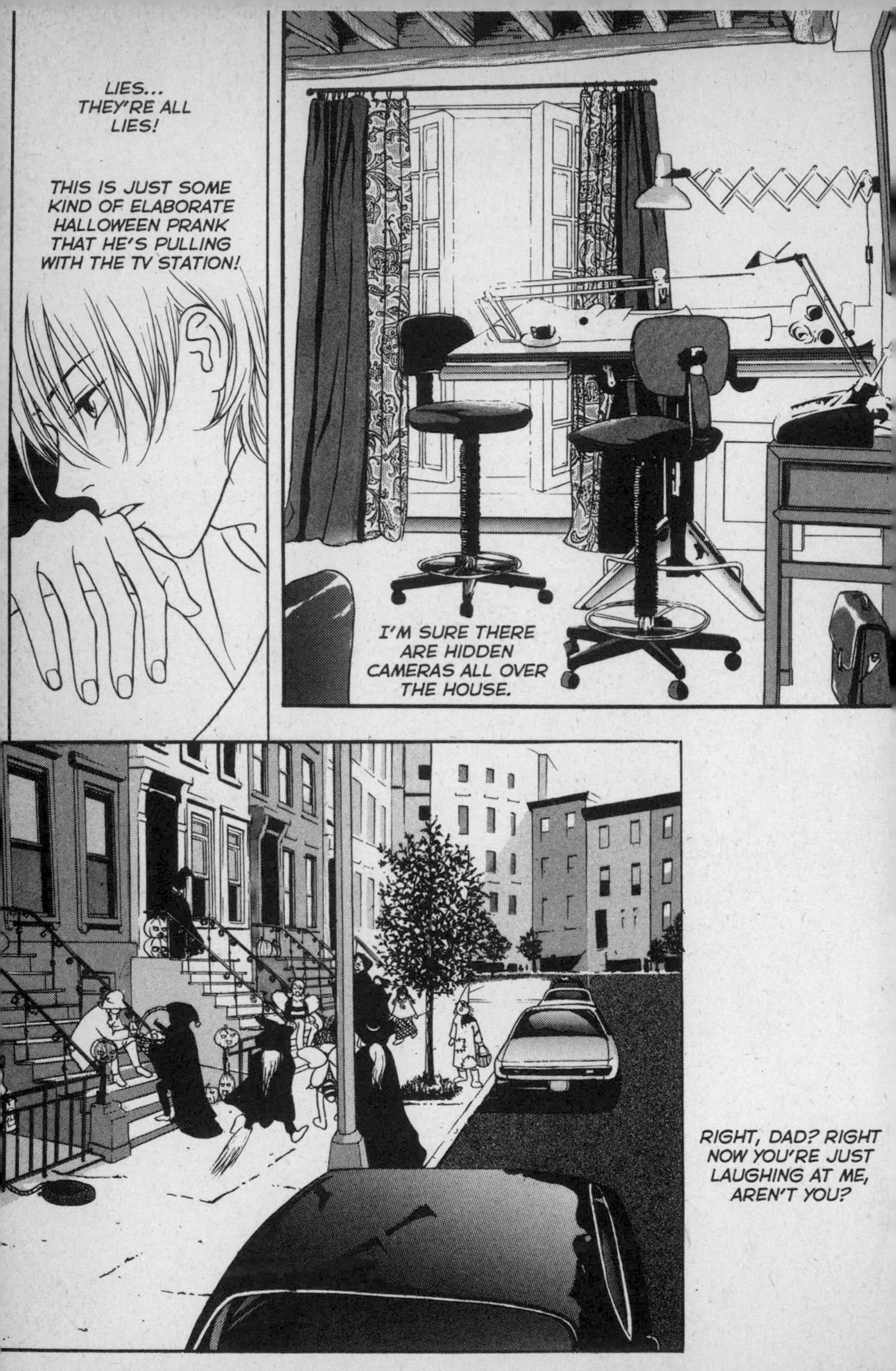
LIES... THEY'RE ALL LIES!
THIS IS JUST SOME KIND OF ELABORATE HALLOWEEN PRANK THAT HE'S PULLING WITH THE TV STATION!
I'M SURE THERE ARE HIDDEN CAMERAS ALL OVER THE HOUSE.
RIGHT, DAD? RIGHT NOW YOU'RE JUST LAUGHING AT ME, AREN'T YOU?

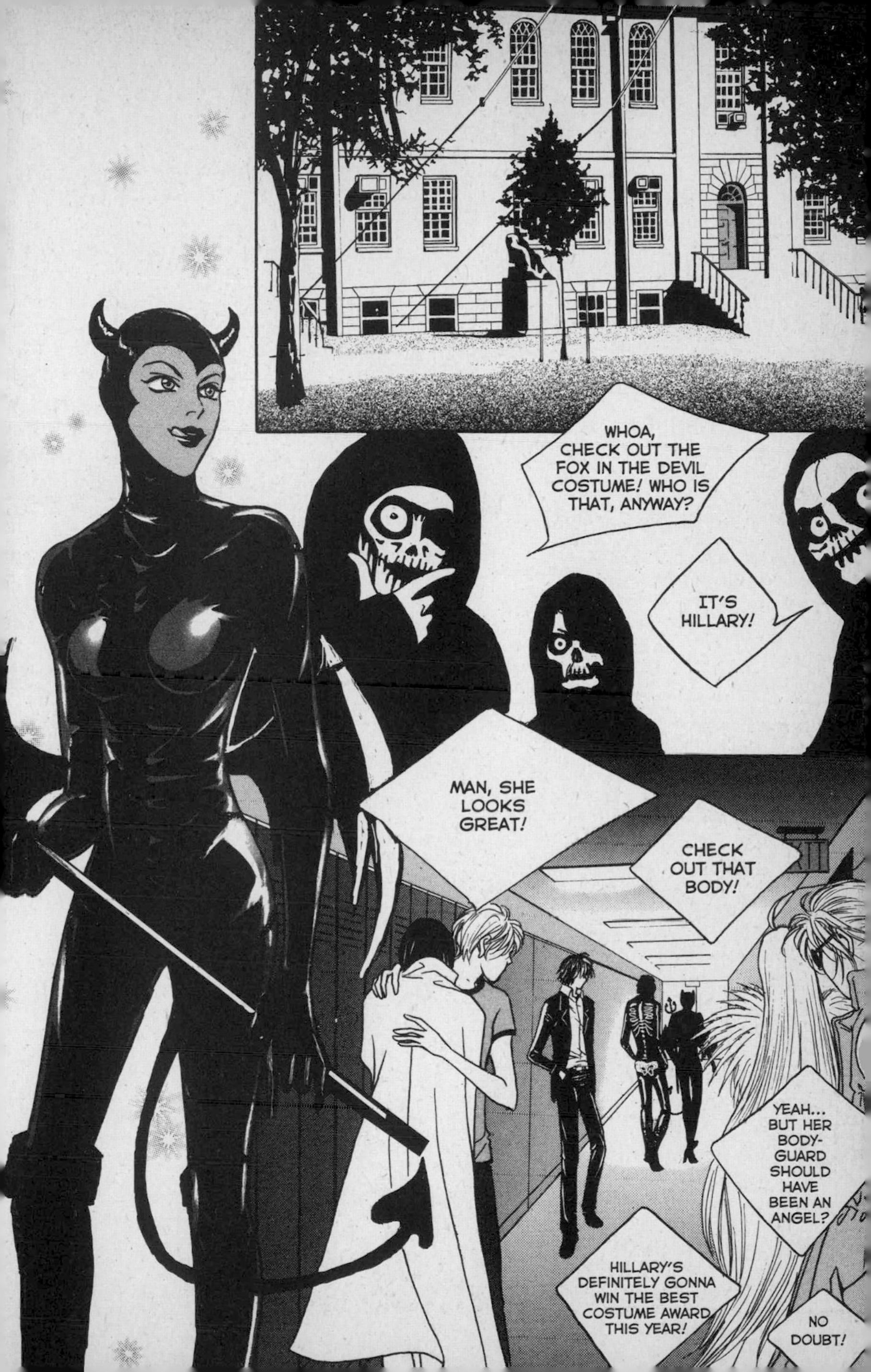
WHOA, CHECK OUT THE FOX IN THE DEVIL COSTUME! WHO IS THAT, ANYWAY?
IT'S HILLARY!
MAN, SHE LOOKS GREAT!
CHECK OUT THAT BODY!
YEAH... BUT HER BODY-GUARD SHOULD HAVE BEEN AN ANGEL?
HILLARY'S DEFINITELY GONNA WIN THE BEST COSTUME AWARD THIS YEAR!
NO DOUBT!

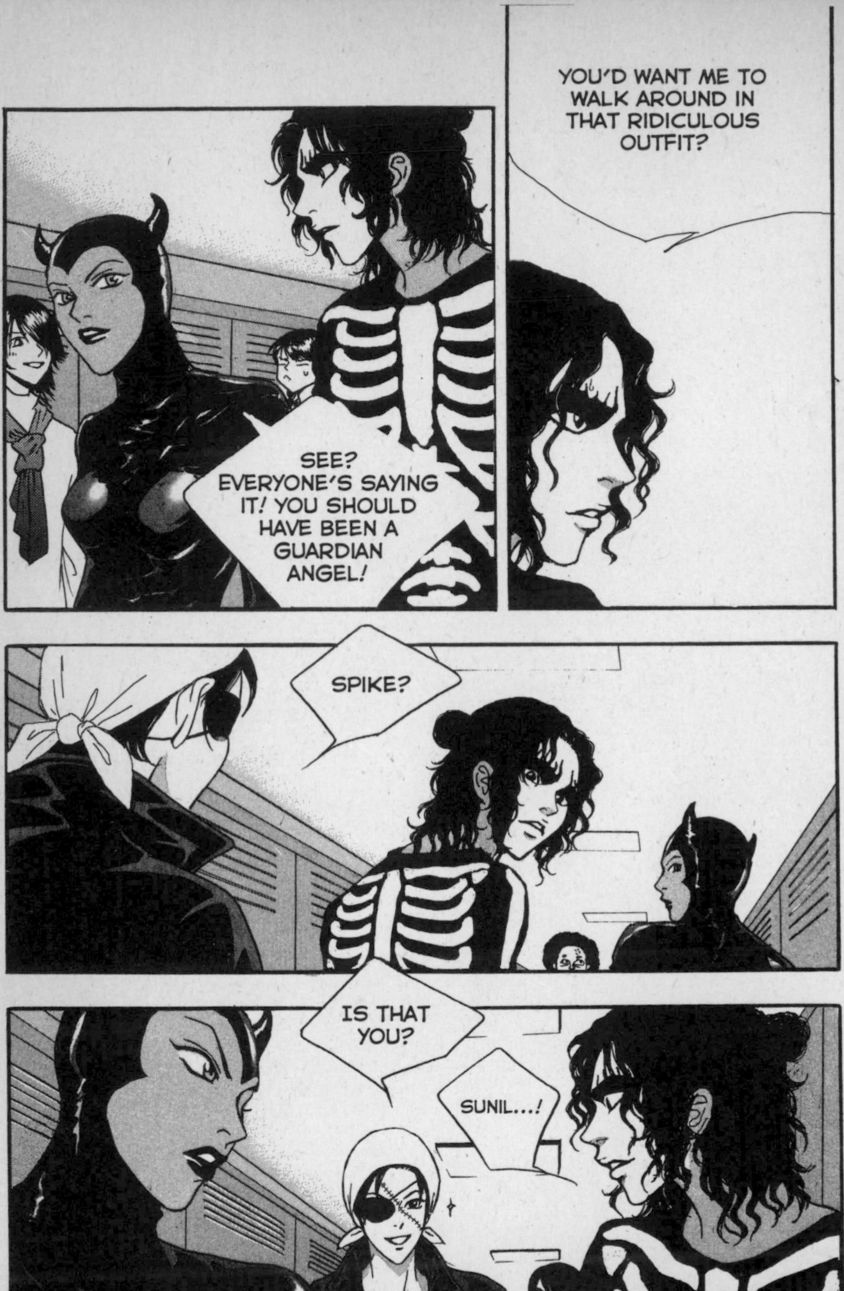
SEE? EVERYONE'S SAYING IT! YOU SHOULD HAVE BEEN A GUARDIAN ANGEL!
YOU'D WANT ME TO WALK AROUND IN THAT RIDICULOUS OUTFIT?
SPIKE?
IS THAT YOU?
SUNIL...!

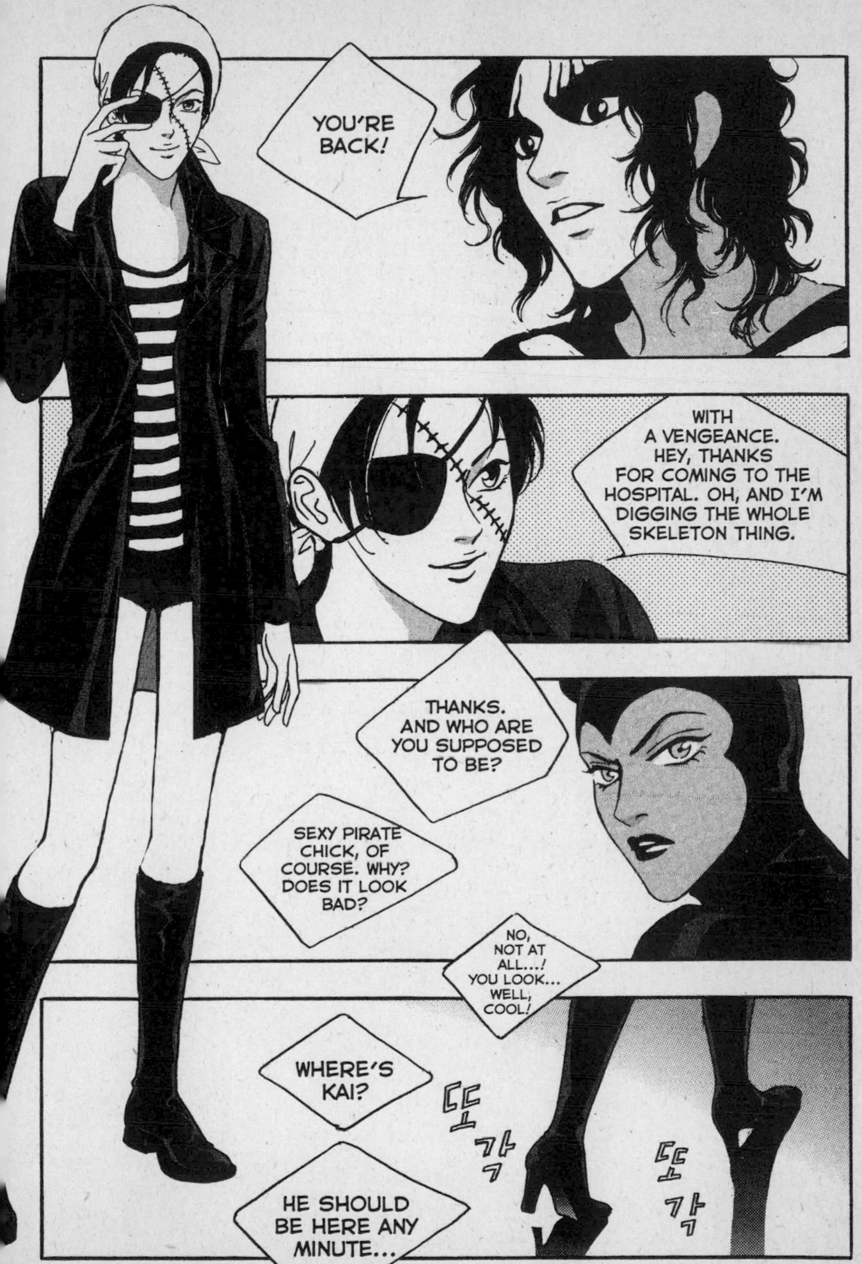
YOU'RE BACK!
WITH A VENGEANCE. HEY, THANKS FOR COMING TO THE HOSPITAL. OH, AND I'M DIGGING THE WHOLE SKELETON THING.
THANKS. AND WHO ARE YOU SUPPOSED TO BE?
SEXY PIRATE CHICK, OF COURSE. WHY? DOES IT LOOK BAD?
NO, NOT AT ALL...! YOU LOOK... WELL, COOL!
WHERE'S KAI?
또각
HE SHOULD BE HERE ANY MINUTE...
또각

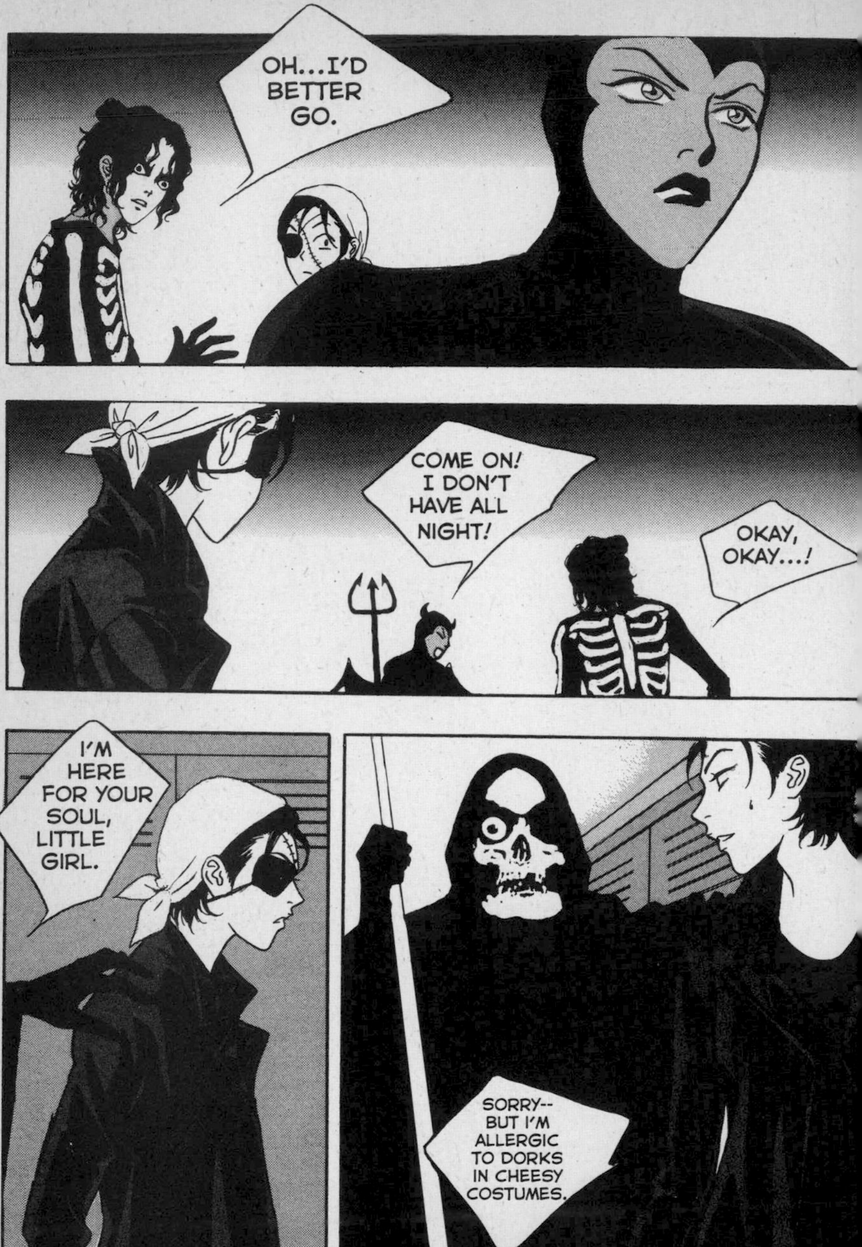
OH...I'D BETTER GO.
COME ON! I DON'T HAVE ALL NIGHT!
OKAY, OKAY...!
I'M HERE FOR YOUR SOUL, LITTLE GIRL.
SORRY-- BUT I'M ALLERGIC TO DORKS IN CHEESY COSTUMES.

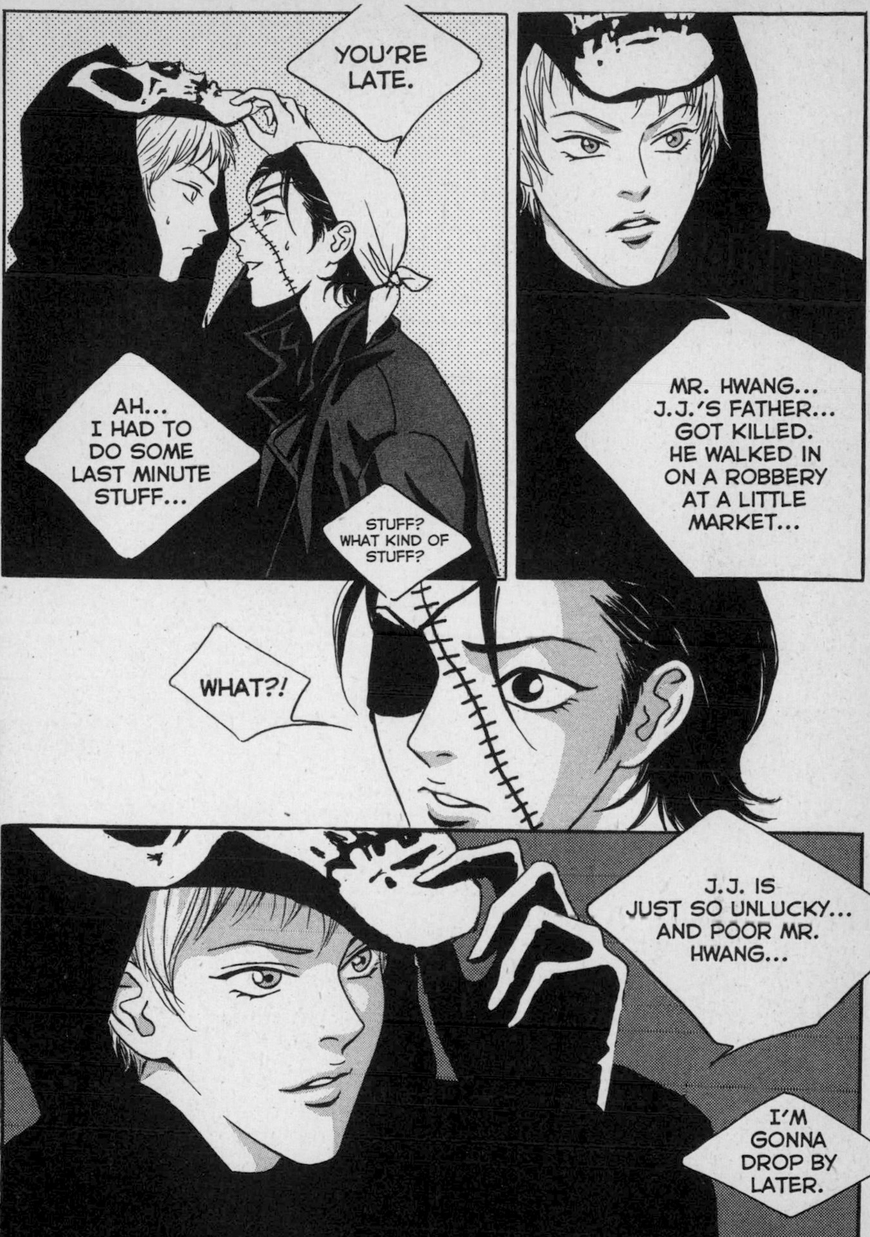
YOU'RE LATE.
AH... I HAD TO DO SOME LAST MINUTE STUFF...
STUFF? WHAT KIND OF STUFF?
MR. HWANG... J.J.'S FATHER... GOT KILLED. HE WALKED IN ON A ROBBERY AT A LITTLE MARKET...
WHAT?!
J.J. IS JUST SO UNLUCKY... AND POOR MR. HWANG...
I'M GONNA DROP BY LATER.

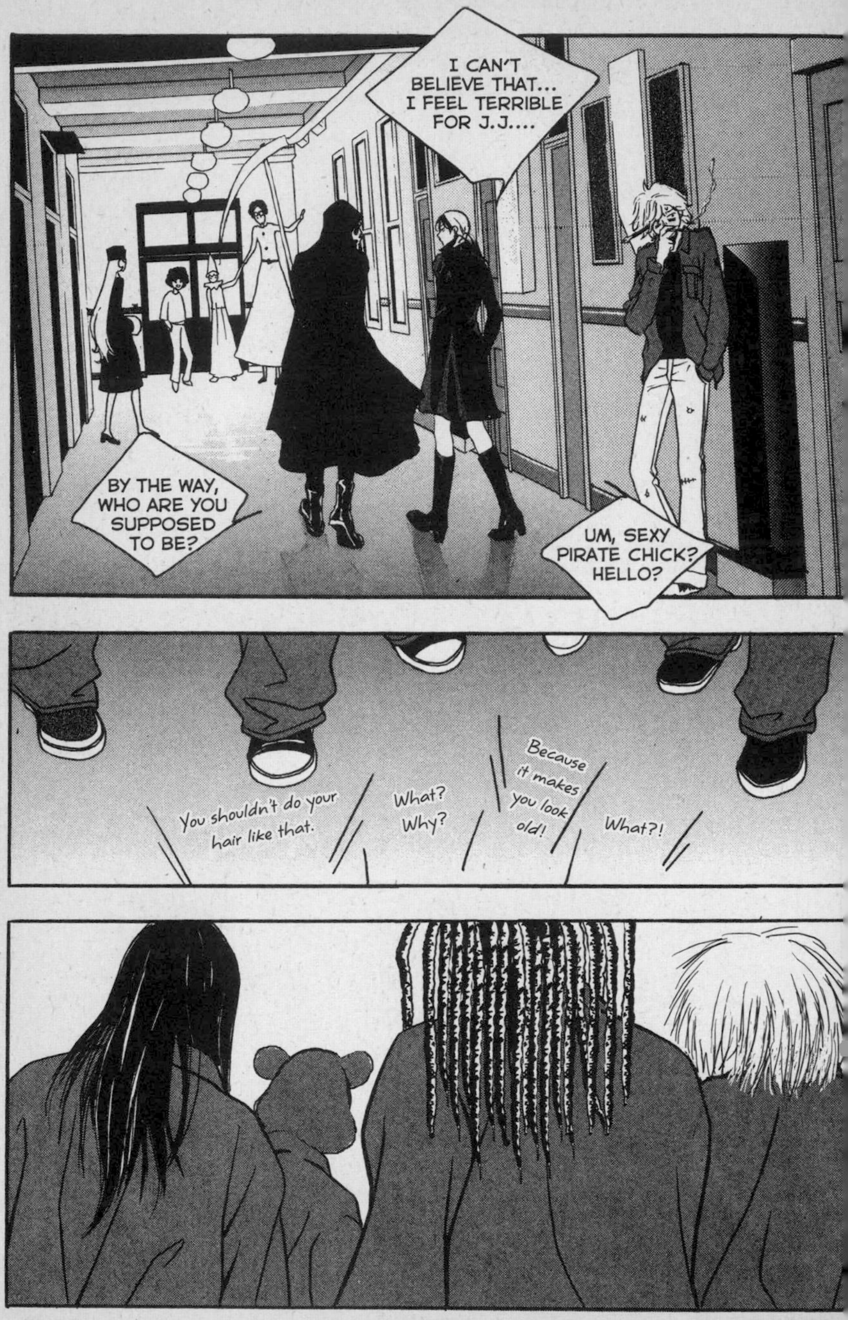
I CAN'T BELIEVE THAT... I FEEL TERRIBLE FOR J.J....
BY THE WAY, WHO ARE YOU SUPPOSED TO BE?
UM, SEXY PIRATE CHICK? HELLO?
You shouldn't do your hair like that.
What? Why?
Because it makes you look old!
What?!

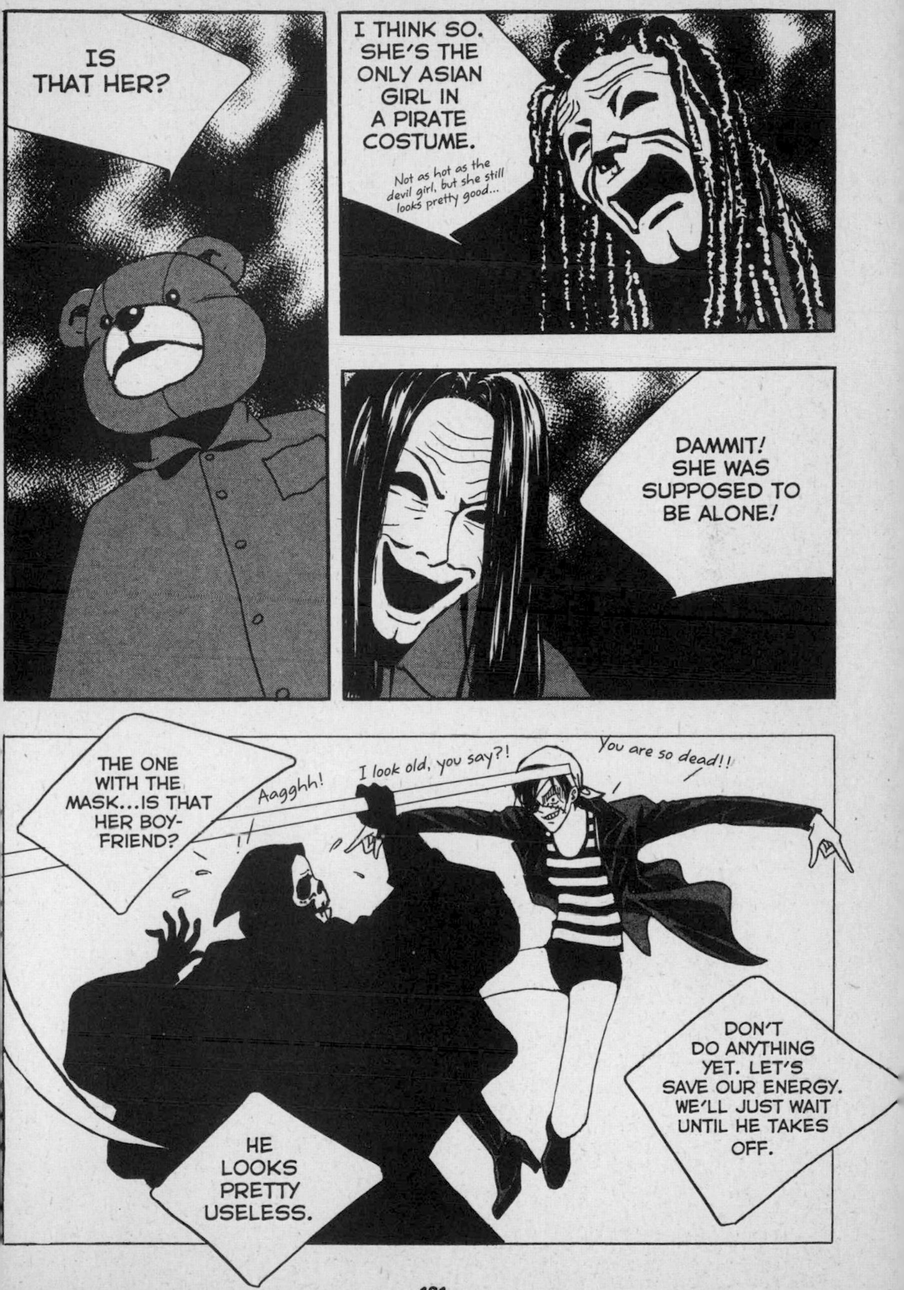
IS THAT HER?
I THINK SO. SHE'S THE ONLY ASIAN GIRL IN A PIRATE COSTUME.
Not as hot as the devil girl, but she still looks pretty good...
DAMMIT! SHE WAS SUPPOSED TO BE ALONE!
THE ONE WITH THE MASK...IS THAT HER BOY-FRIEND?
Aagghh!
I look old, you say?!
You are so dead!!
HE LOOKS PRETTY USELESS.
DON'T DO ANYTHING YET. LET'S SAVE OUR ENERGY. WE'LL JUST WAIT UNTIL HE TAKES OFF.

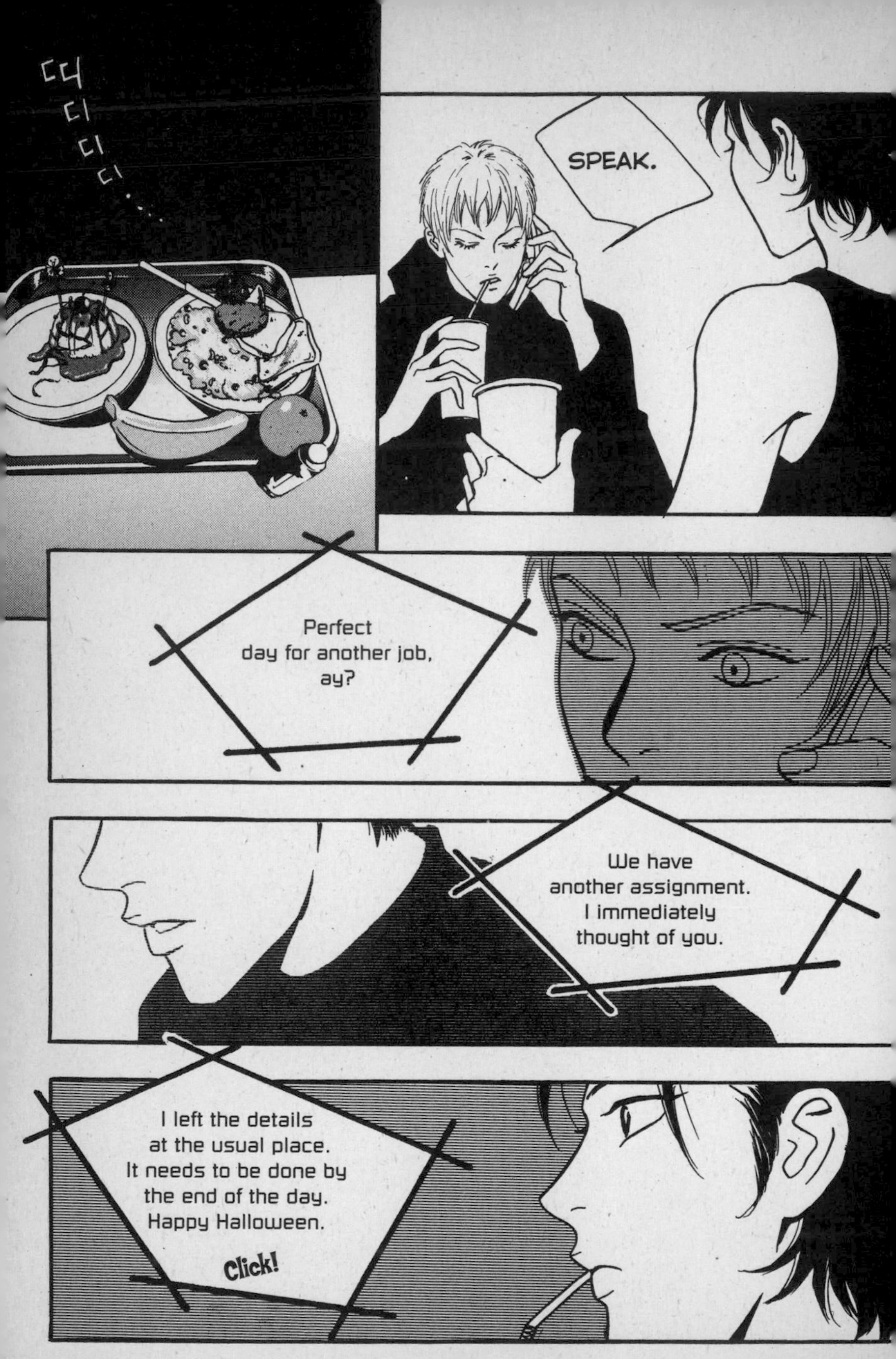
띠디디디...
SPEAK.
Perfect day for another job, ay?
We have another assignment. I immediately thought of you.
I left the details at the usual place. It needs to be done by the end of the day. Happy Halloween.
Click!

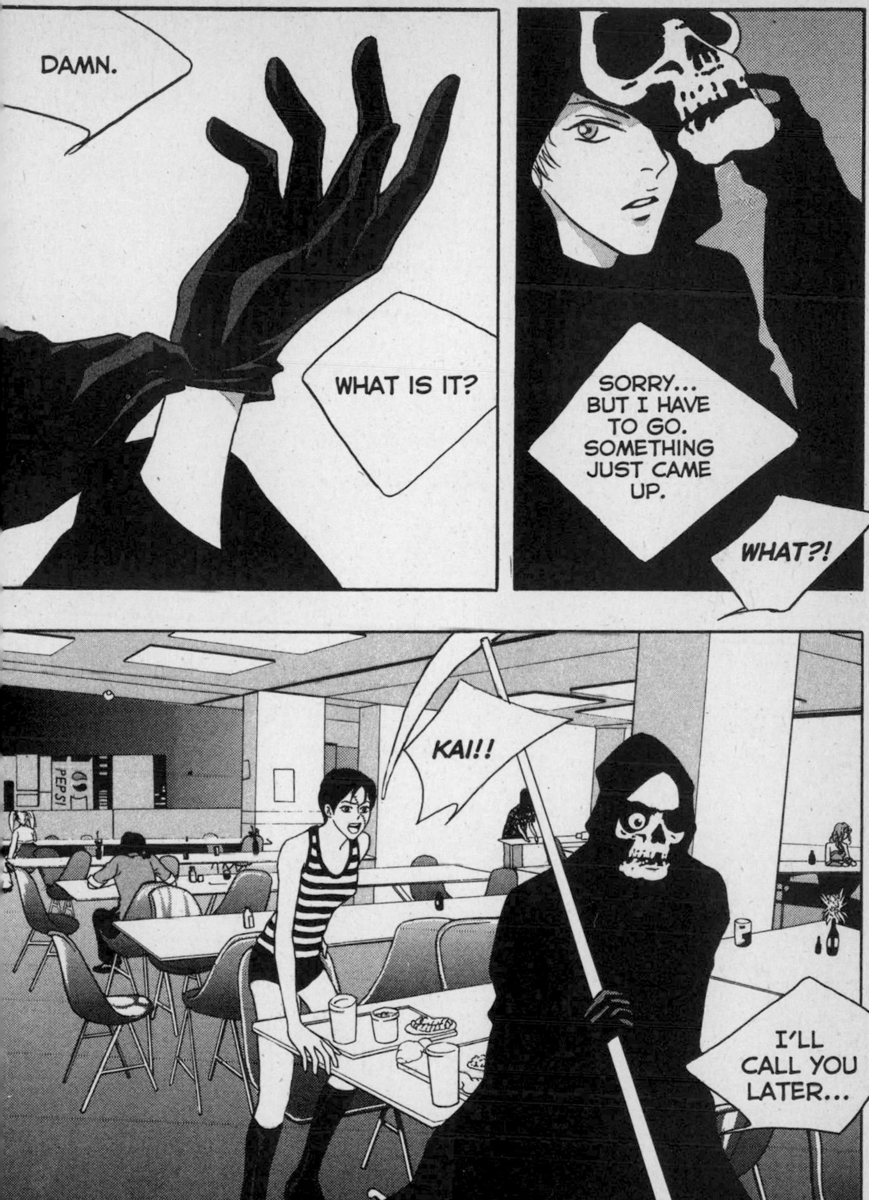
DAMN.
WHAT IS IT?
SORRY... BUT I HAVE TO GO. SOMETHING JUST CAME UP.
WHAT?!
KAI!!
I'LL CALL YOU LATER...

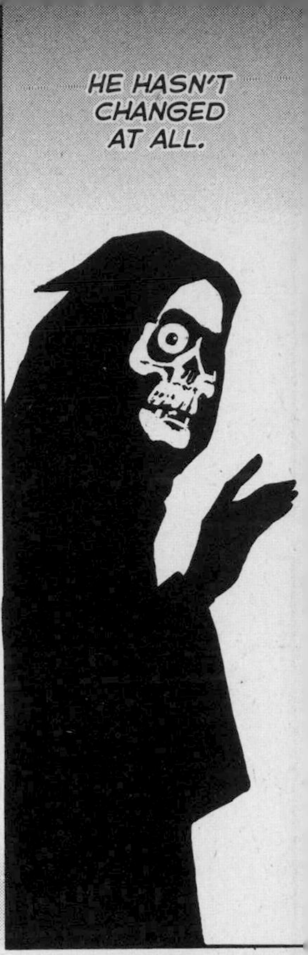
HE HASN'T CHANGED AT ALL.
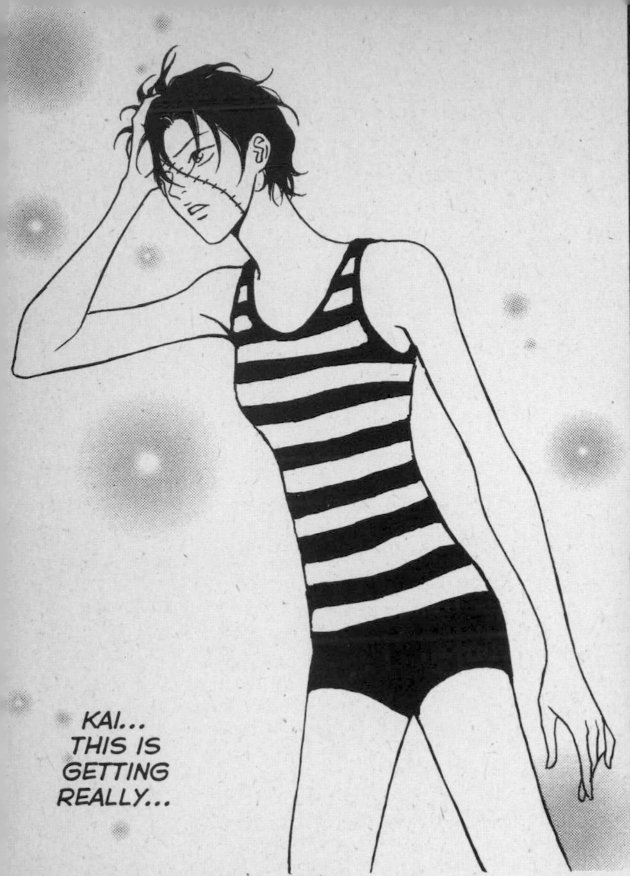
KAI... THIS IS GETTING REALLY...
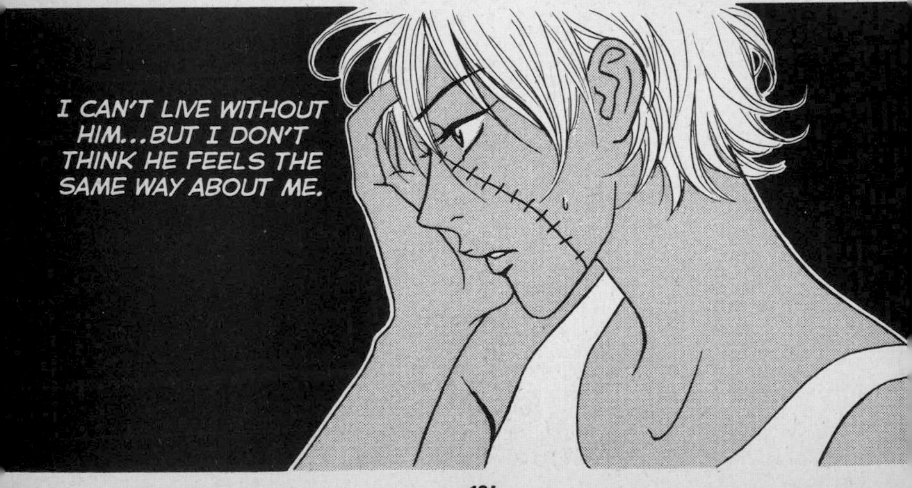
I CAN'T LIVE WITHOUT HIM...BUT I DON'T THINK HE FEELS THE SAME WAY ABOUT ME.

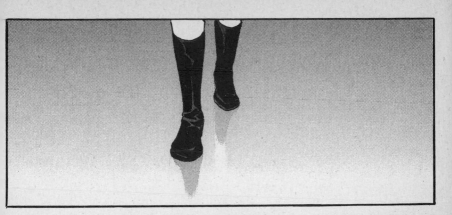

HOW LONG
CAN I KEEP
THIS UP?

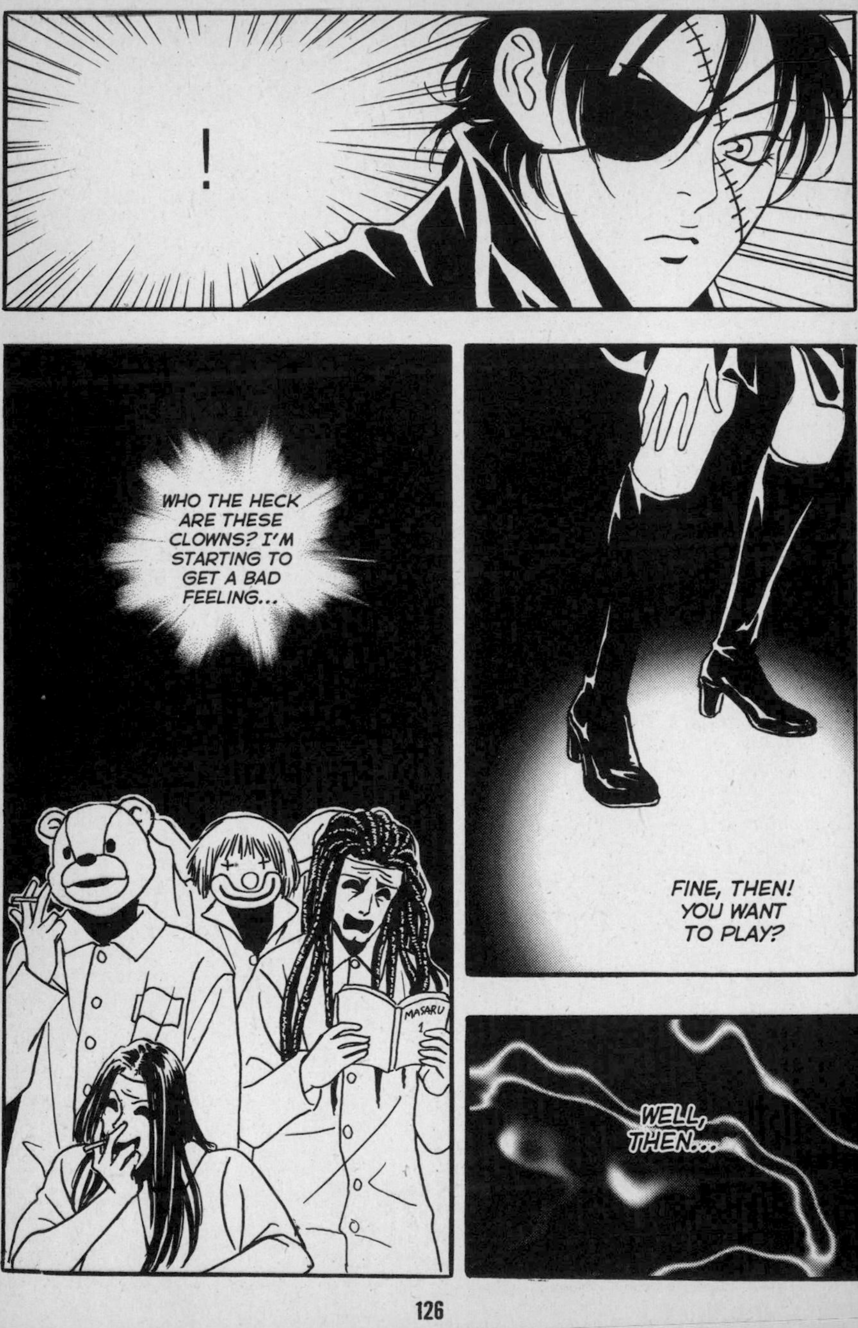
!
FINE, THEN! YOU WANT TO PLAY?
WELL, THEN...
WHO THE HECK ARE THESE CLOWNS? I'M STARTING TO GET A BAD FEELING...
MASARU 1

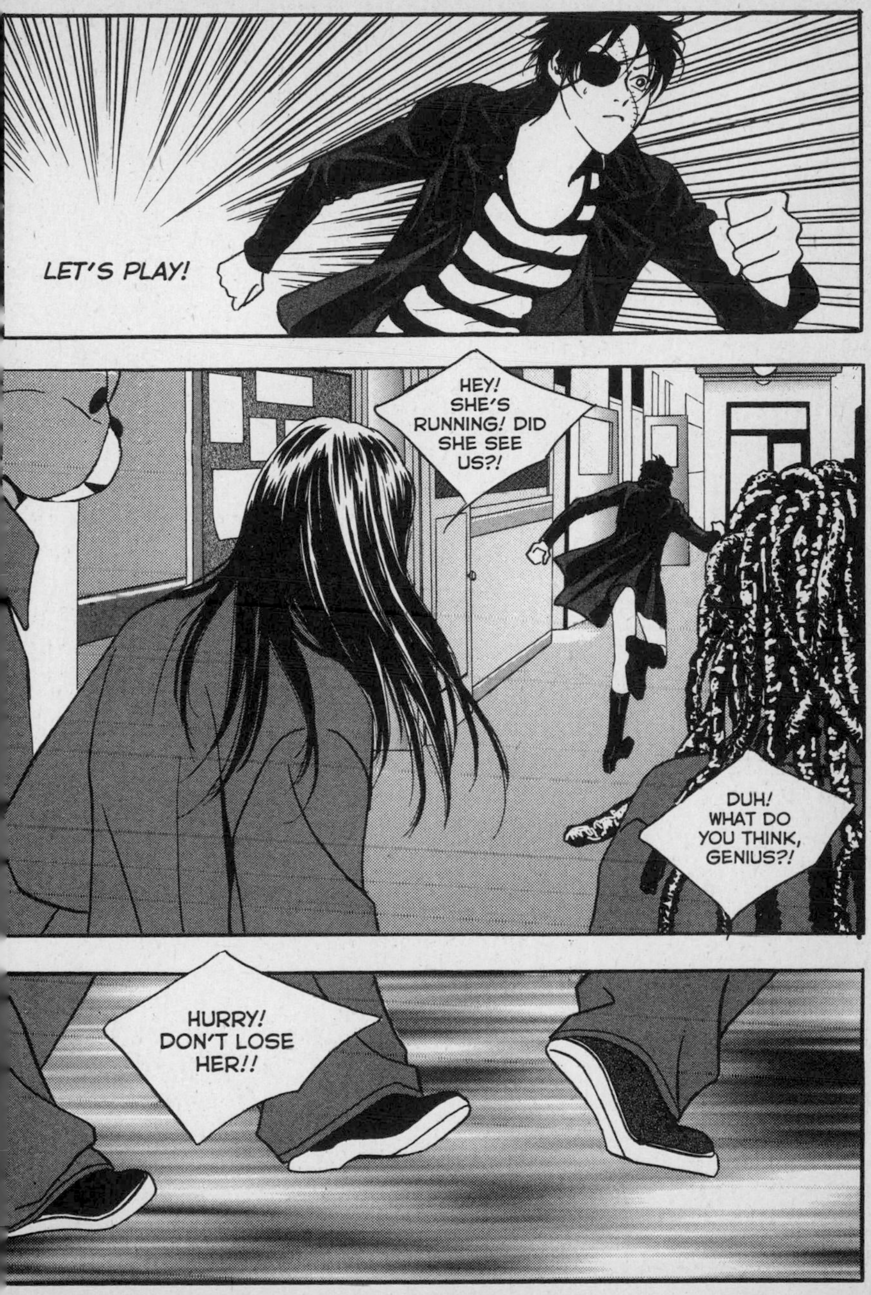
LET'S PLAY!
HEY! SHE'S RUNNING! DID SHE SEE US?!
DUH! WHAT DO YOU THINK, GENIUS?!
HURRY! DON'T LOSE HER!!

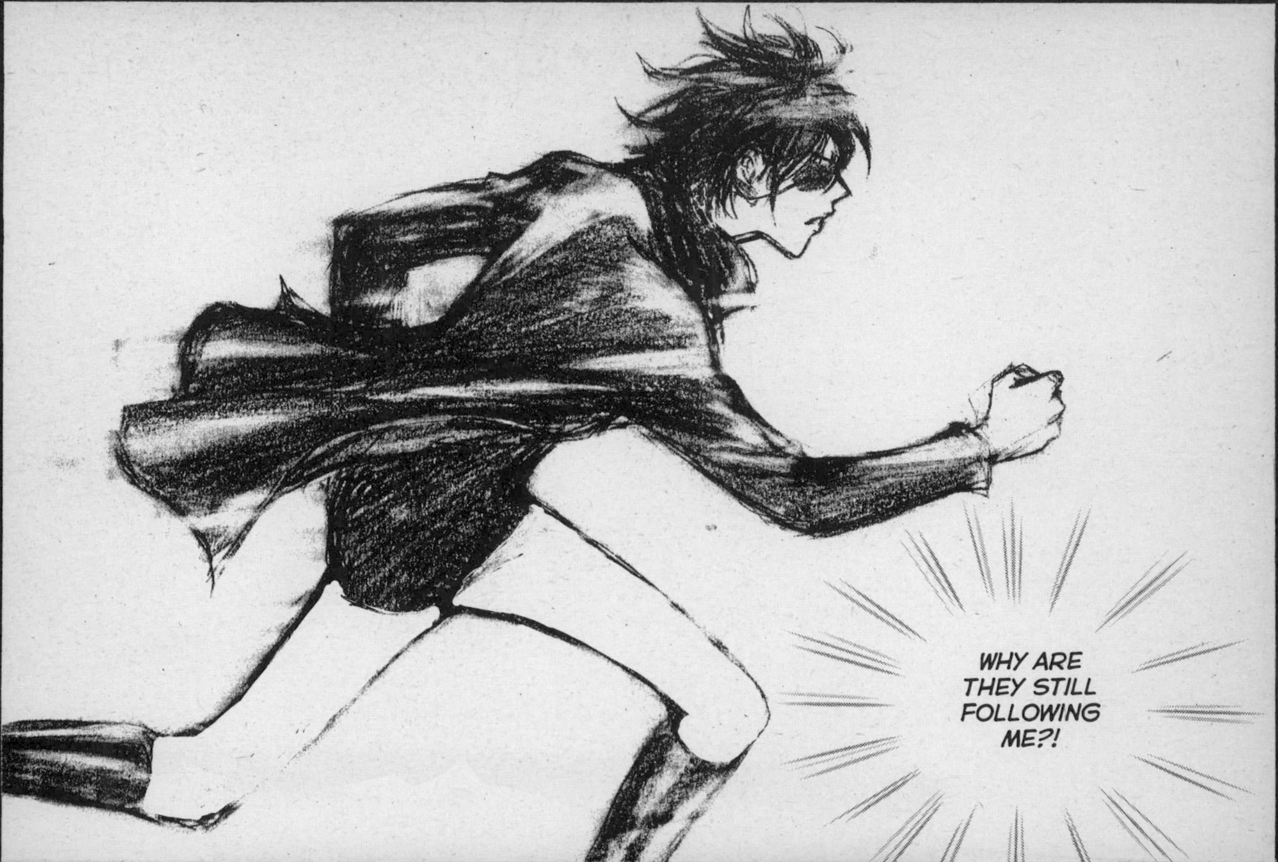
WHY ARE THEY STILL FOLLOWING ME?!

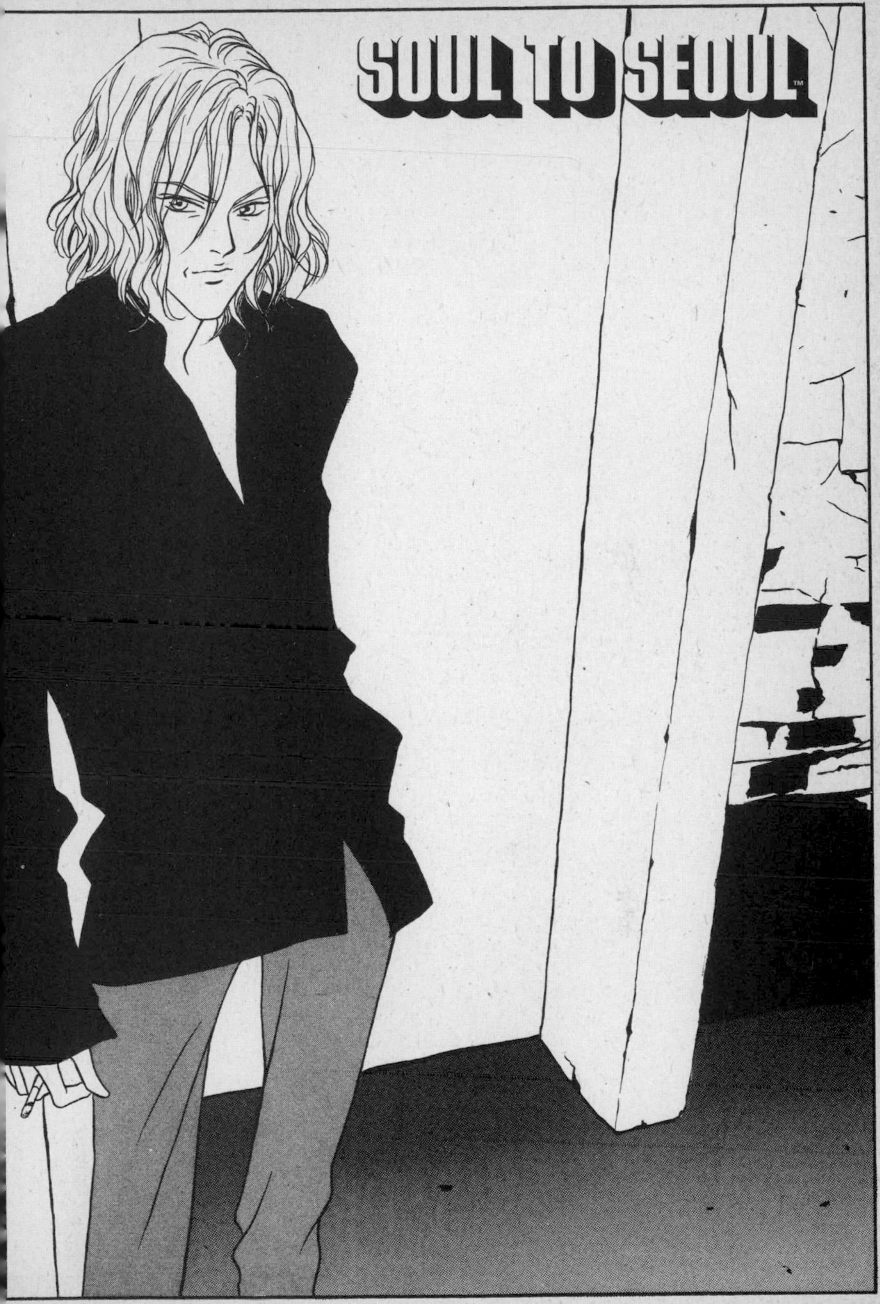
SOUL TO SEOUL™

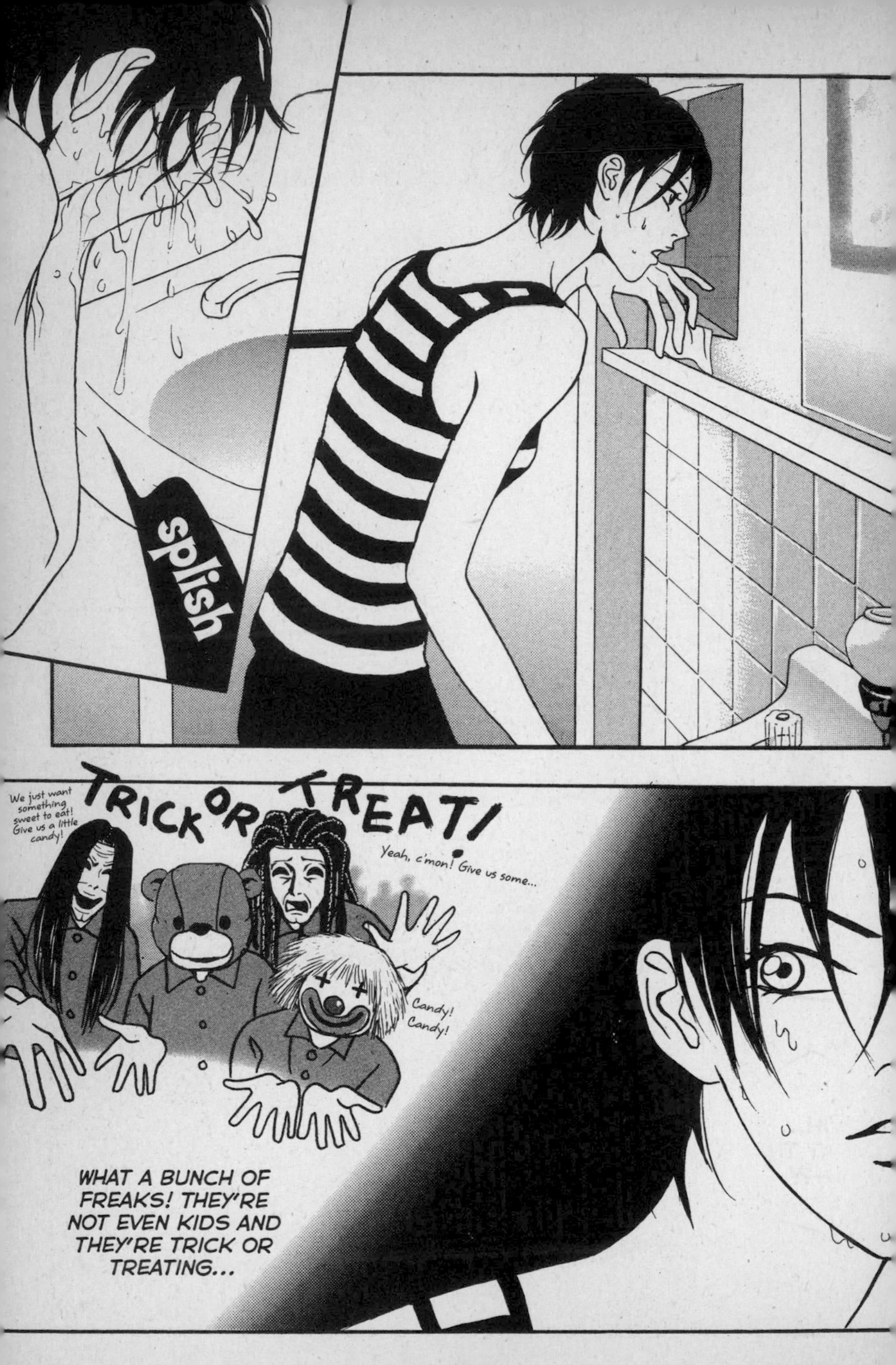
splish
TRICK OR TREAT!
Yeah, c'mon! Give us some...
Candy! Candy!
We just want something sweet to eat! Give us a little candy!
WHAT A BUNCH OF FREAKS! THEY'RE NOT EVEN KIDS AND THEY'RE TRICK OR TREATING...

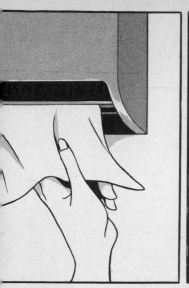

MAYBE I WAS JUST OVER-REACTING.

BUT THEN AGAIN, WHY WOULD THEY RUN AFTER ME?

TRICK OR TREAT!

HUH...? WHAT THE --?!

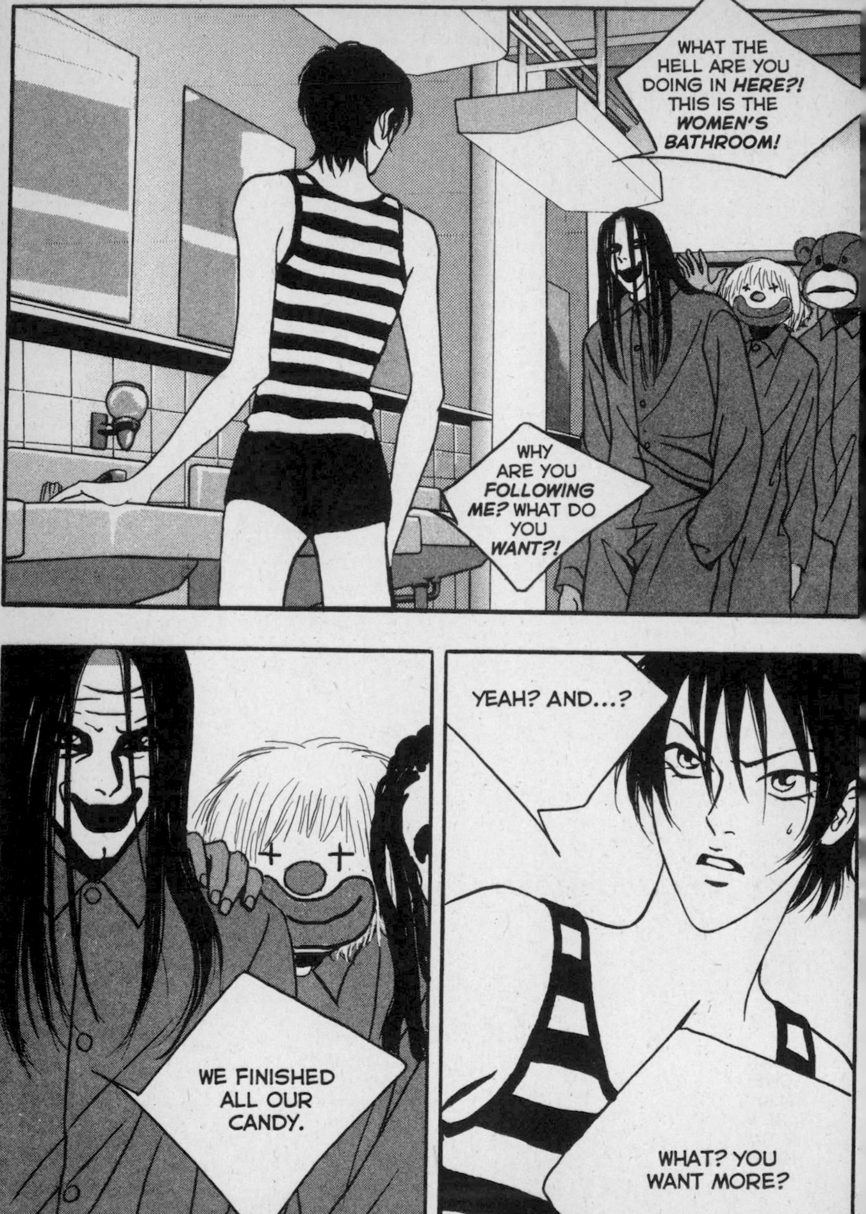
WHAT THE HELL ARE YOU DOING IN *HERE?!* THIS IS THE ***WOMEN'S BATHROOM!***
WHY ARE YOU ***FOLLOWING ME?*** WHAT DO YOU ***WANT?!***
WE FINISHED ALL OUR CANDY.
YEAH? AND...?
WHAT? YOU WANT MORE?

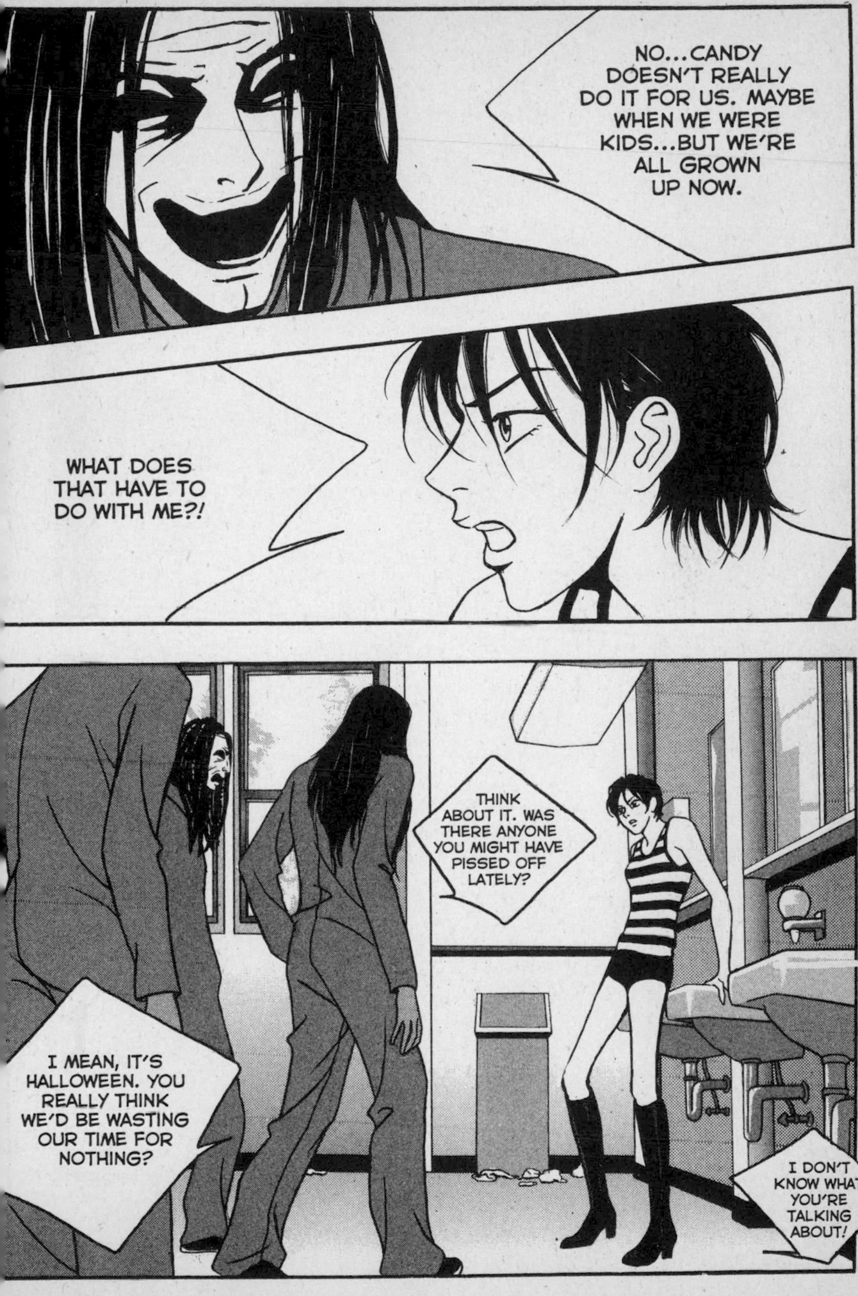
NO...CANDY DOESN'T REALLY DO IT FOR US. MAYBE WHEN WE WERE KIDS...BUT WE'RE ALL GROWN UP NOW.
WHAT DOES THAT HAVE TO DO WITH ME?!
THINK ABOUT IT. WAS THERE ANYONE YOU MIGHT HAVE PISSED OFF LATELY?
I MEAN, IT'S HALLOWEEN. YOU REALLY THINK WE'D BE WASTING OUR TIME FOR NOTHING?
I DON'T KNOW WHAT YOU'RE TALKING ABOUT!

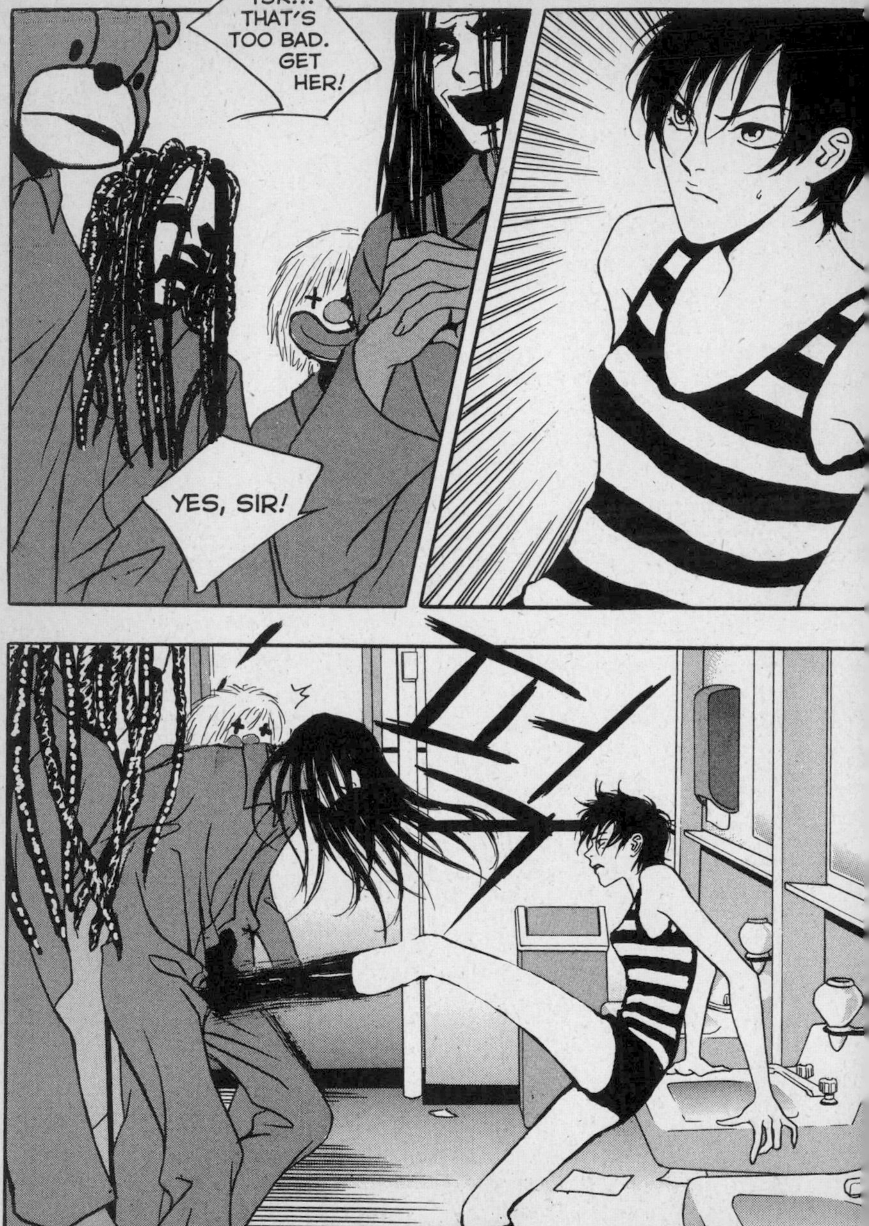
TSK... THAT'S TOO BAD. GET HER!
YES, SIR!

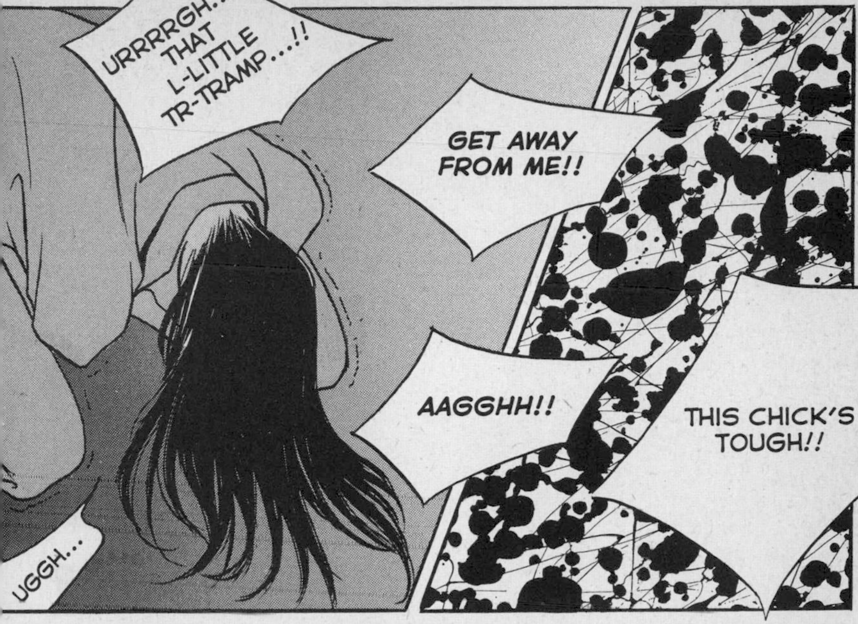
GET AWAY FROM ME!!
THIS CHICK'S TOUGH!!
AAGGHH!!
URRRRGH... THAT L-LITTLE TR-TRAMP...!!
UGGH...

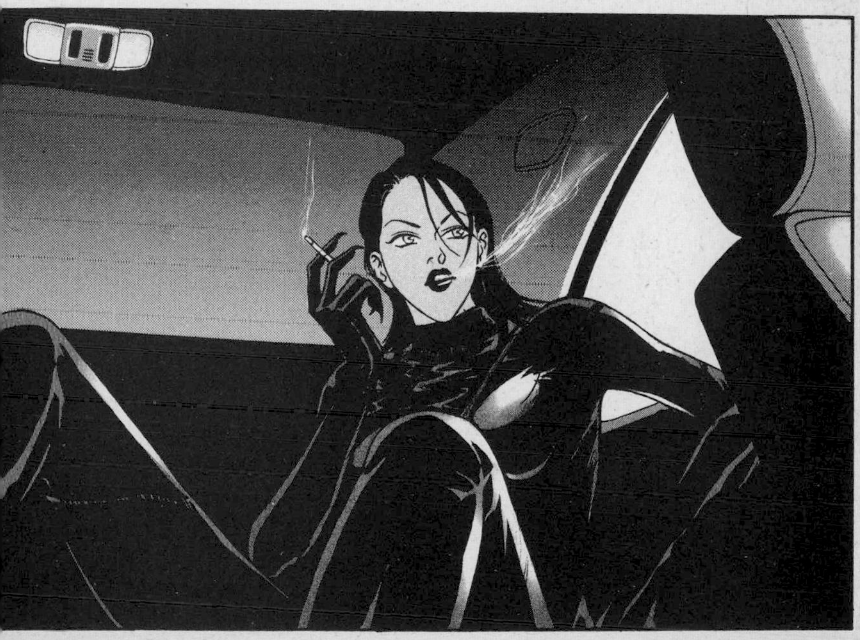

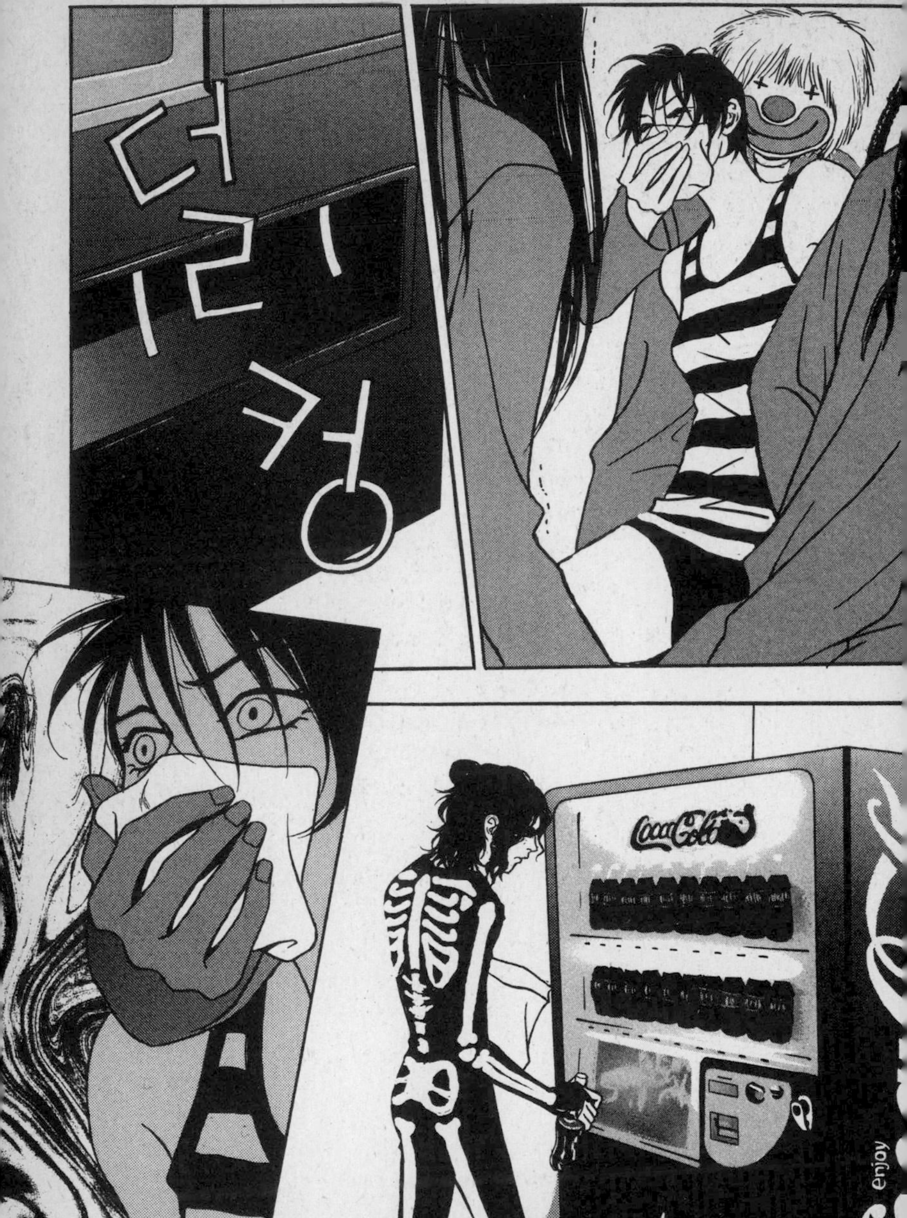
덜컹
Coca-Cola
enjoy

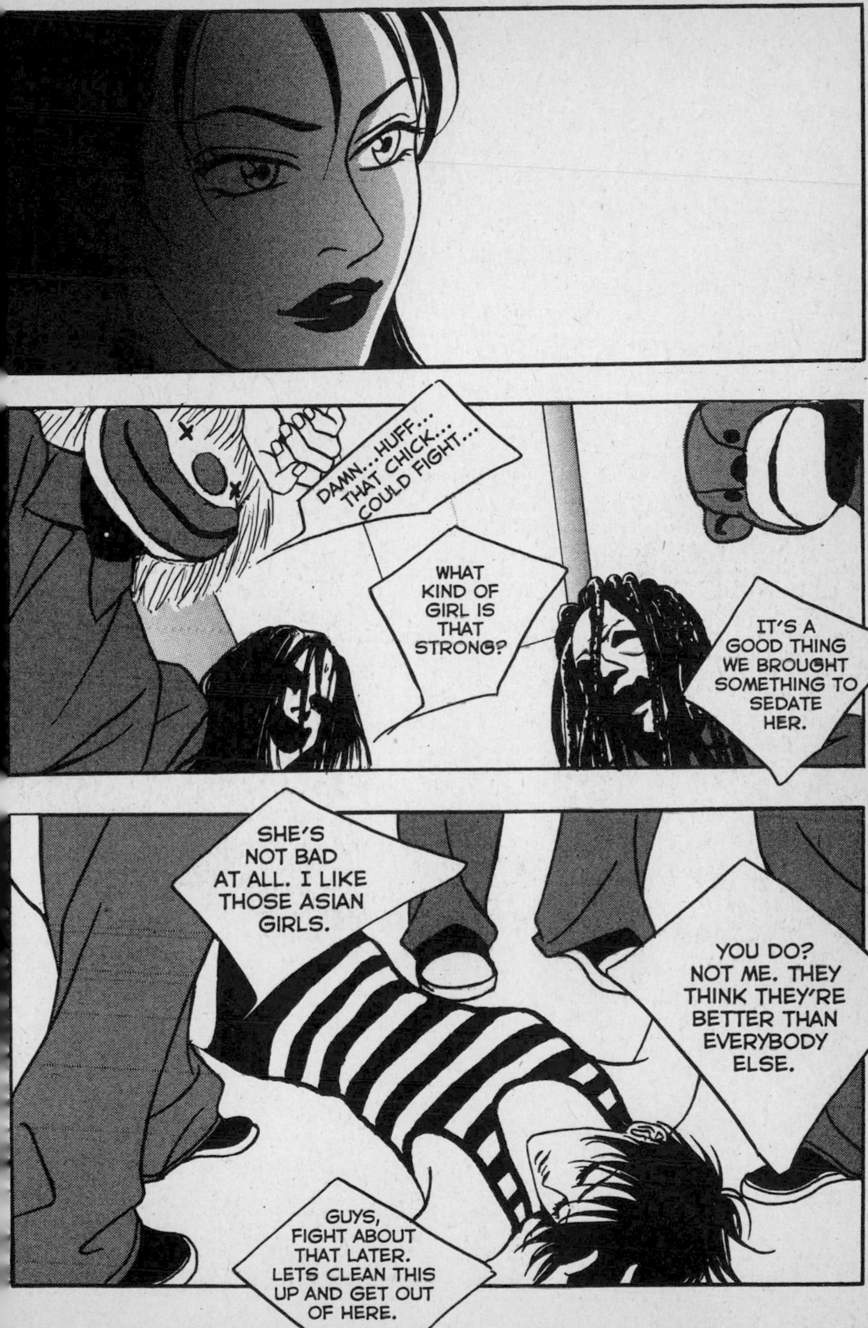
DAMN...HUFF... THAT CHICK... COULD FIGHT...
WHAT KIND OF GIRL IS THAT STRONG?
IT'S A GOOD THING WE BROUGHT SOMETHING TO SEDATE HER.
SHE'S NOT BAD AT ALL. I LIKE THOSE ASIAN GIRLS.
YOU DO? NOT ME. THEY THINK THEY'RE BETTER THAN EVERYBODY ELSE.
GUYS, FIGHT ABOUT THAT LATER. LETS CLEAN THIS UP AND GET OUT OF HERE.

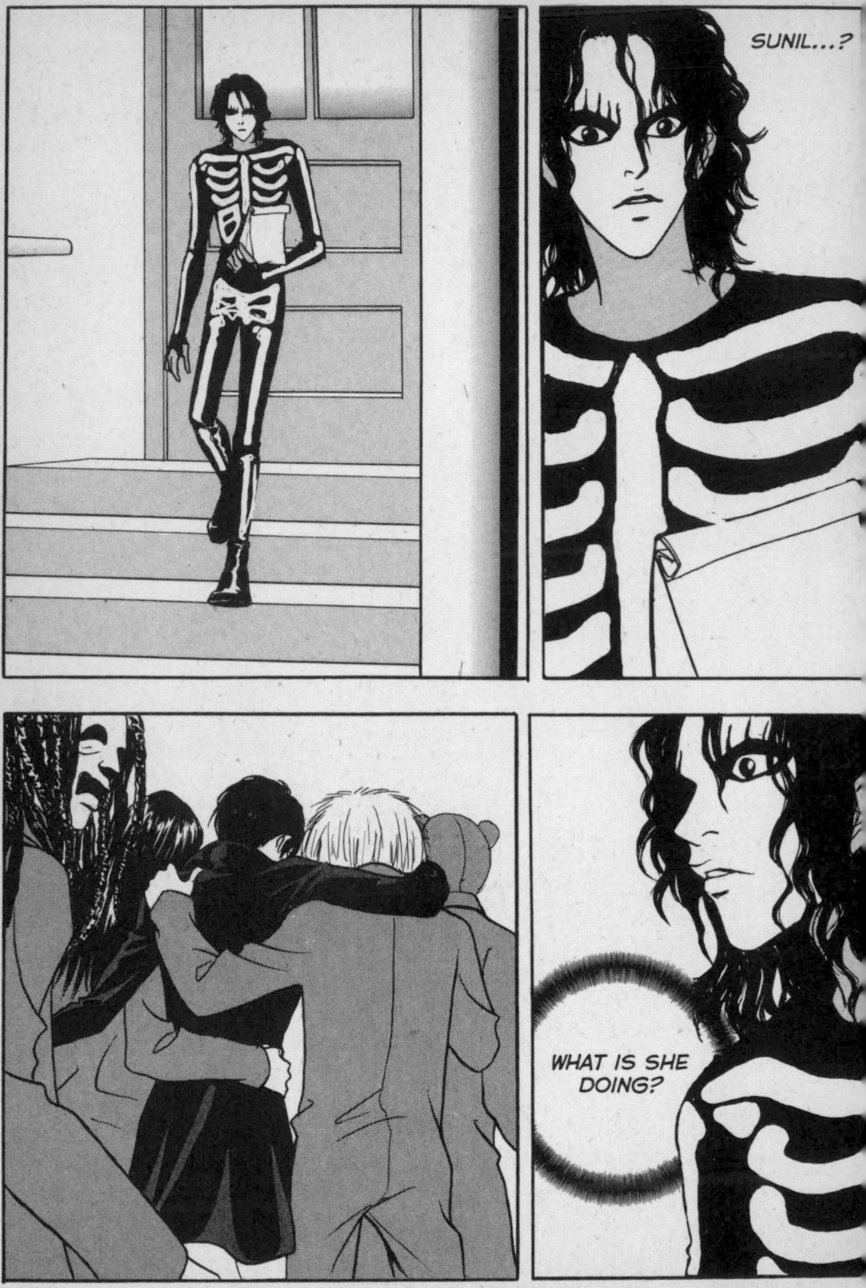
SUNIL...?
WHAT IS SHE DOING?

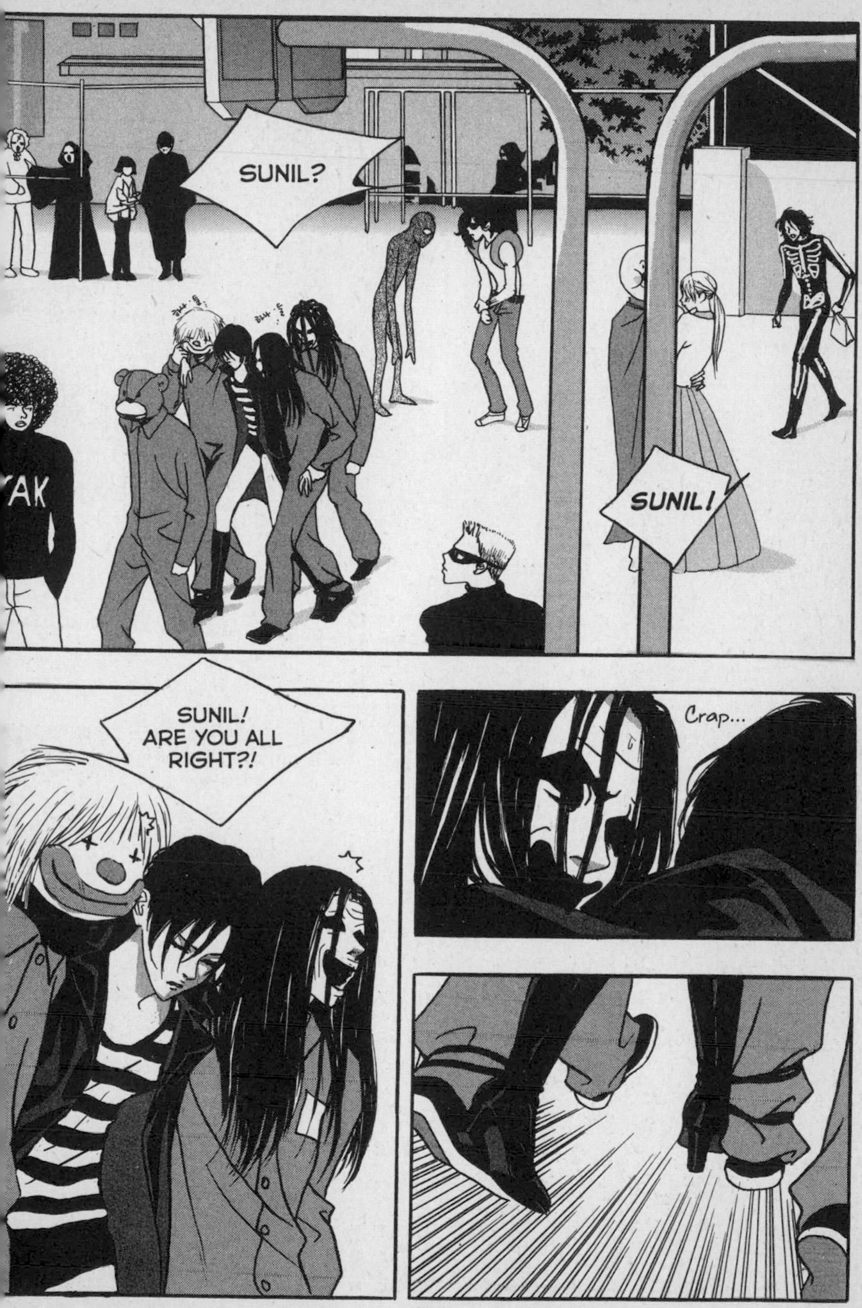
SUNIL?
SUNIL!
SUNIL! ARE YOU ALL RIGHT?!
Crap...

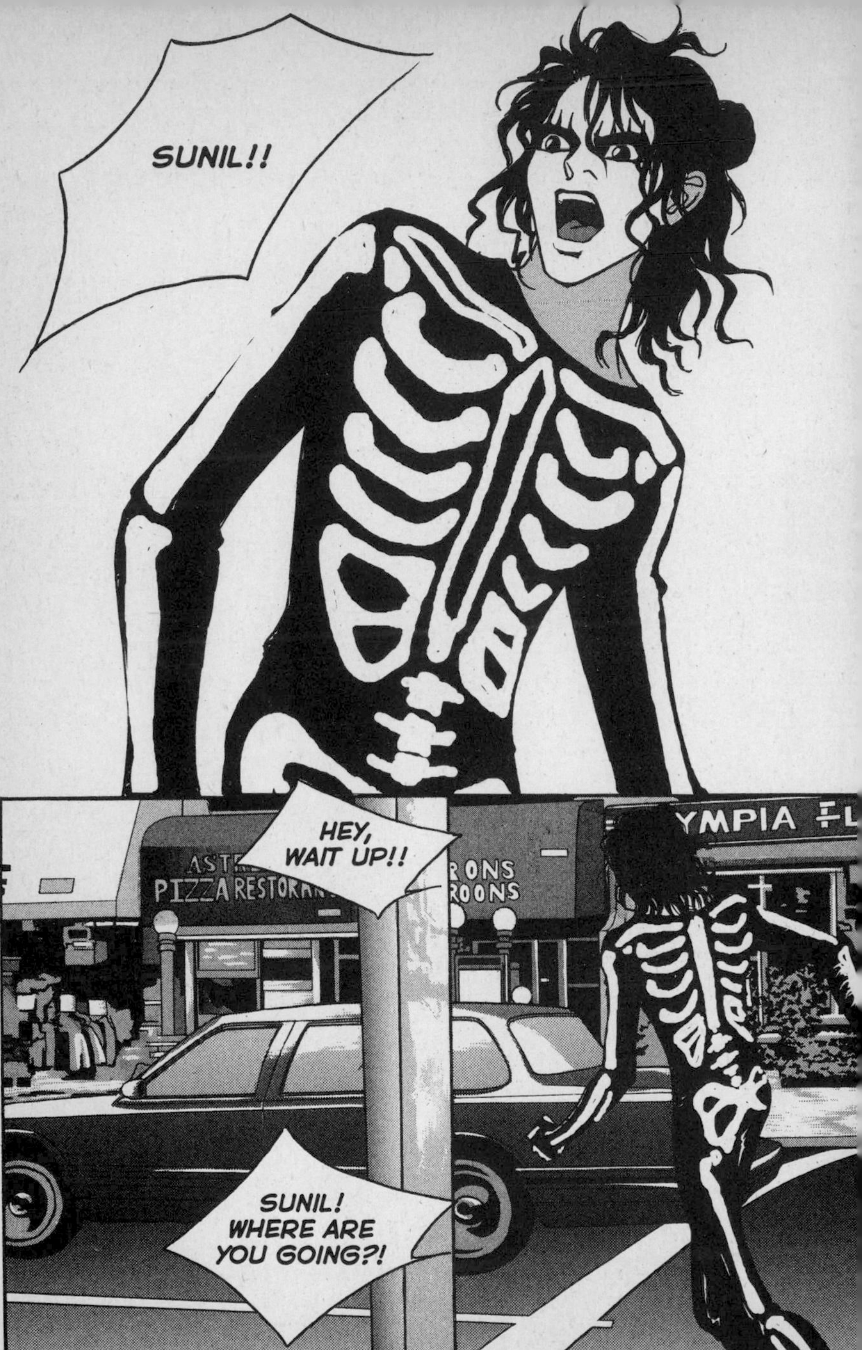
SUNIL!!
HEY, WAIT UP!!
PIZZA
SUNIL! WHERE ARE YOU GOING?!

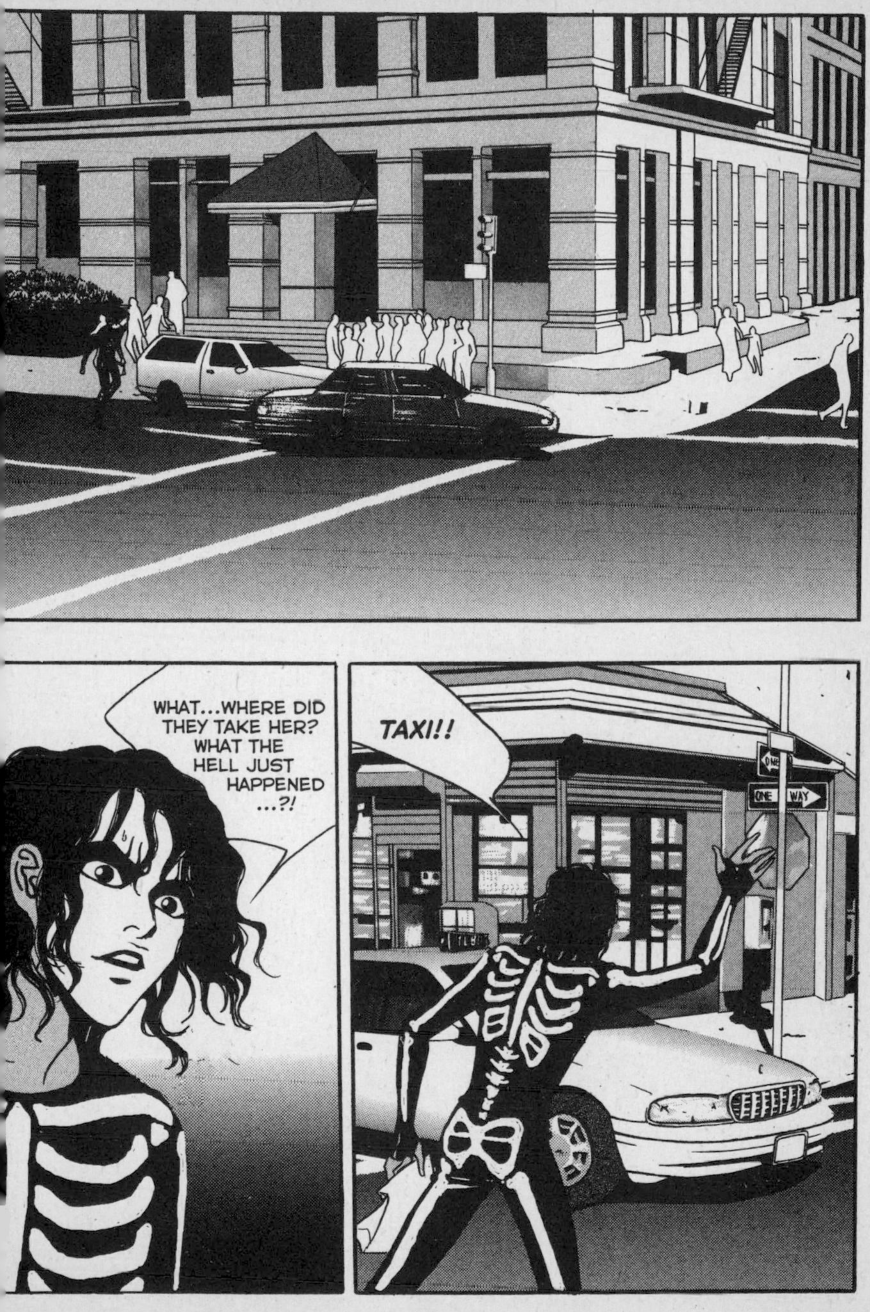
WHAT...WHERE DID THEY TAKE HER? WHAT THE HELL JUST HAPPENED ...?!
TAXI!!
ONE WAY

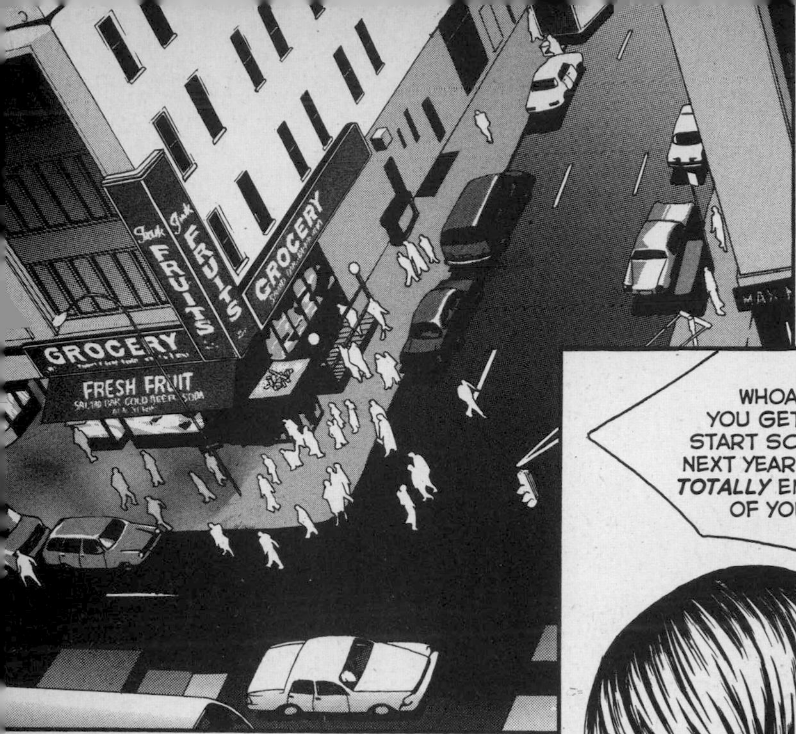
GROCERY
FRUITS
FRUITS
GROCERY
FRESH FRUIT

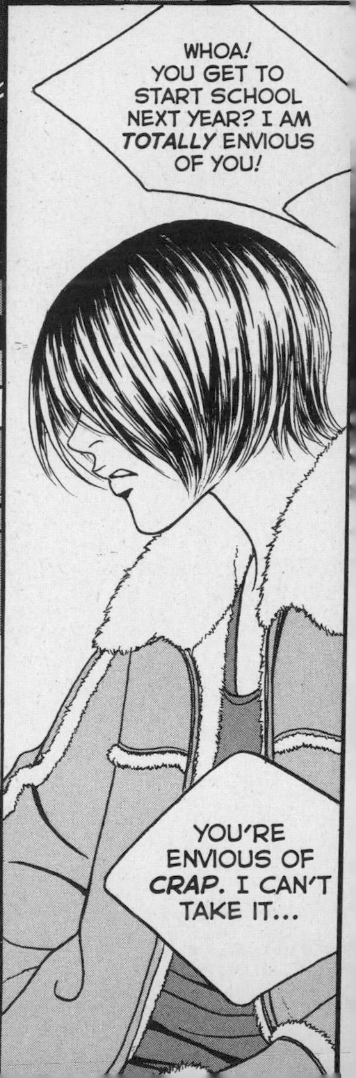
WHOA! YOU GET TO START SCHOOL NEXT YEAR? I AM *TOTALLY* ENVIOUS OF YOU!
YOU'RE ENVIOUS OF *CRAP*. I CAN'T TAKE IT...

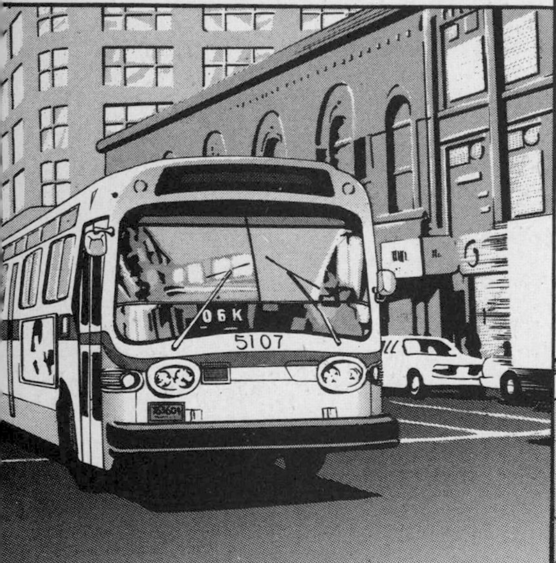
06K
5107

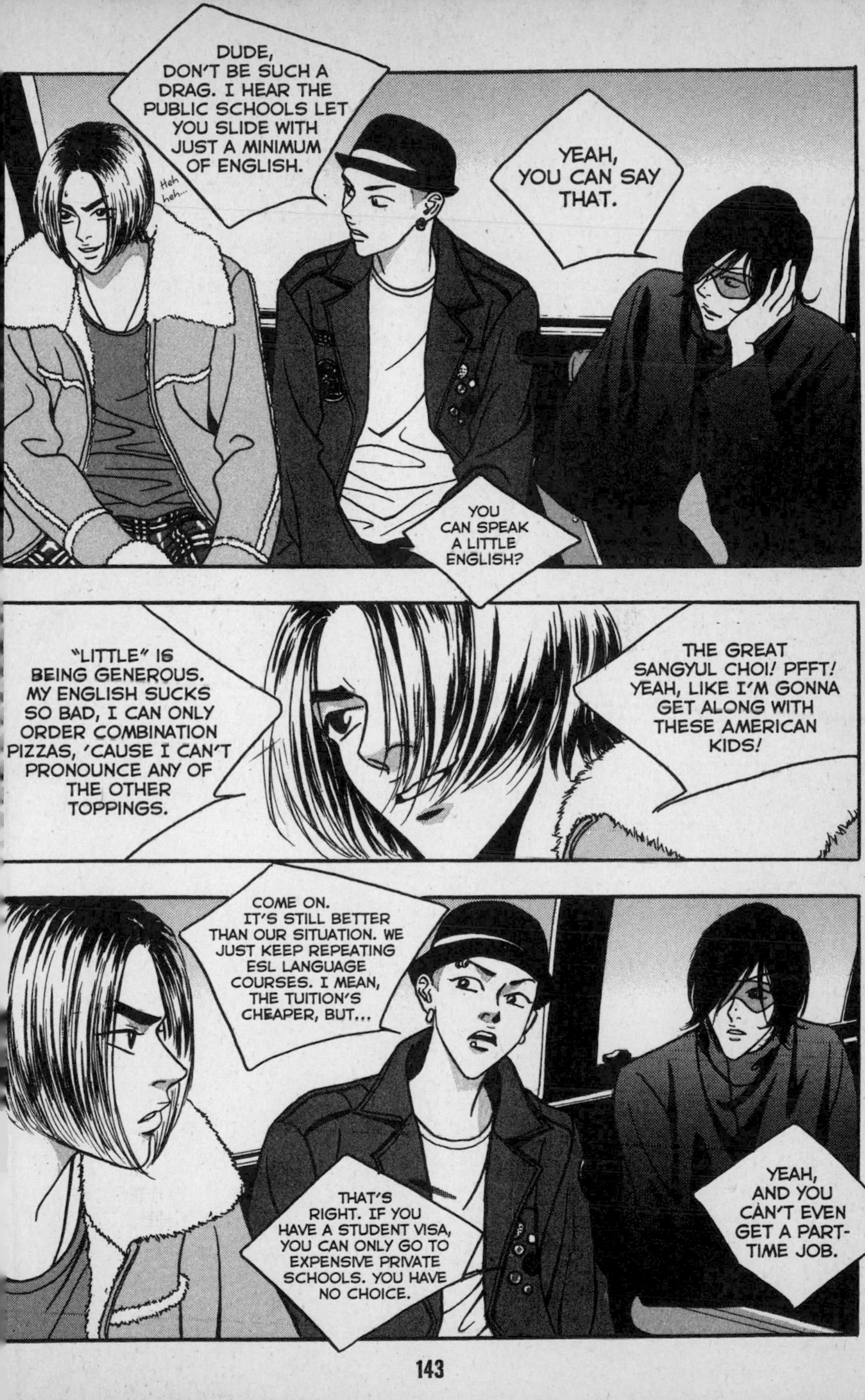
DUDE, DON'T BE SUCH A DRAG. I HEAR THE PUBLIC SCHOOLS LET YOU SLIDE WITH JUST A MINIMUM OF ENGLISH.
Heh heh...
YEAH, YOU CAN SAY THAT.
YOU CAN SPEAK A LITTLE ENGLISH?
"LITTLE" IS BEING GENEROUS. MY ENGLISH SUCKS SO BAD, I CAN ONLY ORDER COMBINATION PIZZAS, 'CAUSE I CAN'T PRONOUNCE ANY OF THE OTHER TOPPINGS.
THE GREAT SANGYUL CHOI! PFFT! YEAH, LIKE I'M GONNA GET ALONG WITH THESE AMERICAN KIDS!
COME ON. IT'S STILL BETTER THAN OUR SITUATION. WE JUST KEEP REPEATING ESL LANGUAGE COURSES. I MEAN, THE TUITION'S CHEAPER, BUT...
THAT'S RIGHT. IF YOU HAVE A STUDENT VISA, YOU CAN ONLY GO TO EXPENSIVE PRIVATE SCHOOLS. YOU HAVE NO CHOICE.
YEAH, AND YOU CAN'T EVEN GET A PART-TIME JOB.

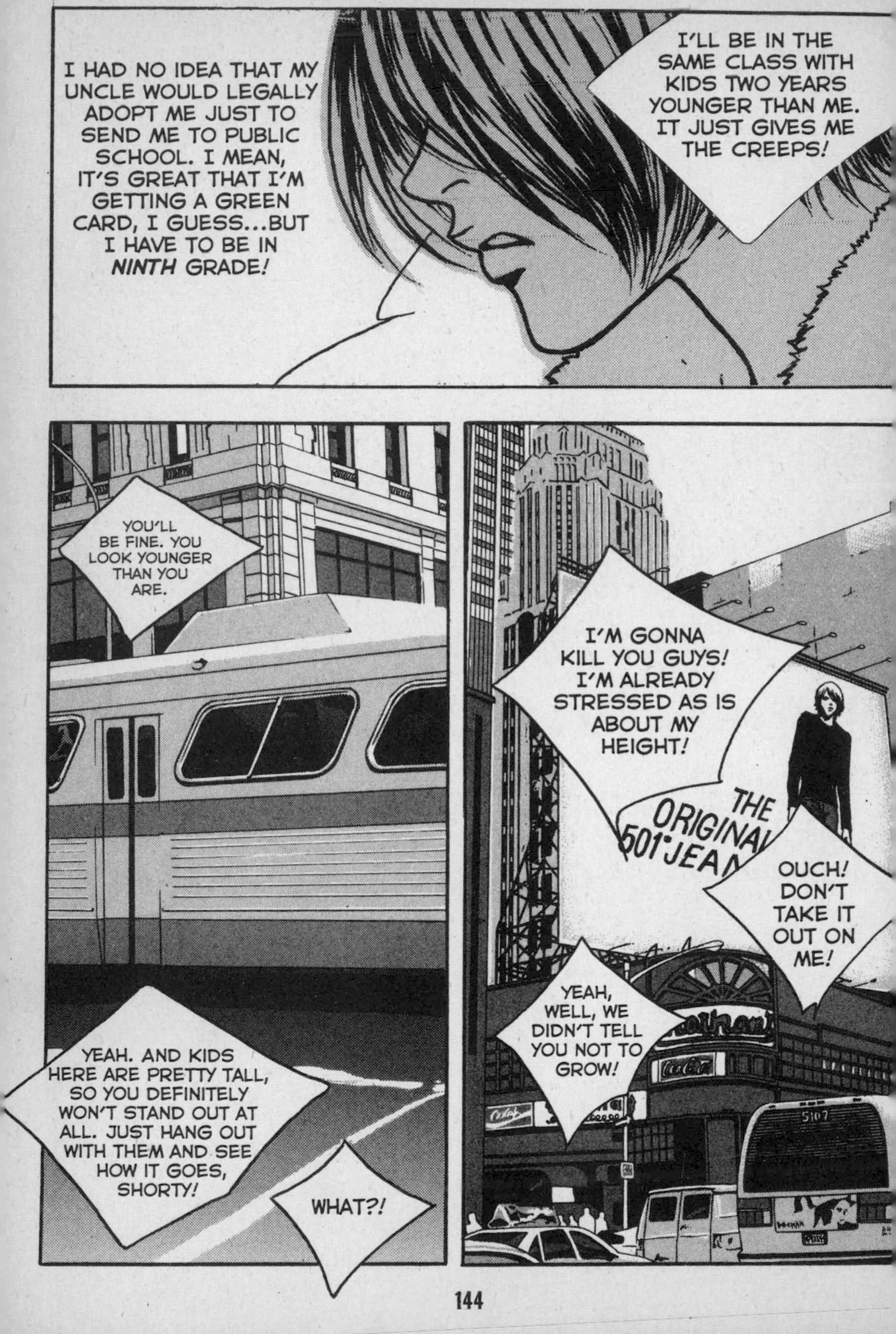
I HAD NO IDEA THAT MY UNCLE WOULD LEGALLY ADOPT ME JUST TO SEND ME TO PUBLIC SCHOOL. I MEAN, IT'S GREAT THAT I'M GETTING A GREEN CARD, I GUESS...BUT I HAVE TO BE IN *NINTH* GRADE!
I'LL BE IN THE SAME CLASS WITH KIDS TWO YEARS YOUNGER THAN ME. IT JUST GIVES ME THE CREEPS!
YOU'LL BE FINE. YOU LOOK YOUNGER THAN YOU ARE.
YEAH. AND KIDS HERE ARE PRETTY TALL, SO YOU DEFINITELY WON'T STAND OUT AT ALL. JUST HANG OUT WITH THEM AND SEE HOW IT GOES, SHORTY!
WHAT?!
I'M GONNA KILL YOU GUYS! I'M ALREADY STRESSED AS IS ABOUT MY HEIGHT!
OUCH! DON'T TAKE IT OUT ON ME!
YEAH, WELL, WE DIDN'T TELL YOU NOT TO GROW!

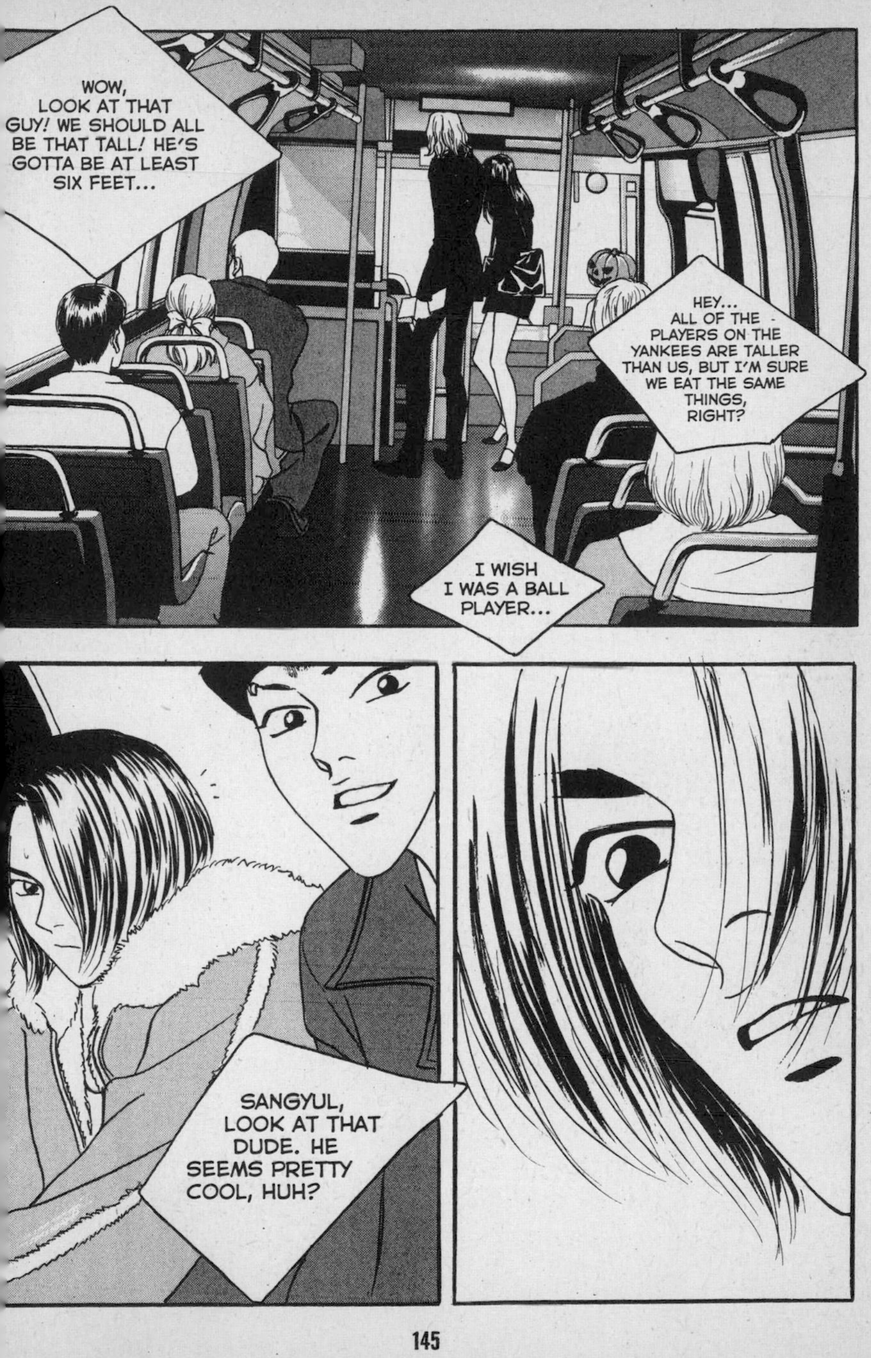
WOW, LOOK AT THAT GUY! WE SHOULD ALL BE THAT TALL! HE'S GOTTA BE AT LEAST SIX FEET...
HEY... ALL OF THE PLAYERS ON THE YANKEES ARE TALLER THAN US, BUT I'M SURE WE EAT THE SAME THINGS, RIGHT?
I WISH I WAS A BALL PLAYER...
SANGYUL, LOOK AT THAT DUDE. HE SEEMS PRETTY COOL, HUH?

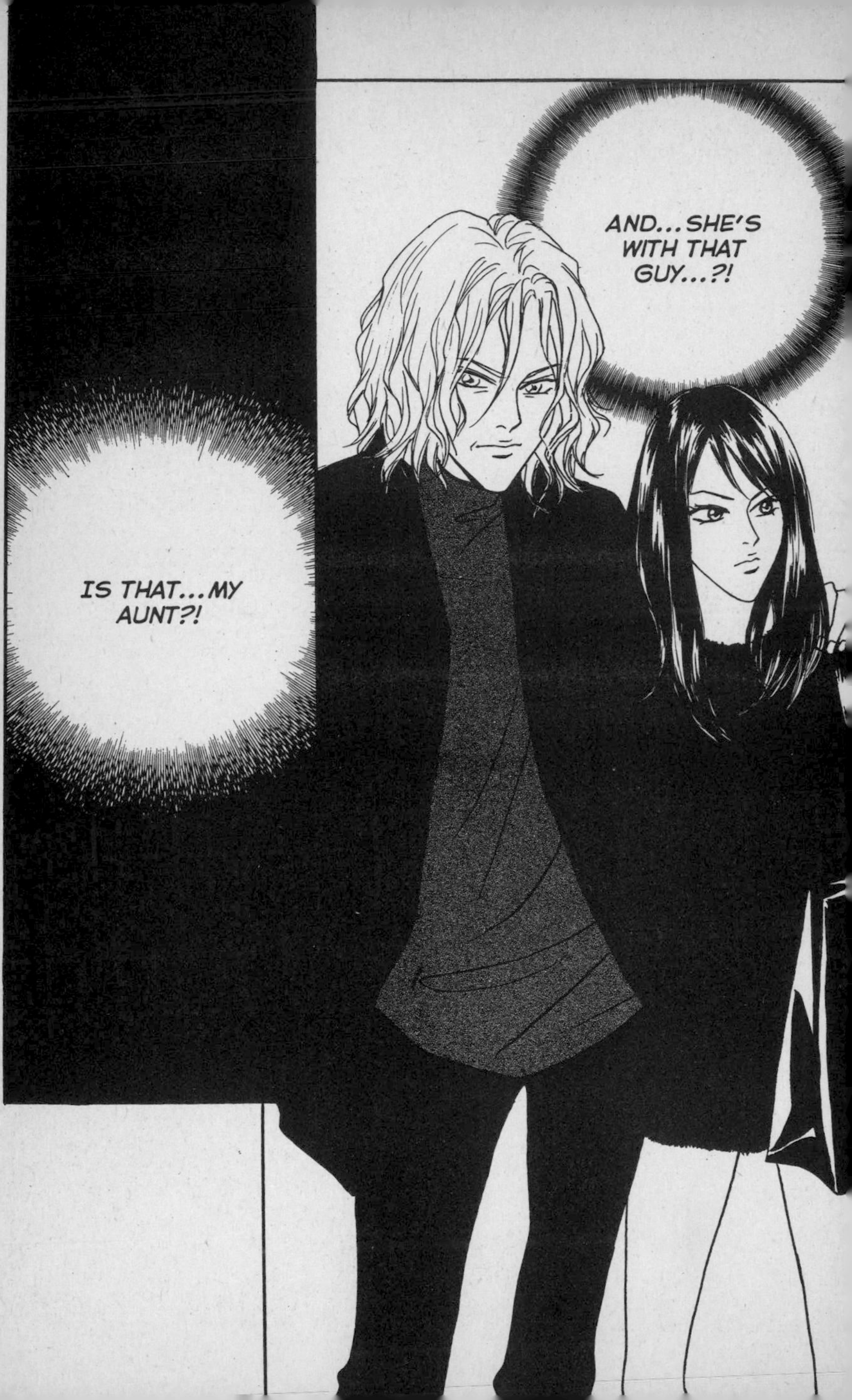
IS THAT...MY AUNT?!
AND...SHE'S WITH THAT GUY...?!

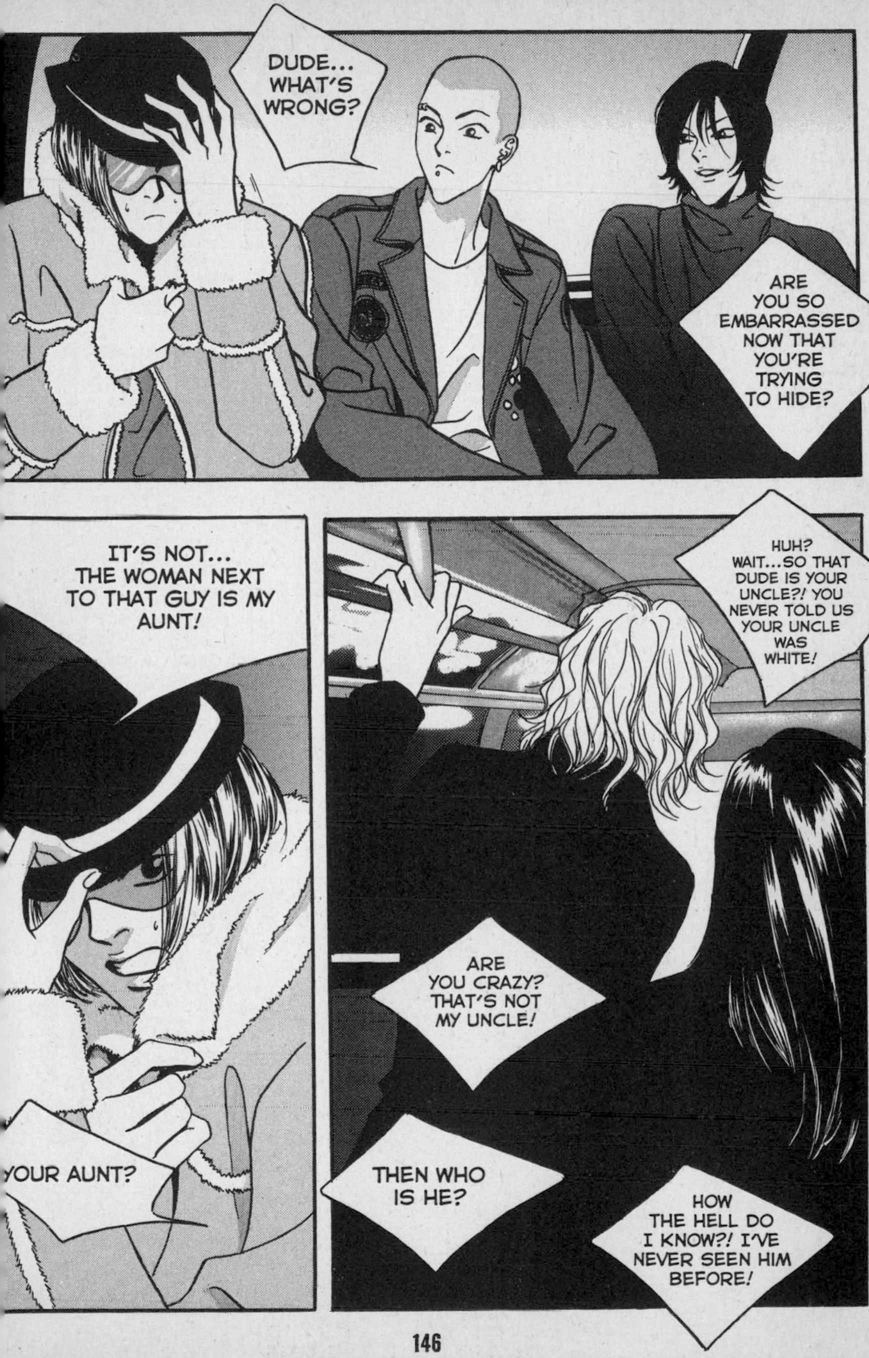
DUDE... WHAT'S WRONG?
ARE YOU SO EMBARRASSED NOW THAT YOU'RE TRYING TO HIDE?
IT'S NOT... THE WOMAN NEXT TO THAT GUY IS MY AUNT!
YOUR AUNT?
HUH? WAIT...SO THAT DUDE IS YOUR UNCLE?! YOU NEVER TOLD US YOUR UNCLE WAS WHITE!
ARE YOU CRAZY? THAT'S NOT MY UNCLE!
THEN WHO IS HE?
HOW THE HELL DO I KNOW?! I'VE NEVER SEEN HIM BEFORE!

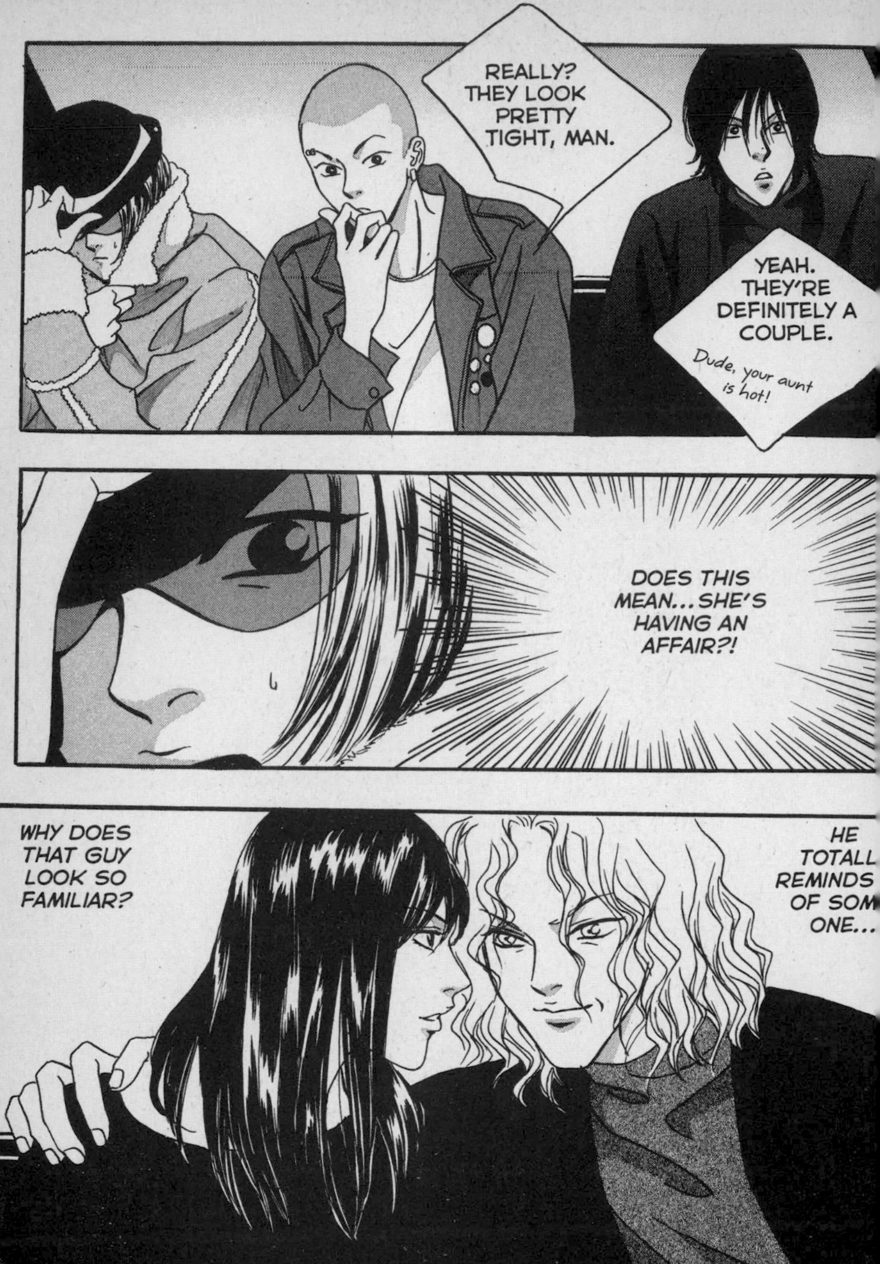
REALLY? THEY LOOK PRETTY TIGHT, MAN.
YEAH. THEY'RE DEFINITELY A COUPLE.
Dude, your aunt is hot!
DOES THIS MEAN...SHE'S HAVING AN AFFAIR?!
HE TOTALL REMINDS OF SOM ONE...
WHY DOES THAT GUY LOOK SO FAMILIAR?

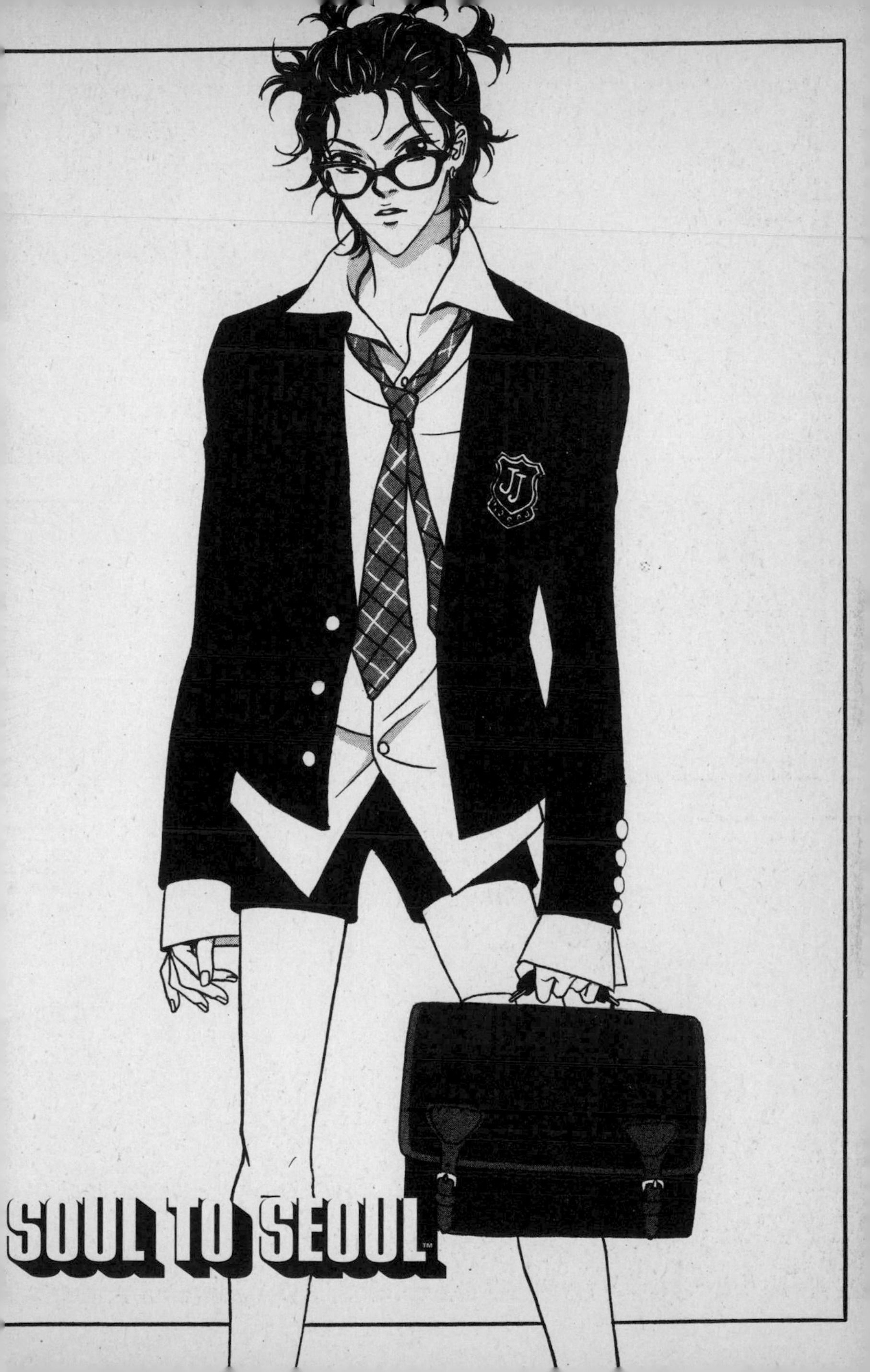
SOUL TO SEOUL™

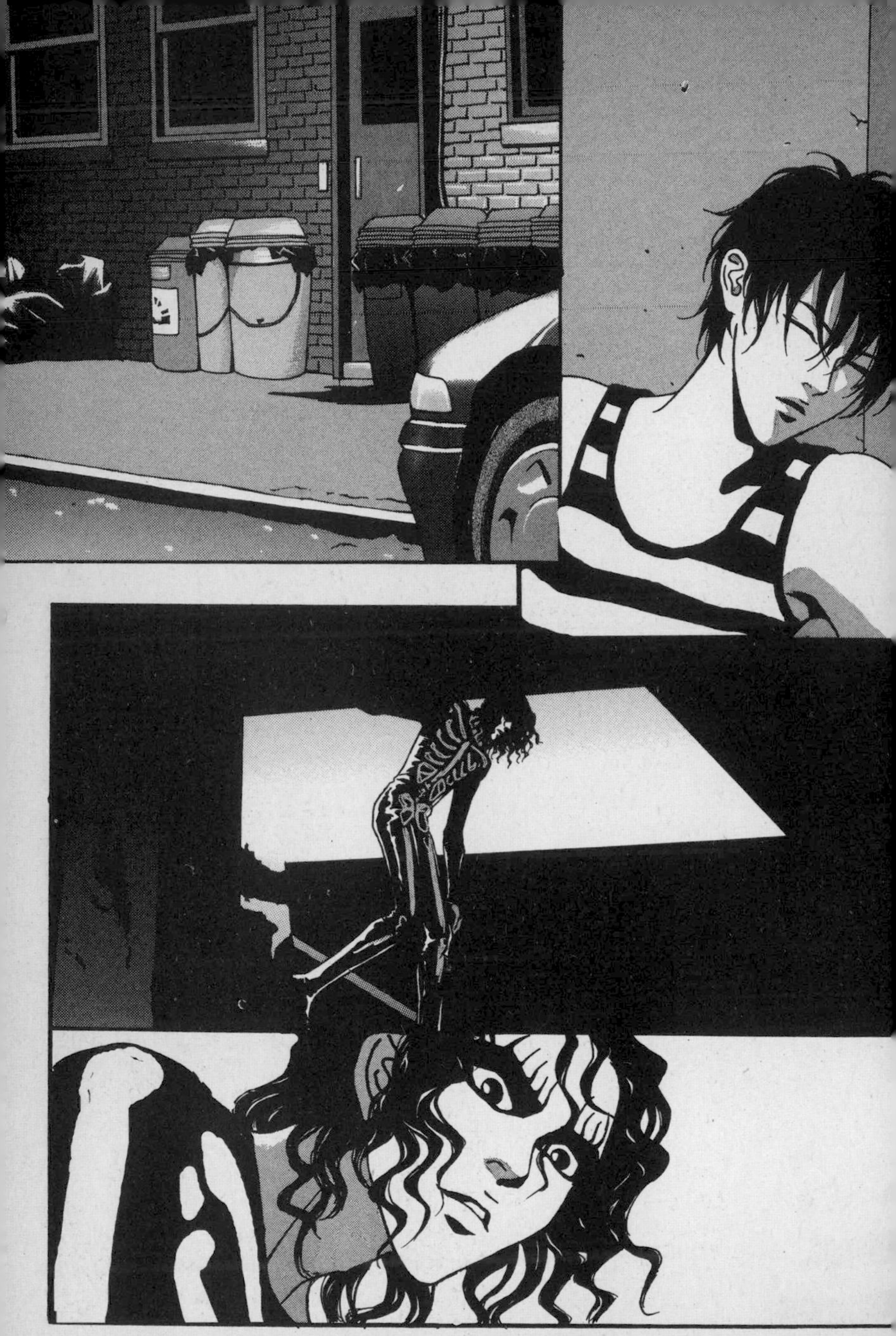

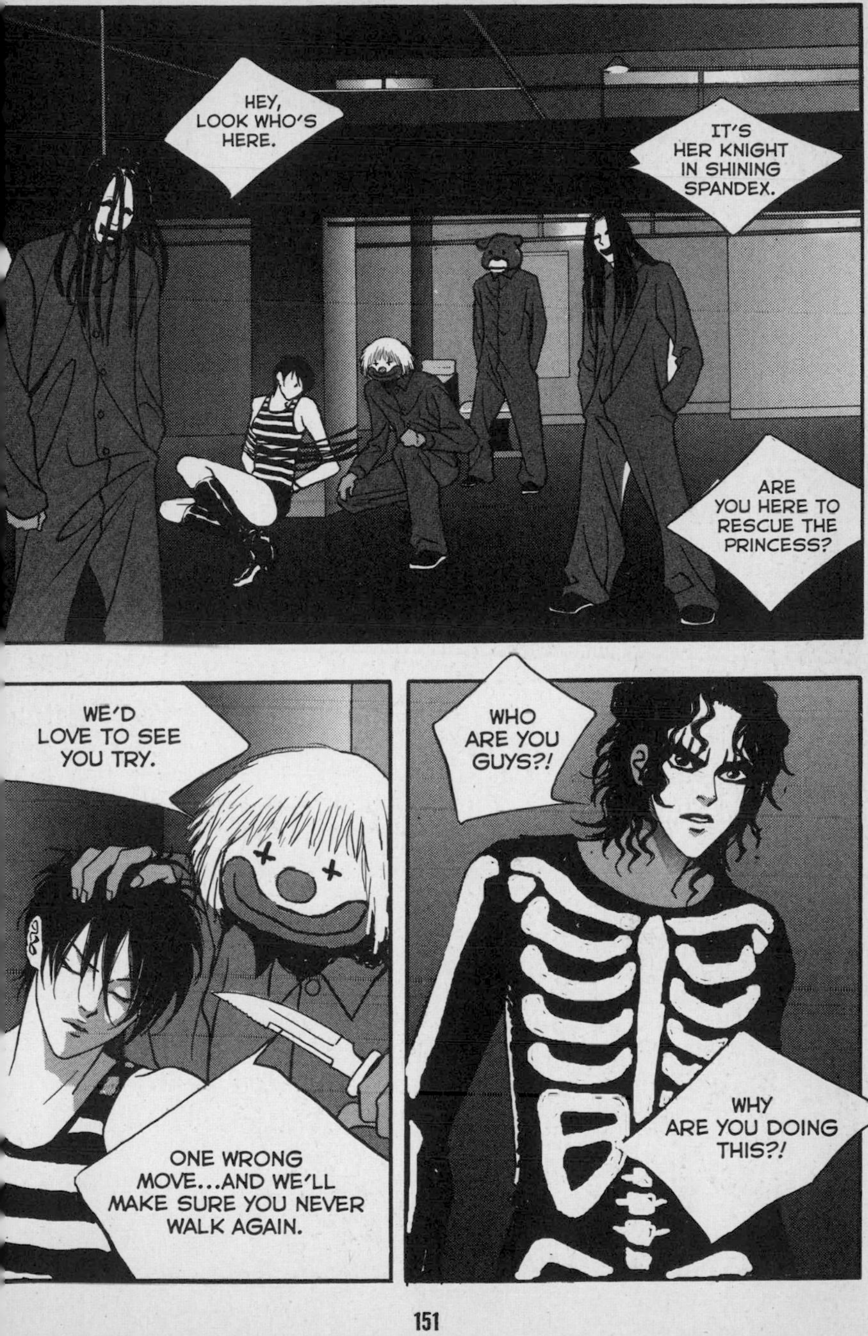
HEY, LOOK WHO'S HERE.
IT'S HER KNIGHT IN SHINING SPANDEX.
ARE YOU HERE TO RESCUE THE PRINCESS?
WE'D LOVE TO SEE YOU TRY.
ONE WRONG MOVE...AND WE'LL MAKE SURE YOU NEVER WALK AGAIN.
WHO ARE YOU GUYS?!
WHY ARE YOU DOING THIS?!

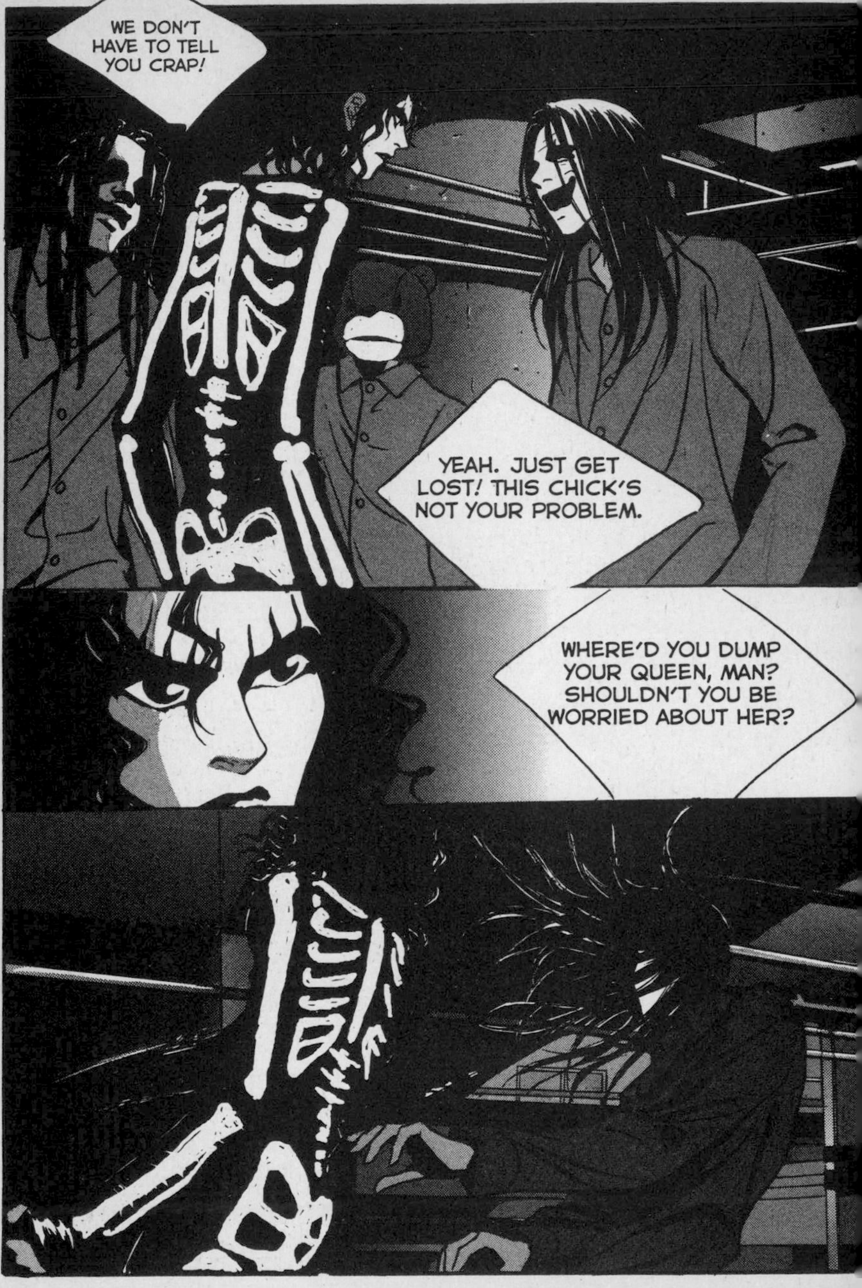
WE DON'T HAVE TO TELL YOU CRAP!
YEAH. JUST GET LOST! THIS CHICK'S NOT YOUR PROBLEM.
WHERE'D YOU DUMP YOUR QUEEN, MAN? SHOULDN'T YOU BE WORRIED ABOUT HER?

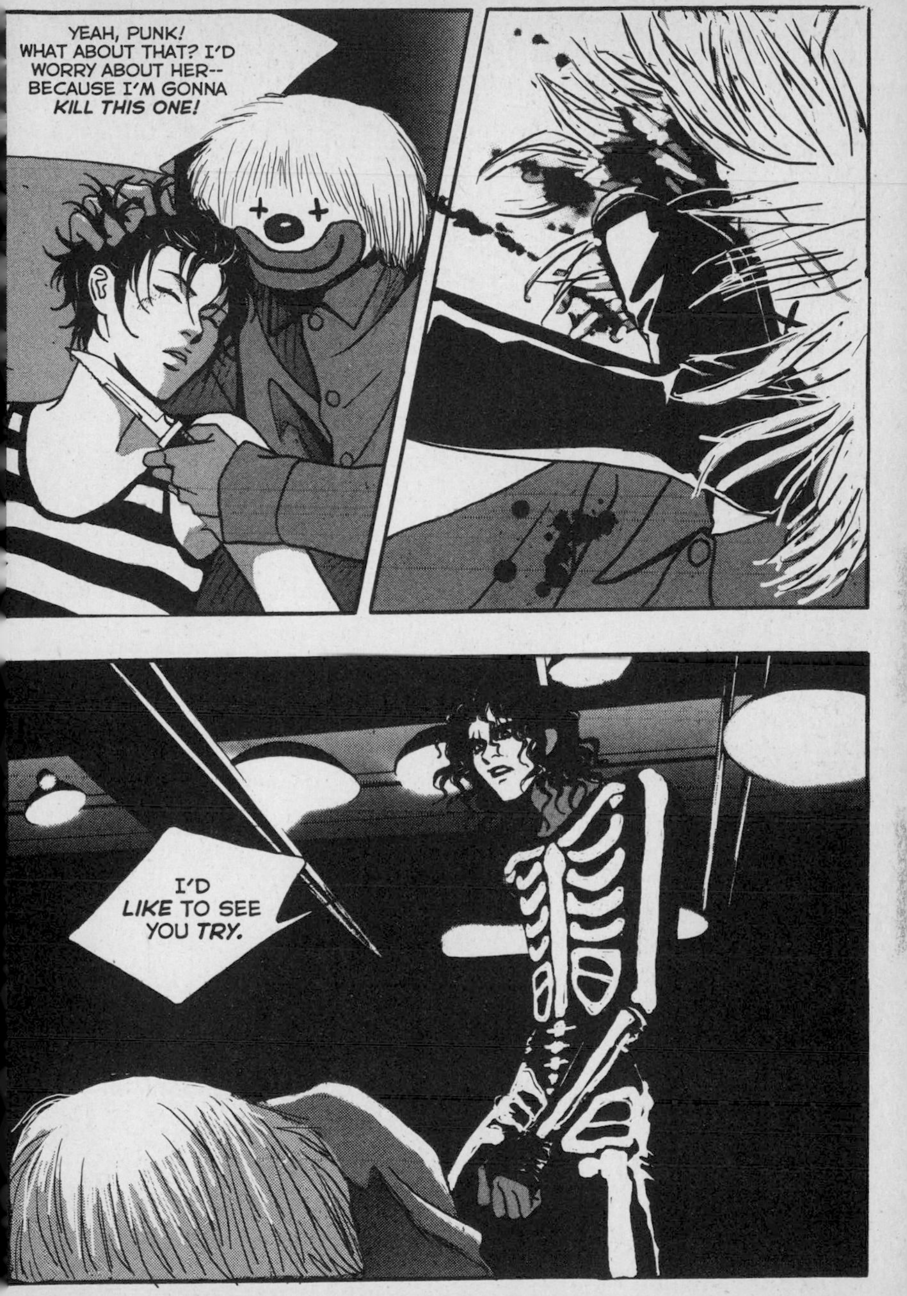
YEAH, PUNK! WHAT ABOUT THAT? I'D WORRY ABOUT HER-- BECAUSE I'M GONNA KILL THIS ONE!
I'D LIKE TO SEE YOU TRY.

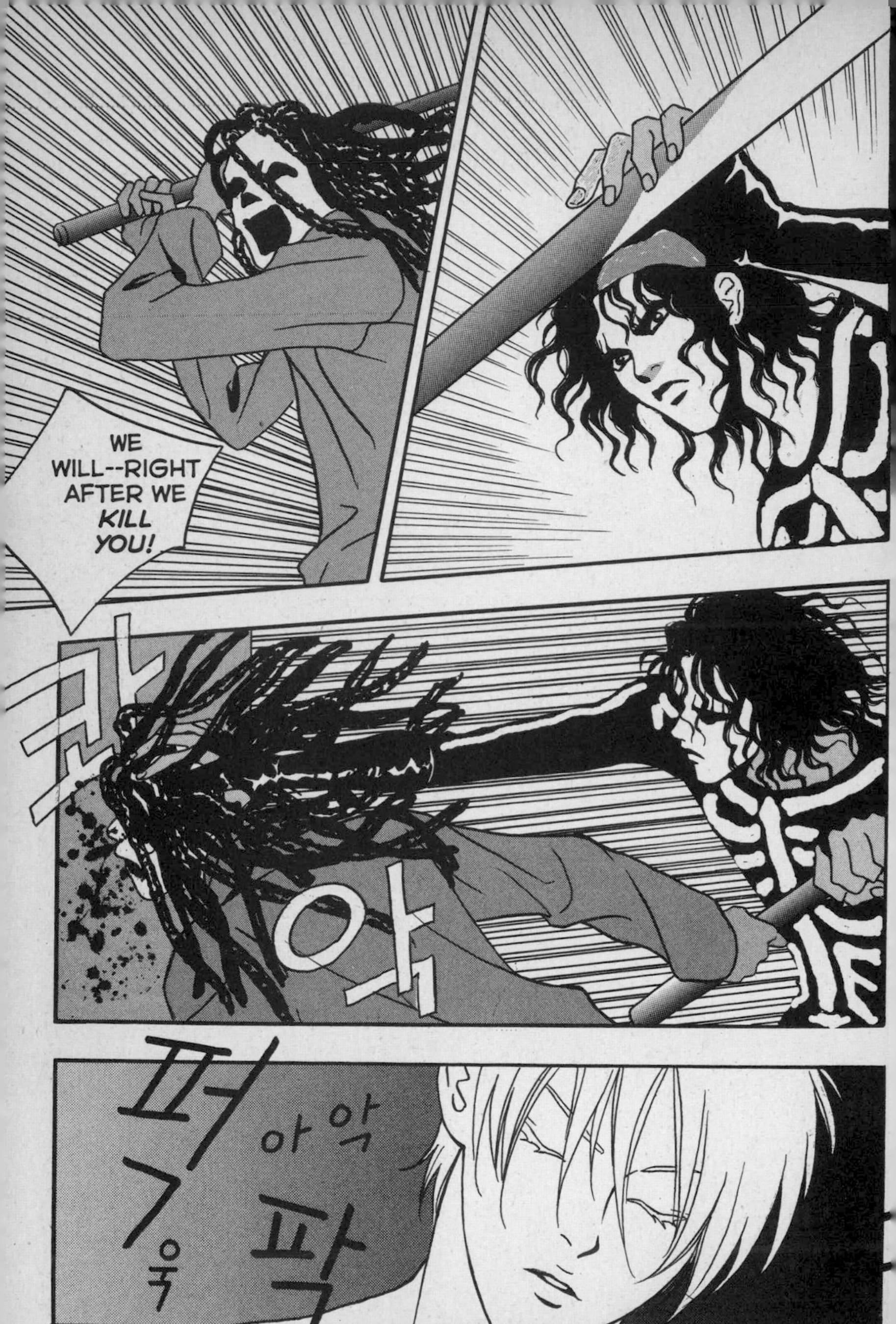
WE WILL--RIGHT AFTER WE KILL YOU!
아악

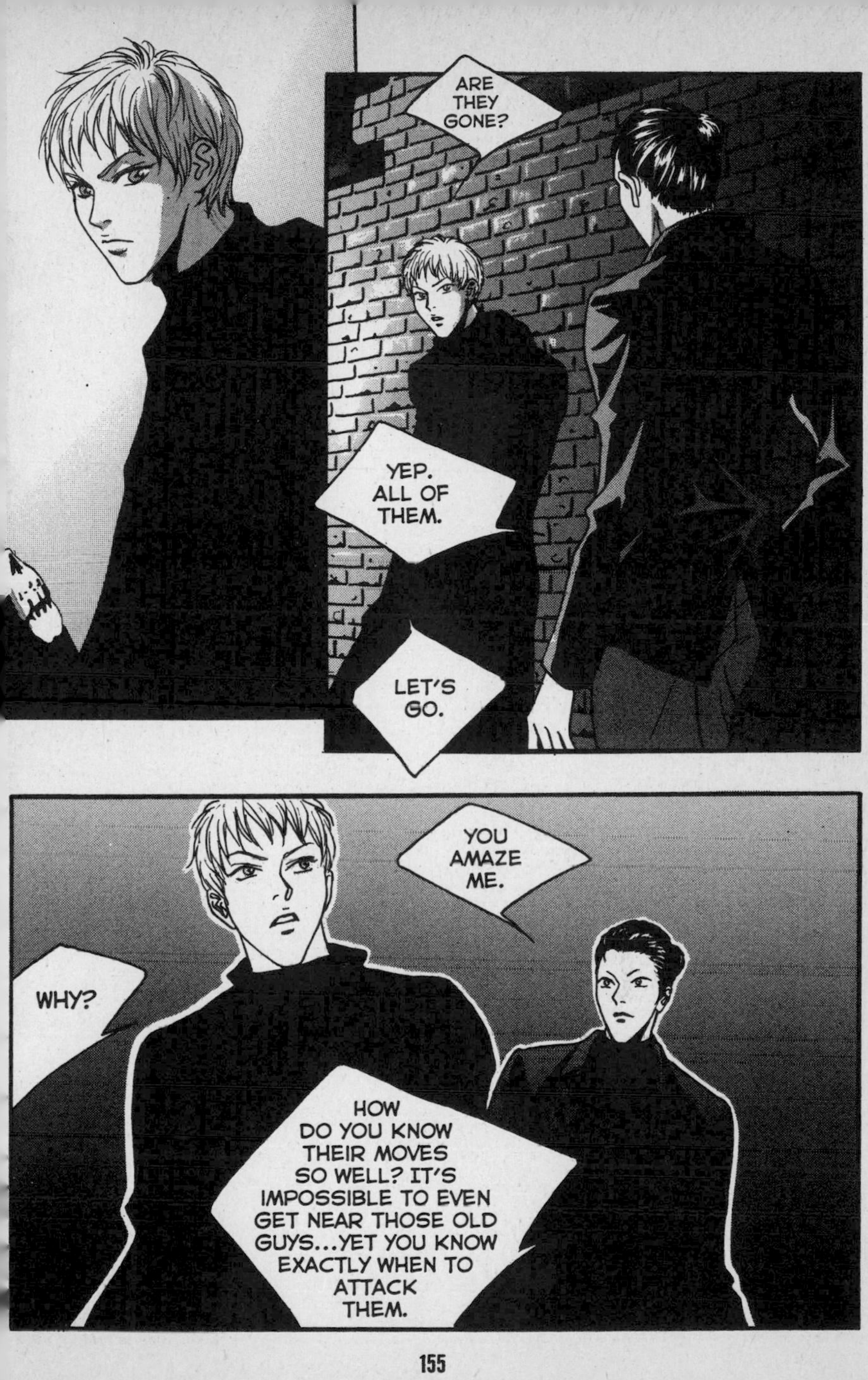
ARE THEY GONE?
YEP. ALL OF THEM.
LET'S GO.
YOU AMAZE ME.
WHY?
HOW DO YOU KNOW THEIR MOVES SO WELL? IT'S IMPOSSIBLE TO EVEN GET NEAR THOSE OLD GUYS...YET YOU KNOW EXACTLY WHEN TO ATTACK THEM.

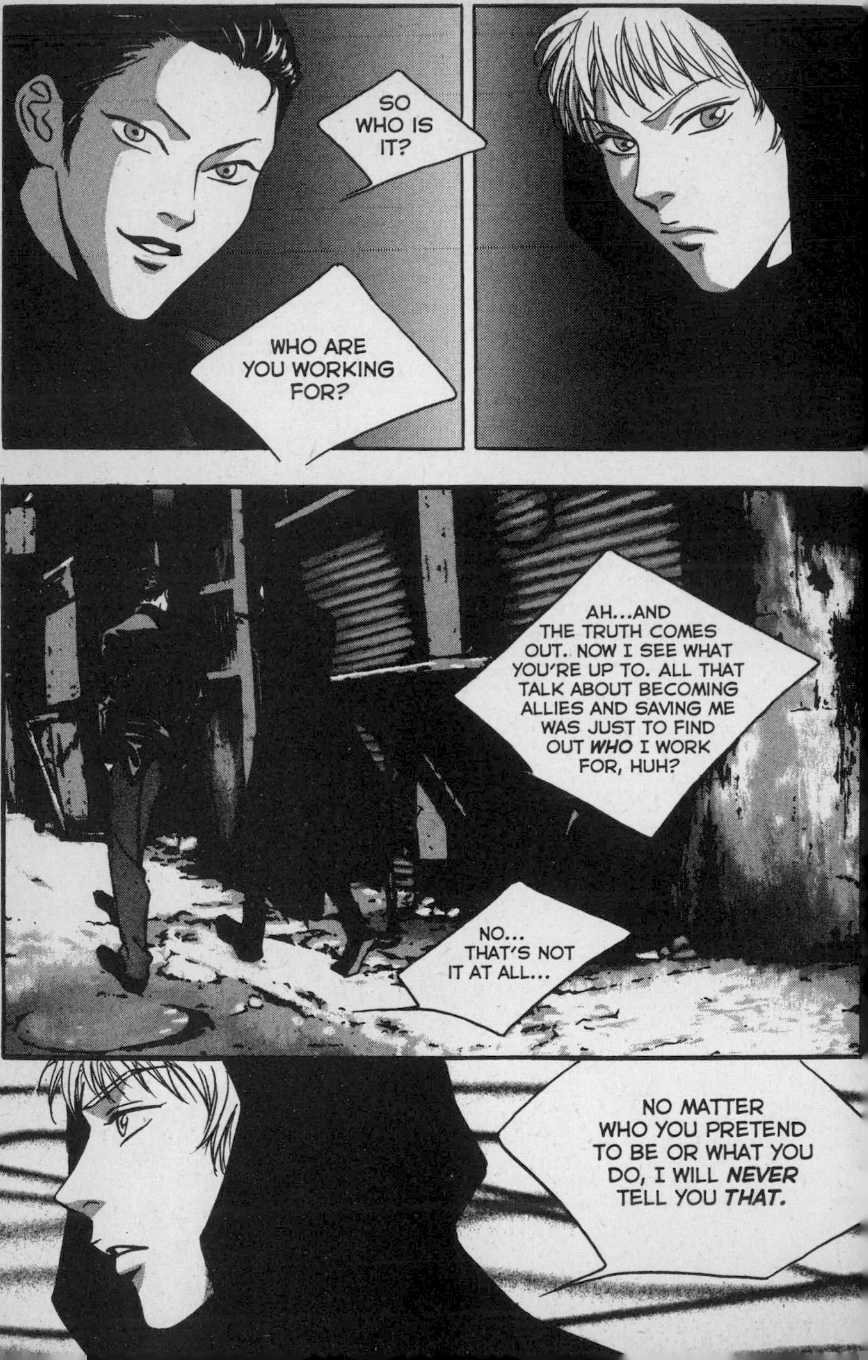
SO WHO IS IT?
WHO ARE YOU WORKING FOR?
AH...AND THE TRUTH COMES OUT.. NOW I SEE WHAT YOU'RE UP TO. ALL THAT TALK ABOUT BECOMING ALLIES AND SAVING ME WAS JUST TO FIND OUT *WHO* I WORK FOR, HUH?
NO... THAT'S NOT IT AT ALL...
NO MATTER WHO YOU PRETEND TO BE OR WHAT YOU DO, I WILL ***NEVER*** TELL YOU ***THAT.***

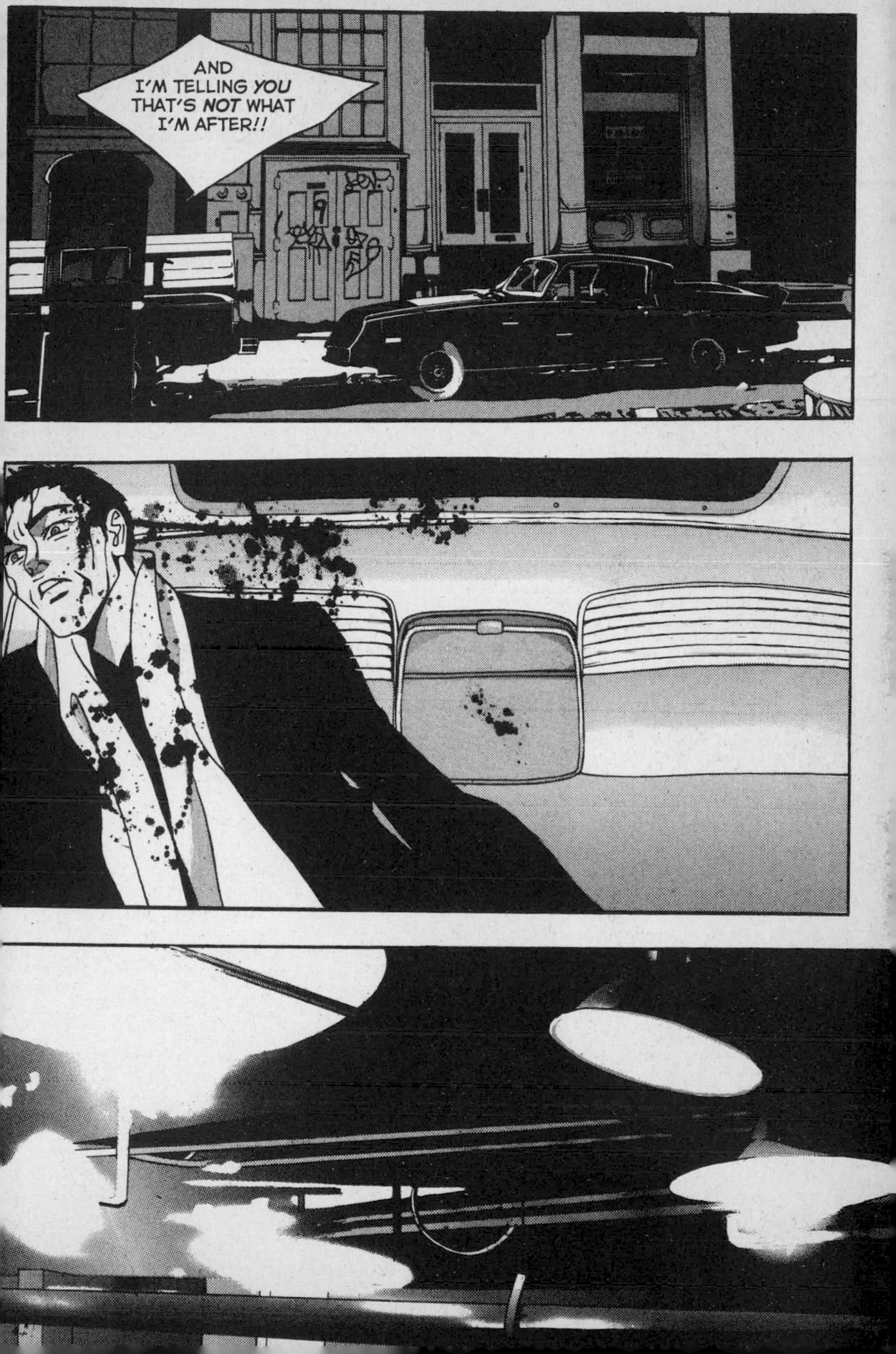
AND I'M TELLING *YOU* THAT'S ***NOT*** WHAT I'M AFTER!!

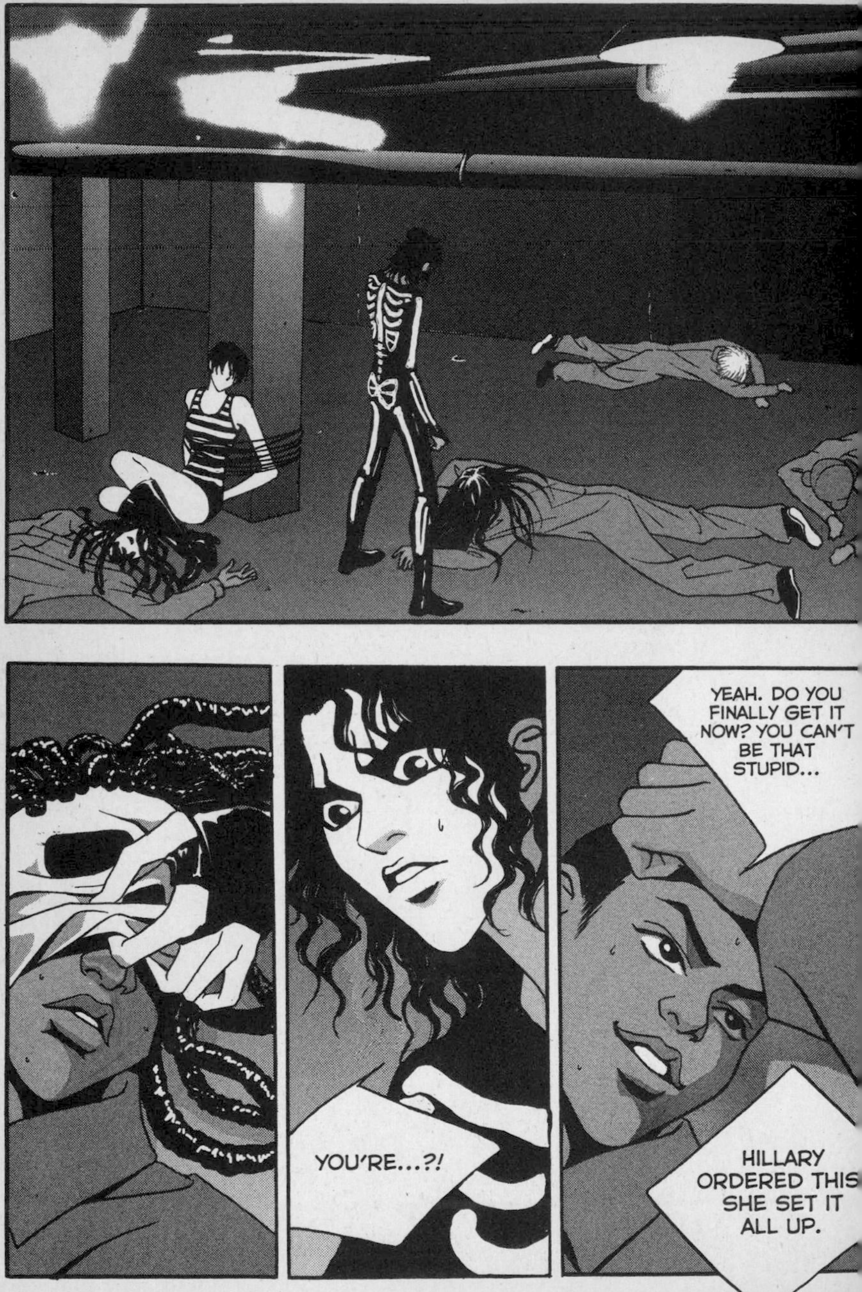
YOU'RE...?!
YEAH. DO YOU FINALLY GET IT NOW? YOU CAN'T BE THAT STUPID...
HILLARY ORDERED THIS SHE SET IT ALL UP.

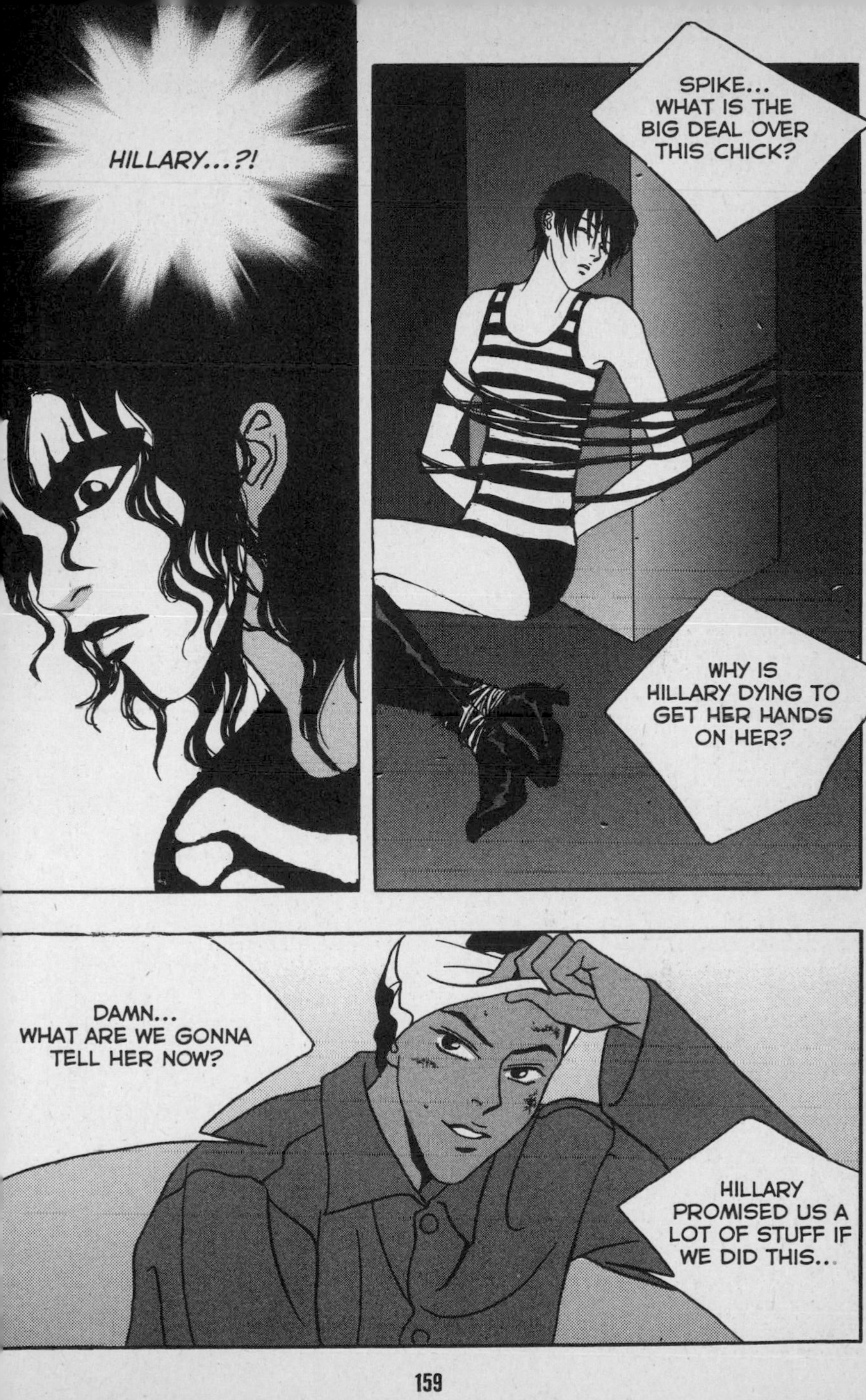
SPIKE... WHAT IS THE BIG DEAL OVER THIS CHICK?
WHY IS HILLARY DYING TO GET HER HANDS ON HER?
HILLARY...?!
HILLARY PROMISED US A LOT OF STUFF IF WE DID THIS...
DAMN... WHAT ARE WE GONNA TELL HER NOW?

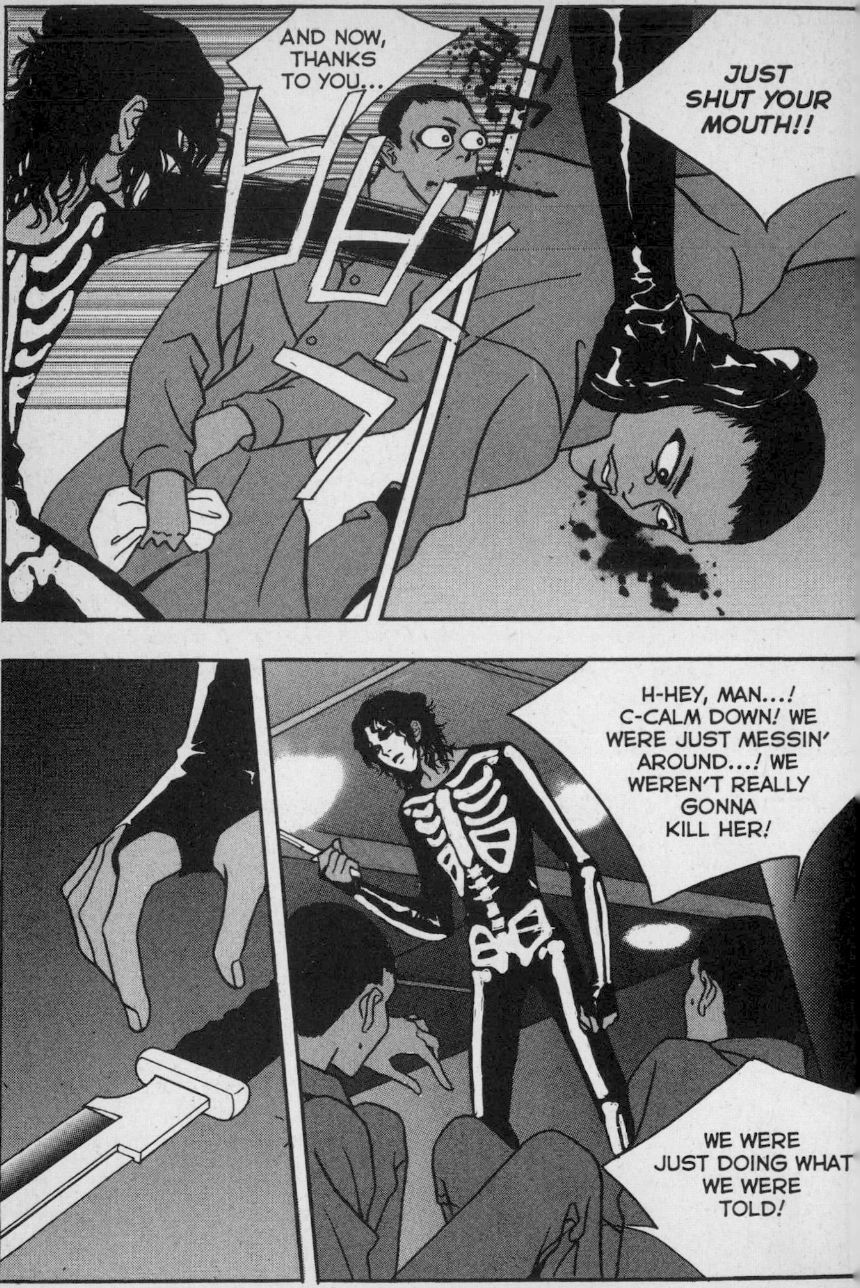
JUST SHUT YOUR MOUTH!!
AND NOW, THANKS TO YOU...
H-HEY, MAN...! C-CALM DOWN! WE WERE JUST MESSIN' AROUND...! WE WEREN'T REALLY GONNA KILL HER!
WE WERE JUST DOING WHAT WE WERE TOLD!

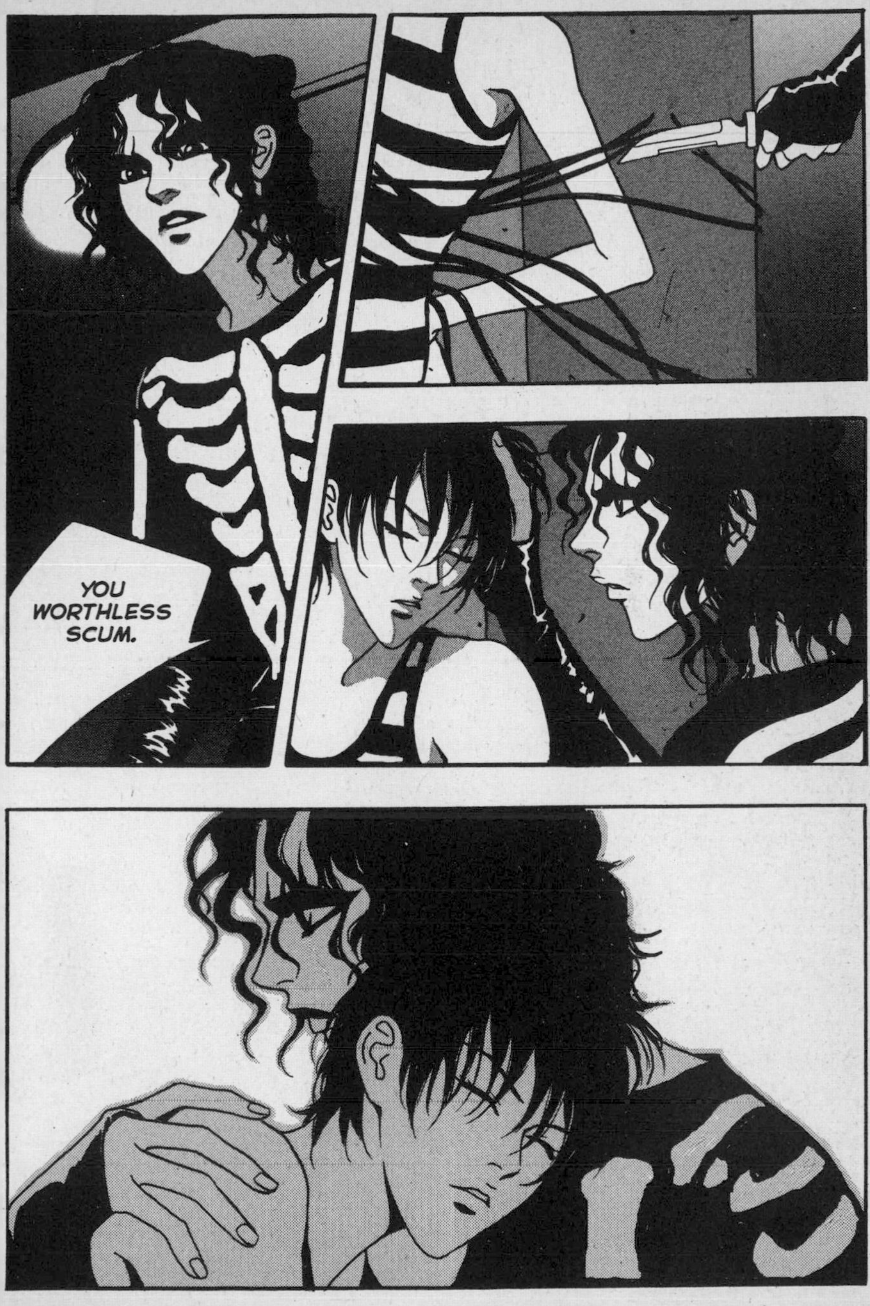
YOU WORTHLESS SCUM.

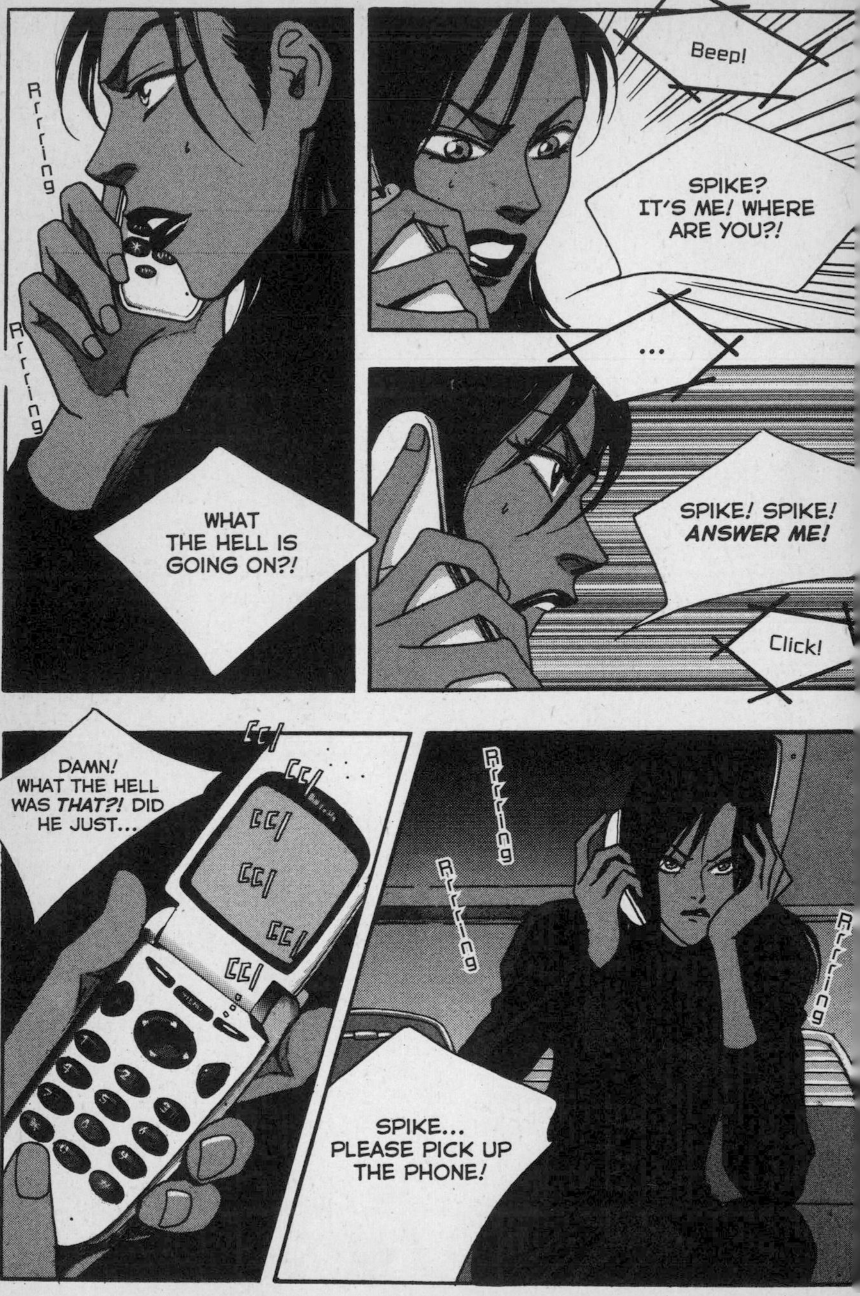
Beep!
SPIKE? IT'S ME! WHERE ARE YOU?!
...
SPIKE! SPIKE! ANSWER ME!
Click!
Rrrring
Rrrring
WHAT THE HELL IS GOING ON?!
Rrrring
Rrrring
Rrrring
SPIKE... PLEASE PICK UP THE PHONE!
DAMN! WHAT THE HELL WAS THAT?! DID HE JUST...

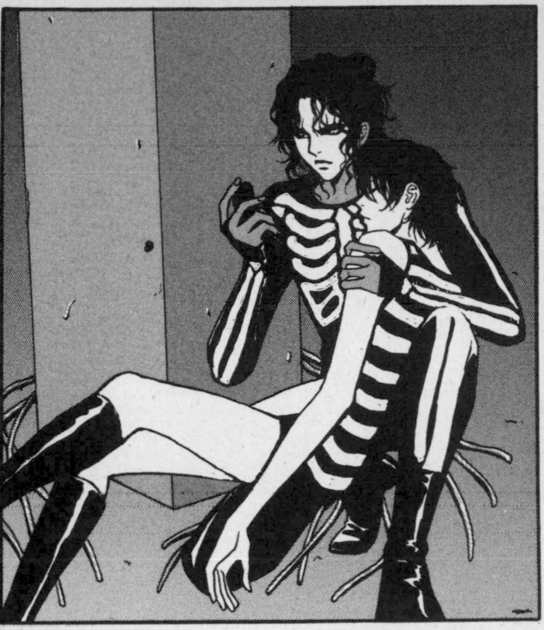

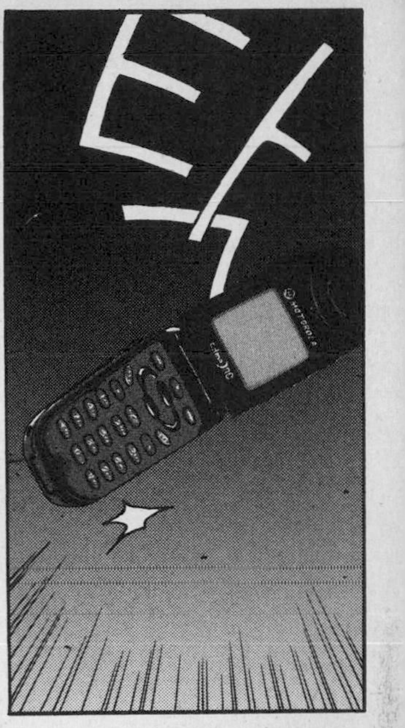
탁

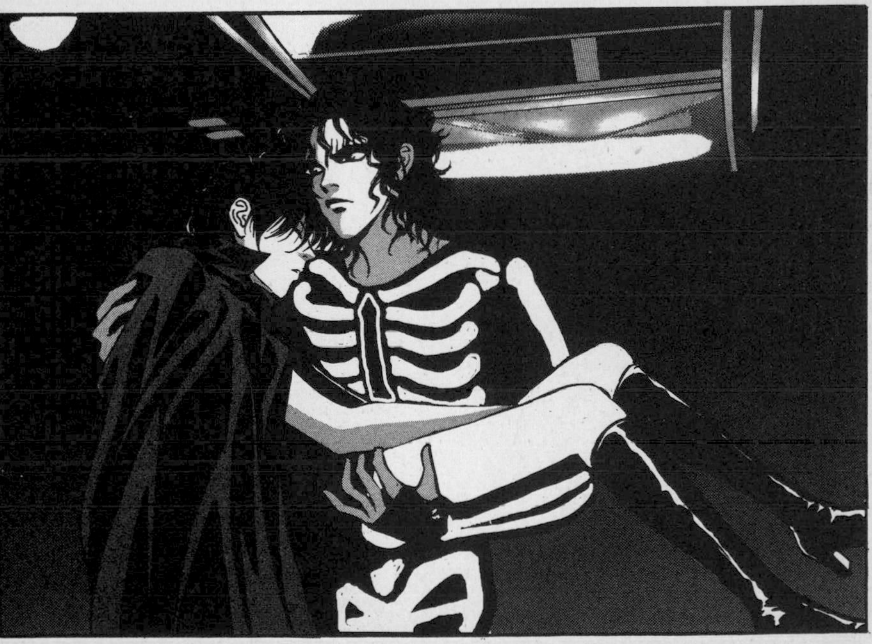

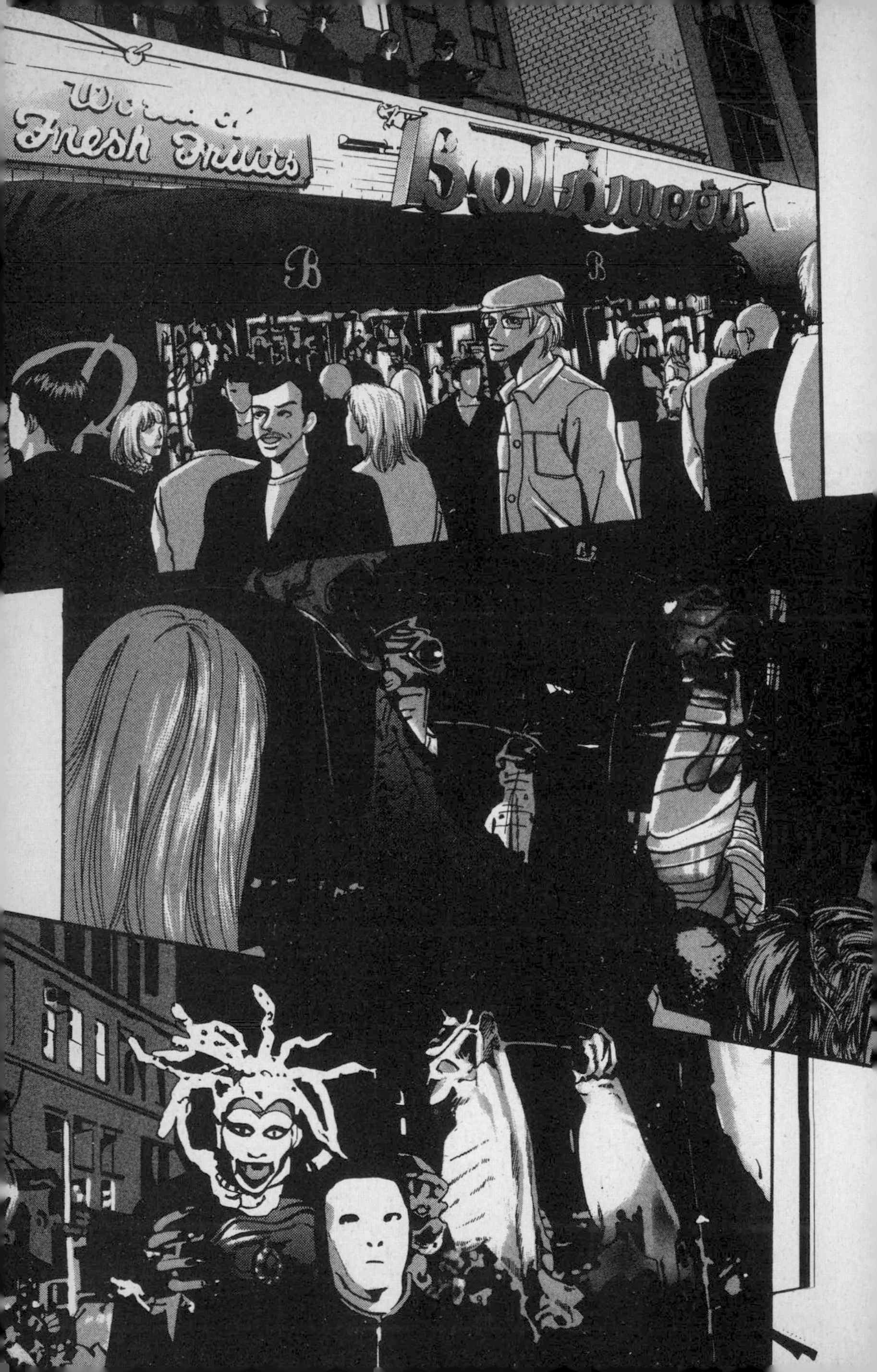
Fresh Fruits

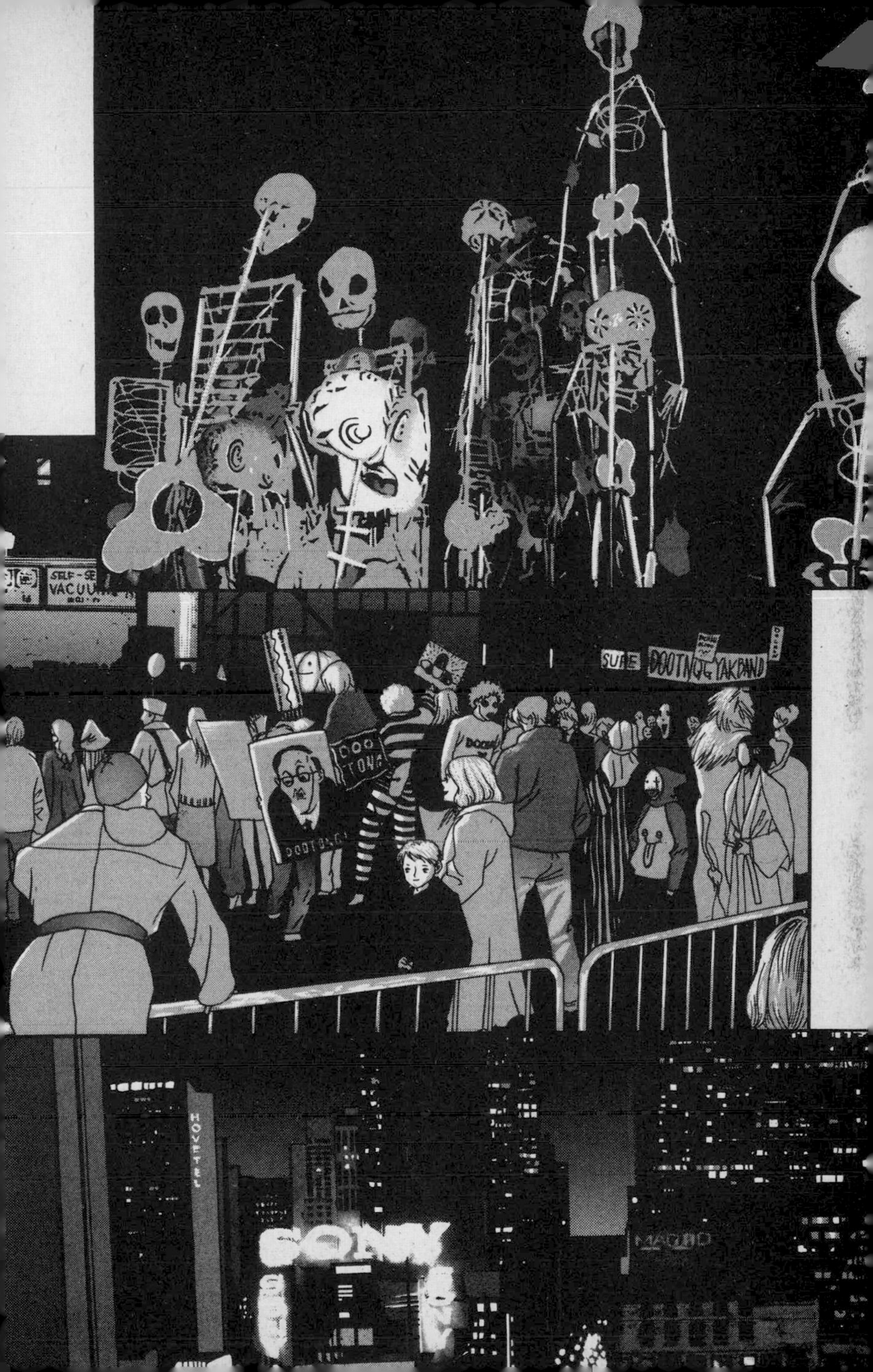
SURE
DOO TONG
HOVETEL
SONY

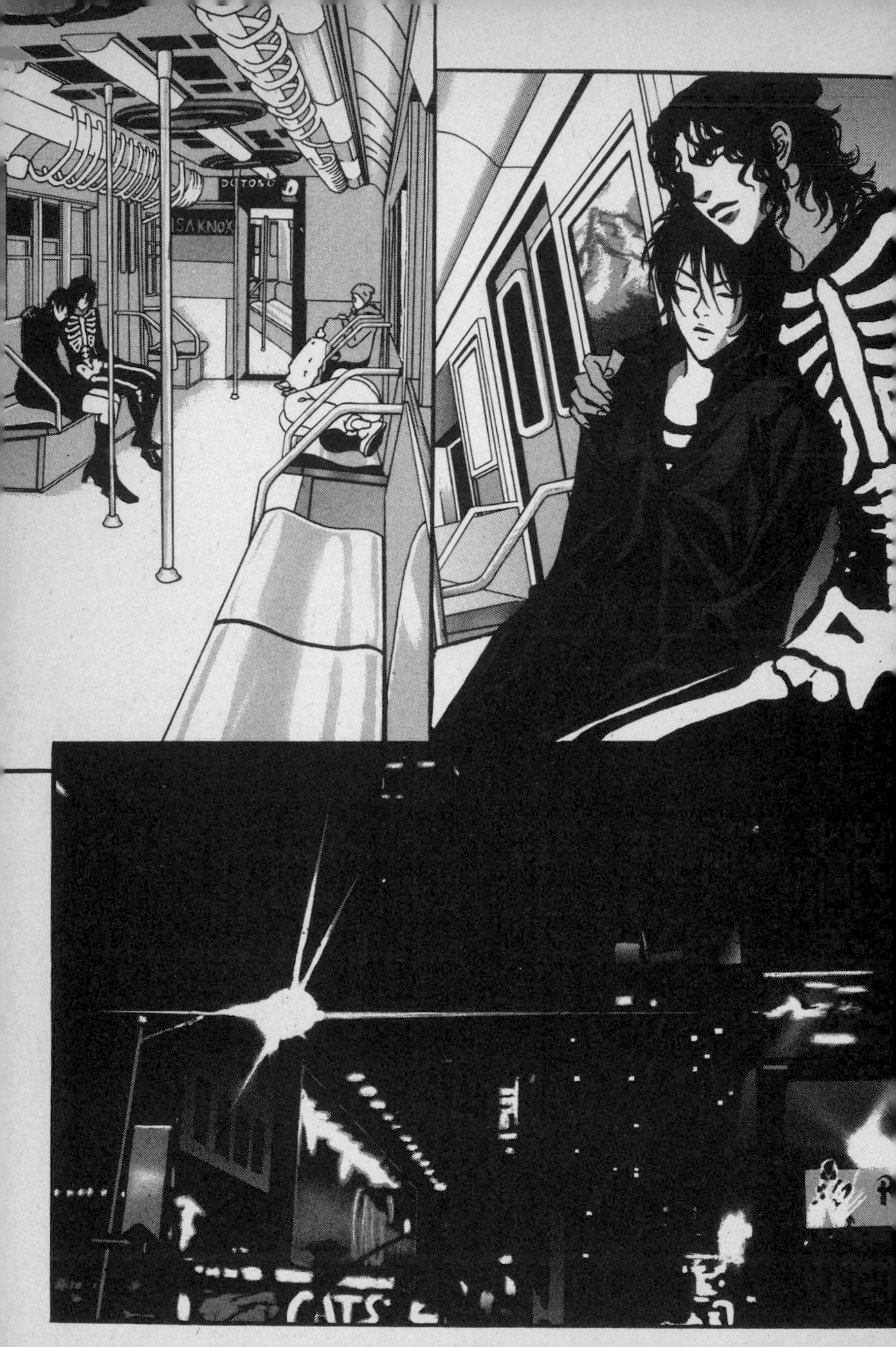
ISA KNOX
CATS

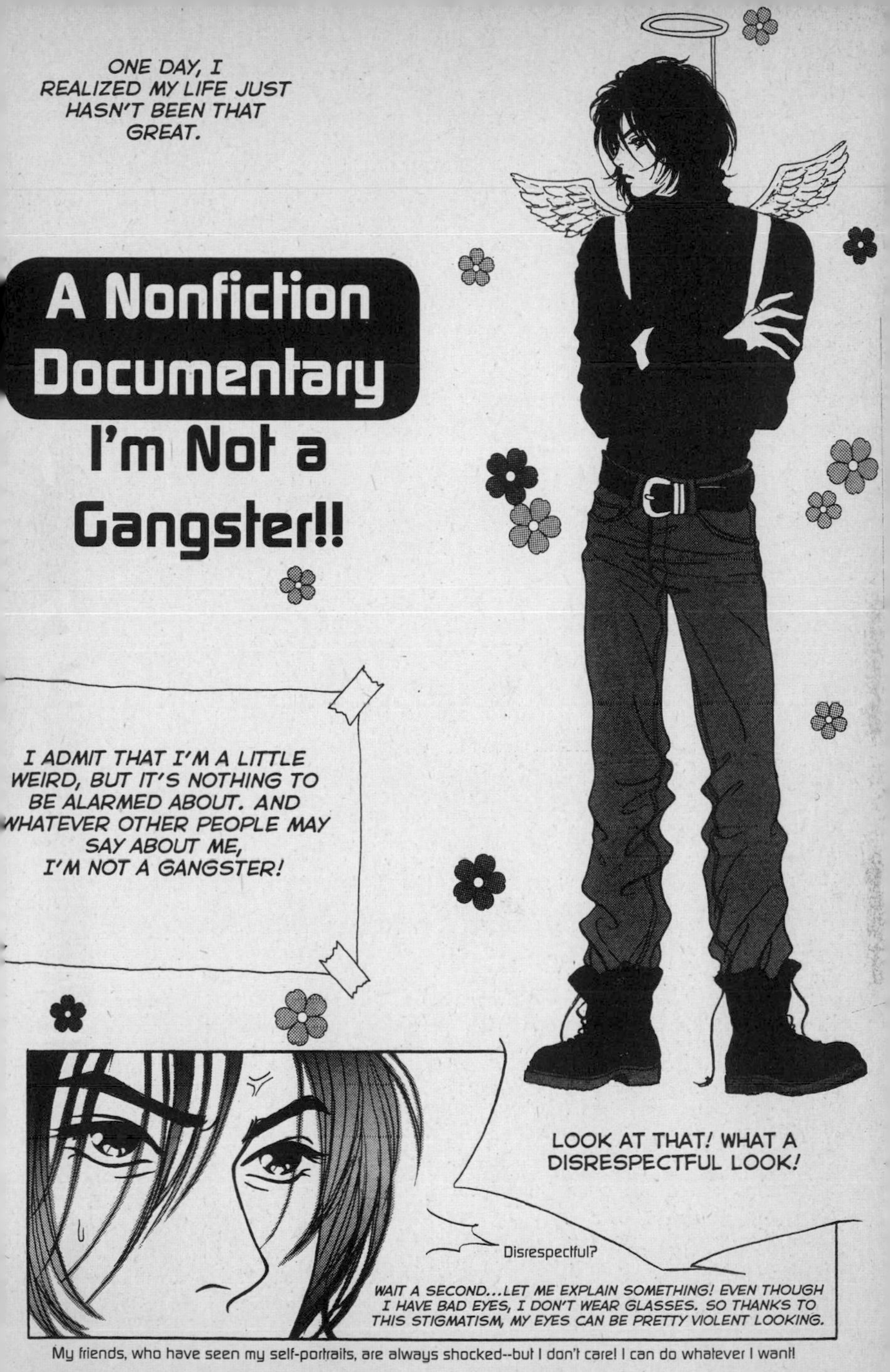
ONE DAY, I REALIZED MY LIFE JUST HASN'T BEEN THAT GREAT.
A Nonfiction Documentary
I'm Not a Gangster!!
I ADMIT THAT I'M A LITTLE WEIRD, BUT IT'S NOTHING TO BE ALARMED ABOUT. AND WHATEVER OTHER PEOPLE MAY SAY ABOUT ME, I'M NOT A GANGSTER!
LOOK AT THAT! WHAT A DISRESPECTFUL LOOK!
Disrespectful?
WAIT A SECOND...LET ME EXPLAIN SOMETHING! EVEN THOUGH I HAVE BAD EYES, I DON'T WEAR GLASSES. SO THANKS TO THIS STIGMATISM, MY EYES CAN BE PRETTY VIOLENT LOOKING.

My friends, who have seen my self-portraits, are always shocked--but I don't care! I can do whatever I want!

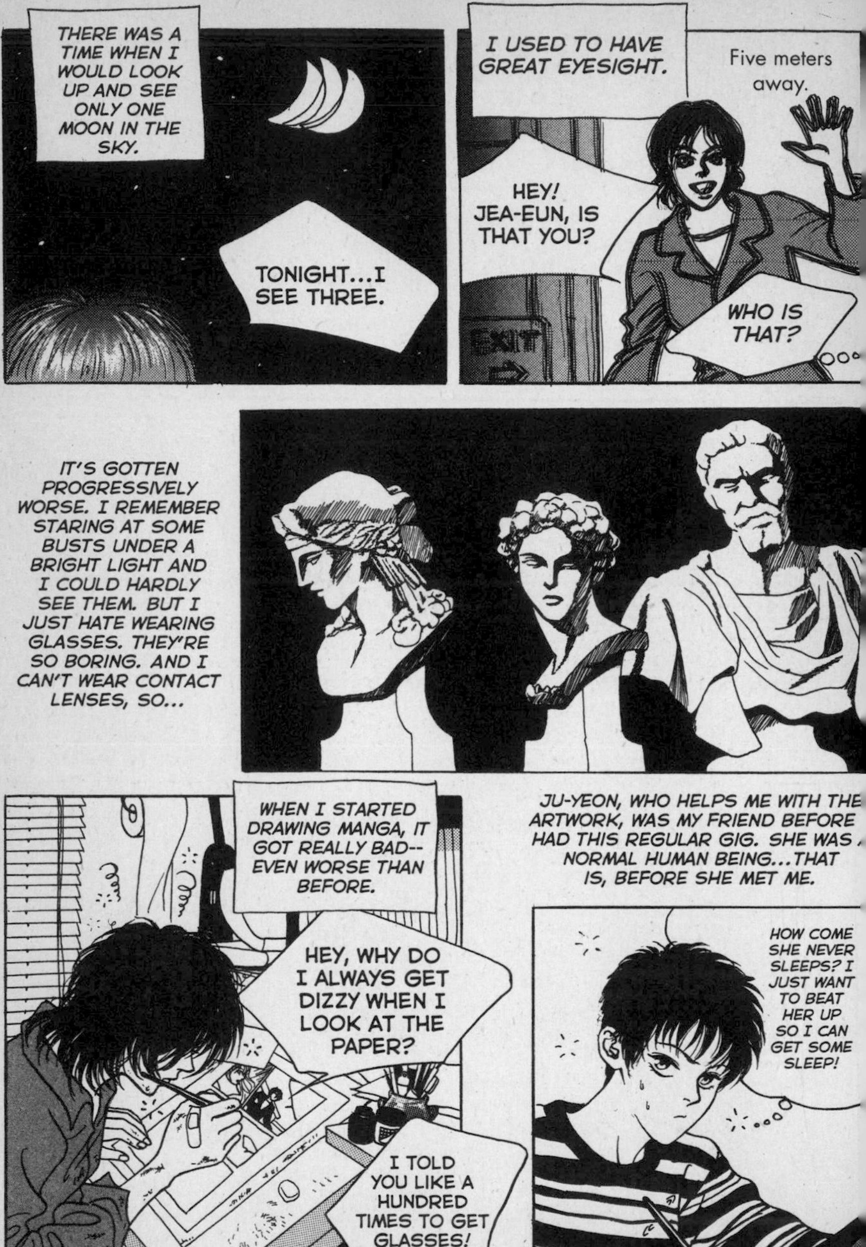
THERE WAS A TIME WHEN I WOULD LOOK UP AND SEE ONLY ONE MOON IN THE SKY.
TONIGHT...I SEE THREE.
I USED TO HAVE GREAT EYESIGHT.
Five meters away.
HEY! JEA-EUN, IS THAT YOU?
WHO IS THAT?
IT'S GOTTEN PROGRESSIVELY WORSE. I REMEMBER STARING AT SOME BUSTS UNDER A BRIGHT LIGHT AND I COULD HARDLY SEE THEM. BUT I JUST HATE WEARING GLASSES. THEY'RE SO BORING. AND I CAN'T WEAR CONTACT LENSES, SO...
WHEN I STARTED DRAWING MANGA, IT GOT REALLY BAD--EVEN WORSE THAN BEFORE.
HEY, WHY DO I ALWAYS GET DIZZY WHEN I LOOK AT THE PAPER?
I TOLD YOU LIKE A HUNDRED TIMES TO GET GLASSES!
JU-YEON, WHO HELPS ME WITH THE ARTWORK, WAS MY FRIEND BEFORE
HAD THIS REGULAR GIG. SHE WAS
NORMAL HUMAN BEING...THAT IS, BEFORE SHE MET ME.
HOW COME SHE NEVER SLEEPS? I JUST WANT TO BEAT HER UP SO I CAN GET SOME SLEEP!

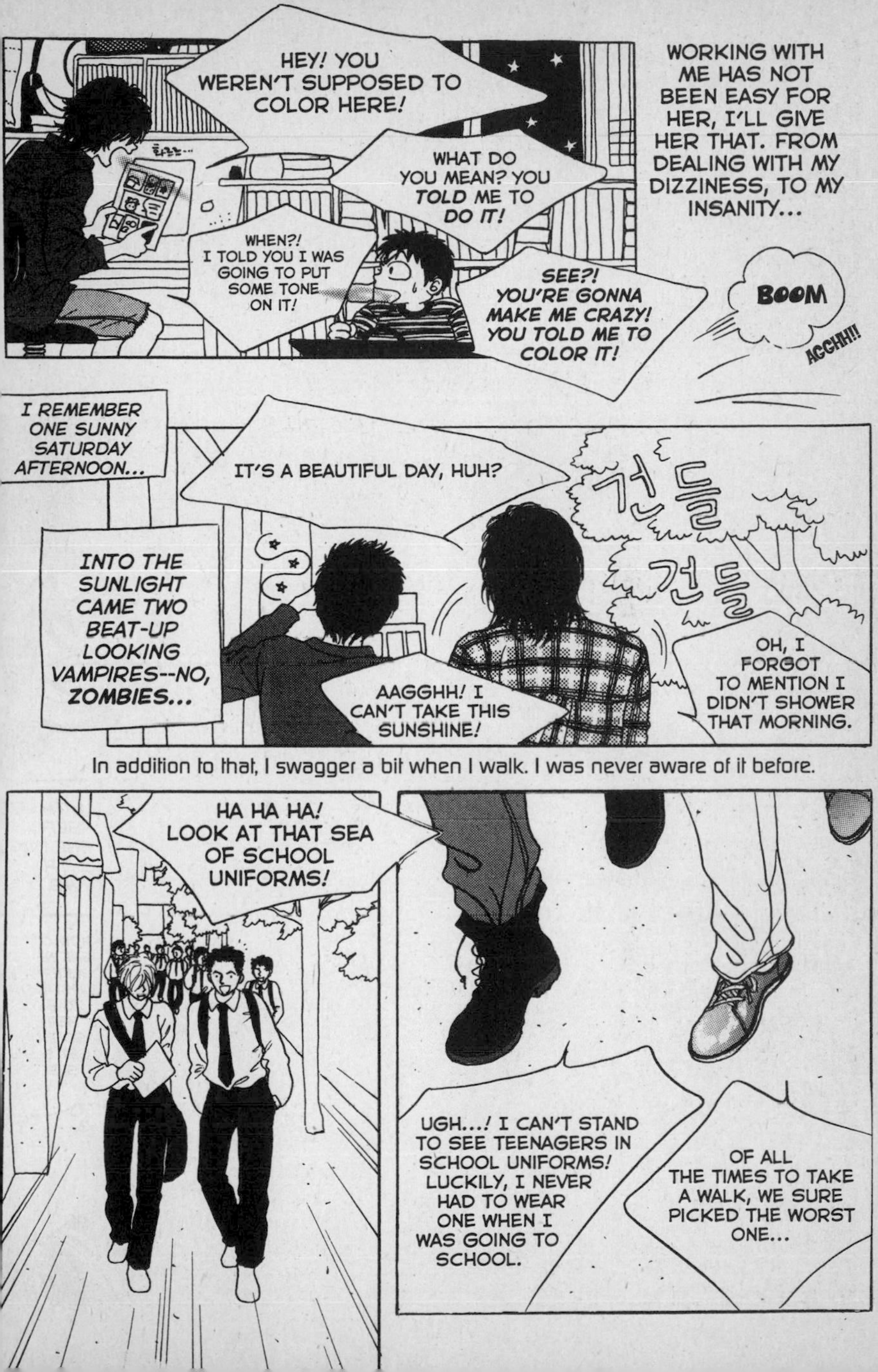
HEY! YOU WEREN'T SUPPOSED TO COLOR HERE!
WHAT DO YOU MEAN? YOU *TOLD* ME TO *DO IT!*
WHEN?! I TOLD YOU I WAS GOING TO PUT SOME TONE ON IT!
SEE?! YOU'RE GONNA MAKE ME CRAZY! YOU TOLD ME TO COLOR IT!
WORKING WITH ME HAS NOT BEEN EASY FOR HER, I'LL GIVE HER THAT. FROM DEALING WITH MY DIZZINESS, TO MY INSANITY...
BOOM
AGCHH!!!
I REMEMBER ONE SUNNY SATURDAY AFTERNOON...
IT'S A BEAUTIFUL DAY, HUH?
INTO THE SUNLIGHT CAME TWO BEAT-UP LOOKING VAMPIRES--NO, ZOMBIES...
AAGGHH! I CAN'T TAKE THIS SUNSHINE!
건들 건들
OH, I FORGOT TO MENTION I DIDN'T SHOWER THAT MORNING.
In addition to that, I swagger a bit when I walk. I was never aware of it before.
HA HA HA! LOOK AT THAT SEA OF SCHOOL UNIFORMS!
UGH...! I CAN'T STAND TO SEE TEENAGERS IN SCHOOL UNIFORMS! LUCKILY, I NEVER HAD TO WEAR ONE WHEN I WAS GOING TO SCHOOL.
OF ALL THE TIMES TO TAKE A WALK, WE SURE PICKED THE WORST ONE...

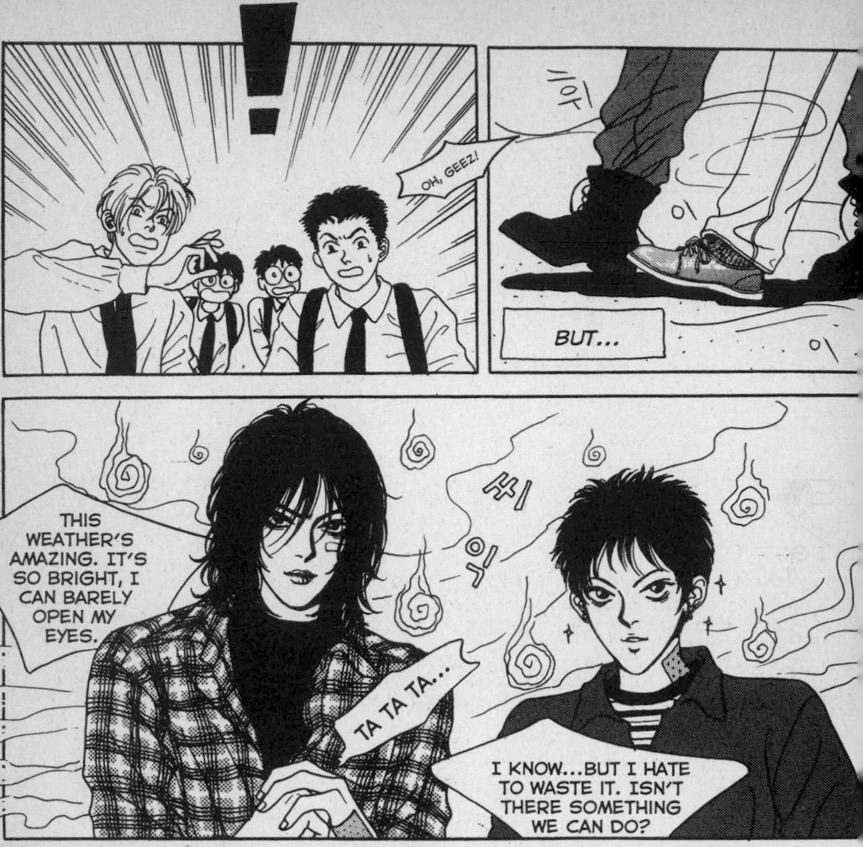
OH, GEEZ!
BUT...
THIS WEATHER'S AMAZING. IT'S SO BRIGHT, I CAN BARELY OPEN MY EYES.
TA TA TA...
씨익
I KNOW...BUT I HATE TO WASTE IT. ISN'T THERE SOMETHING WE CAN DO?

I had no intention of threatening them. We were just so tired after working all night.

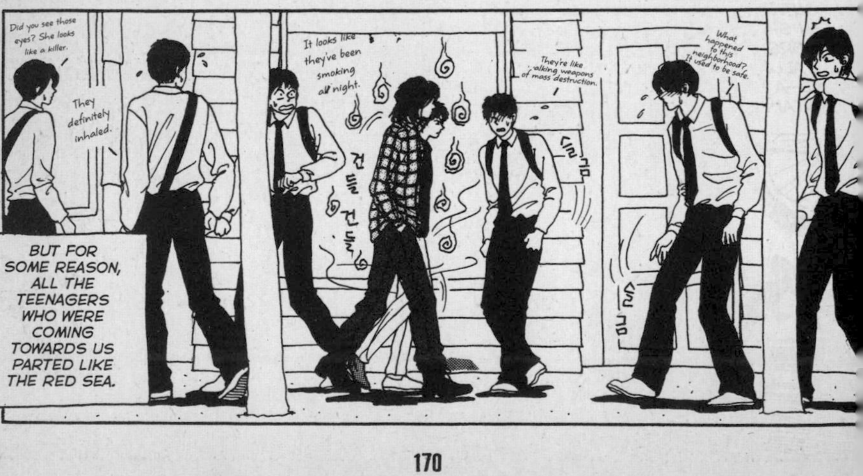
Did you see those eyes? She looks like a killer.
They definitely inhaled.
It looks like they've been smoking all night.
건들건들
They're like walking weapons of mass destruction.
What happened to this neighborhood? It used to be safe.
BUT FOR SOME REASON, ALL THE TEENAGERS WHO WERE COMING TOWARDS US PARTED LIKE THE RED SEA.

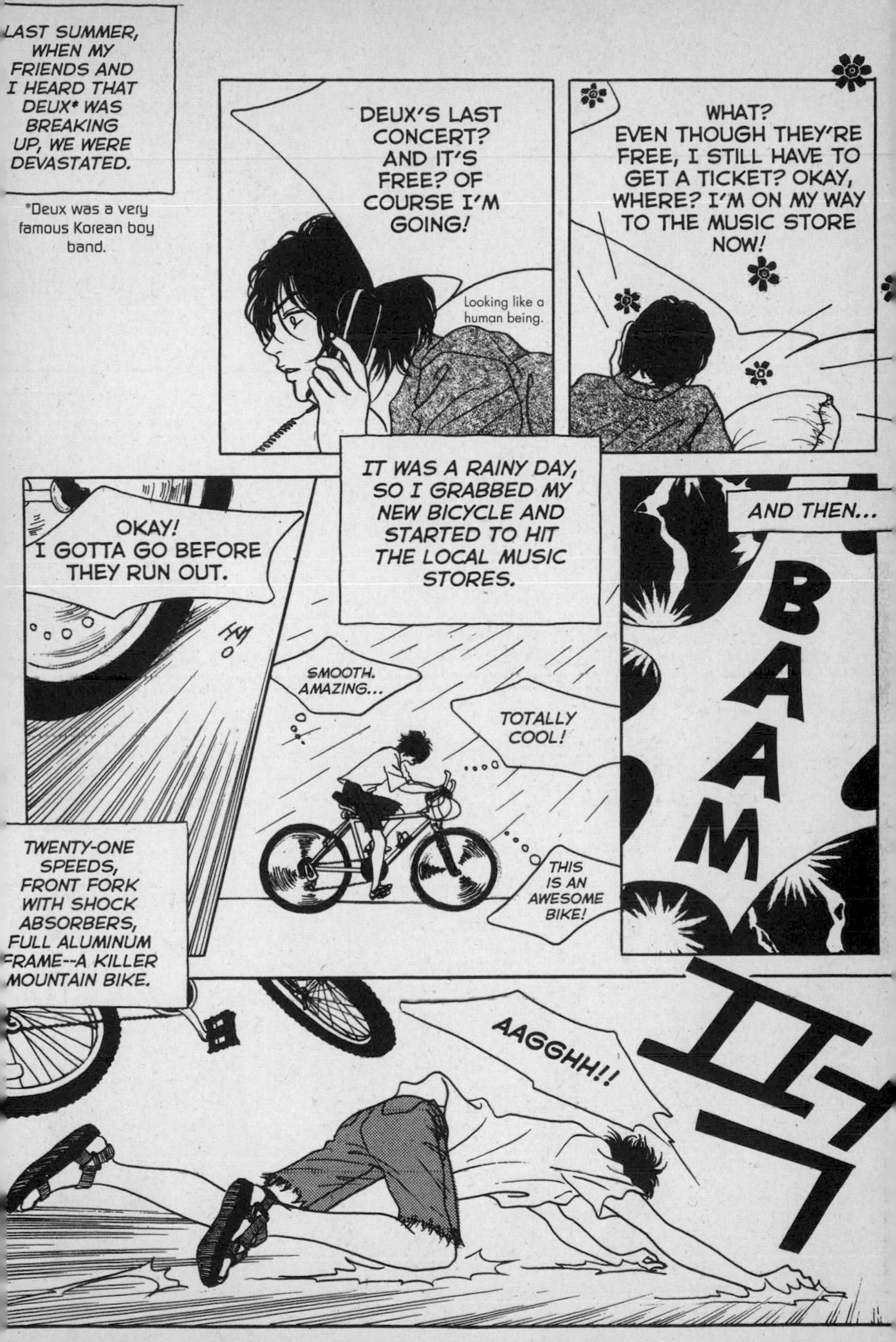
LAST SUMMER, WHEN MY FRIENDS AND I HEARD THAT DEUX* WAS BREAKING UP, WE WERE DEVASTATED.
*Deux was a very famous Korean boy band.
DEUX'S LAST CONCERT? AND IT'S FREE? OF COURSE I'M GOING!
Looking like a human being.
WHAT? EVEN THOUGH THEY'RE FREE, I STILL HAVE TO GET A TICKET? OKAY, WHERE? I'M ON MY WAY TO THE MUSIC STORE NOW!
OKAY! I GOTTA GO BEFORE THEY RUN OUT.
IT WAS A RAINY DAY, SO I GRABBED MY NEW BICYCLE AND STARTED TO HIT THE LOCAL MUSIC STORES.
SMOOTH. AMAZING...
TOTALLY COOL!
THIS IS AN AWESOME BIKE!
TWENTY-ONE SPEEDS, FRONT FORK WITH SHOCK ABSORBERS, FULL ALUMINUM FRAME--A KILLER MOUNTAIN BIKE.
AND THEN...
BAAM
AAGGHH!!

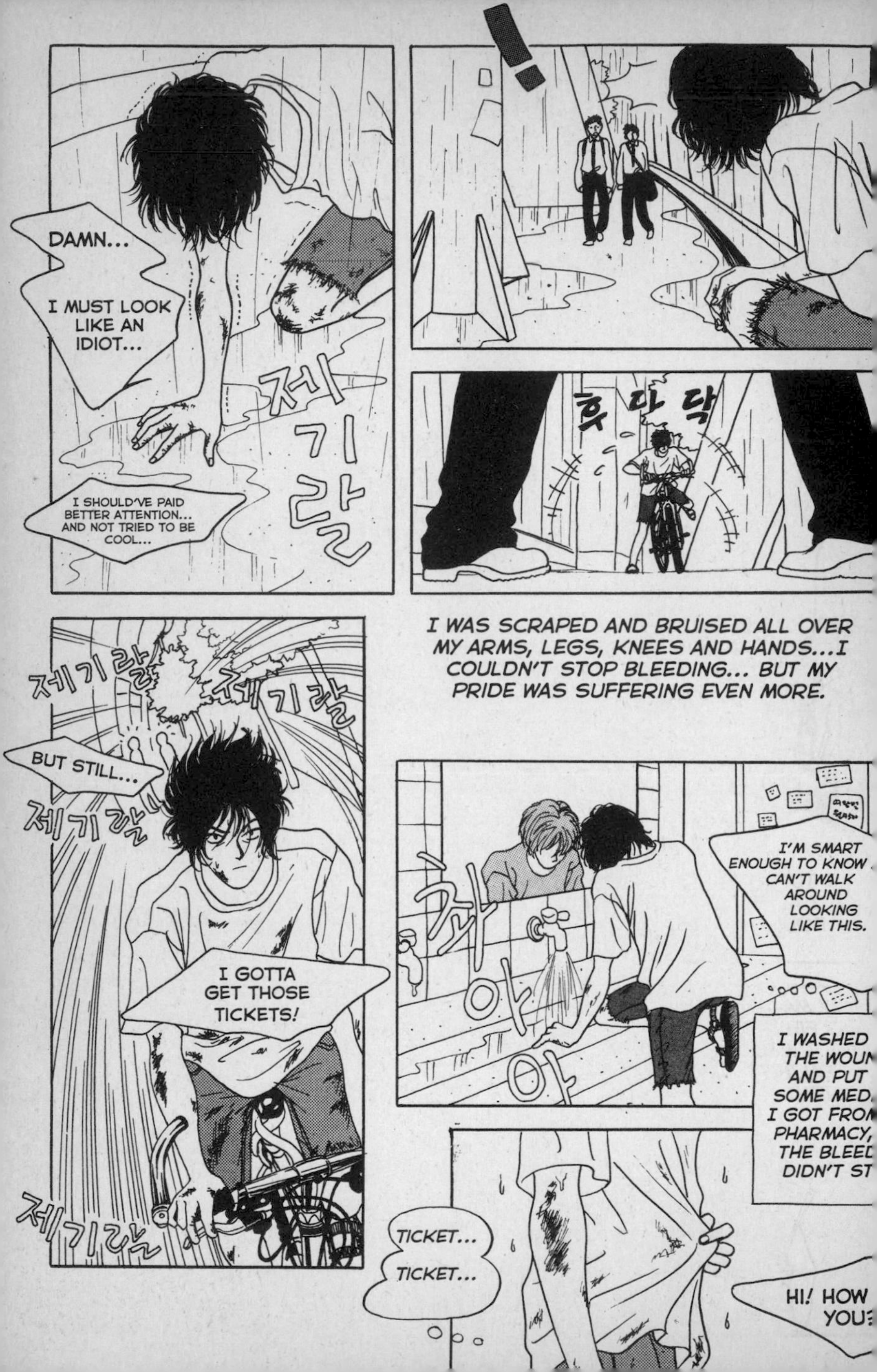
DAMN...
I MUST LOOK LIKE AN IDIOT...
제기랄
I SHOULD'VE PAID BETTER ATTENTION... AND NOT TRIED TO BE COOL...
후다닥
I WAS SCRAPED AND BRUISED ALL OVER MY ARMS, LEGS, KNEES AND HANDS...I COULDN'T STOP BLEEDING... BUT MY PRIDE WAS SUFFERING EVEN MORE.
제기랄
제기랄
BUT STILL...
제기랄
I GOTTA GET THOSE TICKETS!
제기랄
촤아아
I'M SMART ENOUGH TO KNOW CAN'T WALK AROUND LOOKING LIKE THIS.
I WASHED THE WOUN AND PUT SOME MED I GOT FROM PHARMACY, THE BLEED DIDN'T ST
TICKET... TICKET...
HI! HOW YOU?

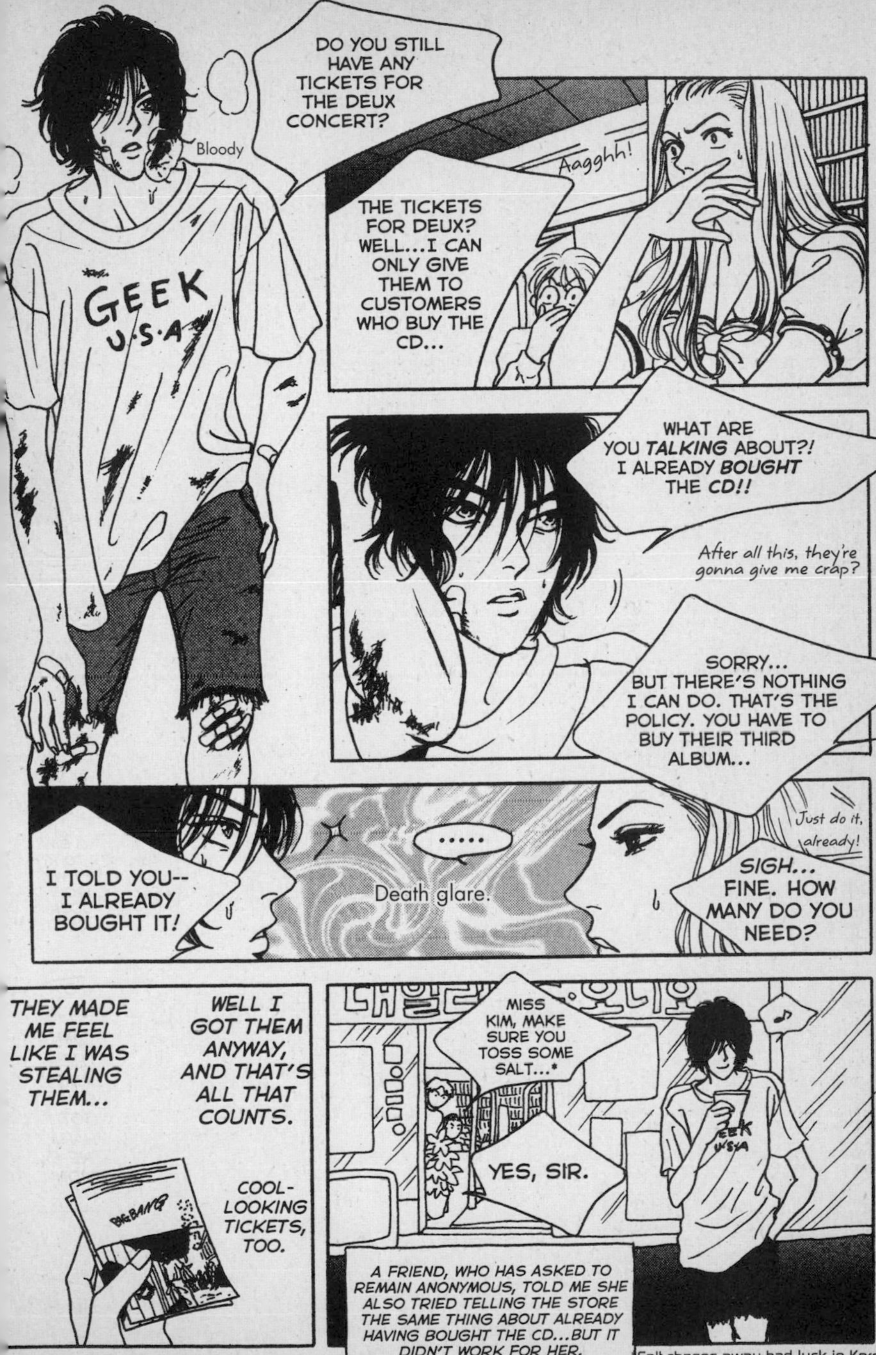
DO YOU STILL HAVE ANY TICKETS FOR THE DEUX CONCERT?
Bloody
GEEK U·S·A
Aagghh!
THE TICKETS FOR DEUX? WELL...I CAN ONLY GIVE THEM TO CUSTOMERS WHO BUY THE CD...
WHAT ARE YOU *TALKING* ABOUT?! I ALREADY *BOUGHT* THE *CD!!*
After all this, they're gonna give me crap?
SORRY... BUT THERE'S NOTHING I CAN DO. THAT'S THE POLICY. YOU HAVE TO BUY THEIR THIRD ALBUM...
I TOLD YOU-- I ALREADY BOUGHT IT!
.....
Death glare.
Just do it, already!
SIGH... FINE. HOW MANY DO YOU NEED?
THEY MADE ME FEEL LIKE I WAS STEALING THEM...
WELL I GOT THEM ANYWAY, AND THAT'S ALL THAT COUNTS.
BIG BANG
COOL-LOOKING TICKETS, TOO.
MISS KIM, MAKE SURE YOU TOSS SOME SALT...*
YES, SIR.
A FRIEND, WHO HAS ASKED TO REMAIN ANONYMOUS, TOLD ME SHE ALSO TRIED TELLING THE STORE THE SAME THING ABOUT ALREADY HAVING BOUGHT THE CD...BUT IT DIDN'T WORK FOR HER.

So a special thanks to "frog."

*Salt chases away bad luck in Korea.

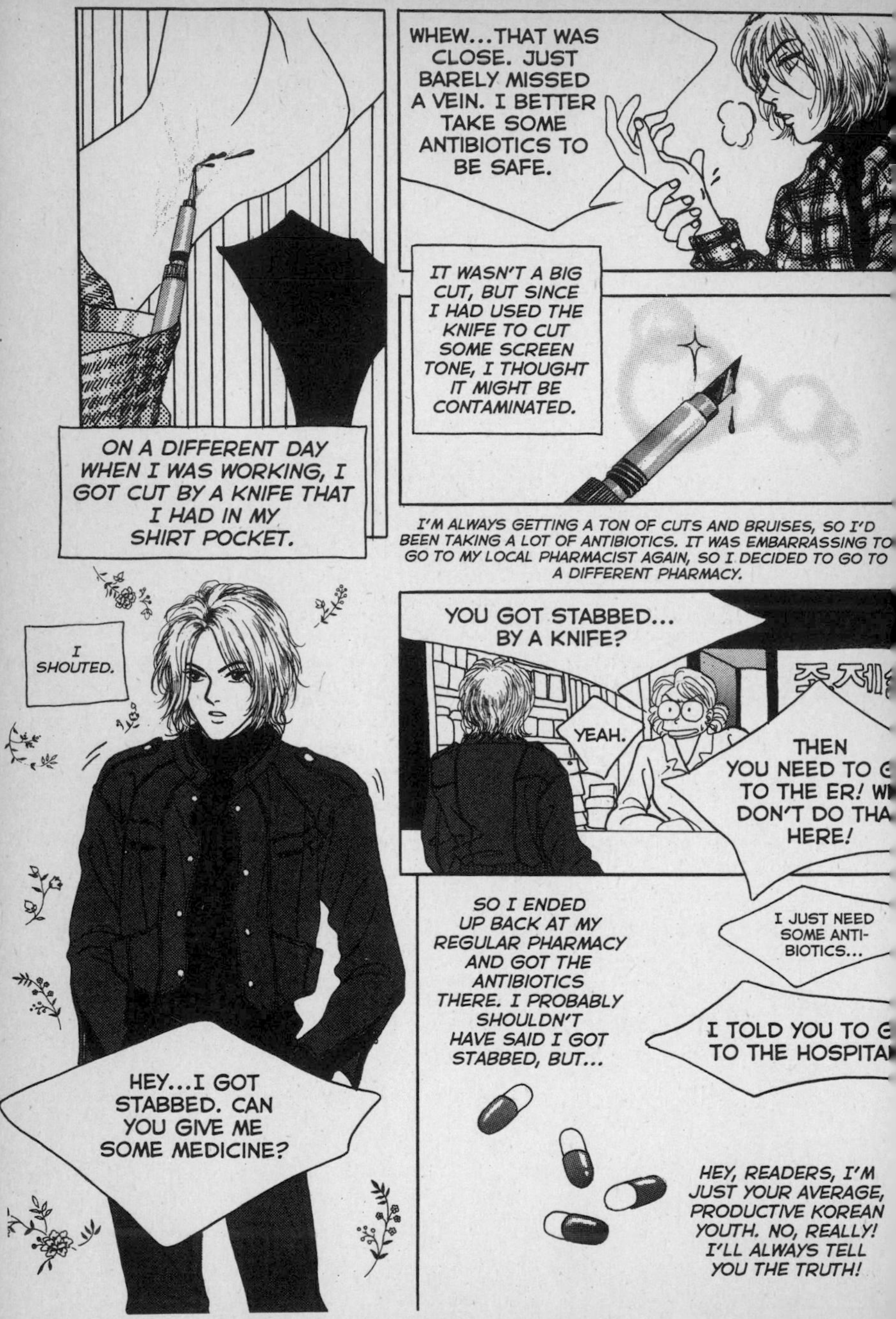
ON A DIFFERENT DAY WHEN I WAS WORKING, I GOT CUT BY A KNIFE THAT I HAD IN MY SHIRT POCKET.
WHEW...THAT WAS CLOSE. JUST BARELY MISSED A VEIN. I BETTER TAKE SOME ANTIBIOTICS TO BE SAFE.
IT WASN'T A BIG CUT, BUT SINCE I HAD USED THE KNIFE TO CUT SOME SCREEN TONE, I THOUGHT IT MIGHT BE CONTAMINATED.
I'M ALWAYS GETTING A TON OF CUTS AND BRUISES, SO I'D BEEN TAKING A LOT OF ANTIBIOTICS. IT WAS EMBARRASSING TO GO TO MY LOCAL PHARMACIST AGAIN, SO I DECIDED TO GO TO A DIFFERENT PHARMACY.
I SHOUTED.
HEY...I GOT STABBED. CAN YOU GIVE ME SOME MEDICINE?
YOU GOT STABBED... BY A KNIFE?
YEAH.
THEN YOU NEED TO G TO THE ER! W DON'T DO THA HERE!
I JUST NEED SOME ANTI-BIOTICS...
I TOLD YOU TO G TO THE HOSPITA
SO I ENDED UP BACK AT MY REGULAR PHARMACY AND GOT THE ANTIBIOTICS THERE. I PROBABLY SHOULDN'T HAVE SAID I GOT STABBED, BUT...
HEY, READERS, I'M JUST YOUR AVERAGE, PRODUCTIVE KOREAN YOUTH. NO, REALLY! I'LL ALWAYS TELL YOU THE TRUTH!

In the next volume of ...

SOUL TO SEOUL™

J.J. still in mourning over the death of his foster father, decides to visit Korea. Will Gelda let the man of her dreams slip through her fingers? Spike finally confesses his feelings for Sunil and announces he's leaving for the west coast...but even more shocking is Kai's confession to him that'll change everything. Meanwhile, Kai is ordered to take on another "assignment"...but his target has more in common with Kai than he realizes. They've saved the best for last in this, the final shocking volume of Soul to Seoul!

Don't miss it!

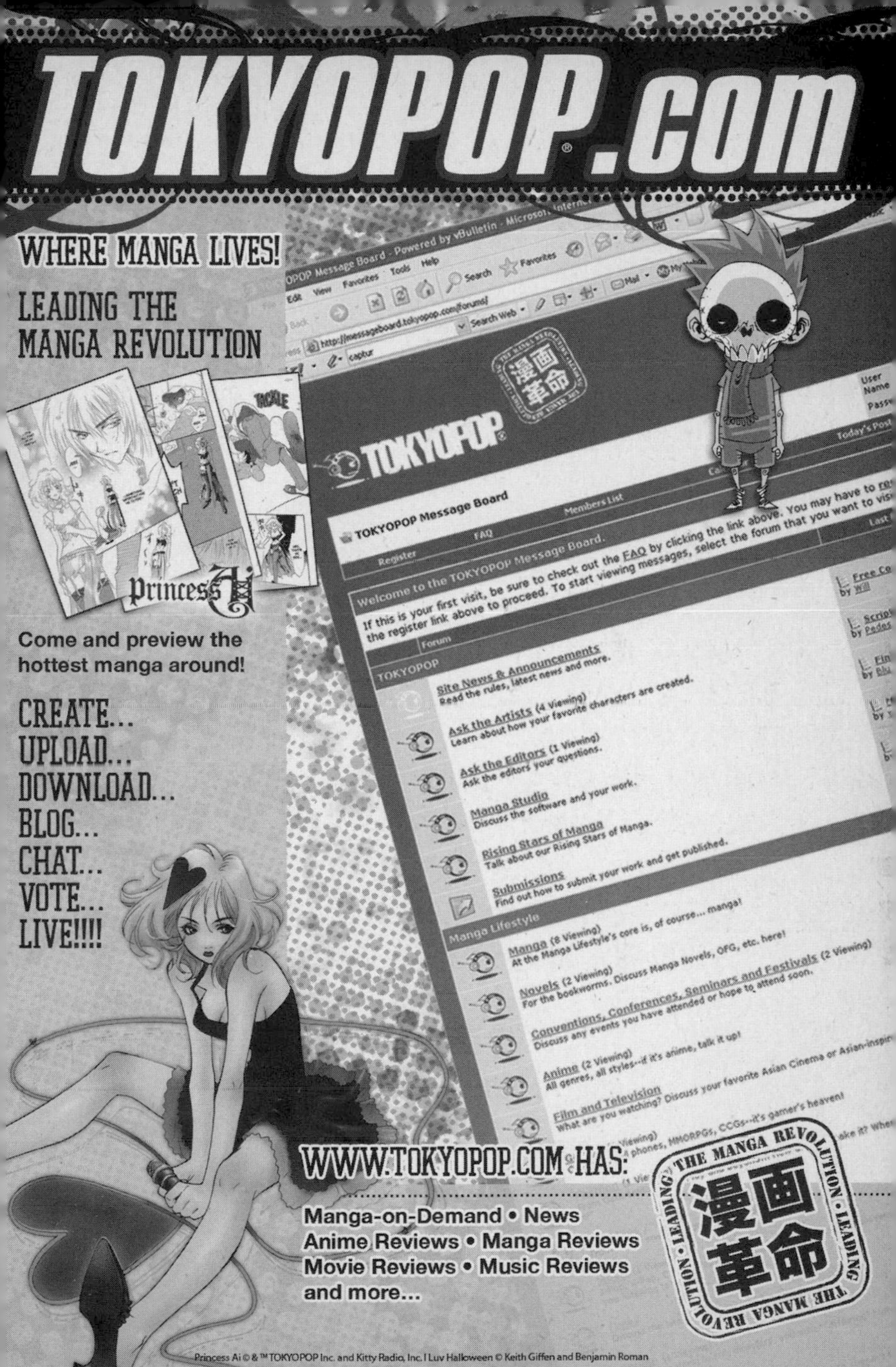
TOKYOPOP.com
WHERE MANGA LIVES!
LEADING THE MANGA REVOLUTION
Princess Ai
Come and preview the hottest manga around!
CREATE...
UPLOAD...
DOWNLOAD...
BLOG...
CHAT...
VOTE...
LIVE!!!!
TOKYOPOP Message Board
Welcome to the TOKYOPOP Message Board.
If this is your first visit, be sure to check out the FAQ by clicking the link above. You may have to register before you can post: click the register link above to proceed. To start viewing messages, select the forum that you want to visit from the selection below.
Site News & Announcements
Read the rules, latest news and more.
Ask the Artists (4 Viewing)
Learn about how your favorite characters are created.
Ask the Editors (1 Viewing)
Ask the editors your questions.
Manga Studio
Discuss the software and your work.
Rising Stars of Manga
Talk about our Rising Stars of Manga.
Submissions
Find out how to submit your work and get published.
Manga Lifestyle
Manga (8 Viewing)
At the Manga Lifestyle's core is, of course... manga!
Novels (2 Viewing)
For the bookworms. Discuss Manga Novels, OFG, etc. here!
Conventions, Conferences, Seminars and Festivals (2 Viewing)
Discuss any events you have attended or hope to attend soon.
Anime (2 Viewing)
All genres, all styles--if it's anime, talk it up!
Film and Television
What are you watching? Discuss your favorite Asian Cinema or Asian-inspired
WWW.TOKYOPOP.COM HAS:
Manga-on-Demand • News
Anime Reviews • Manga Reviews
Movie Reviews • Music Reviews
and more...
THE MANGA REVOLUTION • LEADING
漫画革命

Jim Henson's
RETURN TO
LABYRINTH™

Jim Henson's classic continues...

The Goblin King has kept a watchful eye on Toby: His minions secretly guiding and protecting the child... Legions of goblins working behind the scenes to ensure that Toby has whatever his heart desires... Preparing him for the day when he will return to the Labyrinth and take his rightful place beside Jareth as the heir to the Goblin Kingdom.

That day has come...

...but no one has told Toby.

By Chris Lie
and Jake T. Forbes

FANTASY   TEEN
AGE 13+

Return to Labyrinth
™ & © Henson /
Labyrinth Enterprises
www.HENSON.com

FOR MORE INFORMATION VISIT: WWW.TOKYOPOP.COM

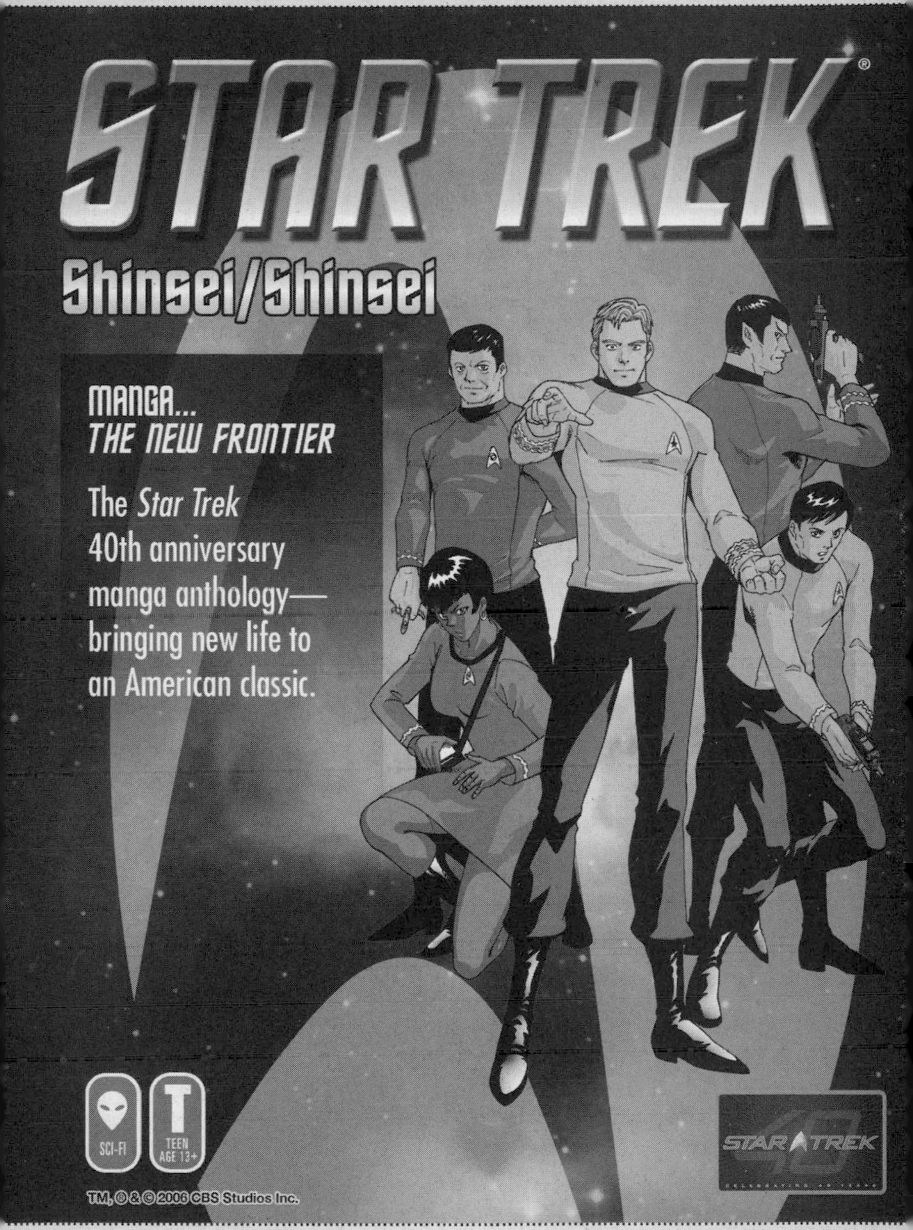
STAR TREK®
Shinsei/Shinsei
MANGA...
THE NEW FRONTIER
The Star Trek 40th anniversary manga anthology—bringing new life to an American classic.
SCI-FI
T
TEEN AGE 13+
STAR TREK
TM, ® & © 2006 CBS Studios Inc.

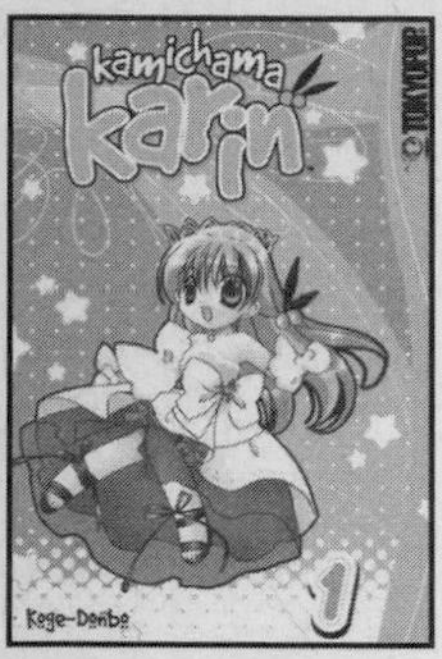
kamichama
karin
TOKYOPOP
Koge-Donbo
1

ROMANCE

Y
YOUTH AGE 10+

KAMICHAMA KARIN

BY KOGE-DONBO

This one was a surprise. I mean, I knew Koge-Donbo drew insanely cute characters, but I had no idea a magical girl story could be so darn clever. *Kamichama Karin* manages to lampoon everything about the genre, from plushie-like mascots to character archetypes to weapons that appear from the blue! And you gotta love Karin, the airheaded heroine who takes guff from no one and screams "I AM GOD!" as her battle cry. In short, if you are looking for a shiny new manga with a knack for hilarity and a penchant for accessories, I say look no further.

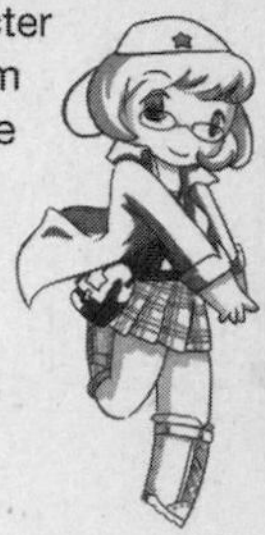

~Carol Fox, Editor

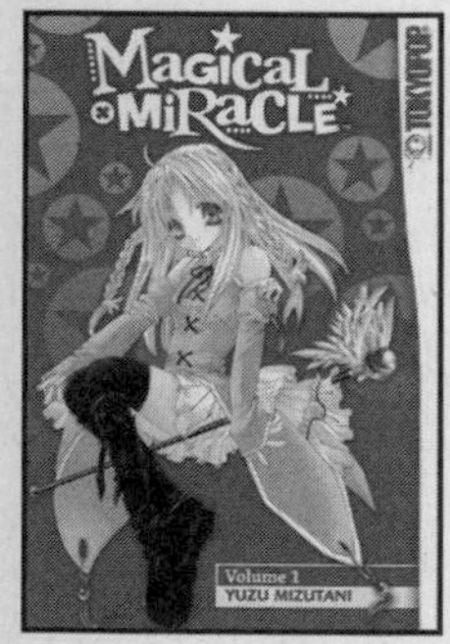
Magical
Miracle
TOKYOPOP
Volume 1
YUZU MIZUTANI

FANTASY

T
TEEN AGE 13+

MAGICAL X MIRACLE

BY YUZU MIZUTANI

Magical X Miracle is a quirky—yet uplifting—tale of gender-bending mistaken identity! When a young girl must masquerade as a great wizard, she not only finds the strength to save an entire kingdom...but, ironically, she just might just find herself, too. Yuzu Mizutani's art is remarkably adorable, but it also has a dark, sophisticated edge.

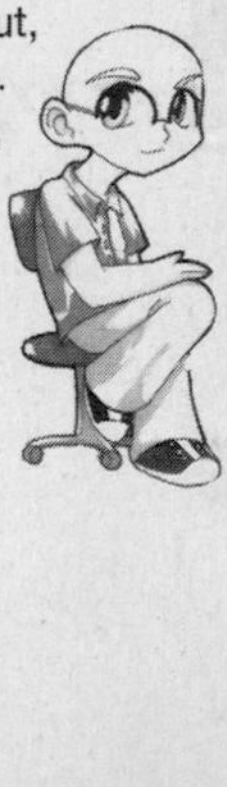

~Paul Morrissey, Editor

Every life has a story...
Every story has a life of its own.

LIFE ™

When Ayumu gets in the school of her choice but her best bud does not, the pain of being separated from her friend is too much to handle...But a new school year begins and a fresh start is presented to her, until she takes solace in her new friend Manami...

OT OLDER TEEN AGE 16+

DRAMA

© Keiko Suenobu

Volumes 1 and 2 Available Now!

FOR MORE INFORMATION VISIT: WWW.TOKYOPOP.COM

THE EPIC STORY OF A FERRET WHO DEFIED HER CAGE.

www.TOKYOPOP.com

© LINDSAY CIBOS, JARED HODGES AND TOKYOPOP INC.

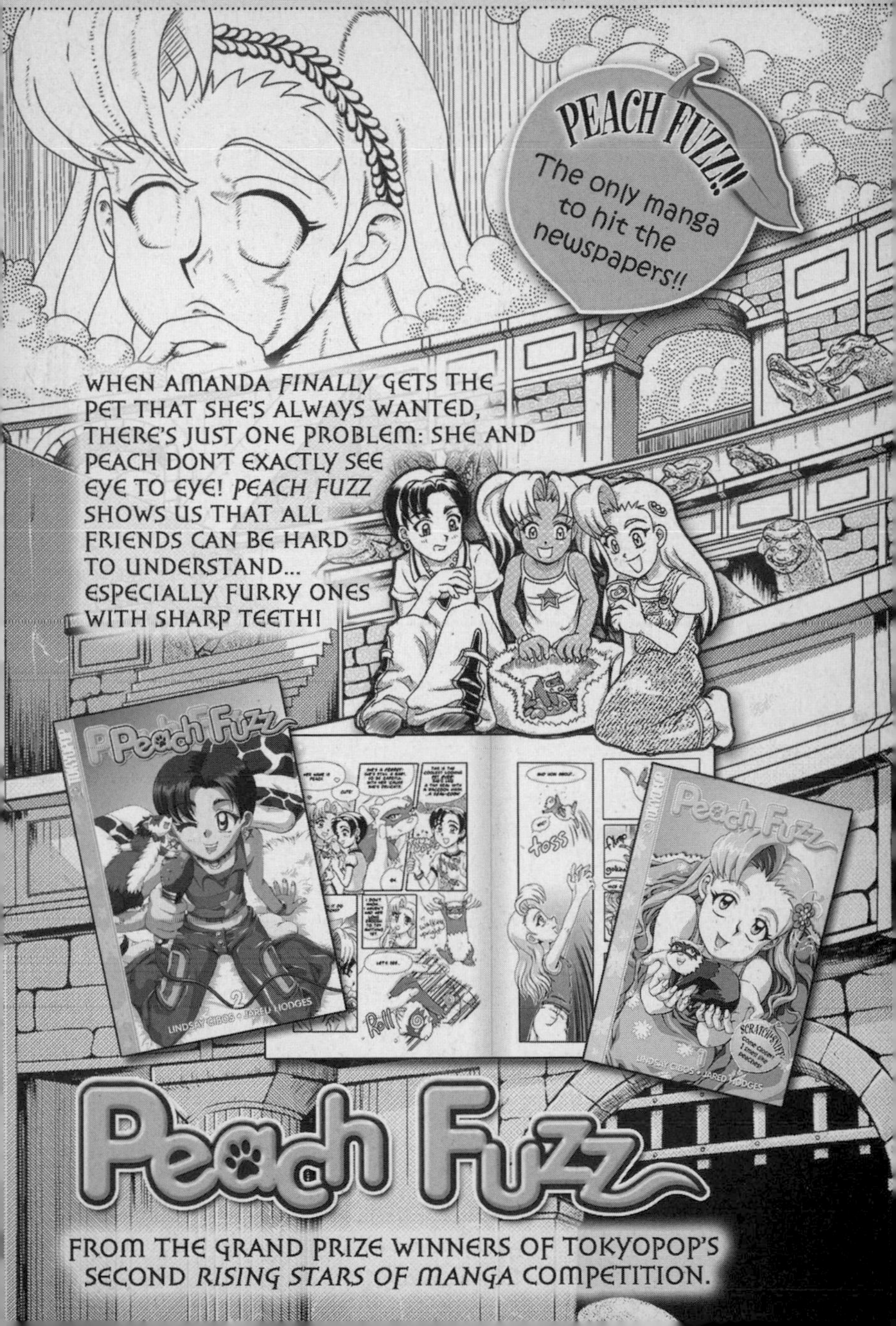
PEACH FUZZ!!
The only manga to hit the newspapers!!
WHEN AMANDA *FINALLY* GETS THE PET THAT SHE'S ALWAYS WANTED, THERE'S JUST ONE PROBLEM: SHE AND PEACH DON'T EXACTLY SEE EYE TO EYE! *PEACH FUZZ* SHOWS US THAT ALL FRIENDS CAN BE HARD TO UNDERSTAND... ESPECIALLY FURRY ONES WITH SHARP TEETH!
Peach Fuzz
Peach Fuzz
Peach Fuzz
FROM THE GRAND PRIZE WINNERS OF TOKYOPOP'S SECOND *RISING STARS OF MANGA* COMPETITION.